MW01419005

Storecupboard VEGAN

Acknowledgements

This book is dedicated to those who are always in a rush...

Laura and Sébastien would especially like to thank Julien for his constant help and support. A massive thank you goes to Alex Sindrome for his music that gets us excited and helped us stay focused each day. (https://alexsindrome.bandcamp.com)

A huge thank you also goes to Un Monde Vegan, Vegan Deli and Wheaty for their trust.

This English language edition published in 2020 by
Grub Street
4 Rainham Close
London
SW11 6SS

Email: food@grubstreet.co.uk
Twitter: @grub_street
Facebook: Grub Street Publishing
Web: www.grubstreet.co.uk
Instagram: grubstreet_books

Copyright this English language edition © Grub Street 2020
Design and illustration by Lucy Thorne © Grub Street 2020

Copyright © 2018 Éditions La Plage, Paris

A CIP record for this title is available from the British Library
ISBN 978-1-911621-41-6

All rights reserved. No part of this book may be reproduced or transmitted in any form or by any means, electronic or mechanical, including photocopying, recording or any information storage and retrieval system, without permission in writing from the publisher.

Printed and bound by Finidr in the Czech Republic

Storecupboard VEGAN

Laura Veganpower
& Sébastien Kardinal

GRUB STREET • LONDON

CONTENTS

Introduction 9
Storecupboard essentials 10

Vegan Meatballs
Riboulade 15
Yakitori 15
Veggie ball gratin 17
Hot & cold salad 17
Oriental vegan meatballs 18
Tomato & vegan meatball soup 18
Vegan meatballs with mustard 18
Surprise vegan meatballs 20
Spicy vegan meatballs 20
Vegan meatballs with capers 20

Grains
Wheatsotto 23
Quinoa with mushrooms 23
Stuffed tomatoes 24
Çiğ köfte 24
Moroccan couscous 24
Buddha bowl 26
Wheat biryani 26
Chocolate granola 29
Semolina cake 29
Morning porridge 29

Charcuterie
'Chorizo' pinwheels 31
'BLT' bagel 31
'Chorizo' & potato tart 32
Chicory gratin 32
Savoury cupcakes 34
Stuffed artichokes 34
Mini aperitif brochettes 34

Meatless strips
Green salad 37
Sauté with Brussels sprouts 37
Fajitas 38
Sweet potato farmer's pie 38
Broccoli rice 38
Pitta waffles 40
Thai soup 40

Vegan cheese
Grilled cheese 43
Pizza pitta 43
Mac & cheese 44
Welsh rarebit 44
Tartiflette 44
Poutine 46
Quesadillas 46
French onion soup 48
Aligot 48
Vegan fondue 48

Ice cream
Decadent milkshake 51
Coffee ice-cream float 51
Cookie sandwich 53
Frozen smoothie 53
Mango mega boost 53
Tomato salad with lemon sorbet 54
Caribbean delight 54

Gnocchi
Gnocchi with pesto 57
Parsley butter gnocchi 57
Gnocchi with creamed leeks 59
Gnocchi with peppers 59
Bollywood gnocchi 59
Gnocchi with spinach 60
Parisian gnocchi 60
Gnocchi alla norma 62
Sea-flavoured gnocchi 62
Bordelaise gnocchi 62

Mixed vegetables
Minestrone 65
Stuffed peppers 65
Vegetable tart 66
Curry 66
Samosas 68
Creamy vegetables 68
Thai style 68

Julienne vegetables
Wok 71

Contents

Crumble 71
Stir fry 73
Avocado roll 73
Puff pastry waffles 73
Vegetable pancakes 74
Comforting broth 74

Lentils & beans
Spicy terrine 77
Avocado cream 77
Jacket potatoes 79
Beetroot hummus 79
Neo-cassoulet 79
Chilli con corn 80
Lentil cream with truffles 80
Lentils with smoked tofu 80
Lentil soup 82
Mediterranean dal 82

Mayonnaise
Gravlaxsas 85
Aioli 85
Andalusian 85
Summer vegetable salad 87
Sauce gribiche 87
Tartare sauce 87
Cocktail sauce 88
Béarnaise sauce 88
Hollandaise sauce 88
Potato salad 88

Miso
Mushroom & herb soup 91
Salted peanut cup 91
Rainbow salad 92
Beetroot ravioli 92
Saffron cauliflower 95
Sautéed mushrooms 95
Miso-glazed aubergines 95

Bread
Toast with mushrooms 97
Club sandwich 97
Avocado toast 98
Garlic bread 98
Chestnut French toast 98
Gazpacho 100
Bread pudding 100
Toastie roll ups 102
Mini bruschetta 102
Bread soup 102

Breaded treats
Caesar salad 105
Spinach escalopes 105
Viennese burger 106
Toasted wraps 106
BBQ pizza 108
Torikatsu 108
Milanese 108
Mini burgers 111
Ocean brochettes 111
Red kebab 111

Pasta
Penne arrabiata 113
Fusilli à la forestière 113
Tagliatelle carbonara 114
Farfalle with broccoli 114
Conchiglie pesto 114
Ink linguine 116
Conchiglie melanzane 116
Tricolour salad 119
One-pot pasta 119
Oven-baked ravioli 119

Pastry dough
Bread sticks 121
Chickpea pasties 121
Vegetable pie 122
Pizza bianca 122
Empanadas 122
Apple & blueberry tart 124
Fruit tart 124
Quick mini croissants 126
Kings' & queens' cake 126
Thin banana tart 126

Contents

Vegan pâtés
Rustic sandwich 129
Puff pastry canapés 129
Posh salad 130
Surprise muffins 130
Black forest toast 132
Quick & fancy sauce 132
Cream of shiitake mushroom soup 132

Chickpeas
Red hummus 135
Moroccan harira soup 135
Falafel terrine 137
Burrito 137
Lebanese salad 138
Spiced 'steaks' 138
Sautéed greens 138

Potatoes
Spanish-style potatoes 141
Potato hotpot 141
Sautéed country veg 142
Aloo pie 142
Potato burger 144
Potato gratin 144
Potato croquettes 144

Textured vegetable protein
Marengo sauté 147
Spaghetti bolognese 147
Florentine lasagne 148
Pumpkin parmentier 148
Ocean sandwich 148
Moussaka 151
Warm broccoli salad 151
Grilled TVP with shallot sauce 152
Modern blanquette 152
Cider casserole 152

Ratatouille
Polenta 155
Rata-toast 155
Savoury porridge 156
Vegetable lasagne 156

Galettes 159
Gourmet sauce 159
Mediterranean vegetable soup 159

Rice
Vineyard risotto 161
Vegetable curry rice 161
Thai rice salad 162
Trio of maki 162
Kimchi onigiri 164
Broccoli & rice 164
Paella 164
Rice tart 167
Cherry matcha rice pudding 167
Jambalaya 167

Vegan sausages
Basquaise 169
Banh mi dog 169
Pea soup 170
'Sausage' rolls 170
Tomato & chilli 'sausages' 170
Grilled 'bacon' & golden mash 173
Brussels sprouts stew 173
Currywurst 174
Choucroute garnie 174
'Sausage' salad 174

Seitan
Quick bourguignon 177
'Steak' tartare 177
BBQ style 178
Sichuan seitan skewers 178
Philly 'cheesesteak' 180
Orange seitan strips 180
'Steak' with peppercorn sauce 180
Italian stew 182
Pot-au-feu 182
Sauté Provençal 182

Meat substitutes
Chinese 'chicken' 185
Traditional French stew 185
'Chicken' & ginger 186

Contents

Bean satay 186
Sautéed 'chicken' with olives 186
Beer stew 189
African peanut stew 189
Flageolet bean casserole 189
Pad thai 190
Tarragon casserole 190

Vegan steak
Jägerburger 193
'Steak' with mash 193
Mitrailette sandwich 194
'Steak' bagel 194
Pistachio-crusted 'steak' 194
Rossini 196
'Steak' pie 196

Egg substitute
Mushroom omelette 199
Tortilla 199
Frittata 200
Jerusalem artichoke & truffle oil cake .. 200
Cointreau French toast 202
Fu-yung 202
Matcha pancakes 202

Tempeh
Spring rolls 205
Tempeh tandoori 205
Cauliflower soup 206
Tempeh stew 206
Smoky burger patty 206
'Bacon' salad 209
Italian-style burger 209
Tempeh sautéed with onions 210
Spicy tempeh balls 210
Tempeh cheese 210

Smoked tofu
Hawaiian salad 213
Carrot & cumin soup 213
Terrine 214
Green peppercorn tofu burger 214
Scandinavian ragout 217

Tofu skewer 217
Baked baguette 217
Autumn rolls 218
Vol-au-vent 218
Red pesto 218

Plain tofu
Sesame grilled tofu 221
Tofu marinière 221
Summer bruschetta 223
Bruschetta 223
Golden nuggets 223
Cretan salad 225
Courgette cannelloni 225
Vegan egg muffin 226
Palak tofu 226
Tofu & vegetable stew 226

Silken tofu
Tofu mayonnaise 229
Asparagus tartlets 229
Kimchi soup 230
Leek & coriander quiche 230
Chive cream & crudités 230
Banana flan 232
Irish coffee cream 232
Hiyayakko 232
Crème brûlée chartreuse 234
Cointreau tiramisu 234

Yogurt
Mango lassi 237
Mojito curd 237
Tzatziki 239
Fromage frais 239
Ktipiti 239
Raita 241
'Chicken' korma 241
Matchatella 241
Yogurt loaf 242
Autumn cake 242

Address book 244
Index 245

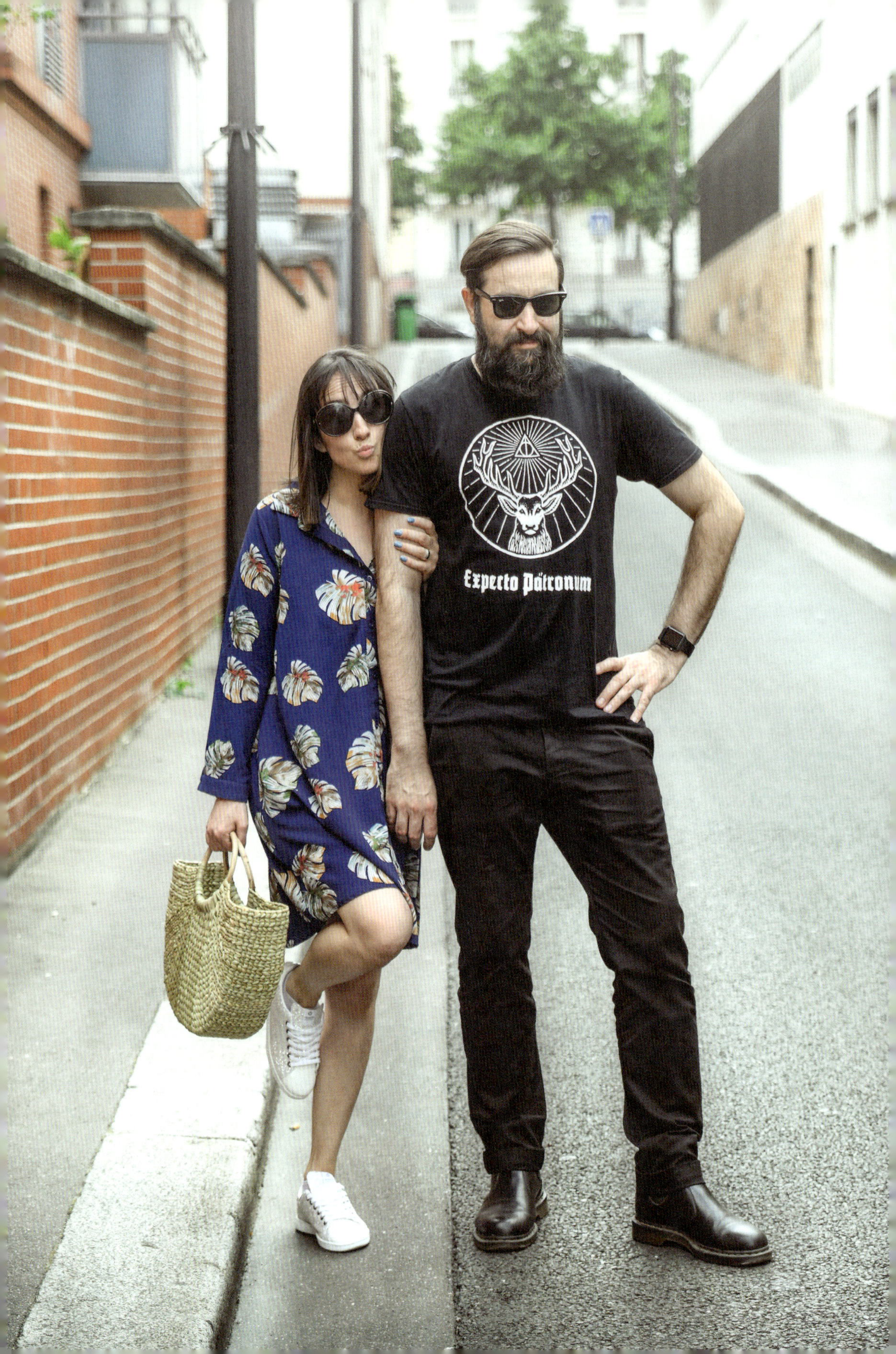
Experto Patronum

INTRODUCTION

This book is designed for busy city dwellers. Let's call them 'urban vegans'. Why? Because there are noticeable differences in access to food according to where we live. In big cities like London, Paris or New York, you can find every possible vegan ingredient, and endless products imported from exotic countries.

On the other hand, since there is rarely local production, it can often be very hard to find top-quality super-fresh fruits and vegetables at reasonable prices. The situation is different in rural towns or villages where fresh fruits and vegetables can be sourced from farmer's markets or by picking your own, but where it will certainly be more difficult to get a simple piece of tempeh ... each has its advantages and disadvantages!

You may also be surprised to find that almost all the vegetables and herbs used in this book are frozen. The first obvious advantage to using frozen is it's time saving! No cleaning, no peeling, no cutting – and available in small quantities, without waste. The second advantage is having the basics on hand for an instant meal. You are always ready to go! Finally, you are assured of having the highest levels of vitamins and nutrients. Quality frozen vegetables are frozen within 24 hours of being picked. While fresh vegetables found in the high street shops and supermarkets unfortunately spend at least more than a week between harvesting and display.

So the aim of this book is to provide recipes for real cooking every day using mainly products that are easily found in neighbourhood shops and supermarkets. The idea is to use what you have on hand, stored in your kitchen cupboards or at the bottom of the fridge.

STORECUPBOARD ESSENTIALS

Ideally, you should never need to go out at the last minute, just because an ingredient is missing. That's why we have a 'basic' shopping list to fill our kitchen. When an ingredient is missing, you can simply pick it up the next time that you're at the shops. This allows you to be ready for any culinary eventuality.

IN THE CUPBOARDS

- Agar-agar
- Agave syrup
- Apple compôte
- Baking powder
- Breadcrumbs
- Coconut milk
- Cornflour
- Couscous
- Fried onions
- Green pesto
- Ground almonds
- Icing sugar
- Malted yeast
- Maple syrup
- Nori sheets
- Pasta (different types)
- Peanut butter
- Polenta
- Porridge
- Quinoa
- Red lentils
- Rice (different types)
- Rice paper sheets
- Tahini
- Tapioca flour
- Textured vegetable protein (different forms)
- Tinned chickpeas
- Tinned chopped tomatoes
- Tinned green lentils
- Tinned haricot beans
- Tinned kidney beans
- Tinned ravioli
- Tinned sweetcorn
- Tomato purée
- Tomato sauce
- Unsweetened cocoa powder
- Vanilla extract
- Vanilla sugar
- Vegan pâté
- Vegetable stock
- Wheat flour
- Xanthan gum

IN THE SPICE RACK

- Bay leaves
- Black pepper
- Cardamom
- Chipotle powder
- Cinnamon
- Cloves
- Coarse salt
- Coriander
- Cumin
- Espelette pepper
- Fine salt
- French four spice mix
- Garam masala
- Garlic powder
- Jalapeño sauce
- Kala namak (black salt)
- Liquid smoke
- Madras curry powder
- Nutmeg
- Oregano
- Pink peppercorns
- Saffron
- Sage
- Smoked paprika
- Sweet paprika
- Thyme

Storecupboard Essentials

- Turmeric
- Worcestershire sauce

IN THE FRIDGE

- Beer
- Button mushrooms
- Capers
- Different meat substitutes
- Dijon mustard
- Fresh herbs
- Grated vegan cheese
- Tomato ketchup
- Lemon juice
- Vegan margarine
- Natural soya milk
- Piccalilli
- Pickles
- Plain tofu
- Seitan
- Sliced vegan cheese
- Smoked tofu
- Soya cream
- Soya yogurts
- Sun-dried tomatoes in oil
- Tempeh
- Variety of plant-based milks
- Vegan mayonnaise
- Wholegrain mustard

IN THE FREEZER

- Carrots
- Courgettes
- Diced potatoes
- Frozen herbs
- Garlic
- Ginger
- Mashed potatoes
- Mixed julienne vegetables
- Mixed mushrooms
- Mixed vegetables
- Onions
- Peas
- Peppers
- Ratatouille
- Shallots
- Sweet potatoes
- Tomatoes

IN THE OTHER CUPBOARD...

- Apple cider vinegar
- Balsamic vinegar
- Calvados
- Cognac
- Jägermeister
- Olive oil
- Port
- Rapeseed oil
- Red wine
- Sriracha
- Tamari
- Toasted sesame oil
- Whisky
- White wine

Of course this isn't an exhaustive list and should be personalised according to your tastes and the space you have available. For example, in our case, you can easily quadruple spices, as well as exotic sauces and chilli-based mixtures. It's a passion! It's up to you to see where your taste buds go. It should be noted that organic versions of the vast majority of products in this list are available.

285 recipes for busy urbanites

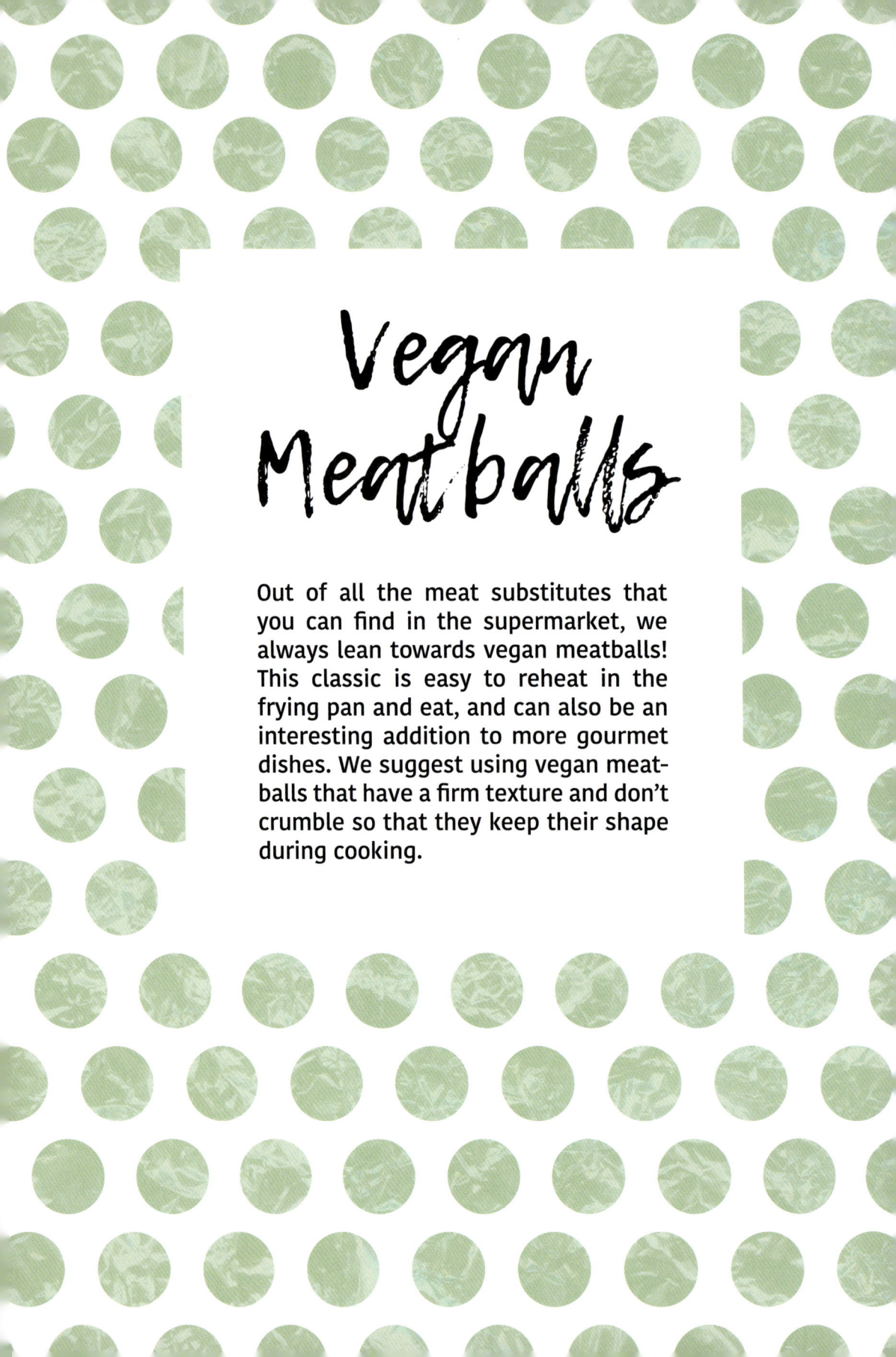

Vegan Meatballs

Out of all the meat substitutes that you can find in the supermarket, we always lean towards vegan meatballs! This classic is easy to reheat in the frying pan and eat, and can also be an interesting addition to more gourmet dishes. We suggest using vegan meatballs that have a firm texture and don't crumble so that they keep their shape during cooking.

Vegan Meatballs

RIBOULADE

- 3 tbsp tomato ketchup
- 2 tsp Cajun spice
- 250 g vegan meatballs
- 2 tbsp rapeseed oil
- 1 garlic clove, crushed
- 150 g basmati rice
- 1½ tsp coarse salt
- 500 g frozen or tinned ratatouille
- 4 tbsp chopped fresh basil

Mix the ketchup with 1 tsp of Cajun spice in a bowl, then add the vegan meatballs. Cover with the sauce and set aside. In a large pot, heat the oil with the crushed garlic and remaining 1 tsp of cajun spice. Add the rice and heat for 1 minute. Add 450 ml of water and the coarse salt. Cook over a medium heat until the liquid completely evaporates (around 10 minutes) then add the ratatouille. Mix well and cover, cook for 10 minutes, then add the chopped basil. Cook the vegan meatballs in a frying pan over a low heat for 5 minutes, turning regularly. Serve the rice in shallow bowls and top with the meatballs.

YAKITORI

- 4 tsp soy sauce
- 4 tsp sake
- 4 tsp agave syrup
- 225 g vegan meatballs
- 1 tbsp sesame seeds
- 2 tbsp chopped fresh chives

Mix the soy sauce, sake and agave syrup in a bowl. Marinate the meatballs in the liquid for 20 minutes. Prepare the yakitori by placing three meatballs on each wooden skewer. Heat a dry non-stick frying pan and grill the skewers, turning them every 10 seconds. When the skewers start to brown, deglaze with the leftover liquid. Turn the skewers in the liquid until it completely evaporates. Scatter with sesame seeds and chives before serving.

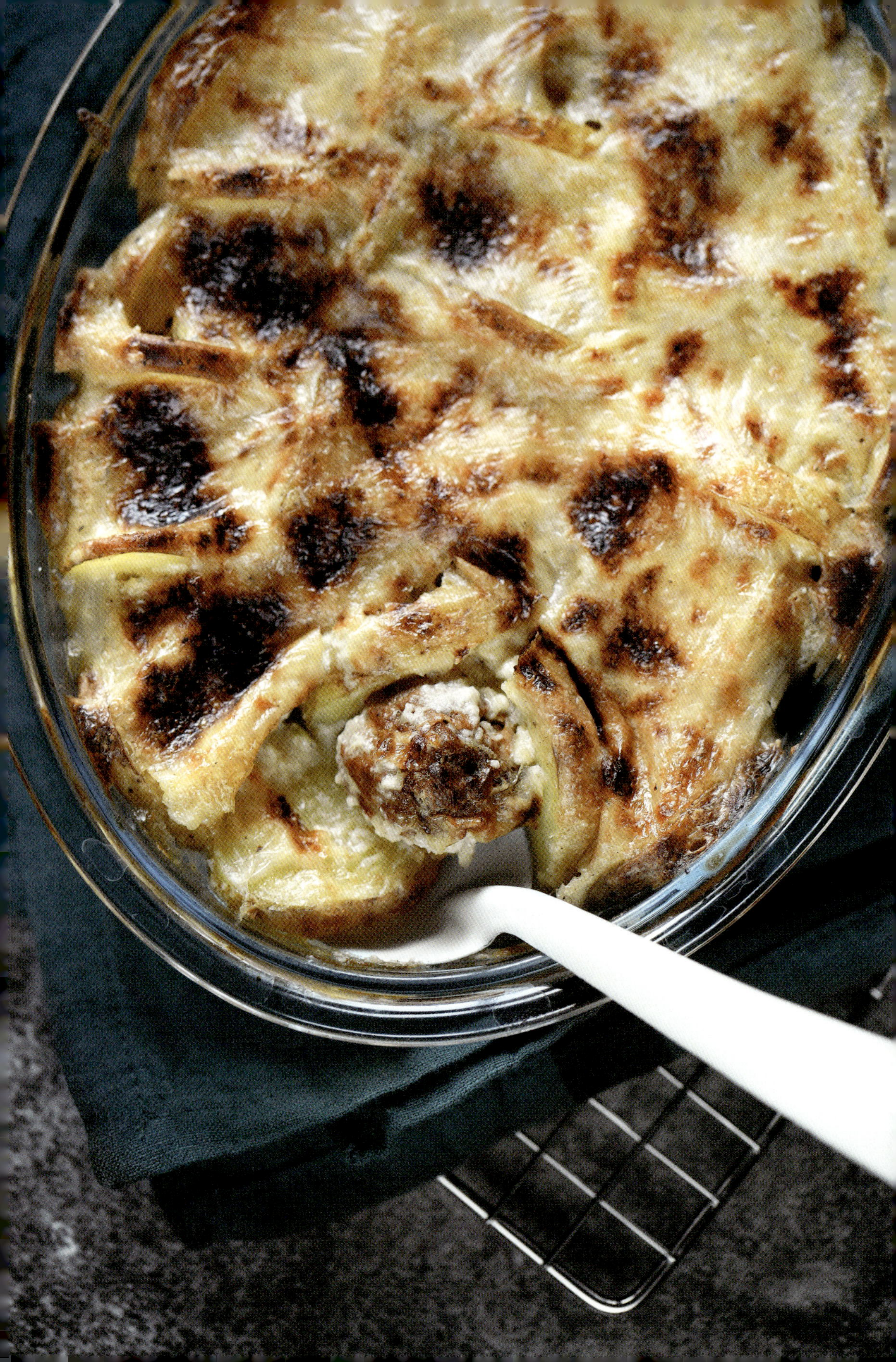

VEGGIE BALL GRATIN

- 225 g vegan meatballs
- 350 g potatoes
- 200 ml soya cream
- 100 g grated vegan cheese
- 1 tsp Dijon mustard
- ¼ tsp grated nutmeg
- Generous pinch of fine salt

Place the meatballs in a gratin dish. Cut the unpeeled potatoes into 0.5-cm thick slices.

Add to the gratin dish, alternating between meatballs and sliced potatoes. Mix the soya cream with the grated cheese, mustard, nutmeg and salt in a bowl. Pour evenly over the potatoes and meatballs. Cover the gratin dish and bake in the oven for 50 minutes at 180°C (gas mark 4) then place under the grill for 10 minutes and serve.

HOT & COLD SALAD

- 250 g small potatoes (pre-cooked)
- 2 medium-sized carrots
- 15 radishes
- 225 g vegan meatballs
- 15 cherry tomatoes
- 8 artichoke hearts in oil
- 150 g spinach leaves
- 200 g cooked green beans
- 4 tsp walnut oil
- 2 tsp balsamic vinegar
- 1 tsp mustard
- Some fresh herbs of your choice

Sauté the potatoes in a frying pan with a drizzle of oil then slice. Coarsely grate the carrots and slice the radishes. Halve the meatballs and brown in a hot frying pan. Halve the cherry tomatoes and quarter the artichoke hearts.

Put the spinach and cooked green beans in a salad bowl and add the rest of the vegetables. For the dressing, pour the oil, vinegar and mustard into a ramekin and mix. Chop the fresh herbs before adding to the salad. Pour in the dressing, mix everything together and serve. Season with salt and pepper if needed.

Vegan Meatballs

ORIENTAL VEGAN MEATBALLS →

- 2 tbsp olive oil • ½ tsp coriander seeds • 100 g onions • 2 tsp chopped garlic • 150 g frozen courgettes • 100 g frozen tomatoes • 2 tsp ras-el-hanout • 225 g vegan meatballs • 500 ml vegetable stock • 4 tsp tomato purée • 2 tbsp chopped fresh coriander

In a large pot, heat the oil with the crushed coriander seeds. Add the onions, garlic, courgettes and tomatoes. Cook until fully defrosted then add the ras-el-hanout. Mix well and cook for 2 minutes. Add the meatballs and sauté over a medium heat for 3 minutes. Add the hot vegetable stock and tomato purée. Stir and cook over a high heat for 10 minutes. Finish by adding the chopped coriander and serve.

TOMATO & VEGAN MEATBALL SOUP

- 2 tsp chopped garlic
- 200 g sliced onions
- Olive oil
- 1 clove
- 1 tsp paprika
- Pepper
- 600 g peeled tomatoes
- 500 ml vegetable stock
- 225 g vegan meatballs

Sauté the garlic and onions with 1 tbsp of olive oil, the clove and the paprika in a large casserole dish. Season with pepper. When the onions start to brown, add the tomatoes and vegetable stock (seasoned). Bring to the boil, cover and reduce over a low heat. Cook for 15 minutes. Blend until smooth and creamy. Brown the meatballs in a pre-heated frying pan with a little olive oil. Serve the soup in bowls and evenly distributed meatballs on top.

VEGAN MEATBALLS WITH MUSTARD

- 3 tbsp soya cream • 1 tsp agave syrup • 4 tsp Dijon mustard • 3 tbsp wholegrain mustard • ½ tsp four spice mix • 2 tbsp chopped chives • 225 g vegan meatballs • 1 tbsp rapeseed oil

Mix the cream with the agave syrup, Dijon mustard and wholegrain mustard in a bowl. Add the four spice mix and chives. Cook the meatballs with the rapeseed oil in a frying pan until crisp. Add the sauce and cook over a low heat for 2 minutes.

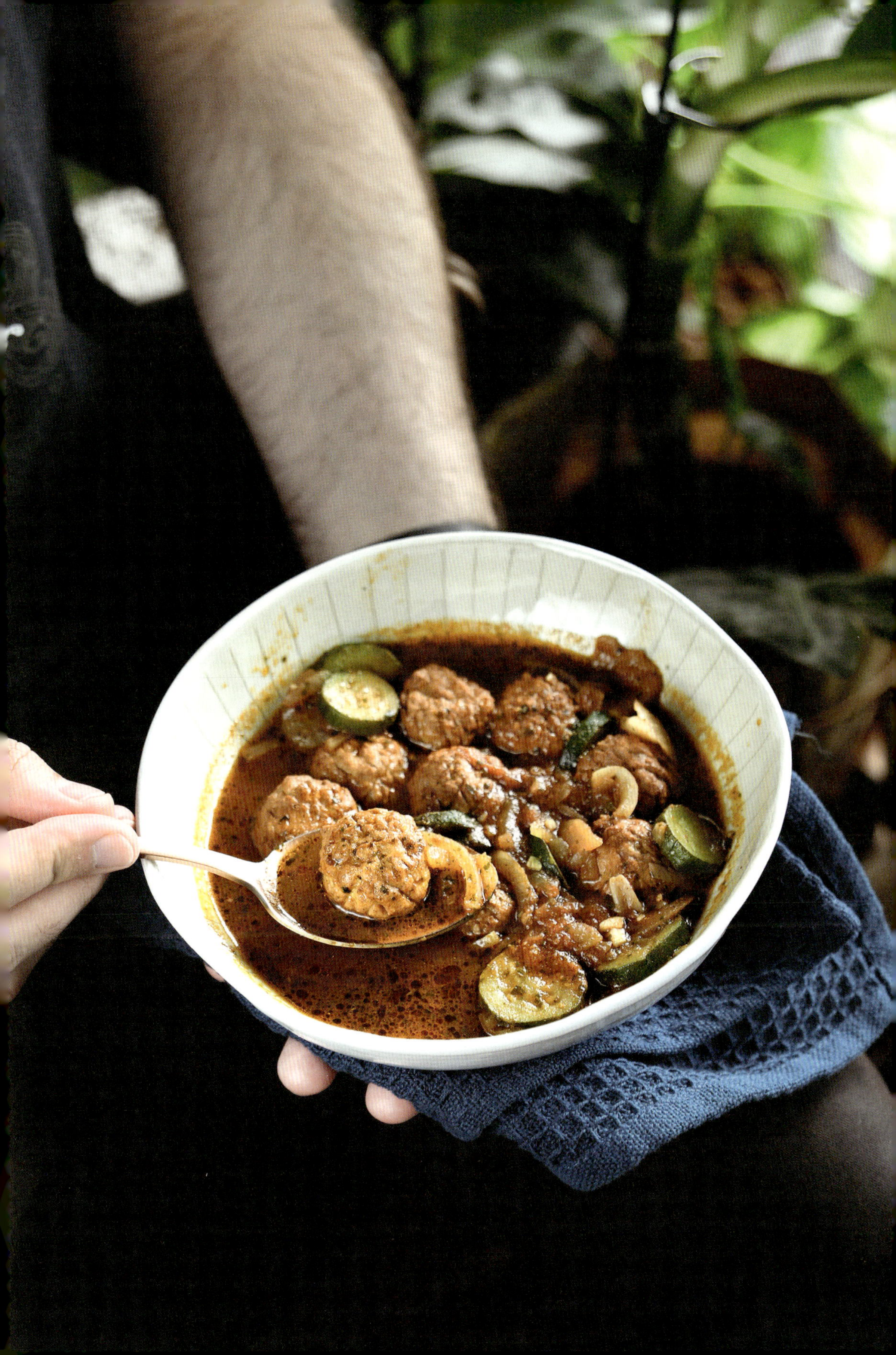

Vegan Meatballs

SURPRISE VEGAN MEATBALLS →

- 225 g vegan meatballs
- 30 g vegan cheese
- 80 g plain flour
- 2½ tbsp cornflour
- 1 tsp garlic powder
- 1 tsp fine salt
- 1¼ tsp Espelette pepper
- 1¼ tsp smoked paprika
- 200 ml soya milk
- 50 g panko breadcrumbs

Use a small knife to remove a small piece from the outside of the meatball and make a hole in the centre. Place 2 g vegan cheese in the centre and close with the removed outer part of the meatball. Mix the flour with the cornflour, garlic powder, salt, Espelette pepper and smoked paprika in a large mixing bowl. Pour in the soya milk and whisk until the flour and spices dissolve. Put the panko breadcrumbs in another bowl. Dip the meatballs in the batter, then coat in panko breadcrumbs. Repeat. Heat oil in a deep fryer to 180°C. Deep fry the meatballs for 3 minutes, place on kitchen paper to absorb any excess oil and serve.

SPICY VEGAN MEATBALLS

- 2 tbsp olive oil • 150 g onions
- 2 tsp chopped garlic • 1 tbsp grated ginger • 225 g vegan meatballs • ½ tsp fine salt • 1 tbsp Cognac • 400 g tomato sauce • 2 tsp Worcestershire sauce • 1 tbsp jalapeño sauce

Heat the oil in a pan with the onions, garlic and ginger. When the onions become translucent, add the meatballs, salt and stir. Cook over a medium heat for 5 minutes, stirring occasionally. Deglaze with Cognac, then add the tomato sauce, Worcestershire sauce and jalapeño sauce. Stir and simmer over a low heat for 10 minutes.

VEGAN MEATBALLS WITH CAPERS

- 200 ml soya cream • 1 tbsp lemon juice • 25 g capers in vinegar • 3 tbsp chopped flat-leaf parsley • Salt
- 225 g vegan meatballs • Cornflour
- 4 tsp vegan margarine

Heat the cream with the lemon juice in a small pan. Add the drained capers, chopped parsley and salt. Heat the sauce over a low heat for 5 minutes. Coat the meatballs in cornflour. Melt the margarine in a hot frying pan. Cook the meatballs in the frothy margarine over a medium heat. Pour the sauce over the meatballs, heat through and serve.

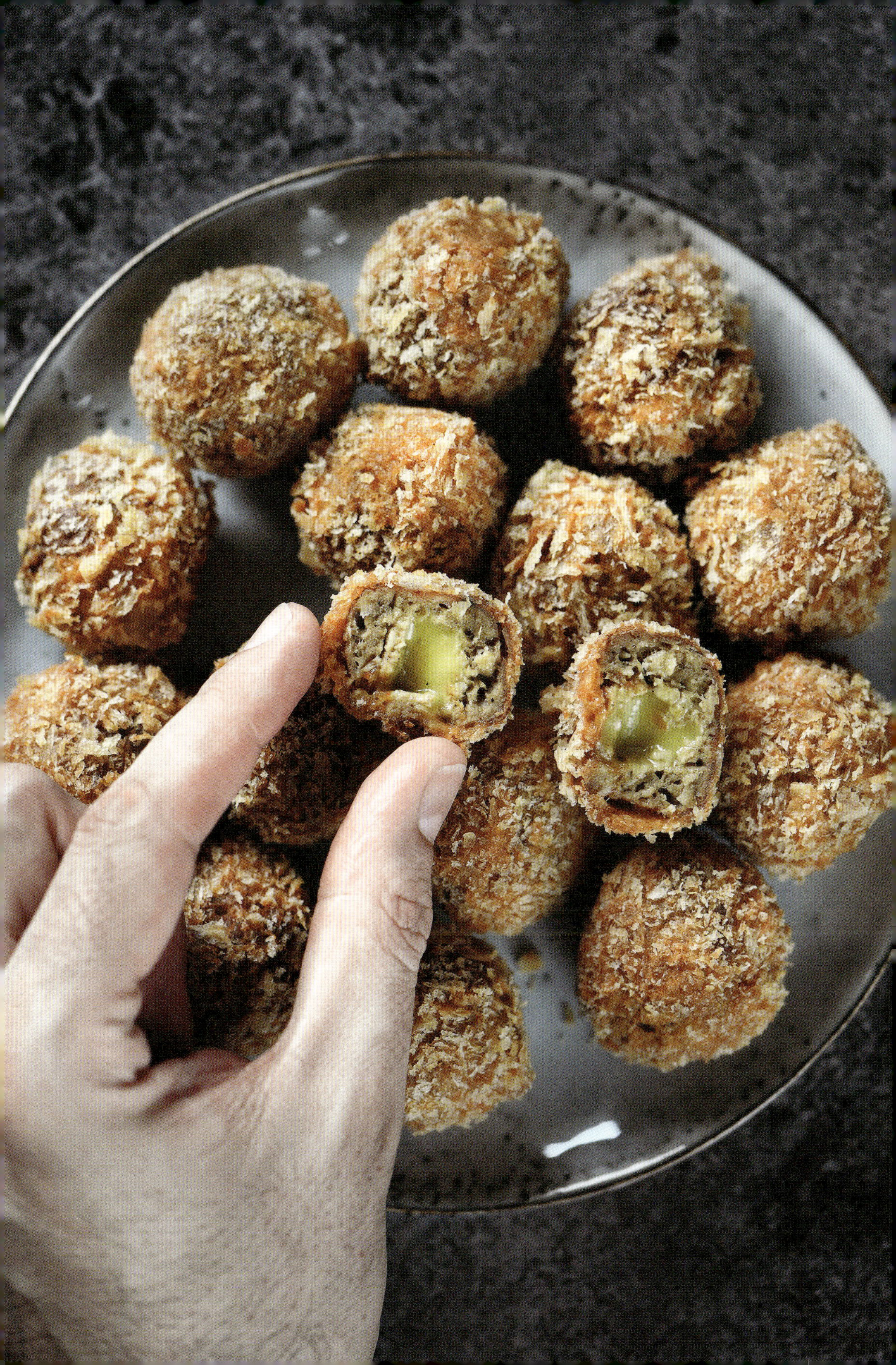

Grains

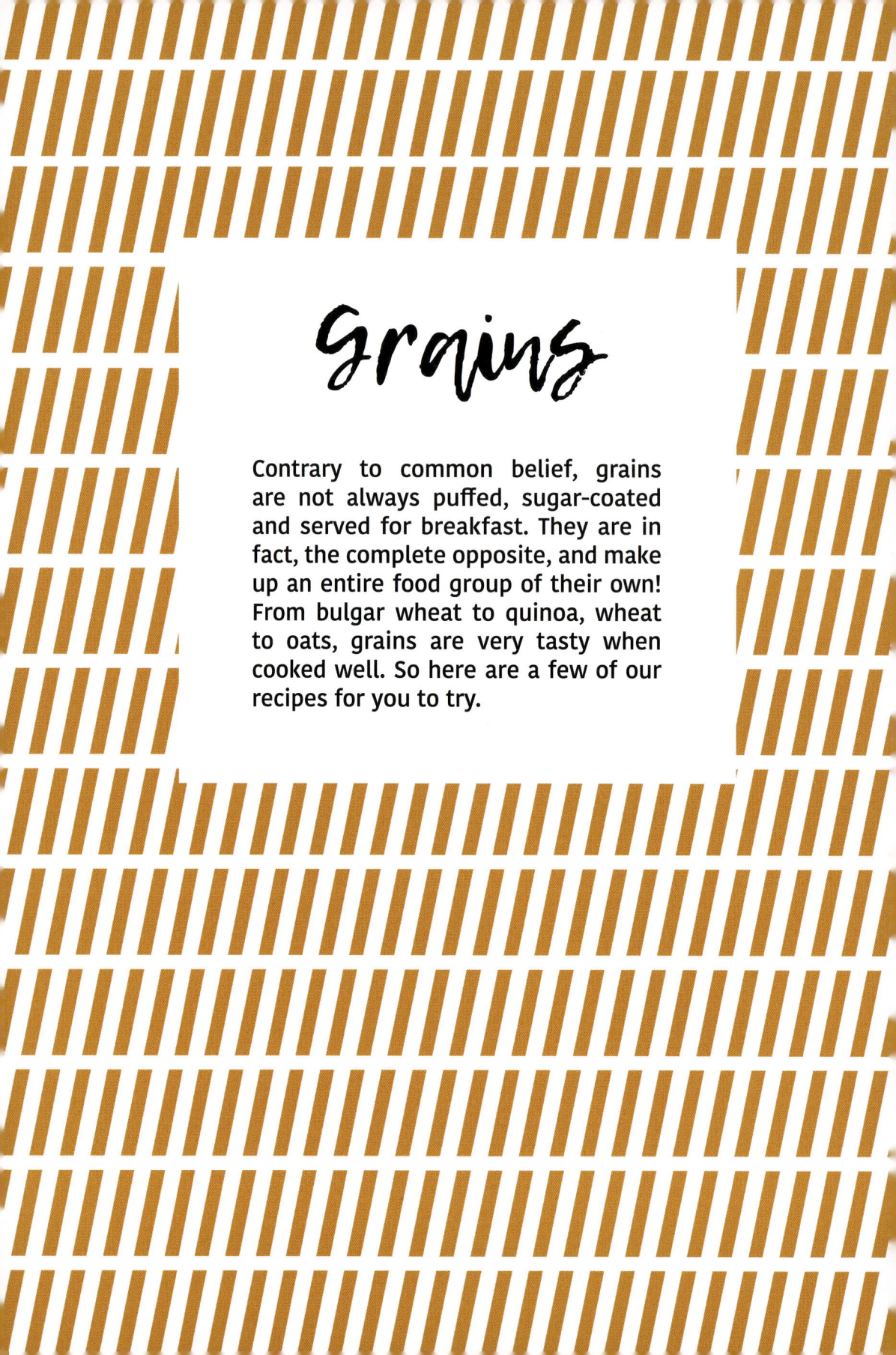

Contrary to common belief, grains are not always puffed, sugar-coated and served for breakfast. They are in fact, the complete opposite, and make up an entire food group of their own! From bulgar wheat to quinoa, wheat to oats, grains are very tasty when cooked well. So here are a few of our recipes for you to try.

Grains

WHEATSOTTO

- 3 tbsp olive oil
- 40 g frozen shallots
- 2½ tsp ground coriander
- 400 g Ebly pure durum wheat or quick cook farro di cocco
- 1 litre vegetable stock
- 4 tsp soya cream
- 2 tbsp malted yeast
- Black pepper
- 300 g mixed frozen mushrooms

In a large pot, sauté the shallots and coriander in the olive oil. Once the shallots are lightly browned, add the dried wheat and stir. Pour in just enough stock to cover the wheat and cook until it evaporates, stirring regularly so that it doesn't stick to the bottom of the pan. Add 100 ml of stock, leave to evaporate and repeat. This should take about 12 minutes for wheat or 20 minutes for spelt or barley. Add the soya cream, yeast and season with pepper. Cook the mushrooms in a frying pan and add to the wheatsotto.

QUINOA WITH MUSHROOMS

- 30 g dried mushrooms (around 80 g when rehydrated)
- 200 g quinoa
- 1 litre vegetable stock
- 2 tbsp toasted sesame oil
- 1 tbsp tamari sauce
- 4 tbsp chopped fresh chives
- 1 tbsp black sesame seeds

Cover the mushrooms in warm water for 15 minutes to rehydrate them. If mushrooms are whole, chop into bite-size pieces. Cook the quinoa in the vegetable stock for about 13 minutes, then drain. Heat the sesame oil in a wok and sauté the drained mushrooms. Add the quinoa, mix well over a medium heat, drizzle with 1 tbsp of tamari and scatter with chopped chives and black sesame seeds.

Grains

STUFFED TOMATOES →

• 4 tomatoes (1.5 kg) • Olive oil • 450 g frozen chopped vegetables • 120 g green pesto • 150 g pre-cooked quinoa • Salt • 1 tbsp balsamic vinegar • Pepper

Cut the tops off the tomatoes, then remove the flesh with a spoon and cut it into small pieces. Don't keep the tomato juice. Place the tomatoes in an ovenproof dish and set aside. Heat a little olive oil in a wok and sauté the chopped vegetables. Allow it to reduce, then add half of the pesto, stir and add the quinoa and the tomato flesh. Cover and reduce for 5 minutes stirring occasionally. Season with salt, add the balsamic vinegar, the remaining pesto, season with pepper and stir. Generously stuff the tomatoes, cover with the tomato tops and bake in the oven at 180°C (gas mark 4) for 30 minutes.

ÇIG KÖFTE

• 150 g walnuts • 250 g cooked bulgar wheat • 2 garlic cloves • 3 tbsp frozen parsley • 1¼ tsp Espelette pepper • 1¼ tsp sweet paprika • 2¾ tsp ground cumin • ¼ tsp fine salt • 1 tbsp olive oil • 2½ tbsp tomato purée

Soak the walnuts in a bowl of warm water for 20 minutes. Blend the walnuts, bulgar wheat, crushed garlic, parsley, pepper, paprika, cumin and salt together in a food processor with an S blade. Blend at full power until a grainy dough is formed. Add the olive oil and tomato purée. Blend again to ensure that the mixture is evenly mixed. Shape with your hands (using gloves) by placing a heaped tablespoon of mixture in your hand. Lightly squeeze your fingers to give the köfte their characteristic ridged shape. Serve with, for example, a green salad of mint, flat-leaf parsley, pickled peppers, fresh tomatoes and grenadine syrup.

MOROCCAN COUSCOUS

• 1 kg mixed frozen vegetables • 1 tbsp olive oil • 2 tsp ras-el-hanout • 1½ tbsp frozen parsley • 1.5 litres vegetable stock • 1 tsp harissa paste • 500 g pre-cooked couscous • 4 tsp vegan margarine • 200 g vegan meatballs • 200 g spicy vegan sausage

Sauté the vegetables with the oil in a large pot for 5 minutes. Add the ras-el-hanout, parsley and vegetable stock. Stir and cook over a medium heat for 20 minutes. Once cooked, add the harissa and stir. Remove the vegetables from the broth. Reheat the couscous with the margarine in a frying pan. Grill the vegan meatballs and merguez in a separate pan. On a large plate, arrange the couscous around outside of the plate, place the vegetables in the centre and top with the meatballs and merguez sausages. Serve the broth on the side.

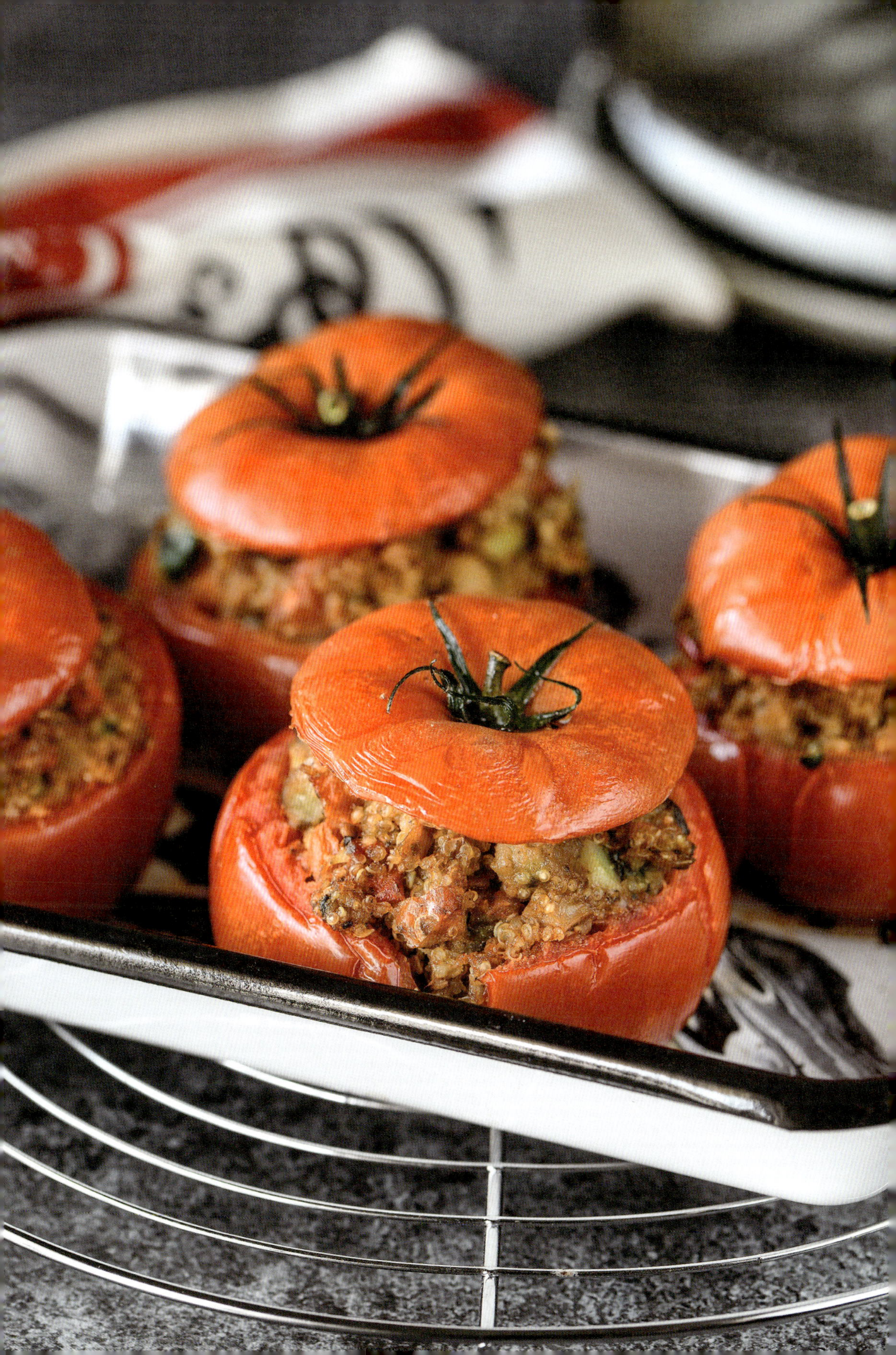

grains

BUDDHA BOWL

- 400 g Ebly pure durum wheat or quick cook farro di cocco
- 20 g chopped chives
- 1 apple
- 120 g celery
- 400 g broccoli
- Olive oil
- 4 tbsp tamari
- 400 g tempeh
- 4 tsp agave syrup
- 1 tsp smoked paprika
- 2 tbsp apple cider vinegar
- 40 g mayonnaise
- Pinch salt
- ½ tsp Espelette pepper
- 2 avocados
- 100 g baby spinach leaves
- Fresh mint

Mix the wheat with the chives in a bowl and set aside. Peel the apple, remove the core, cut into small pieces and set aside. Cut the celery into small pieces and set aside. Cut the broccoli into florets and sear over a high heat in a wok with a dash of olive oil for 5 minutes. Deglaze with half the tamari and cook for a few more minutes over a medium heat, stirring regularly. Set aside. Slice the tempeh. Mix together the remaining tamari, 2 tbsp of olive oil, the agave syrup and smoked paprika. Pour over the tempeh and mix. Sauté in a hot frying pan for 2 minutes on each side to caramelise the tempeh. Set aside. Mix 4 tbsp of olive oil with the apple cider vinegar, mayonnaise, salt, Espelette pepper and 2 tbsp of water in a bowl. Halve the avocados and cut into thin slices. Distribute the spinach and the other ingredients equally and arrange tastefully in four large bowls. Drizzle with a little vinaigrette, garnish with fresh mint and enjoy.

WHEAT BIRYANI

- 50 g frozen peas
- 200 g frozen cauliflower
- 100 g frozen carrots
- 4 tbsp sunflower oil
- 2 bay leaves
- 1½ tsp cumin seeds
- 3 cloves
- 10 cardamom pods
- 100 g frozen onions
- 100 g natural soya yogurt
- 2 tbsp tomato purée
- 2 tsp turmeric
- 2 tsp garam masala
- 400 g Ebly pure durum wheat or quick cook farro di cocco
- 1 bunch fresh coriander

Put the peas, cauliflower and carrots into a large bowl and fill with hot water. Soak for 5 minutes, then drain. Chop up the cauliflower and cut the carrots into small pieces, then set aside. In a large pot, heat the oil with the bay leaves, cumin seeds, cloves and crushed cardamom pods. Add the onions and cook for 5 minutes, then add the vegetables. Mix the yogurt with the tomato purée, turmeric and garam masala in a bowl. Pour into the pot and stir. Add the wheat and 100 ml of cold water. Cook for 5 minutes over a medium heat. Garnish with chopped coriander and serve.

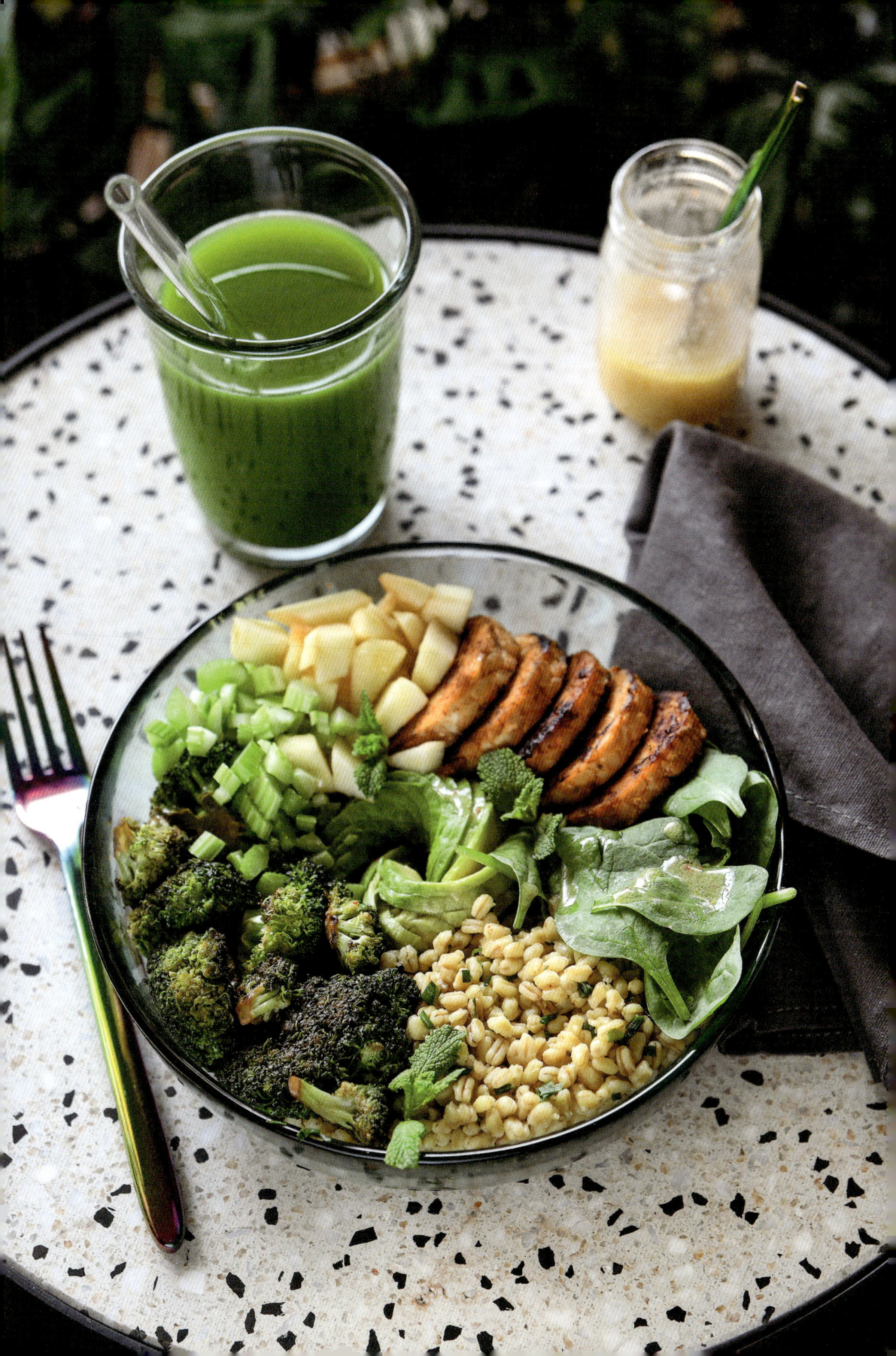

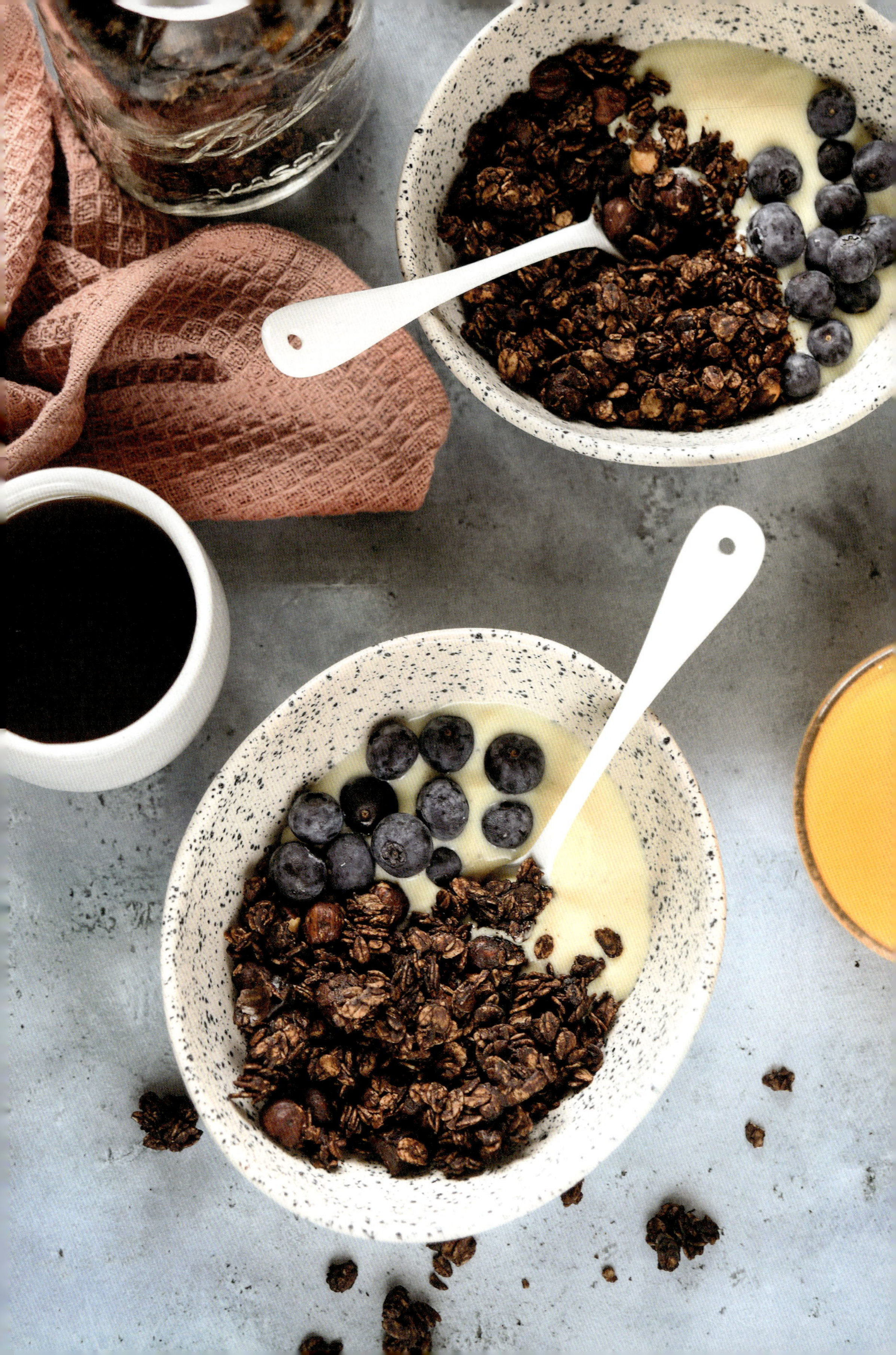

Grains

CHOCOLATE GRANOLA

- 300 g jumbo rolled oats
- 40 g desiccated coconut
- 40 g cocoa powder
- 100 g chocolate chips
- 100 g hazelnuts
- 2 pinches of salt
- 6 tbsp maple syrup
- 60 g coconut oil
- 1 tbsp vanilla extract

Preheat the oven to 180°C (gas mark 4). Pour the oats, grated coconut and cocoa powder in a large mixing bowl and mix together. Add the chocolate chips and whole hazelnuts, then mix and add the salt. Mix the maple syrup, melted coconut oil and vanilla extract in a bowl. Pour over the dry mixture, mix well to coat evenly and spread out on a baking tray lined with baking parchment. Bake for 30–45 minutes. Check after 30 minutes, the granola should be crunchy. Leave to cool and store in a large airtight container.

SEMOLINA CAKE

- 400 g fresh pineapple
- 1 tbsp vegan margarine
- 110 g caster sugar
- 2 tbsp rum
- 250 ml non-dairy milk
- 250 ml coconut milk
- 1 tbsp vanilla extract
- 80 g fine semolina

Cut the pineapple into small dice. Melt the margarine in a hot frying pan, add the diced pineapple and mix. Add 60 g of sugar and caramelise for several minutes, stirring regularly. Deglaze with the rum, allow to reduce and pour into a 20-cm cake tin. Heat the milks, 50 g of sugar and vanilla extract in a pan over a low heat. Add the semolina in a fine stream and stir constantly until it begins to thicken. Pour over the diced pineapples and refrigerate overnight. Remove from the cake tin and enjoy.

MORNING PORRIDGE

- 100 g rolled oats
- 1 tbsp raw cane sugar
- 500 ml natural soya milk
- 1 tsp vanilla extract
- A pinch of cinnamon
- 30 g almonds
- 30 g cashew nuts
- 30 g peeled pistachio nuts
- 30 g dried cranberries
- Maple syrup

In a heavy-based pan, mix together the oats, sugar, soya milk, vanilla and cinnamon. Bring to the boil, stirring regularly. Lower the heat and allow to thicken. It should be a similar texture to risotto. Meanwhile, chop the almonds, cashew nuts and pistachios. Toast them in a dry, hot pan for 1 minute. Divide the porridge between two bowls, add equal amounts of almonds, cashews, pistachios and dried cranberries. Top with a generous dash of maple syrup.

Charcuterie

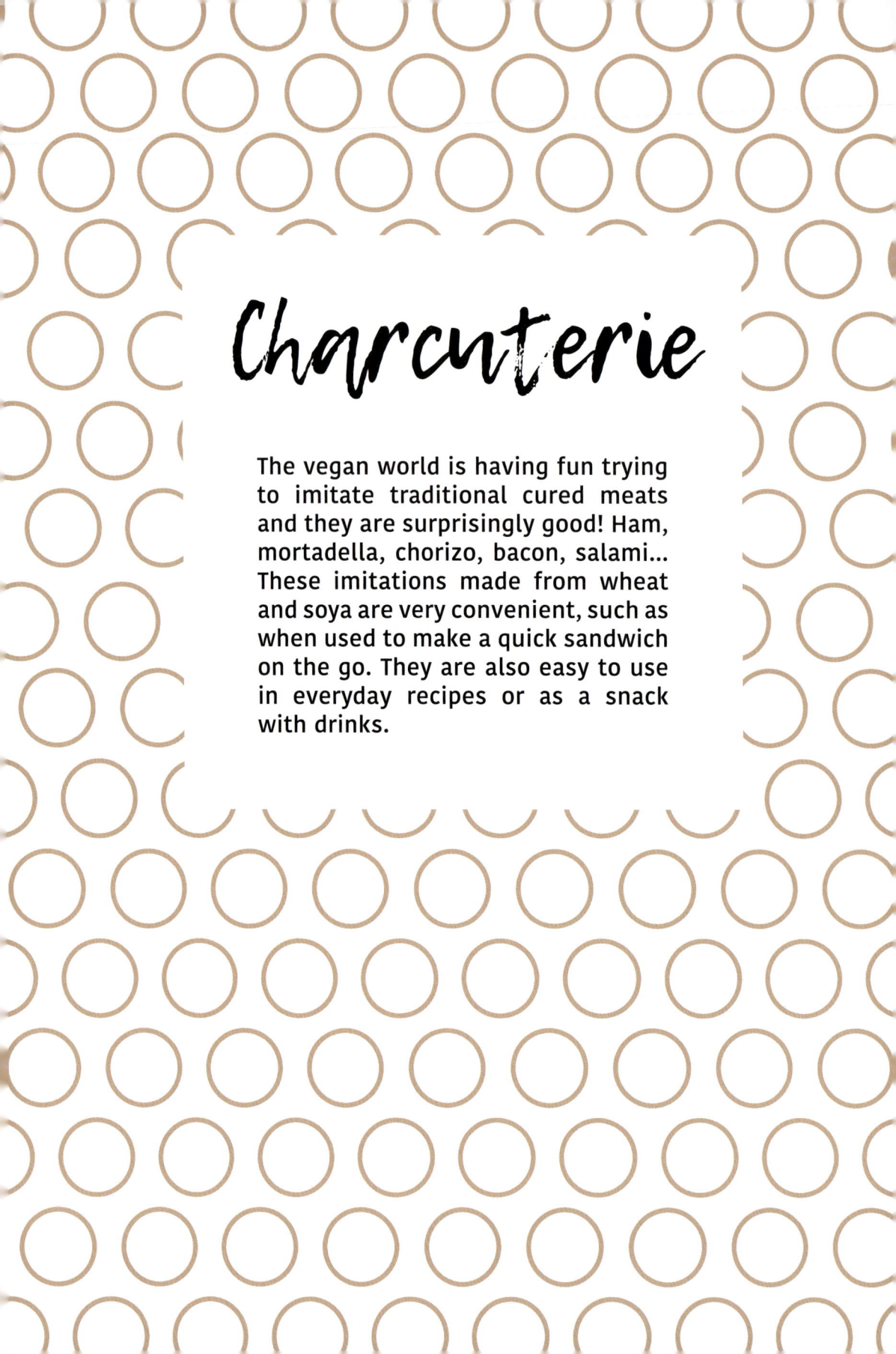

The vegan world is having fun trying to imitate traditional cured meats and they are surprisingly good! Ham, mortadella, chorizo, bacon, salami... These imitations made from wheat and soya are very convenient, such as when used to make a quick sandwich on the go. They are also easy to use in everyday recipes or as a snack with drinks.

'CHORIZO' PINWHEELS

- 200 g vegan chorizo
- 200 g silken tofu
- 2 tbsp malted yeast
- ½ tsp dried oregano
- 1 ready-rolled vegan puff pastry sheet

Dice the chorizo and mix with the silken tofu and malted yeast to make a thick cream. Add the oregano and mix well. Spread an even layer of cream over the unrolled pastry. Roll tightly starting from one end to make a thick sausage shape. Wrap in baking parchment and freeze for 20 minutes. Preheat the oven to 200°C (gas mark 6). Cut the sausage into 2-cm-thick slices and place on a baking tray lined with baking parchment or a baking mat. Bake for 30–40 minutes. Allow to cool before serving.

'BLT' BAGEL

- 12 slices smoked vegan ham
- 1 tbsp olive oil
- 100 g vegan mayonnaise
- 1 tsp jalapeño sauce
- 4 tbsp frozen chives
- 2 tomatoes
- 4 poppy seed bagels
- 1 fresh lettuce

Sear the ham slices in a hot frying pan with olive oil. Cut into thick strips. Mix the mayonnaise, jalapeño sauce and chives in a bowl. Slice the tomatoes into 1-cm-thick slices. Halve the bagels, toast them and spread a layer of mayonnaise on the insides.

Assembly: place the tomato slices on the bottom half of the bagel, then add a few lettuce leaves and finish with three slices of vegan ham. Close with the top half of the bagel, press gently and cut in half vertically with a serrated knife.

Charcuterie

'CHORIZO' & POTATO TART

- 6 tbsp soya cream
- 2 tsp cornflour
- 2 tbsp frozen chives
- 2 tbsp malted yeast
- Salt
- Pepper
- 200 g vegan chorizo
- 1 sheet ready-rolled vegan puff pastry
- 400 g pre-cooked sliced potatoes
- Olive oil
- Fresh herbs

Preheat the oven to 180°C (gas mark 4). Mix the soya cream with the cornflour, chives and malted yeast, then season with salt and pepper. Set aside. Cut the chorizo into 3-mm-thick slices. Unroll the puff pastry on a baking tray and fold over the edge to make a 1 cm border. Prick the pastry with a fork and spread the cream on top. Place alternating potato and chorizo slices, letting them overlap, until the whole pastry is covered up to the border. Season with pepper, drizzle with olive oil and bake in the oven for 45 minutes. Take the tart out of the oven, use a brush to coat with another layer of oil, scatter with fresh herbs and serve immediately.

CHICORY GRATIN

- 8 chicory heads (about 800 g)
- Salt
- Pepper
- 2 tbsp olive oil
- 1 tbsp caster sugar
- 16 slices vegan ham
- 500 ml soya milk
- ¼ tsp grated nutmeg
- 3¼ tbsp cornflour
- 6 tbsp malted yeast

Cut the chicory heads in two lengthways, remove the core, then season with salt and pepper. Sauté the chicory, flat side down in a hot frying pan with olive oil. Season with salt and pepper, cover and cook over a low heat for about 10 minutes. Turn over and continue cooking for another 10 minutes. Dust with sugar, deglaze with 2 tbsp of water and caramelise for a few more minutes. Roll the chicory in the vegan ham and place in a gratin dish. Heat the soya milk in a small pan, season with salt and pepper, then add the grated nutmeg. Mix well and once simmering, add the cornflour diluted with a little water. Whisk continuously and allow to thicken over a medium heat. Off the heat, add the yeast and olive oil, mix well, then pour over the chicory. Bake for 35 minutes in an oven preheated to 180°C (gas mark 4).

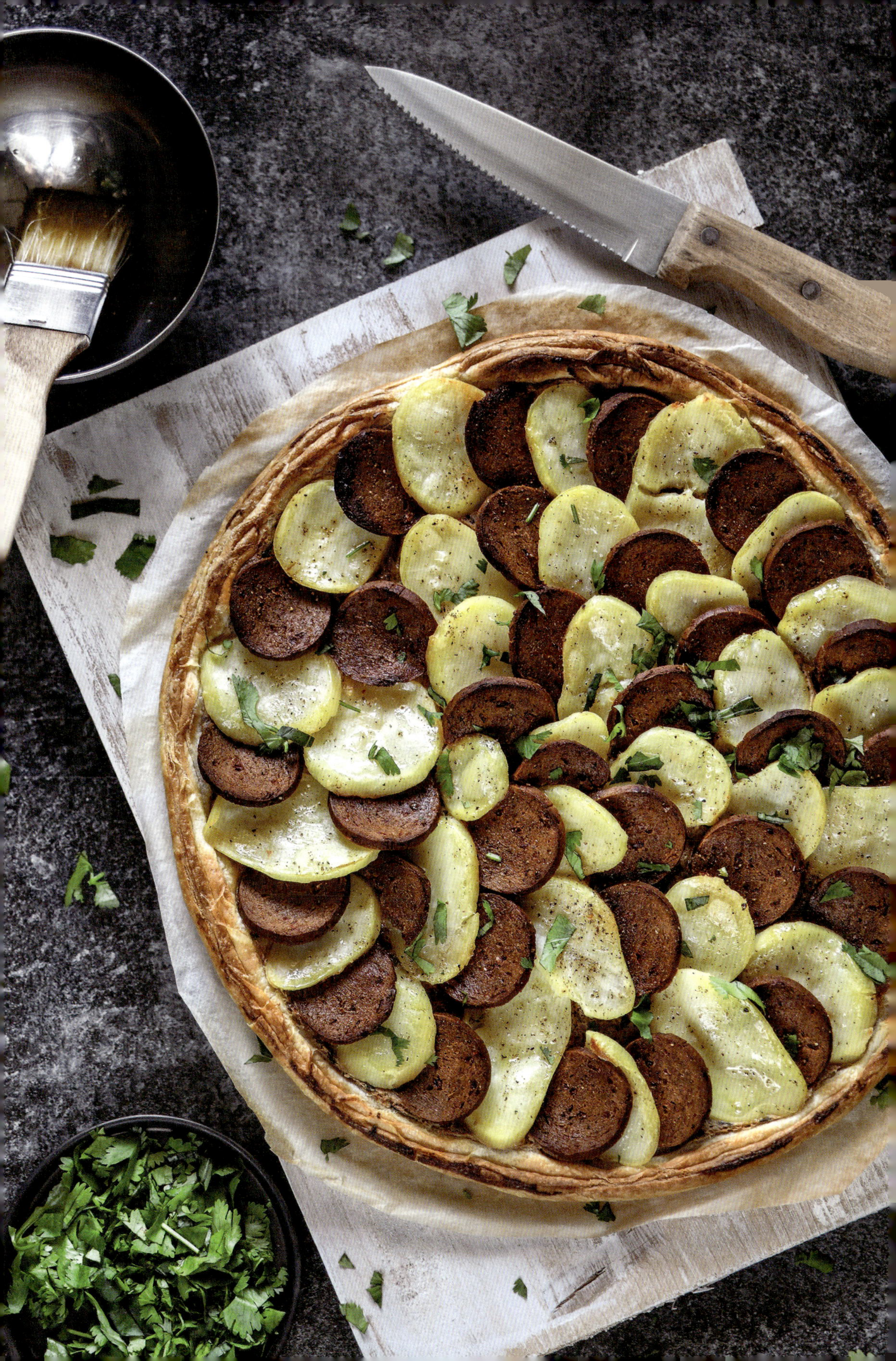

Charcuterie

SAVOURY CUPCAKES →

- 200 g smoked vegan ham
- 200 g cooked lentils
- 4 tbsp soya cream
- 4 tsp mustard
- 40 g tahini
- 150 g plain flour, sifted
- 2½ tbsp cornflour
- 2¼ tsp baking powder
- 2 tbsp malted yeast
- Pinch of salt
- ½ tsp cumin seeds
- ½ tsp coriander seeds
- Black pepper
- 200 ml non-dairy milk
- 3 tbsp olive oil
- Vegan cheese cubes

Chop the ham into small pieces, then blend with the lentils, soya cream, mustard and tahini to make a thick cream. Spoon the cream into a pastry bag with a round tip and refrigerate. Preheat the oven to 180°C (gas mark 4). In a large bowl, mix together the flour, cornflour, baking powder, malted yeast, salt, cumin and coriander seeds, then season generously with pepper. In another bowl, mix the dairy-free milk and oil. Combine the two mixtures, mix well and fill 6 muffin cases until three-quarters full, then push a cube of vegan cheese into the middle. Bake for 20-25 minutes without opening the oven. Let cool before piping on the topping.

STUFFED ARTICHOKES

- 300 g frozen artichoke hearts
- 300 g frozen red onions
- 1 tbsp olive oil
- 100 ml red wine
- ¼ tsp fine salt
- 150 g vegan bacon
- Zest 1 lemon
- Horseradish

Cook the artichoke hearts in a pan of boiling salted water. Boil for 10 minutes, then remove from the water, drain and allow to dry. Sauté the onions in a frying pan with the oil. Once the onions are translucent, deglaze with red wine and season with salt. Leave to reduce until the liquid has evaporated. Add the bacon cut into 1 cm squares. Finish by adding the lemon zest, stir and turn off the heat. Spread a thin layer of horseradish in the centre of the artichoke heart, fill with the onion and bacon mixture, then serve.

MINI APERITIF BROCHETTES

- 120 g spicy vegan sausage
- Cherry tomatoes • 2 tbsp olive oil
- 1 tbsp balsamic vinegar • 1½ tsp herbes de Provence • Pickled onions

Preheat the oven to 200°C (gas mark 6). Cut the sausages into pieces that are the same size as the cherry tomatoes. Mix the olive oil, balsamic vinegar and herbes de Provence in a bowl. Place a piece of sausage, a cherry tomato, another piece of sausage and a pickled onion on a cocktail stick. Brush the brochettes with the sauce. Place on a baking tray and bake for 15–20 minutes.

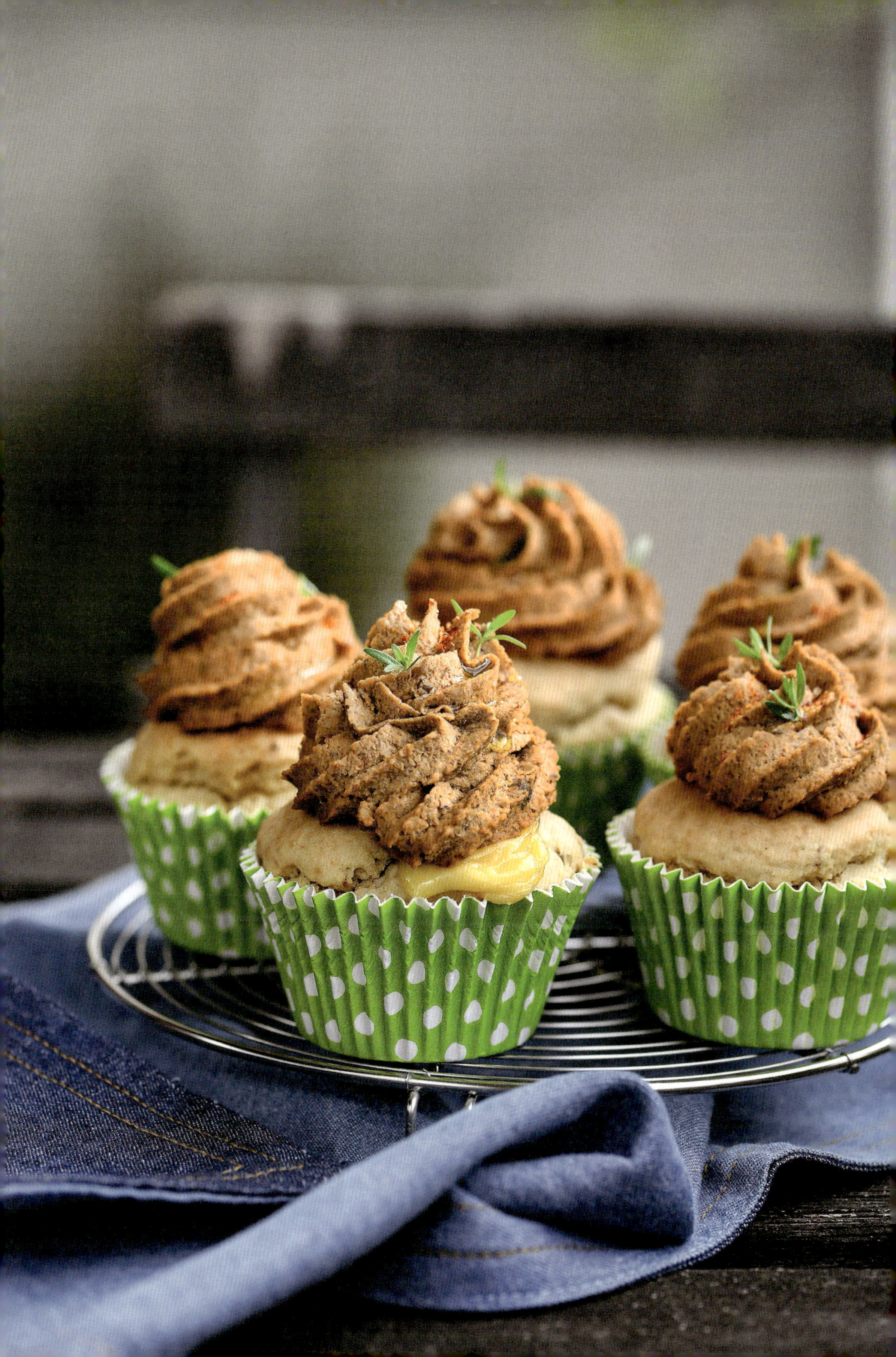

Meatless strips

Under this generic name, we include a range of different meat alternatives such as gyros, sliced meat, kebab... Basically, long, thin slices with quite a firm texture. They often come lightly seasoned and go perfectly with many recipes. But it all depends on what you do with it!

Meatless strips

GREEN SALAD

- 150 g meatless strips
- 150 g lamb's lettuce
- 200 g fennel
- 200 g green apples
- 200 g cucumber
- 4 tsp olive oil
- 4 tsp toasted sesame oil
- 2 tbsp balsamic vinegar
- 1 tbsp frozen chives
- Salt • Pepper

Brown the meatless strips in a hot pan then set aside. Place the lamb's lettuce in a large bowl. Finely slice the fennel and cut the apples into medium-size pieces and add to the salad. Seed the cucumber and cut into medium-sized pieces. Add the cucumber and the meatless strips. Mix the two oils, vinegar, chives and a pinch of salt and pepper in a bowl. Pour over the ingredients, mix well and serve.

SAUTÉ WITH BRUSSELS SPROUTS

- Olive oil
- 70 g frozen shallots
- 300 g frozen Brussels sprouts
- Salt
- Pepper
- 300 g frozen button mushrooms
- 3 tbsp white wine
- 400 g meatless strips
- Fresh coriander

Sauté the shallots in a wok with a dash of olive oil over a medium heat. Add the Brussels sprouts, mix, then season with salt and pepper. Add 2 tbsp of water and cover for 15–20 minutes. Add the mushrooms, mix and cover for 5 minutes. Deglaze with the white wine and let it evaporate. Sauté the meatless strips in a hot pan then set aside. Check that the vegetables are cooked, adjust the seasoning and add a handful of chopped coriander. Add the meatless strips, mix everything together and serve.

Meatless Strips

FAJITAS →

- 2 tbsp rapeseed oil
- 1 tsp oregano
- 2 tsp chopped frozen garlic
- 300 g mixed frozen peppers
- 200 g frozen onions
- 200 g tinned red kidney beans
- 40 g chopped tomatoes
- 300 g meatless strips
- 3 tbsp fajita seasoning
- Fine salt • 2 tsp lime juice
- 4 tortilla wraps

Heat the oil in a wok with the oregano and garlic. Sauté the peppers and onions for 5 minutes over a high heat. Drain and rinse the kidney beans, then pour into the wok. Add the tinned tomatoes, meatless strips and fajita seasoning. Cook for 5 minutes over a medium heat. Season with salt according taste and add the lime juice. Place the tortillas over two oven rack wires with the edges hanging down to form a U shape. Reheat in the oven for 5 minutes at 180°C (gas mark 4). Fill the tortillas with the filling and serve.

SWEET POTATO FARMER'S PIE

- 600 g frozen sweet potatoes
- 500 g pre-cooked potatoes
- 4 tbsp olive oil
- Salt • Pepper
- 75 g grated vegan cheese
- 4 tbsp frozen coriander
- 80 g frozen onions
- 150 g frozen peas
- 400 g meatless strips
- 2 tbsp white wine
- 1 tsp garam masala
- 3 tbsp soya cream

Steam the diced sweet potato then mash with the pre-cooked potatoes and add 3 tbsp of olive oil. Mix well, then season with salt and pepper. Add the grated cheese, coriander and mix one last time. Sauté the onions in 1 tbsp of olive oil and brown for a few minutes, add the peas, mix and cook for a few more minutes, then add the meatless strips. Sauté, deglaze with the white wine, then leave to evaporate slightly before adding the garam masala and soya cream. Mix one last time and remove from the heat. Transfer to an ovenproof dish and cover with the mashed potatoes. Bake for 30 minutes at 180°C (gas mark 4).

BROCCOLI RICE

- 400 g meatless strips
- 600 g broccoli
- 2 red peppers
- 40 fresh mint leaves
- 2 shallots
- 160 g cucumber
- 140 ml olive oil
- 120 ml lemon juice
- 2 tsp ginger juice
- Salt
- Pepper

Sauté the meatless strips in a hot frying pan until golden brown and set aside. Blend the broccoli florets in a food processor with an S blade until it resembles rice. Halve the peppers, remove the seeds and cut into small pieces. Next, chop the mint, finely chop the shallots and dice the cucumber. Put everything in a large bowl and mix well. Mix the olive oil, lemon juice, ginger juice and a pinch of salt and pepper in a bowl. Pour over the vegetables, mix and add the cooked meatless strips. Mix once more then serve.

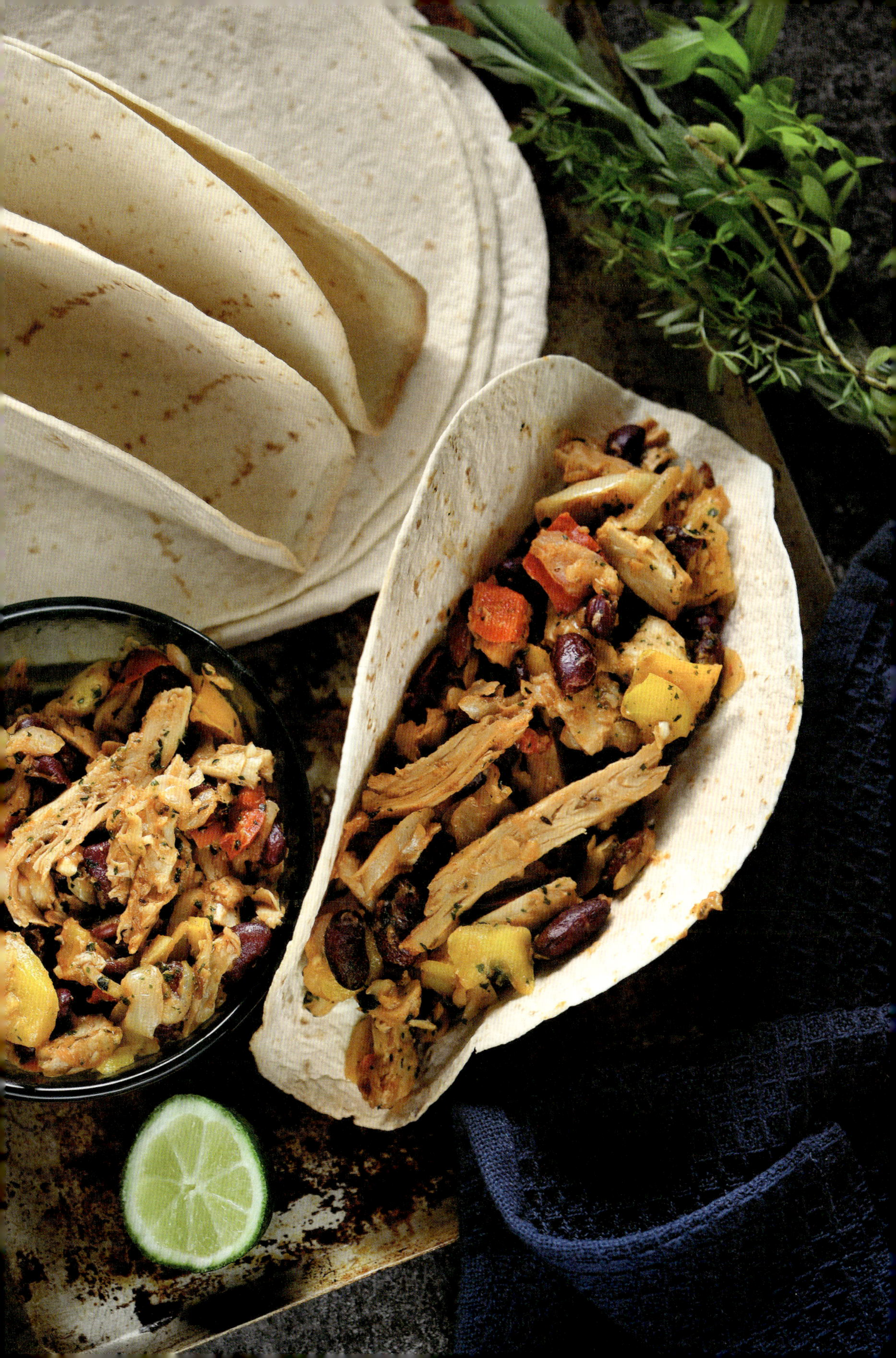

Meatless strips

PITTA WAFFLES

- 150 g meatless strips
- Olive oil
- 100 g frozen peas
- 80 ml soya cream
- 1 tsp Madras curry powder
- 1 tbsp frozen coriander
- 4 pitta breads
- Salt
- Pepper

Lightly brown the meatless strips in a hot pan with a splash of olive oil, then set aside. Add the frozen peas and mix, then cook over a low heat for several minutes. Mix the soya cream with the curry powder and chopped coriander. Pour into the frying pan, mix everything together and allow to reduce slightly. Remove from the heat and generously fill the already cut pitta breads. Toast in a hot waffle iron on medium heat for 5 minutes.

THAI SOUP

- 4 spring onions
- Olive oil
- 10 g frozen ginger
- 1 tbsp frozen lemon grass
- 60 g frozen mushrooms
- 1 tbsp red curry paste
- 200 g meatless strips
- 3½ tbsp red miso
- 300 ml coconut milk
- 100 g rice vermicelli
- Salt
- Fresh basil
- 40 g peanuts, chopped
- 1 lime

Finely slice the spring onions. Sauté for several minutes over a low heat in a large pot with a splash of olive oil. Add the ginger, lemon grass, mix well and add the mushrooms. Cook for several minutes. Add the red curry paste and meatless strips, mix again, then cook for 3-5 minutes before covering with the miso diluted in 1.5 litres of boiling water. Simmer for 5 minutes over medium heat. Next, add the coconut milk and the vermicelli, then mix. Cook for 3 minutes. Adjust the salt seasoning as required. Serve the soup, add the chopped basil, chopped peanuts, and squeeze the lime on top.

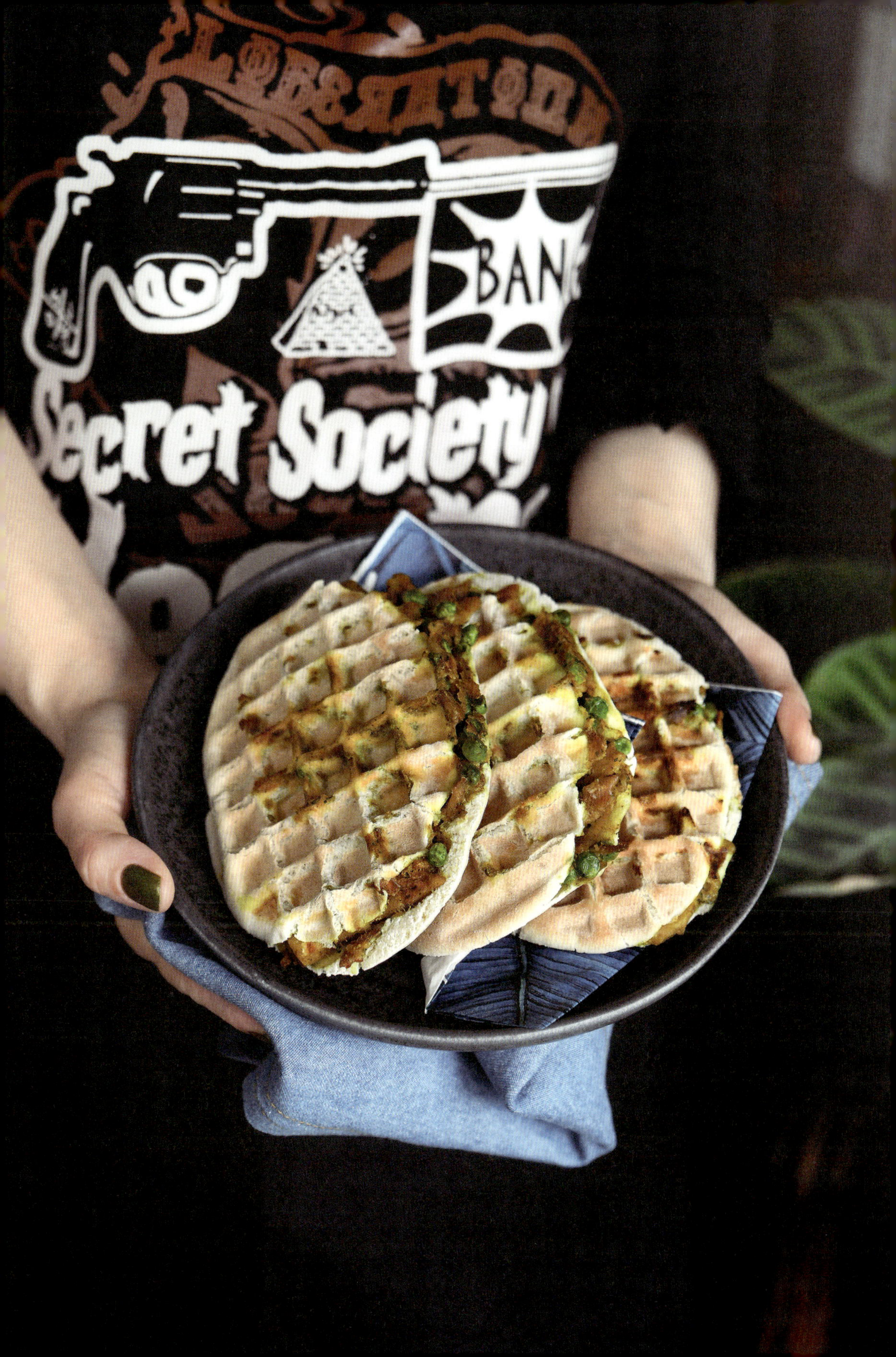
Secret Society

Vegan Cheese

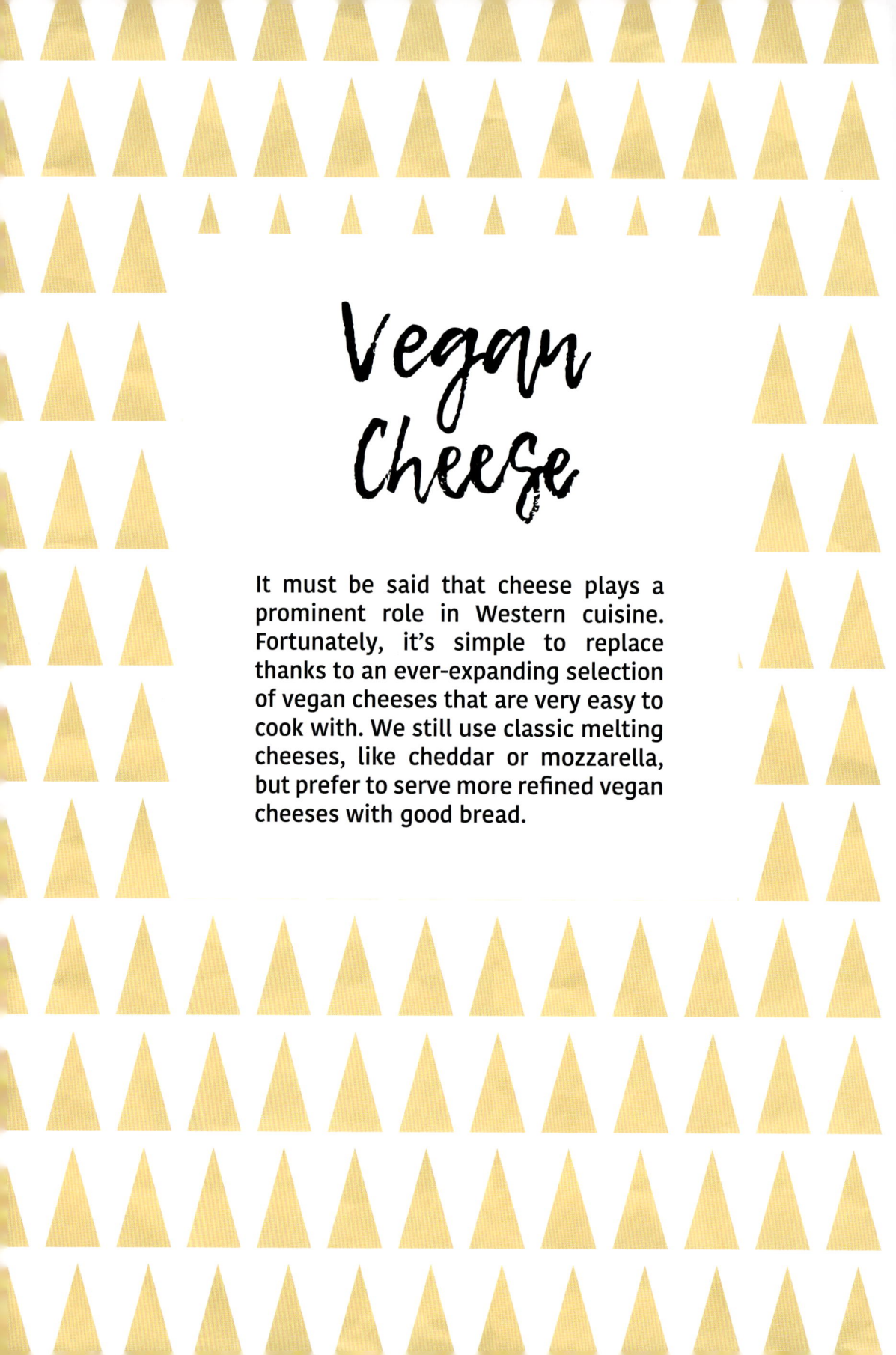

It must be said that cheese plays a prominent role in Western cuisine. Fortunately, it's simple to replace thanks to an ever-expanding selection of vegan cheeses that are very easy to cook with. We still use classic melting cheeses, like cheddar or mozzarella, but prefer to serve more refined vegan cheeses with good bread.

Vegan Cheese

GRILLED CHEESE

- 100 ml soya cream
- 100 g grated vegan cheddar
- 100 g grated vegan mozzarella
- 2 tbsp fried onions
- 1 tsp black pepper
- Vegan margarine
- 8 slices wholemeal bread

Mix together the soya cream, cheddar, mozzarella, fried onions and pepper in a large mixing bowl. Spread a layer of margarine on both sides of each bread slice. Assembly: place a quarter of the cheese mixture in the centre of a slice of bread, then spread it to the edges. Place a second slice of bread on top and press down lightly. Repeat with the other slices of bread to make 4 grilled cheeses. Heat a frying pan without any oil over a high heat. Place a sandwich in the pan and cook for 2 minutes on each side. Place a lid on the pan and lower the heat. Cook for another 3 minutes. Cut in half diagonally and serve.

PIZZA PITTA

- 100 g frozen grilled aubergine
- 200 g tomato passata
- ½ tsp garlic powder
- 1 tbsp olive oil
- 4 pitta breads
- 1 tbsp za'atar seasoning
- 8 vegan mozzarella slices
- 8 fresh basil leaves

Preheat the oven to 200ºC (gas mark 6). Defrost the aubergine in a hot frying pan. Mix together the tomato passata, garlic powder and olive oil in a bowl. Place the pitta breads on a baking tray and spread around 50 g of sauce on top of each. Top with the aubergine slices and scatter with the za'atar seasoning and cover with mozzarella slices. Bake for 10 minutes. Garnish each pitta with 2 basil leaves and serve.

Vegan Cheese

MAC & CHEESE

- 250 g macaroni pasta
- 2 tbsp cornflour
- ¼ tsp grated nutmeg
- 500 ml natural soya milk
- 1 tbsp rapeseed oil
- 1 tbsp Dijon mustard
- 150 g vegan cheddar
- Black pepper

Cook the pasta in 2 litres of boiling salted water for the time shown on the packet. Put the cornflour, grated nutmeg, soya milk, rapeseed oil and mustard into a pan. Mix well with a whisk. Place on a medium heat and whisk continuously until the sauce thickens. Add the cheese, continuing to whisk until it melts, then turn off the heat. Drain the pasta, add to the sauce and season with pepper. Mix well and serve hot.

WELSH RAREBIT

- 4 slices wholemeal bread
- 4 slices smoked vegan ham
- 200 ml pale ale
- 300 g grated vegan cheddar
- 2 tsp Dijon mustard

Preheat the oven to 180°C (gas mark 4). Place the slices of bread in a gratin dish. Cover with the vegan ham. In a pan, bring the beer to the boil, remove from the heat and add the cheddar. Add the mustard and mix with a whisk. Pour into the gratin dish and bake in the oven for 15–20 minutes. Place under the grill for 5 minutes to finish.

TARTIFLETTE

- 100 g frozen onions
- Olive oil
- 200 g smoked tofu
- 1 garlic clove
- 3 tbsp soya cream
- ½ tsp fine salt
- ½ tsp black pepper
- 300 g vegan cheese for melting
- 500 g pre-cooked potatoes

Sweat the onions for 5 minutes in a hot frying pan, then add a splash of oil and the smoked tofu cut into small pieces. Rub the sides of a gratin dish with the garlic clove. Mix together the soya cream, salt, pepper and diced cheese in a large mixing bowl. Slice the potatoes into rounds and add to the cream. Mix everything together gently. In the casserole dish, alternate between layers of potatoes and layers of onion and tofu. There should be three layers of potatoes and two layers of onion and tofu. Bake in the oven for 30-40 minutes at 180°C (gas mark 4) and finish under the grill for 5 minutes.

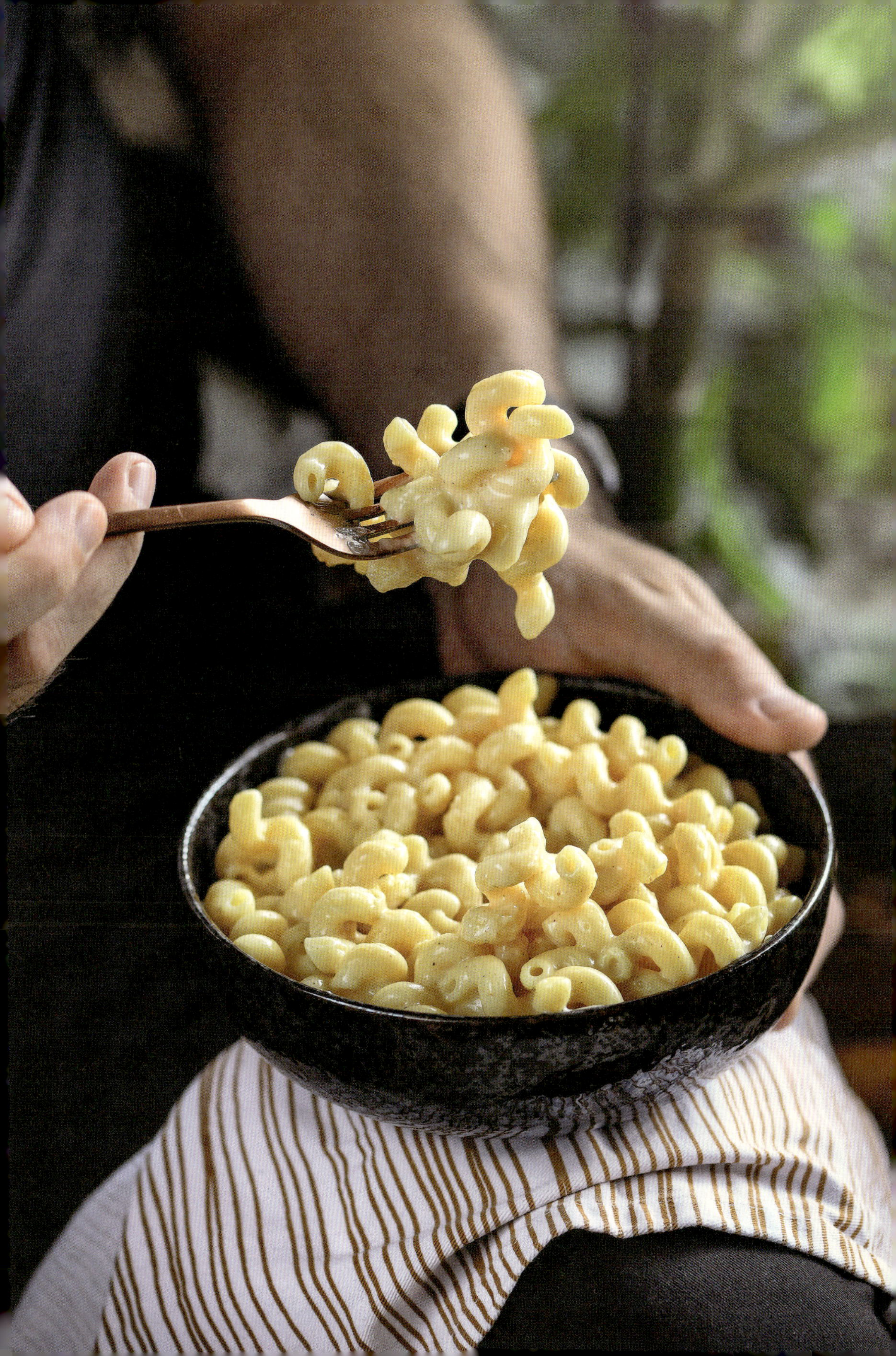

Vegan Cheese

POUTINE

- 1 kg frozen chips
- 200 g vegan mozzarella (block)
- 30 g vegan margarine
- 2½ tbsp frozen shallots
- 2 tsp chopped frozen garlic
- 1 tbsp apple cider vinegar
- 1 tbsp tomato purée
- 2 tsp Worcestershire sauce
- 2 tsp Dijon mustard
- 1¾ tbsp red miso
- 500 ml vegetable stock
- 3 tbsp cornflour

Preheat the oven to 200°C (gas mark 6). Spread the chips out on a baking tray and place in the middle oven shelf for 25 minutes. Cut the cheese into cubes and set aside. In a pan, melt the margarine and sauté the shallots and garlic. Deglaze with vinegar and add the tomato purée, Worcestershire sauce and mustard, then mix together. Dissolve the miso in hot vegetable stock and pour into the pan. Leave to simmer. Dissolve the cornflour in a little water and add to the mixture. Stir with a whisk until the liquid starts to thicken. Pass the gravy through a conical strainer. Mix the chips and cheese on a plate, then top with the gravy.

QUESADILLAS

- 150 g cherry tomatoes
- 100 g tinned sweetcorn
- 100 g vegan chorizo
- 4 wholemeal tortilla wraps
- 300 g grated vegan cheddar
- 1 tbsp jalapeño sauce

Cut the tomatoes in half. Rinse and drain the corn. Cut the chorizo into small pieces. Place the tortilla in a hot pan without any oil. Sprinkle a quarter of the cheese on top and melt. Distribute half of the tomatoes, chorizo and corn on top. Add a few drops of jalapeño sauce. Cover with another quarter of the cheese and a tortilla. Cover and wait for 2 minutes before turning over. Repeat the process with the remaining ingredients. Cut into triangles and serve.

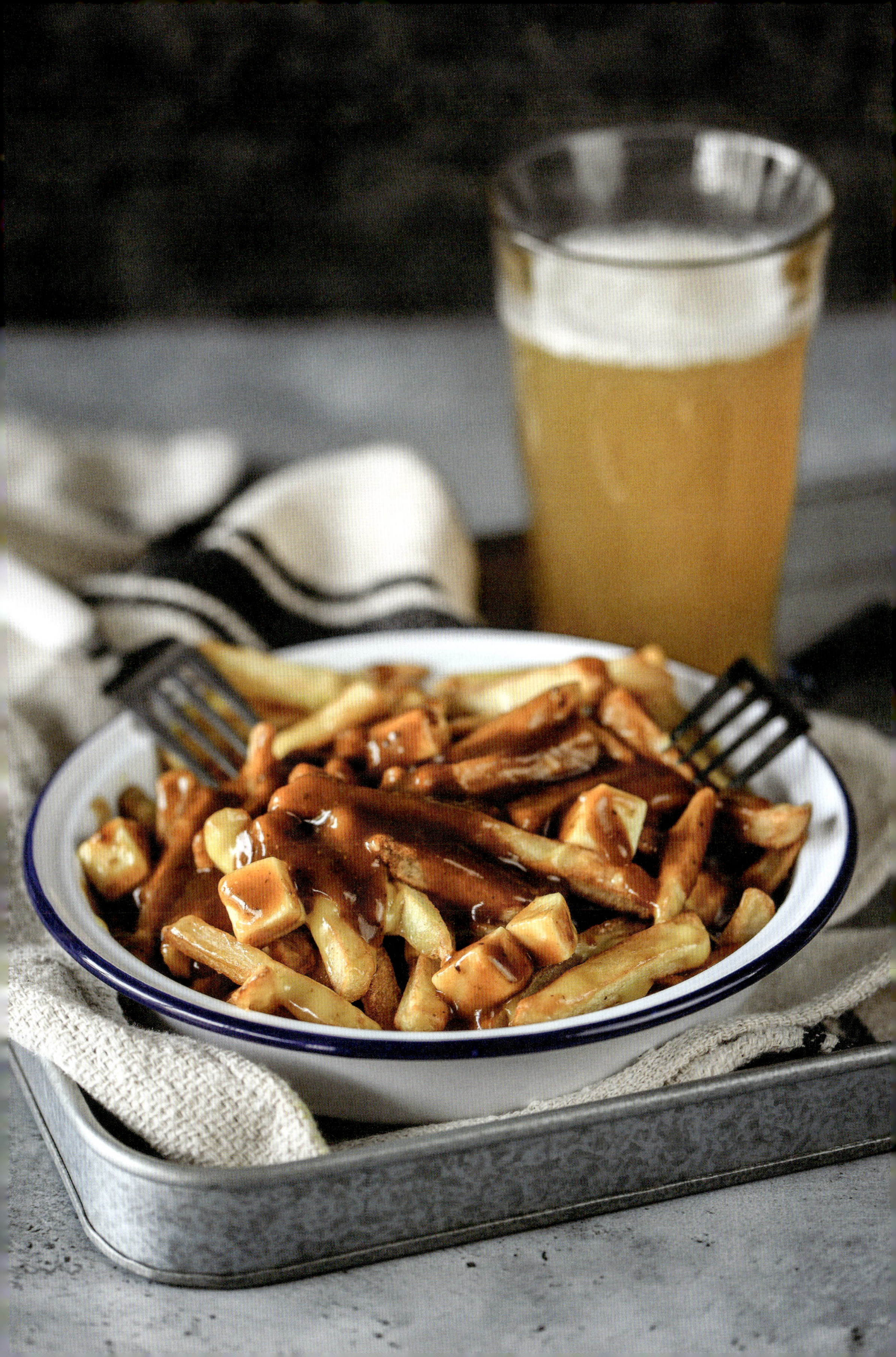

Vegan Cheese

FRENCH ONION SOUP

- 500 g frozen onions
- 400 ml white wine
- 1 litre vegetable stock
- 2 tbsp red miso
- 40 g vegan margarine
- ½ baguette
- 100 g grated vegan cheese
- Black pepper

In a large pot, sweat the onions for 15 minutes. Deglaze with the white wine, then add the vegetable stock and miso. Stir and cook for 15 minutes over a medium heat, then add the margarine. Cut the bread into 3-cm slices. Place on a baking tray, cover with cheese and bake for 5 minutes under the grill. Serve the soup in bowls, season with pepper, add the cheese and mix well. Add a slice of bread to each bowl and serve.

ALIGOT

- 300 g vegan cheese for melting
- 500 g frozen mashed potatoes
- 2 garlic cloves
- 200 ml soya cream
- 40 g vegan margarine
- Black pepper

Cut the cheese into small pieces. In a high-sided frying pan, heat the mashed potatoes. Once the potatoes are defrosted and hot, add the crushed garlic, soya cream and margarine softened at room temperature. Add the cheese in 50 g portions, mixing well in between. Season with a little pepper and serve very hot.

VEGAN FONDUE

- 1 baguette
- 1 garlic clove
- 300 ml white wine
- 1 tbsp cornflour
- ¼ tsp grated nutmeg
- ½ tsp black pepper
- 500 g grated vegan cheese
- 1 tbsp kirsch

Cut the bread into small pieces and leave to dry at room temperature. Rub the sides of the fondue pot with the garlic clove. Heat the pot and add the white wine. Once simmering, add the cornflour diluted with a little cold water. Stir with a whisk. Add the grated nutmeg, pepper and 100 g of cheese. Mix, and once the cheese has melted, add another 100 g of cheese. Repeat the process with the remaining cheese. Add the kirsch. Reduce the heat of the fondue to a minimum. Dip the bread pieces in the fondue with cocktail sticks and serve.

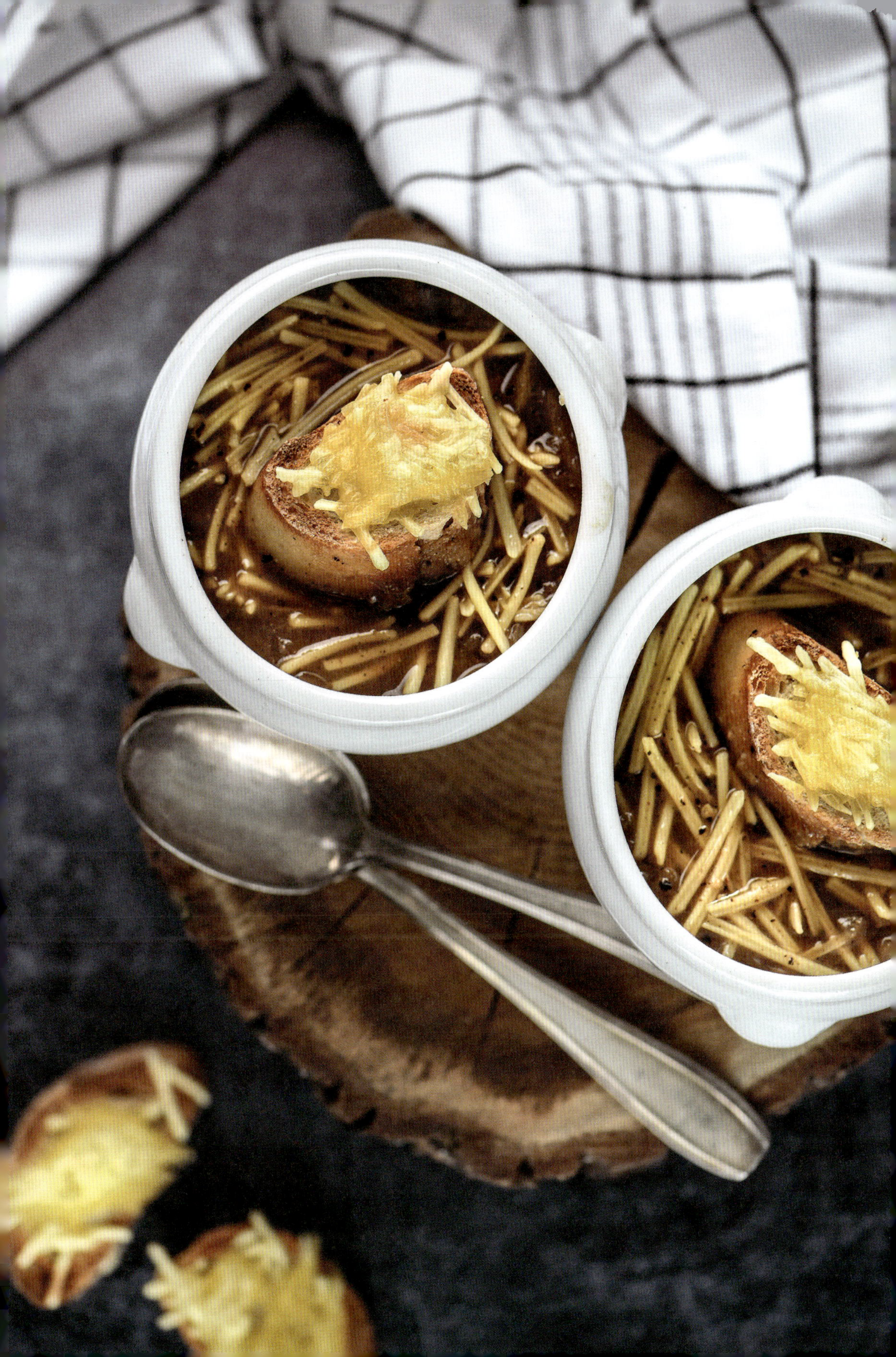

Ice Cream

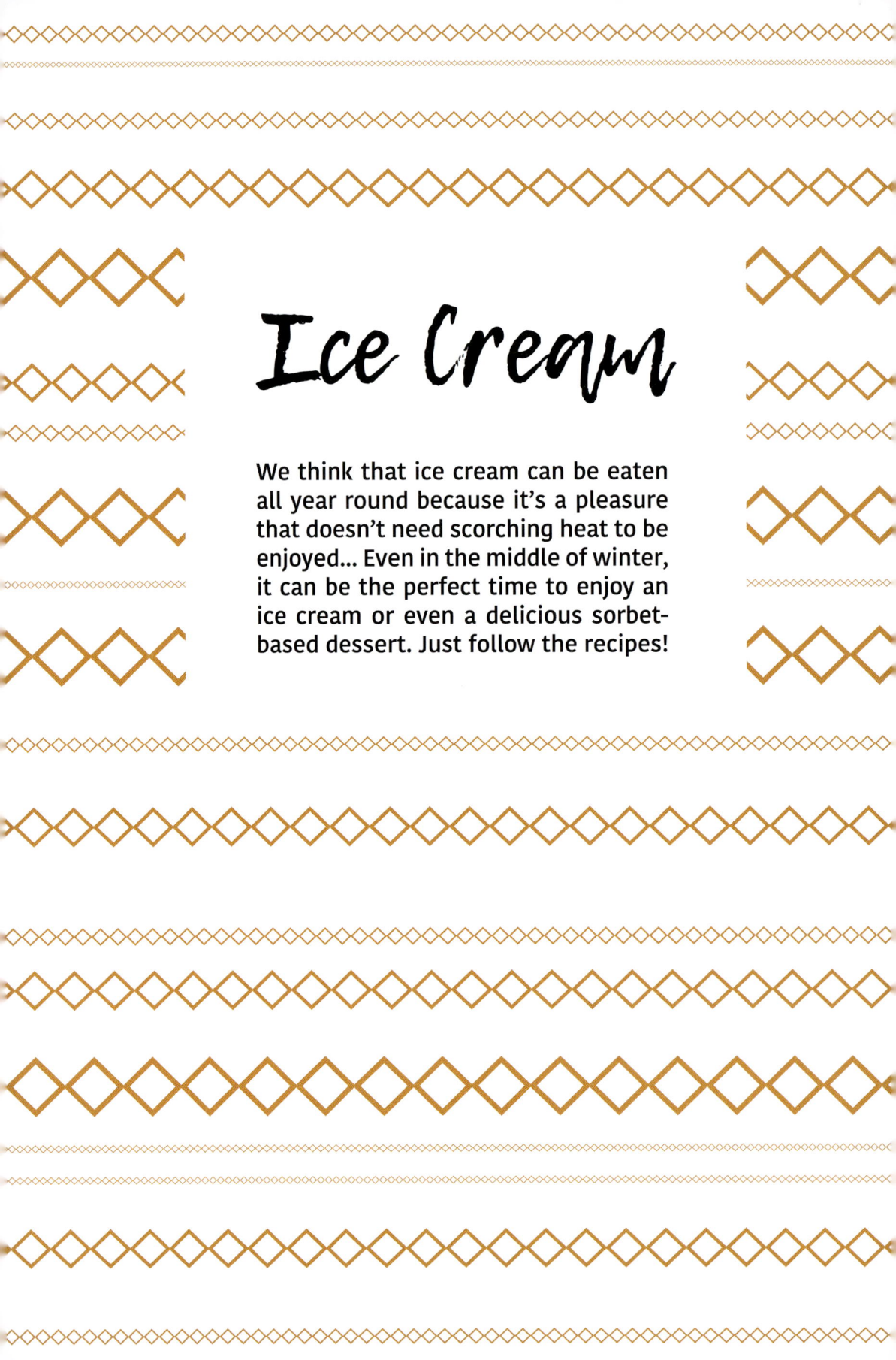

We think that ice cream can be eaten all year round because it's a pleasure that doesn't need scorching heat to be enjoyed... Even in the middle of winter, it can be the perfect time to enjoy an ice cream or even a delicious sorbet-based dessert. Just follow the recipes!

Ice Cream

DECADENT MILKSHAKE

- 300 ml unsweetened almond milk
- 500 g dairy-free cookies ice cream
- 4 tbsp caramel
- Dairy-free whipped cream
- 4 squares praline-filled chocolate

Put four large glasses in the freezer to chill. Pour the very cold almond milk and cookies ice cream into a blender. Blend to make a thick liquid. Drizzle a spiral of caramel on the inside of the glasses (1 tbsp per glass). Pour in the milkshake, cover with whipped cream and scatter with pieces of chocolate. Serve with a straw.

COFFEE ICE-CREAM FLOAT

- 50 g ground coffee beans
- 500 ml sparkling water
- 3 tbsp maple syrup
- 3 tbsp oat milk
- 200 g dairy-free vanilla ice cream

Place the freshly ground coffee in a large clip-top glass jar and gently pour in the sparkling water. Tightly seal the jar and refrigerate for at least 6 hours. Filter the infusion, then add the maple syrup and oat milk. Serve 150 ml in a glass and top with a large scoop of ice cream.

COOKIE SANDWICH

- 8 chocolate chip cookies
- 1 tub of dairy-free ice cream of your choice
- Peanut butter

Take a cookie cutter the same size as the cookies. Fill 3-cm-high with ice cream. Place the ice cream disc on the flat side of a cookie. Use a teaspoon to make a dip in the centre of the ice cream. Fill with peanut butter, place a second cookie on top and press down gently. Cover with cling film and put in the freezer until ready to serve.

FROZEN SMOOTHIE

- 200 ml fresh orange juice
- 1 tbsp lemon juice
- 2 tsp ginger juice
- 4 tbsp frozen mint
- 300 g strawberry sorbet

Pour the orange, lemon and ginger juices into a blender. Add the mint and blend. Add the strawberry sorbet in three parts so that it is well mixed with the juice. Serve immediately in large glasses.

MANGO MEGA BOOST

- 650 g mango sorbet
- 50 g frozen basil
- 1 tbsp sriracha sauce

Take the mango sorbet out of the freezer 10 minutes before use. Transfer the mango sorbet to a large mixing bowl and add the basil. Mix with a spatula. Sprinkle sriracha on top. Gently mix again with the spatula. Put back in the freezer for 15 minutes before serving.

Ice Cream

TOMATO SALAD WITH LEMON SORBET →

- 300 g cherry tomatoes
- 200 g cucumber
- 1 tbsp frozen shallots
- 4 tbsp frozen basil
- Ground black pepper
- 100 g lemon sorbet

Halve the tomatoes, cut the cucumber into small pieces and mix in a large mixing bowl with the shallots and basil. Divide equally between 4 small bowls, season with pepper, add a scoop of sorbet on top, and serve.

CARIBBEAN DELIGHT

- 650 g coconut sorbet
- 100 g dark chocolate chips
- 50 g dessicated coconut
- 4 tsp white rum

Take the coconut sorbet out of the freezer 10 minutes before use. Transfer the sorbet to a large bowl and add the chocolate chips and dessicated coconut. Mix with a spatula. Add the rum. Gently mix again with the spatula. Put back in the freezer for 15 minutes before serving.

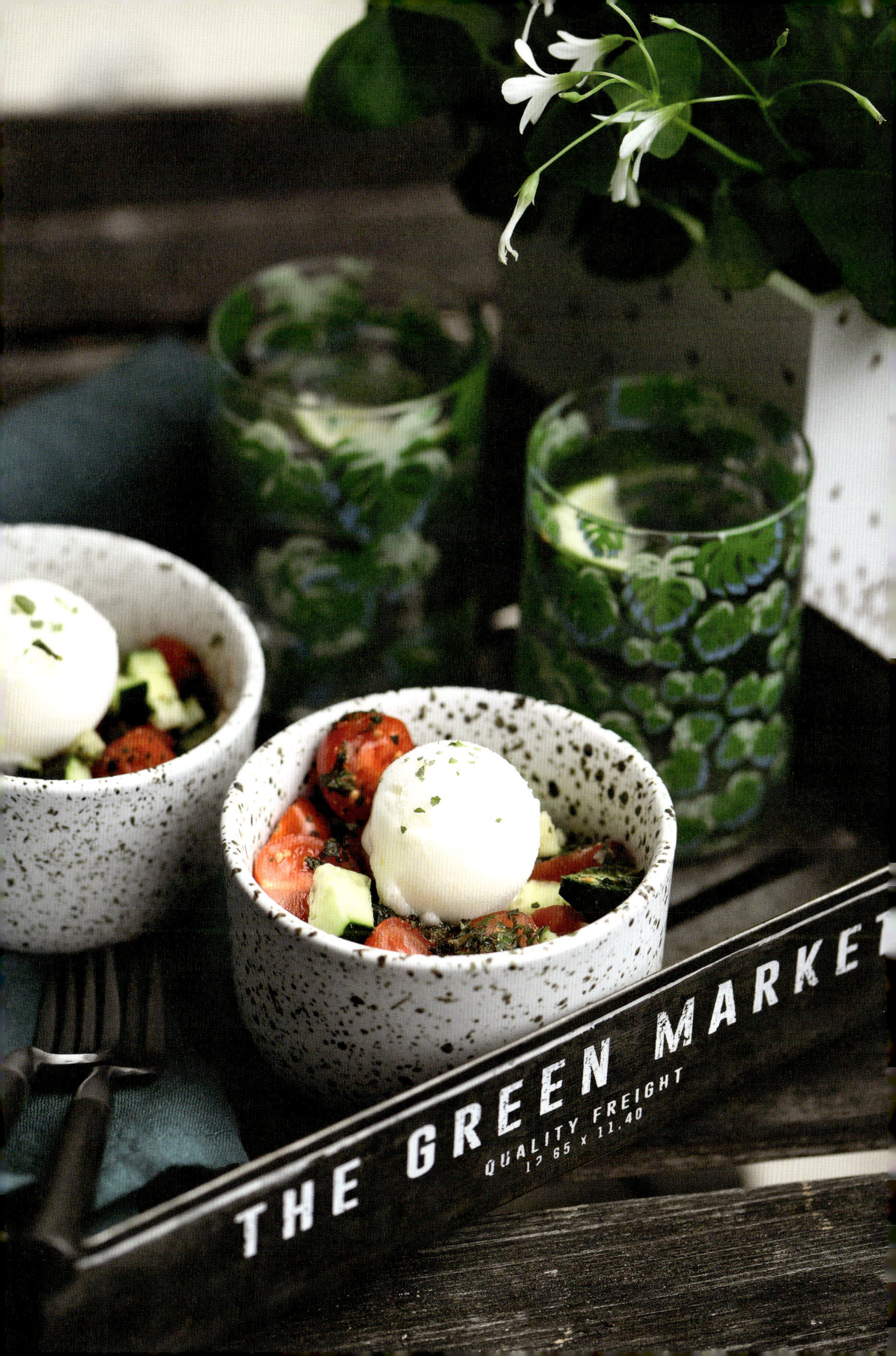
THE GREEN MARKET
QUALITY FREIGHT

Gnocchi

This Italian speciality is made with potatoes and flour. It can be found packaged in the fresh pasta section in supermarkets. Gnocchi doesn't normally contain eggs or milk but it's always best to check the ingredients first before trusting a brand. They are very easy to cook; just place in boiling water, and wait for 1 minute once they rise to the surface then drain. To stop them from sticking together, it's best to mix them immediately with the sauce.

GNOCCHI WITH PESTO

- 1 tbsp olive oil
- 1 garlic clove
- 150 g onions
- 150 g frozen courgettes
- Fine salt
- 3 tbsp white wine
- 90 g vegan green pesto
- 5 tbsp soya cream
- Espelette pepper
- 800 g gnocchi

In a wok, heat the oil then add the crushed garlic, onions and courgettes. Season with salt and cook for another 10 minutes. Add the white wine and reduce for 5 minutes. Mix the pesto, soya cream and a good pinch of Espelette pepper in a bowl. Mix the sauce with the vegetables and set aside.

Cook the gnocchi in a large pot of salted boiling water. Drain and mix with the vegetables before serving.

PARSLEY BUTTER GNOCCHI

- 200 g fennel
- 50 g vegan margarine
- 2 garlic cloves
- 1 tbsp frozen shallots
- 3 tbsp frozen flat-leaf parsley
- 2 tbsp dried sage
- ½ tsp fine salt
- 2 tsp lemon juice
- 800 g gnocchi

Slice the fennel and blanch in boiling water for 3 minutes, drain and set aside. In a large frying pan, melt the margarine over a low heat, then add the crushed garlic, shallots, parsley, sage and salt. Cook for two minutes and add the fennel. Add the lemon juice and mix. Cook over a low heat until the gnocchi is ready. Cook the gnocchi in a large pot of salted boiling water. Drain and transfer to the frying pan with the fennel and herbs. Quickly sauté over a high heat and serve.

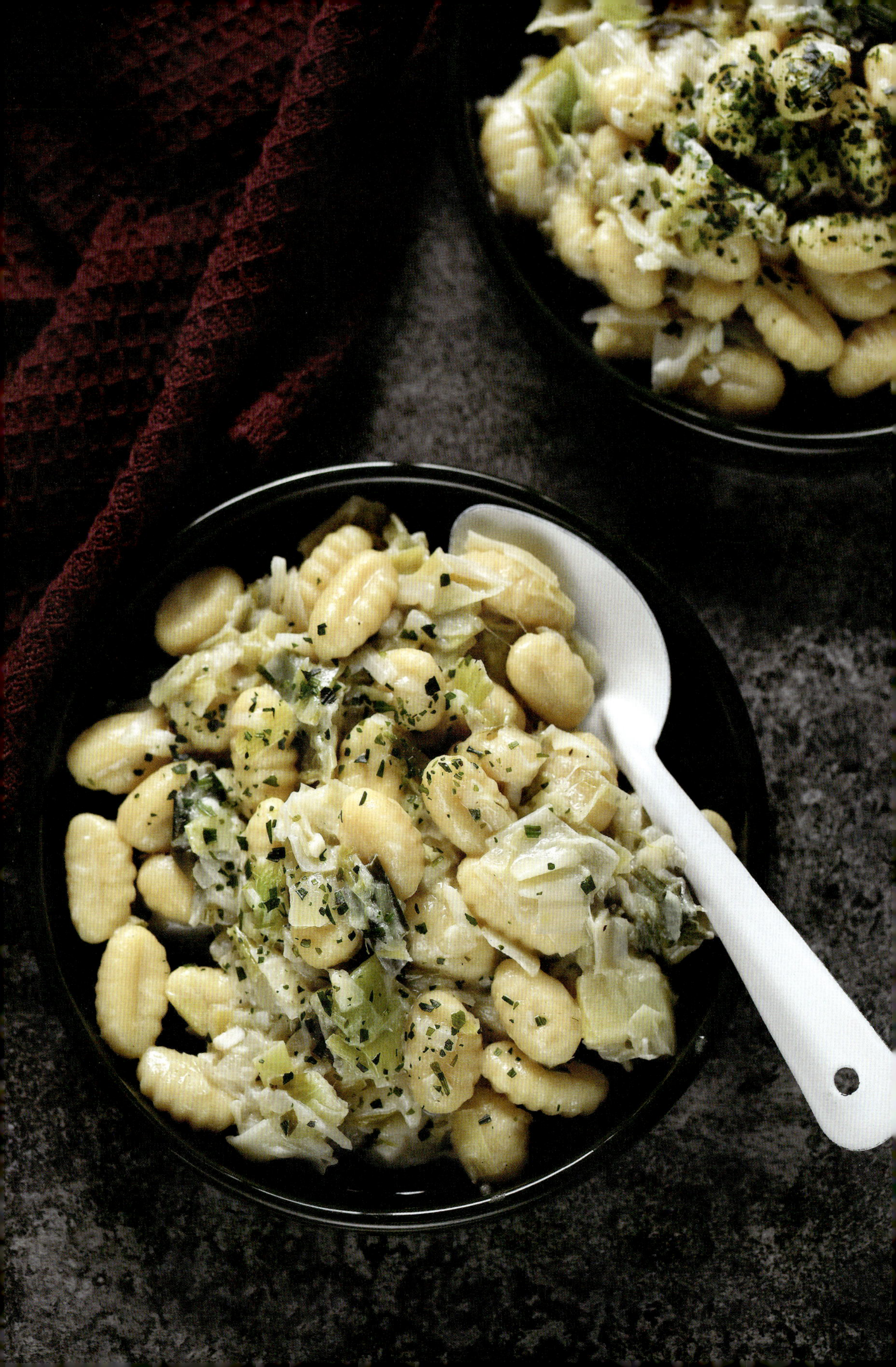

GNOCCHI WITH CREAMED LEEKS

• 2 tbsp olive oil • 3 cloves • 100 g frozen onions • 1 tbsp chopped garlic • 500 g frozen leeks • Fine salt • 4 tsp vegan margarine • 100 ml dry white wine • 100 ml soya cream • Black pepper • 800 g gnocchi

In a large pot, heat the oil with the cloves, then add the onions, garlic and leeks. Cook over a high heat for 10 minutes. Season with salt, add the margarine and white wine, then reduce over a low heat for another 10 minutes. Add the cream, season with pepper and remove from the heat.

Cook the gnocchi in a large pot of salted boiling water. Drain and mix with the creamed leeks before serving.

GNOCCHI WITH PEPPERS

• 2 tbsp olive oil • 300 g sliced peppers • 150 g onions • 2 tsp smoked sweet paprika • ½ tsp fine salt • 180 g tomato sauce • 800 g gnocchi

In a wok, heat the oil then add the peppers, onions and paprika. Add salt and cook for another 10 minutes. Add the sauce, stir and reduce over a low heat.

Cook the gnocchi in a large pot of salted boiling water. Drain and mix with the sauce before serving.

BOLLYWOOD GNOCCHI

• 2 tbsp olive oil • 600 g sliced peppers • 8 cardamom pods • ½ tsp fine salt • 1 tbsp tomato purée • 2 tsp curry powder • 200 g coconut milk • 800 g gnocchi • 1 tbsp coriander

In a wok, heat the oil, then add the peppers and crushed cardamom pods. Add the salt and cook for another 10 minutes. Add the tomato purée, curry powder and coconut milk. Stir and simmer over a low heat.

Cook the gnocchi in a large pot of salted boiling water. Drain, mix with the sauce and sprinkle with chopped coriander before serving.

GNOCCHI WITH SPINACH ➔

- 600 g frozen spinach
- 250 ml soya cream
- ¼ tsp nutmeg • ½ tsp fine salt
- 75 g grated vegan cheese
- Black pepper • 800 g gnocchi

In a large pot, defrost the spinach in 1 tbsp of water over a medium heat. Add the cream, nutmeg and salt. Leave to reduce for 3 minutes and add the cheese. Remove from the heat, add pepper, cover and set aside. Cook the gnocchi in a large pot of salted boiling water. Drain and mix with the spinach before serving.

PARISIAN GNOCCHI

- 1 tbsp olive oil
- 1 garlic clove
- 100 g frozen onions
- 200 g frozen button mushrooms
- Fine salt
- 1 tbsp cornflour
- 3 tbsp flat-leaf parsley
- ¼ tsp nutmeg
- Pepper
- 200 ml soya cream
- 800 g gnocchi
- 100 g grated vegan cheese

In a wok, heat the oil, then add the crushed garlic, onions and mushrooms. Season with salt and cook for another 15 minutes. Add the cornflour mixed with a splash of cold water. Mix and let thicken for 1 minute. Add the chopped parsley and nutmeg, then season generously with pepper. Add the cream, mix and remove from the heat.

Cook the gnocchi in a large pot of salted boiling water. Drain and mix with the sauce.

Transfer to a gratin dish, cover with cheese and place under the grill for 5 minutes before serving.

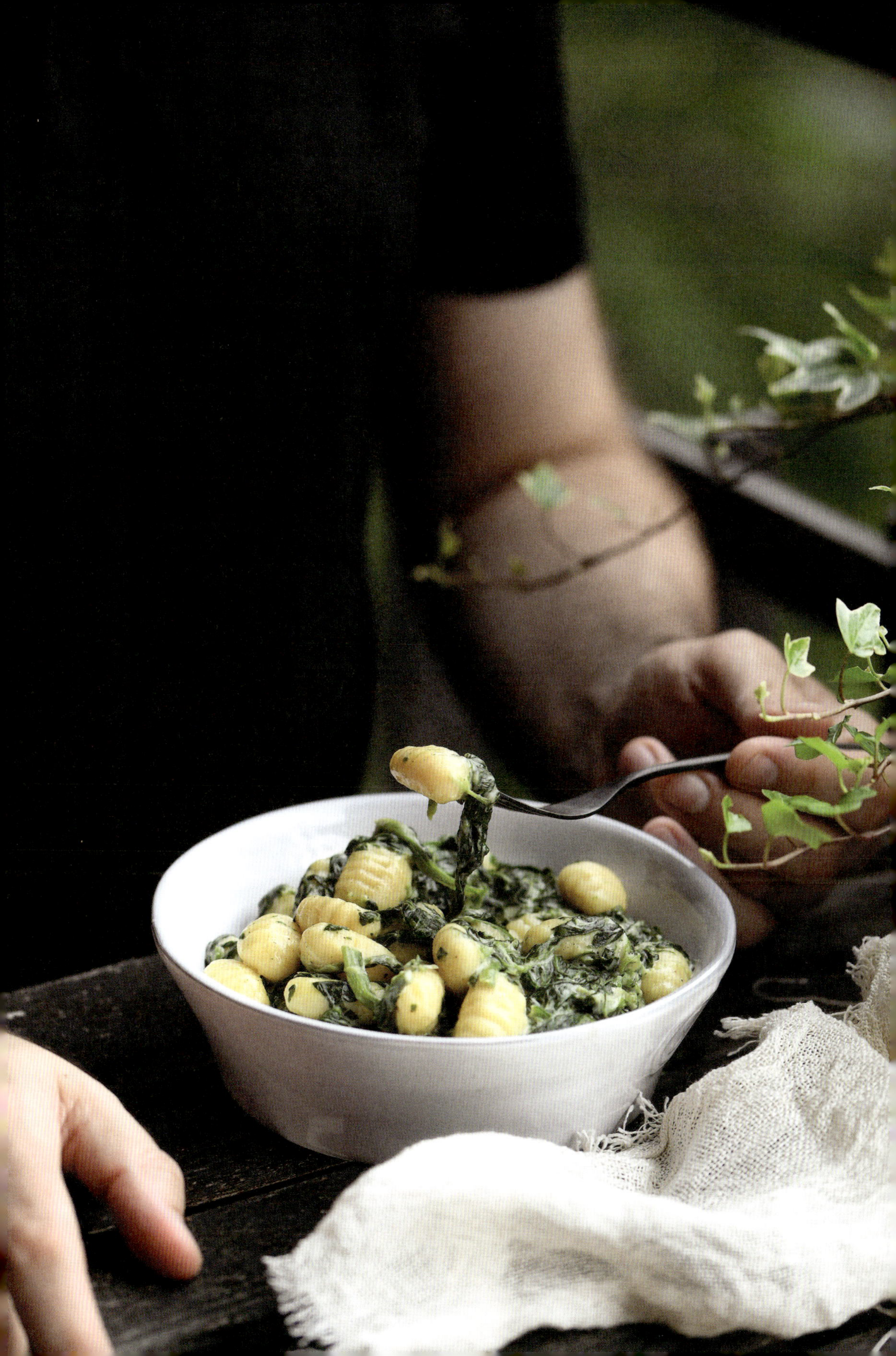

Gnocchi

GNOCCHI ALLA NORMA →

- 1 tbsp olive oil • 2 tsp chopped garlic • 1 tbsp oregano • 200 g chopped tomatoes • 400 g tomato sauce • ½ tsp fine salt • 100 g green olives • 4 tbsp chopped basil • 300 g frozen grilled aubergine • 800 g gnocchi • Malted yeast

Heat the oil in a large casserole dish with the garlic and oregano. Add the tomatoes, tomato sauce and salt. Cook for 5 minutes over a medium heat, then add the olives and basil. Leave to simmer for 10 minutes over a low heat. Cook the aubergine in a frying pan with a splash of oil. Slice the aubergines then add to the sauce. Cook the gnocchi in a large pot of salted boiling water. Drain and mix with the sauce. Dust with malted yeast and serve.

SEA-FLAVOURED GNOCCHI

- 100 g frozen mixed julienne vegetables
- 1 tbsp olive oil
- 1 tsp creamed horseradish sauce
- 2 tbsp frozen basil
- 1 tbsp rice vinegar
- 1 sheet nori
- 1 litre vegetable stock
- 800 g gnocchi
- Toasted sesame oil

Sauté the vegetables in a wok with olive oil. Once defrosted, add the horseradish, basil and deglaze with the rice vinegar. Finely chop the nori and add to the wok. Pour in the hot vegetable stock and simmer. Cook the gnocchi in a large pot of salted boiling water. Once the gnocchi rise to the surface, immediately transfer to the broth. Serve in soup bowls and add 5 drops of sesame oil.

BORDELAISE GNOCCHI

- 50 g frozen shallots
- 50 g frozen red onions
- 2 g frozen thyme
- ½ tsp black pepper
- 400 ml red wine • 1 tbsp white miso • 4 tsp vegan margarine
- 800 g gnocchi

In a dry casserole dish, sweat the shallot and red onion with the thyme and black pepper Add the red wine and miso, then mix. Reduce for 15 minutes over a low heat. Off the heat, whisk in the margarine. Cook the gnocchi in a large pot of salted boiling water. Drain and mix with the sauce.

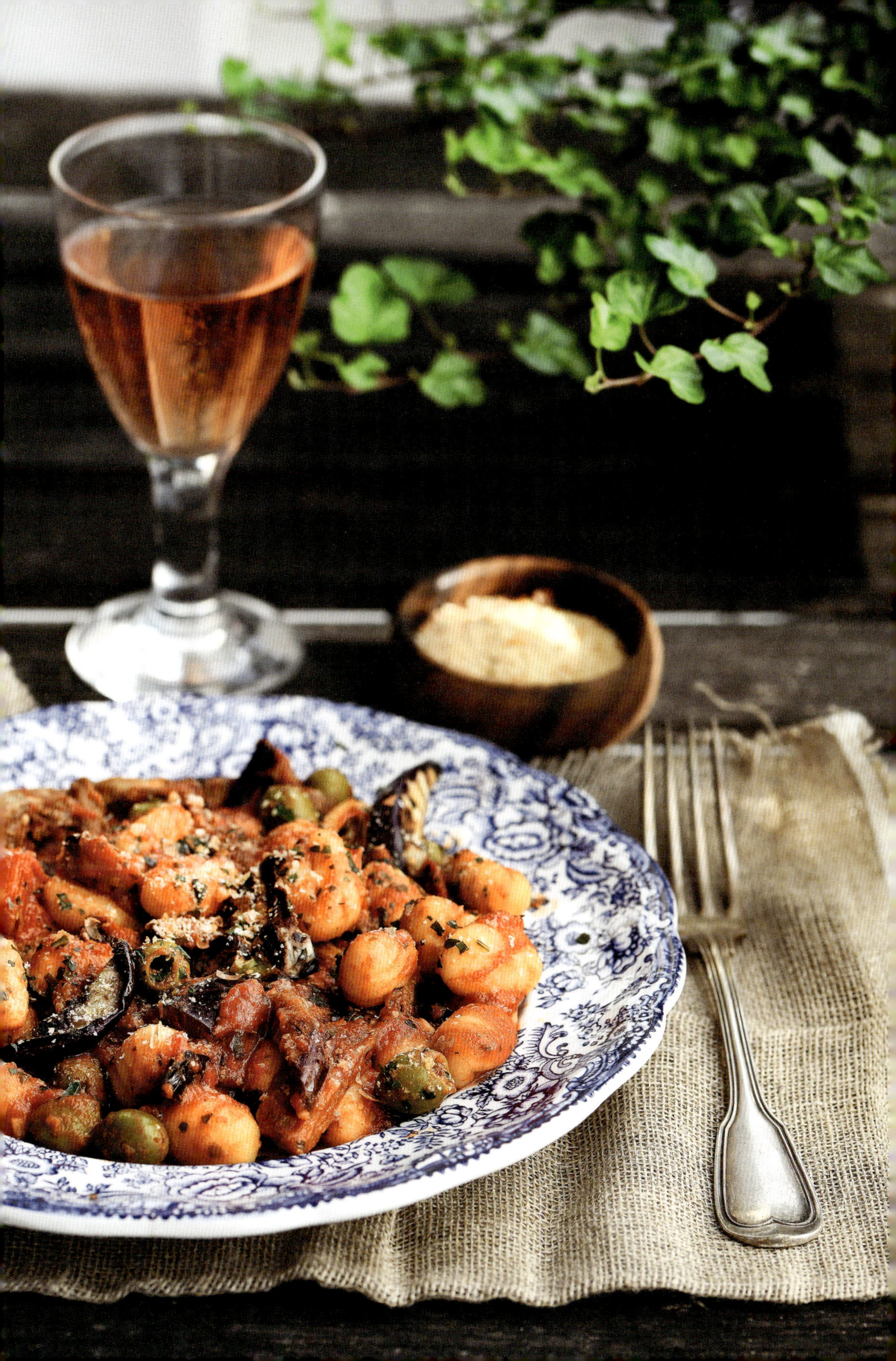

Mixed Vegetables

This name is given to a mixture of vegetables, cut into pieces and ready to be cooked. Are you trying to get your five a day? Not a problem: potatoes, peas, cauliflower, green beans, carrots, this is the magic formula! Find it pre-bagged in the frozen aisle.

Mixed Vegetables

MINESTRONE

- 1 onion
- Olive oil
- 2 garlic cloves
- 400 g frozen mixed vegetables
- 2 vegetable stock cubes
- 90 g green pesto
- 80 g tinned haricot beans
- 240 g peeled tomatoes
- 100 g pasta (small tubes)

Finely slice the onion and sweat in a casserole dish with a splash of olive oil.

Crush the garlic in a garlic press, add to the onion, and mix. Add the frozen vegetables, mix well and cook for 5 minutes before covering with water. Add the vegetable stock cubes, green pesto, beans, peeled tomatoes and pasta. Cover and simmer for around 10 minutes. Check that the pasta is cooked. Serve immediately.

STUFFED PEPPERS

- 2 red peppers
- 400 g frozen mixed vegetables
- Olive oil
- Salt
- Pepper
- 1 tbsp red wine vinegar
- 2 tbsp fried onions
- Espelette pepper
- 2 tbsp tomato ketchup
- 150 g cooked quinoa
- Fresh coriander

Halve the peppers lengthways and remove the seeds. Blanch for 2 minutes in salted boiling water. Transfer immediately to a large bowl of ice water to stop the cooking process. Sauté the mixed veg in a wok with a splash of olive oil and cover for 10 minutes. Season with salt and pepper, deglaze with vinegar and let the liquid evaporate. Add the fried onions with a few pinches of Espelette. Mix well and cook for a few more minutes. In a bowl, mix the ketchup and pre-cooked quinoa. Add the vegetables and garnish with a little chopped coriander. Fill the four pepper halves and bake in the oven preheated to 180°C (gas mark 4) for 15-20 minutes. Serve hot or warm, although it can also be served cold.

Mixed Vegetables

VEGETABLE TART

- 600 g frozen mixed vegetables
- 300 ml soya cream
- 40 g cornflour
- ½ tsp fine salt
- ¼ tsp grated nutmeg
- ½ tsp Espelette pepper
- 1 tsp dried sage
- 4 tbsp frozen basil
- 100 g grated vegan cheese
- 1 vegan ready-rolled shortcrust pastry sheet

Defrost the vegetables in a large pot without any fat. Cook for 10 minutes and set aside. Preheat the oven to 180°C (gas mark 4). In a large bowl, mix the soya cream and the cornflour already dissolved in a splash of cold water. Add the salt, grated nutmeg, Espelette pepper, sage and basil. Add the cooked vegetables, vegan cheese and mix. Line a tart tin with the pastry without removing from the baking parchment. Prick the pastry with a fork and spread the vegetable mixture evenly on top. Cook for 1 hour. Finish by browning lightly under the grill.

CURRY

- 3 tbsp rapeseed oil
- 1¼ tsp coriander seeds
- 1 tsp cumin seeds
- ½ tsp turmeric
- ½ tsp fine salt
- 200 g frozen spinach leaves
- 600 g frozen mixed vegetables
- 1 tsp curry powder
- 2 tbsp tomato purée
- 400 ml coconut milk
- 2 tbsp fresh coriander

In a large pot, heat the oil with the crushed coriander and cumin seeds. Add the turmeric, salt and spinach. Cook over a high heat for 2 minutes then add the mixed vegetables. Cover and cook for 10 minutes. Add the curry powder, tomato purée and coconut milk. Mix well and simmer for 5 minutes over a medium heat. Garnish with chopped coriander.

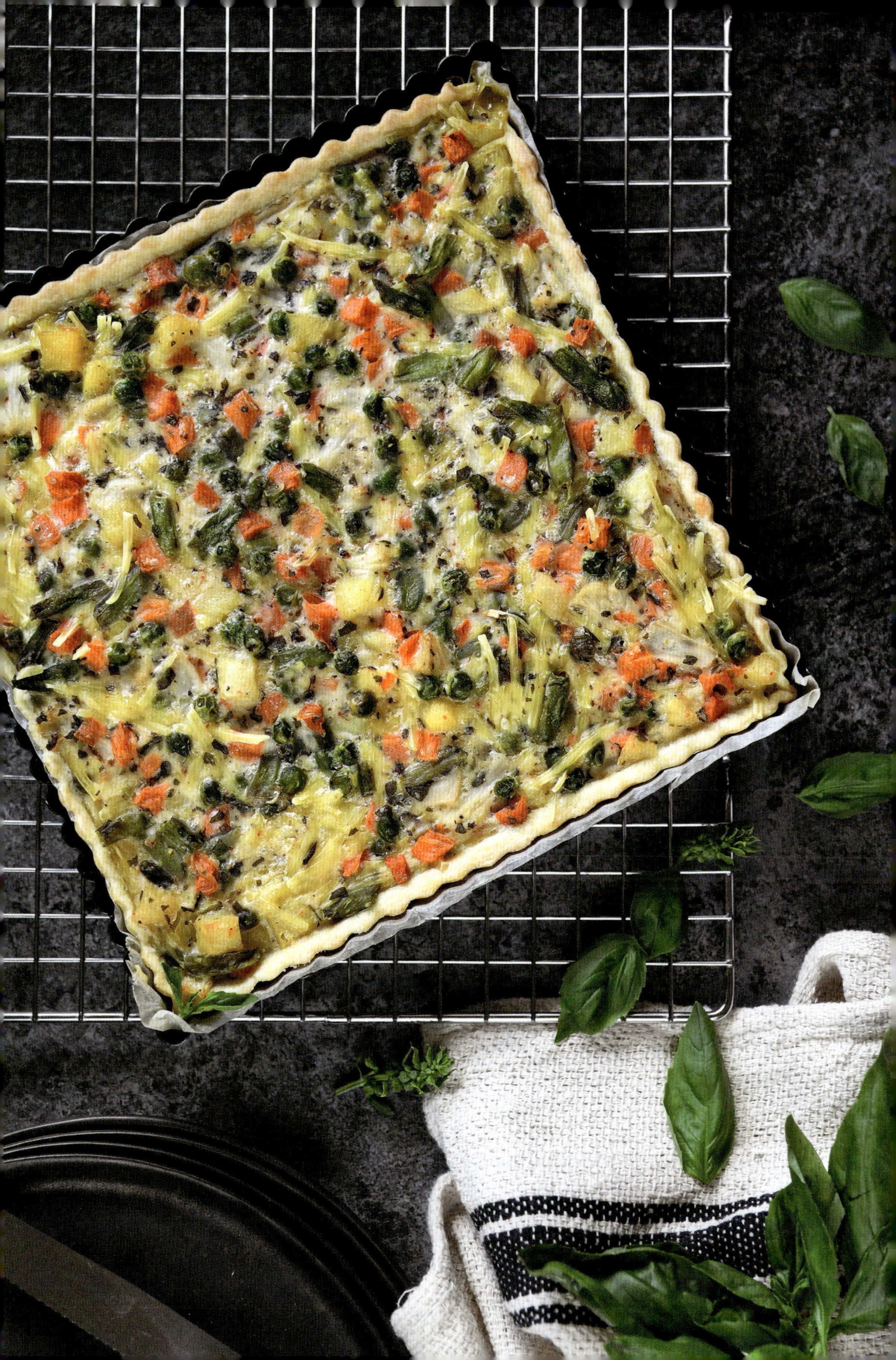

Mixed Vegetables

SAMOSAS →

- 1 tbsp olive oil
- 1 tsp turmeric
- 1 tsp garam masala
- ½ tsp salt
- 600 g frozen mixed vegetables
- 1½ tbsp chopped mint
- 8 vegan filo pastry sheets

Heat the oil in a pan with the turmeric, garam masala and salt. Add vegetables, mix and cover and cook for 10 minutes. Add 100 ml water, mix and cook again until the liquid evaporates. You should be able to crush the potatoes with a fork. Add the mint and lightly crush the vegetables. Leave to cool. Preheat the oven to 180°C/ (Gas mark 4). To make the samosas cut each filo sheet in two. Place a spoonful of the filling off centre, approx 1.5 cm from the end of the pastry nearest to you. Fold over the left-hand corner of the pastry to cover the filling. Fold over the wrapped filling to give a triangular shape. Continue folding the triangle, ensuring the points are tucked in to avoid the filling seeping out. Then cook on a baking tray for 20 minutes.

CREAMY VEGETABLES

- 4 tsp olive oil
- 4 tsp chopped frozen garlic
- 2 tsp frozen thyme
- 1½ tsp rosemary
- 600 g frozen mixed vegetables
- 1 tsp fine salt
- 100 ml white wine
- 3 tbsp soya cream

Heat the oil in a large pot with the garlic, thyme and rosemary. Add the vegetables, season with salt and mix. Cook over a high heat for 10 minutes, stirring occasionally. Add the white wine and the soya cream. Cover and cook over a low heat for 5 minutes.

THAI STYLE

- 2 tsp vegetable oil
- 600 g frozen mixed vegetables
- Fine salt
- 3 tbsp cold water
- 150 ml coconut cream
- 3 tbsp Thai green curry paste
- 4 tbsp fresh coriander

Heat the oil in a wok and sauté the vegetables for 10 minutes. Season with salt. Add the water, coconut cream and green curry paste. Mix and simmer over a medium heat for 10 minutes. Cover with coarsely chopped coriander.

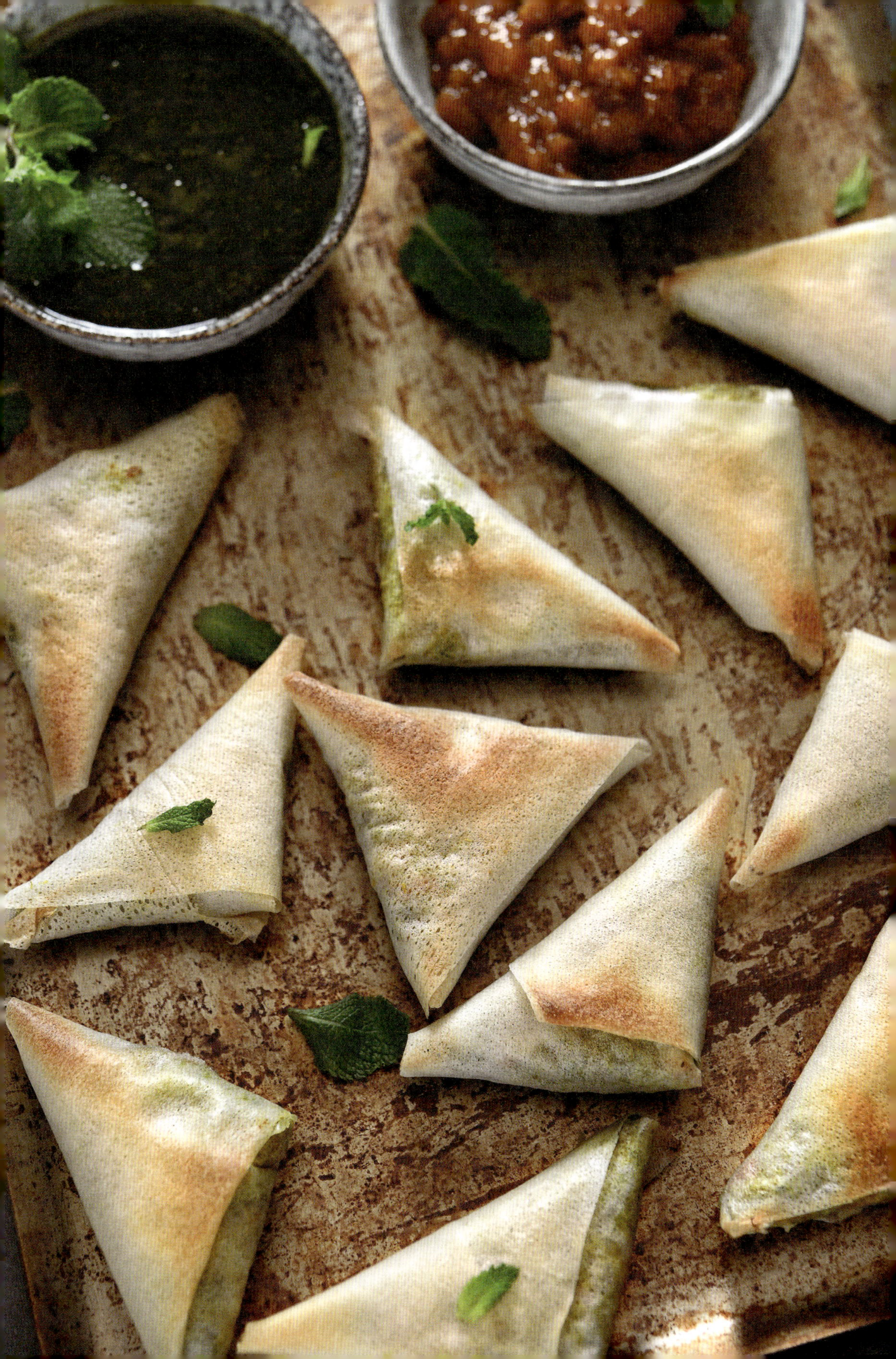

Julienne Vegetables

It's this mix of vegetables cut into thin strips that gives a dish a more sophisticated look straight away. Generally consisting of carrots, celeriac and courgettes, julienne vegetables are a great garnish. But it's even more interesting to use them to make dishes.

Julienne Vegetables

WOK

- 1 tbsp toasted sesame oil
- 2 tsp chopped frozen garlic
- 2½ tsp grated frozen ginger
- 1 tbsp frozen lemon grass
- 450 g frozen mixed julienne vegetables
- 150 g frozen button mushrooms
- 1 tbsp tamari
- 1½ tsp sesame seeds
- 2 tbsp chopped frozen chives

Heat the sesame oil in a wok with the garlic, ginger and lemon grass. Add the mixed vegetables and the mushrooms. Stir and cook over a high heat for 10 minutes. Remove the excess liquid then add the tamari. Cook again for 5 minutes then sprinkle with sesame seeds and chives.

CRUMBLE

- 500 g mixed frozen julienne vegetables
- 200 ml soya cream
- 100 g green pesto
- 100 g plain flour
- 40 g vegan margarine
- 4 tbsp malted yeast

In a frying pan, sweat the mixed vegetables for 10 minutes over a medium heat. Add the soya cream and pesto. Mix and heat for 5 minutes. In a bowl, rub the flour, margarine and yeast with your fingertips until it is a sandy texture. Preheat the oven to 180°C (gas mark 4). Pour the vegetable mixture into a gratin dish and cover with the crumble. Bake in the oven for 25-30 minutes.

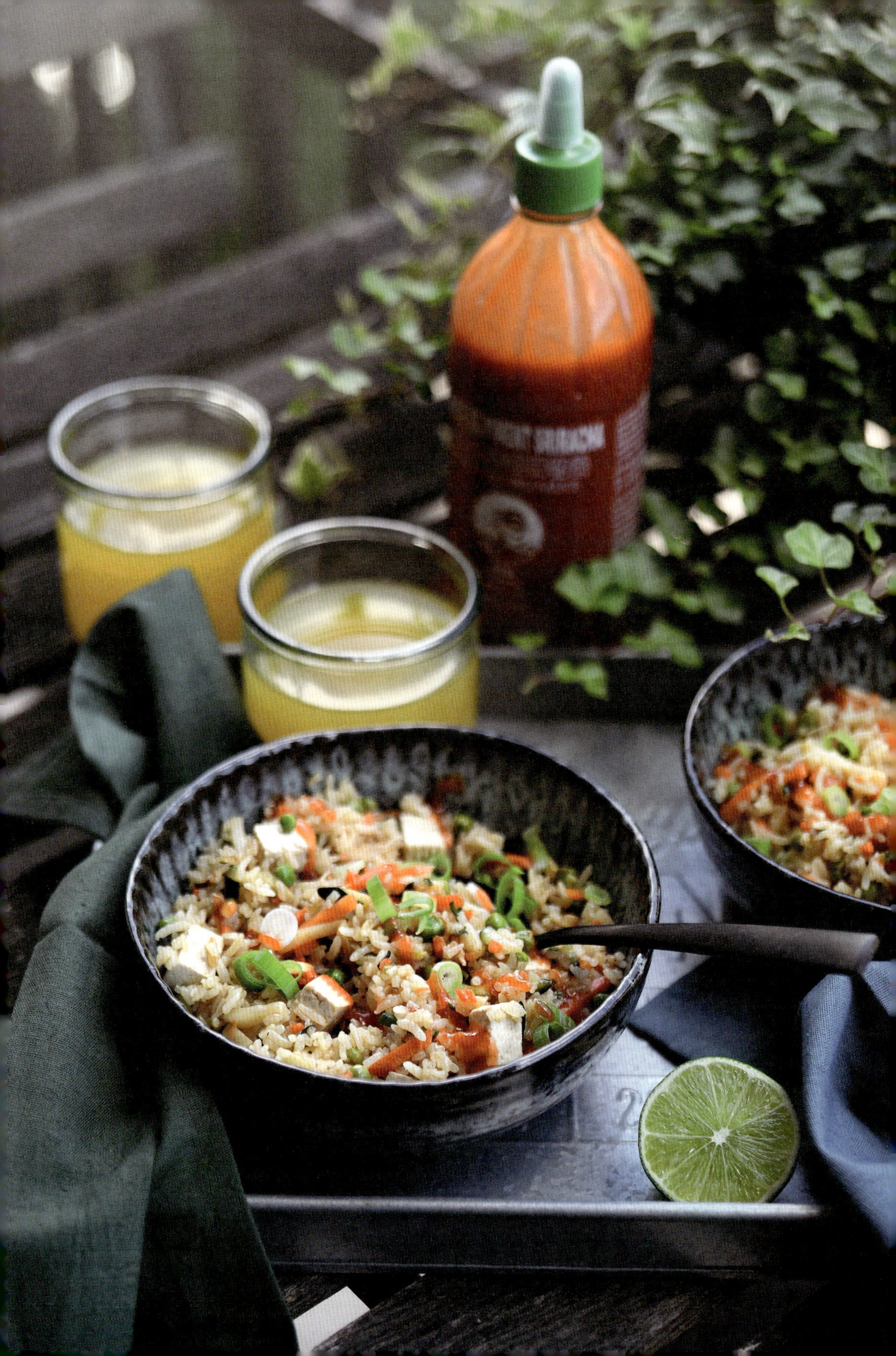

Julienne Vegetables

STIR FRY

- 300 g frozen julienne vegetable mix
- 50 g frozen peas
- 2 tbsp sesame oil
- 100 g plain tofu
- 1 tbsp agave syrup
- 1 tbsp tamari
- 300 g pre-cooked jasmine rice
- 1 tbsp lime juice
- 20 g spring onions
- Sriracha

In a frying pan, sweat the mixed vegetables and peas over a high heat for 5 minutes. Clear the centre of the wok by pushing the vegetables to the sides. Pour the oil into the centre and sauté the diced tofu. Add the agave syrup and tamari, then mix everything together. Add the rice, mix and drizzle with lime juice. Serve in bowls, scatter with finely chopped spring onions and garnish with a few dashes of sriracha.

AVOCADO ROLL

- 200 g frozen mixed julienne vegetables
- 1 tbsp olive oil
- ½ tsp fine salt
- 2 tbsp tomato coulis
- 300 g avocados
- 1 tbsp lime juice
- 2 tsp jalapeño sauce
- ½ tsp cumin seeds
- 4 wholemeal tortilla wraps

Sauté the vegetables with the oil in a frying pan for 5 minutes. Season with salt and add the tomato coulis. Reduce for 2 minutes over a high heat. Leave to cool. Crush the avocados in a bowl, add the lime juice, jalapeño sauce, cumin seeds and mix. Once the vegetables have cooled down, add the crushed avocado. Spread the mixer over the wraps and roll. Cut into 5-cm slices and serve on a large plate.

PUFF PASTRY WAFFLES

- 2 tsp olive oil
- 1 tsp garlic powder
- 200 g frozen mixed julienne vegetables
- ½ tsp salt
- 1 tbsp port
- 1 tsp Worcestershire sauce
- 2 tbsp chopped frozen chives
- 50 g grated vegan cheddar cheese
- 2 sheets ready-rolled vegan puff pastry

Heat the oil in a wok with the garlic powder. Sauté the vegetables over a high heat. Once thawed, season with salt and add the port wine and Worcestershire sauce. Allow to reduce over a medium heat. Add the chives and let the mixture cool before adding the cheddar.

Unroll the first sheet of pastry and cut it into a square shape. Repeat with the other sheet of pastry. Cut a sheet into 4 squares and place the filling in the centre of each square. Cut the second sheet into 4 squares and place on top of the bottom 4 squares with the filling. Seal the edges and cook in a waffle iron on a medium heat for 5 minutes. Serve immediately.

Julienne Vegetables

VEGETABLE PANCAKES

- 180 g plain flour
- 2 tbsp malted yeast
- 1 tbsp caster sugar
- 1 tsp baking powder
- ½ tsp salt
- 1 tsp smoked paprika
- 375 ml soya milk
- 2 tsp tamari
- Olive oil
- ½ tsp cumin seeds
- 300 g frozen julienne vegetable mix
- 4 tbsp frozen chives
- Pepper

Mix together the flour, malted yeast, sugar, and baking powder, salt and the smoked paprika.

Add the milk, tamari, 2 tbsp of olive oil, and mix with a whisk to make a smooth batter. Allow the batter to rest while preparing the next step. Sauté the cumin seeds in a wok with a splash of olive oil and then add the mixed vegetables. Once thawed, add the chives. Season with salt and pepper according to taste. Cook for a few minutes over a high heat, remove from the heat and transfer to a bowl. To cook the pancakes, heat a little oil in a small frying pan, pour in a small ladle of pancake batter and top with vegetables. Cook for 2-3 minutes on each side and repeat with the remaining pancakes and vegetables to make about 10 pancakes. Serve immediately, for example, with salad.

COMFORTING BROTH

- 4 tsp vegan margarine
- 50 g frozen onions
- 300 g frozen julienne vegetable mix
- 100 g vermicelli pasta
- 1 litre vegetable stock
- Fresh chervil

In a pan, melt the margarine and sauté the onions. Once the onions are translucent, add the mixed vegetables and cook for 5 minutes. Add the pasta and the hot stock. Stir and simmer for 5 minutes. Garnish with a few chervil leaves and serve.

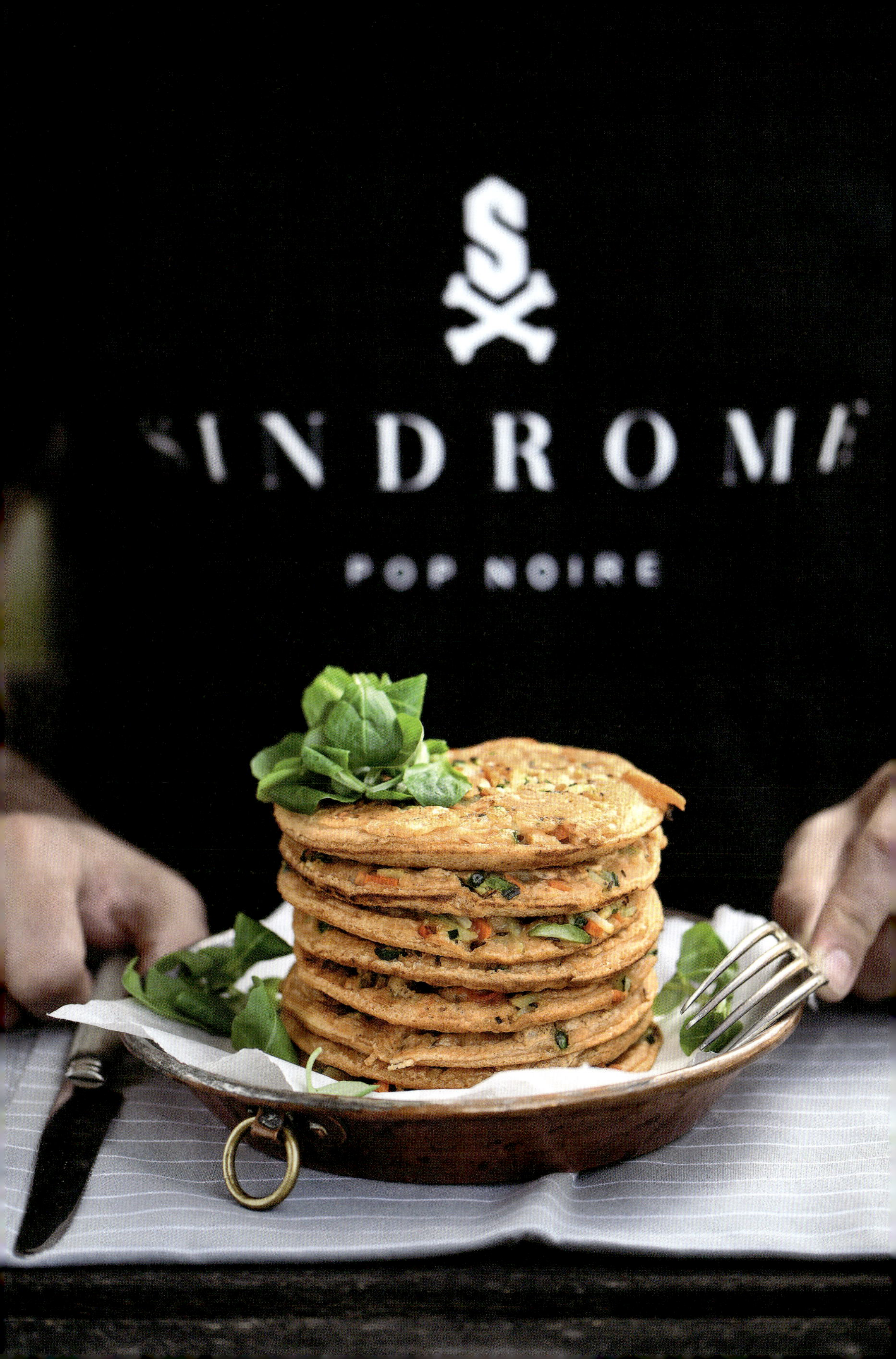
POP NOIRE

Lentils & Beans

We have grouped these two legumes together because they are easy to find ready-to-eat in supermarkets. Haricot and kidney beans, baked beans, brown, green and red lentils are all available tinned, vacuum cooked or even frozen; so you'll never be able to use soaking or cooking time as an excuse not to eat them regularly. These legumes are very practical and so simple to customise.

Lentils & Beans

SPICY TERRINE

- 300 g cooked kidney beans
- 2 medium tomatoes, chopped
- 2 tbsp balsamic vinegar
- 1 tbsp white miso paste
- 1½ tbsp onion powder
- 1 tsp Espelette pepper
- 3 tbsp smoked paprika

Use a food processor to blend the beans to a very smooth purée. Add the chopped tomatoes, balsamic vinegar and white miso paste. Add the onion powder, Espelette pepper and paprika. Blend again until smooth. Transfer to a glass jar and refrigerate for up to a week.

AVOCADO CREAM

- 1 ripe avocado
- 250 g cooked haricot beans
- 50 g basil
- 4 tsp lemon juice
- Fine salt
- 1 tsp sweet jalapeño sauce
- 1 tbsp olive oil

Remove the avocado skin and pit, then cut the flesh into large pieces before transferring to a food processor with an S blade. Add the haricot beans, chopped basil and lemon juice, then blend on a high speed. Season with salt, jalapeño sauce and olive oil. Blend again to obtain a perfectly smooth cream.

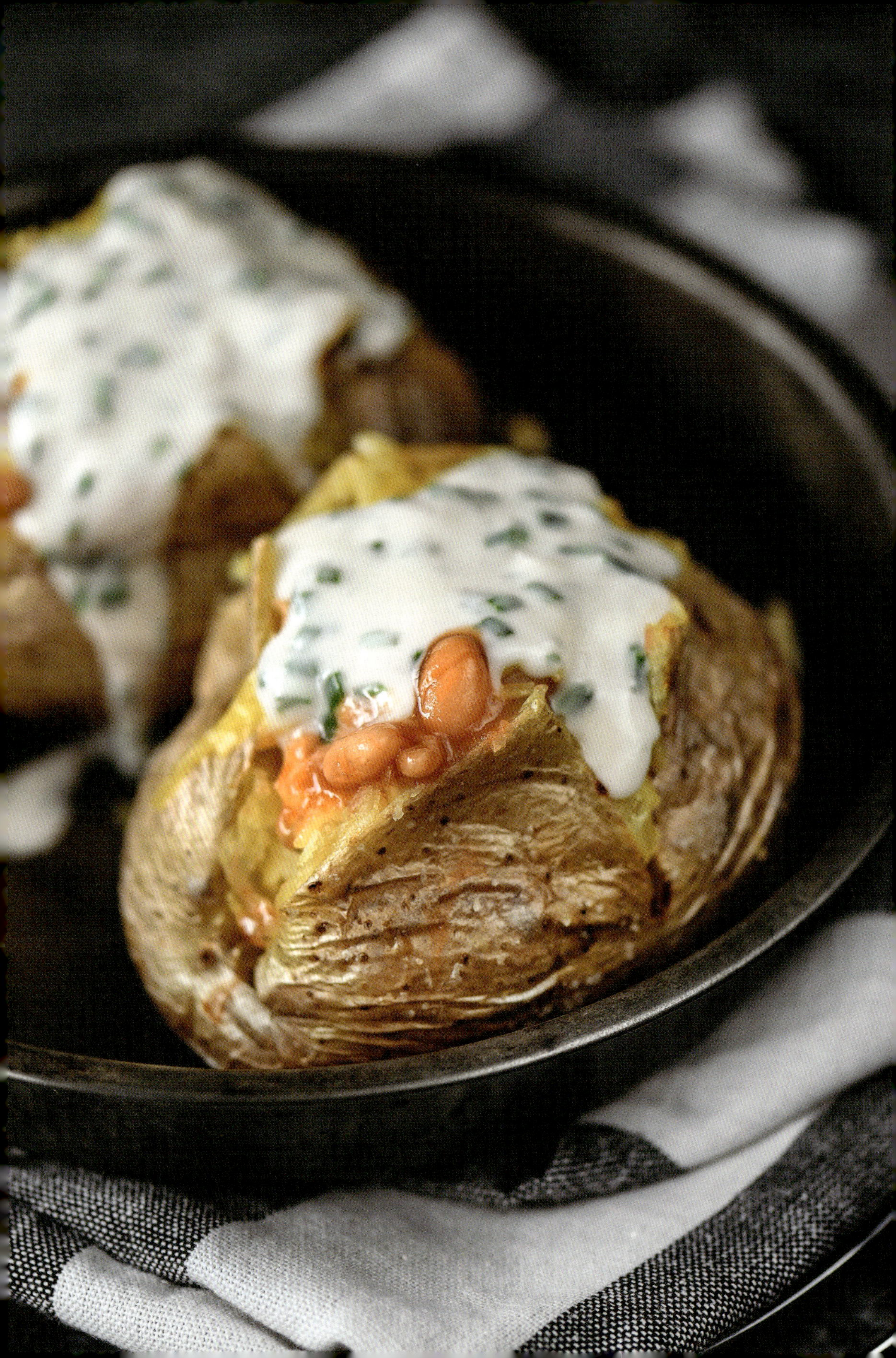

Lentils & Beans

JACKET POTATOES

- 4 baking potatoes (1.5 kg)
- 1 tsp fine salt
- 4 tsp sunflower oil
- 150 g grated vegan cheddar cheese
- 250 g baked beans
- 50 g thick soya cream
- 2 tbsp chopped frozen chives
- 1 tsp apple cider vinegar

Preheat the oven to 200°C (gas mark 6). Wash the potatoes, then dry. Score an x in the skin with a knife. Place the potatoes on a baking tray and rub with fine salt. Then coat the potatoes in oil. Bake in the oven for 1 hour. Check that the potatoes are cooked by pricking them with a knife. Use a tablespoon to remove the potato flesh. Mix with 100 g of cheddar and put back in the potato skins, making an indent. Fill with preheated baked beans. Top the beans with the remaining cheese and put under the grill for 5 minutes. Mix the thick soya cream, chives and apple cider vinegar in a bowl. Top each potato with a tablespoon of cream and serve.

BEETROOT HUMMUS

- 500 g tinned haricot beans
- 100 g cooked beetroot • 2 garlic cloves • 1 tsp ground cumin • 1 tbsp lemon juice • ½ tsp fine salt • 2 tsp creamed horseradish sauce • 1 tbsp olive oil

Blend the beans and beetroot to a fine purée in a food processor with an S blade. Add the crushed garlic, cumin, lemon juice and salt, and blend again. Add the horseradish and olive oil, then blend one last time.

NEO-CASSOULET

- 2 tbsp olive oil • 1 sprig of thyme
- 2 cloves • 1 tbsp black peppercorns
- 2 garlic cloves • 100 g frozen onions
- 100 g frozen carrots • 100 g smoked tofu • 150 g 'chicken' alternative meat • 200 g vegan sausages
- 800 g baked beans

Heat the oil in a large pot with the thyme, cloves and peppercorns. Add crushed garlic, onions and carrots. Cover and cook over a medium heat for 10 minutes. Add the chopped tofu, meat alternative and sausages. Mix gently and add the beans. Cover and simmer over a low heat for 15 minutes. Remove the thyme and serve.

Lentils & Beans

CHILLI CON CORN →

- 2 tbsp olive oil • 4 tsp chopped frozen garlic • 1½ tsp cumin seeds
- 1 tbsp oregano • 1 tsp chipotle chilli flakes • 100 g mixed frozen peppers • 100 g frozen carrots
- 100 g frozen onions • 300 g tinned sweetcorn • 800 g tinned kidney beans • 1 tsp fine salt • 1 tsp liquid smoke • 3 tbsp tomato purée • 1 tbsp lime juice • 2 tbsp basil

Heat the oil in a large pot with the garlic, cumin seeds, oregano and chilli flakes. Add the peppers, carrots and onions. Sauté for 10 minutes and add the drained corn and kidney beans with their liquid. Add the salt, liquid smoke and tomato purée. Mix well, cover and simmer over a low heat for 20 minutes. Garnish with the lime juice and chopped basil.

LENTIL CREAM WITH TRUFFLES

- 400 g pre-cooked brown lentils
- 4 tsp tahini
- 2 tsp tamari
- ¾ tsp black pepper • Fine salt
- 1 tbsp truffle-infused olive oil

Drain the lentils. Transfer the lentils to a bowl and add the tahini, tamari and black pepper. Use a stick blender to blend the ingredients to a very smooth purée. Adjust the seasoning according to taste. Add the truffle-infused olive oil and blend rapidly. Rest the mixture for 20 minutes in the fridge before serving on toasted bread.

LENTILS WITH SMOKED TOFU

- 300 g pre-cooked brown lentils
- 200 g pre-cooked carrots
- 3 tbsp chopped frozen shallots
- 2 tsp chopped frozen garlic
- 200 g smoked tofu
- 1 tbsp oil
- ¼ tsp fine salt
- 1½ tbsp chopped flat-leaf parsley

In a large bowl, mix the lentils, carrots, shallots and garlic. Tear the tofu into small pieces by hand. In a large frying pan, heat the oil and sauté the tofu pieces over a high heat for 5 minutes. Set the tofu aside and add the contents of the bowl to the pan. Season with salt and cook for another 5 minutes, stirring regularly. Once cooked, add the smoked tofu and chopped parsley.

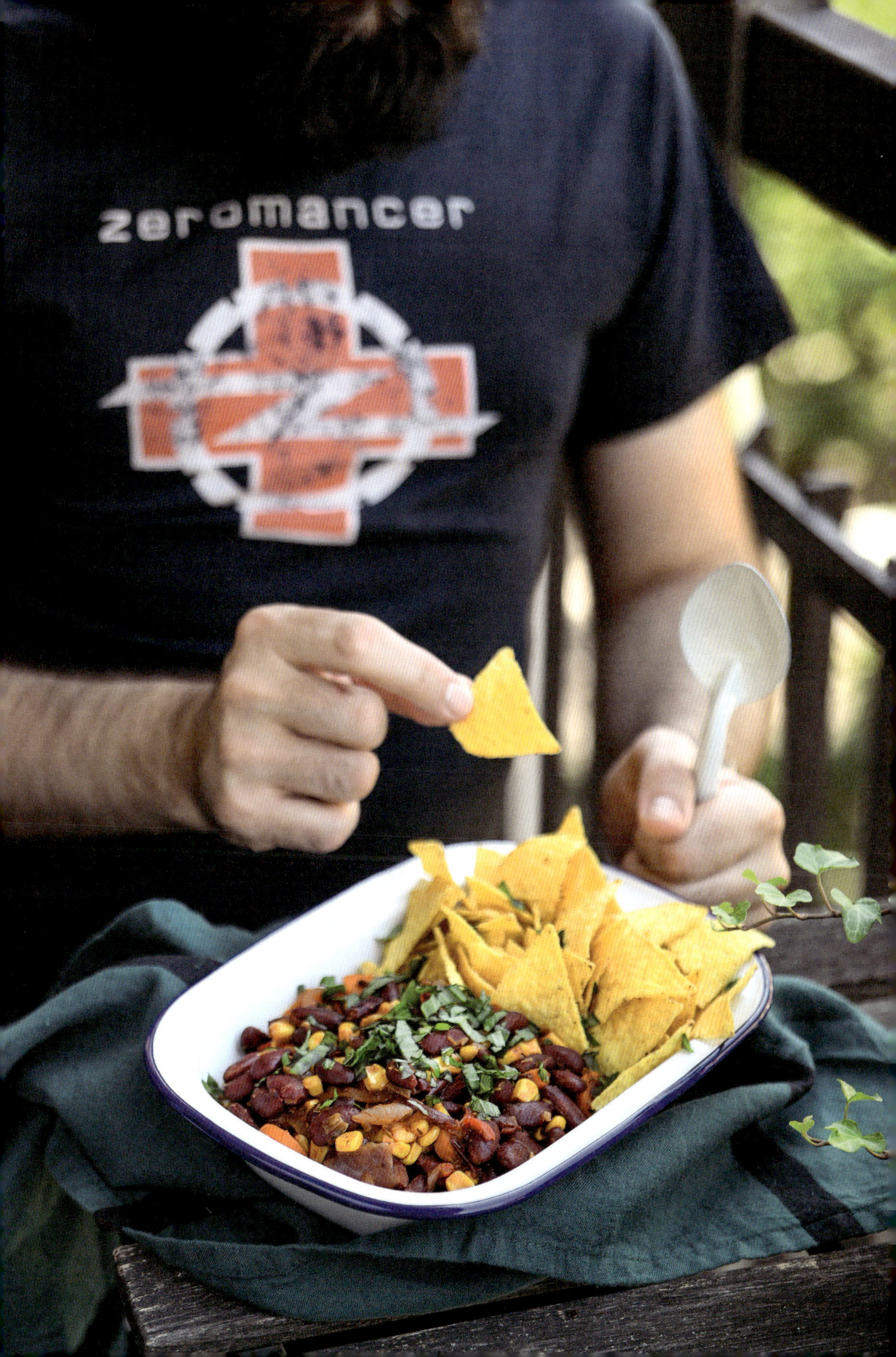
zeromancer

Lentils & Beans

LENTIL SOUP

- 100 g frozen parsnips
- 100 g frozen onions
- 2 tsp chopped frozen garlic
- 1 sprig thyme
- 3 bay leaves
- 2½ tsp dried sage
- 450 g cooked green lentils
- 800 ml vegetable stock
- Black pepper

In a large pot, cook the parsnips, onions and garlic over a high heat. Add the thyme, bay leaves, and sage. Brown the vegetables until they start to stick to the bottom of the pot. Add the lentils and pour in the hot vegetable broth. Stir and simmer for 15 minutes. Finish with a few twists of black pepper.

MEDITERRANEAN DAL

- 300 g courgettes
- 100 g red peppers
- 150 g onions
- Olive oil
- 1 tsp sweet paprika
- 3 garlic cloves
- Fine salt
- 1 sprig thyme
- Fresh basil
- 1 tsp Espelette pepper
- 1 tbsp coriander seeds
- 400 g red lentils
- 1.5 litres vegetable stock

Cut the courgettes, peppers and onions into small pieces. Heat a splash of oil in a wok with the paprika and crushed garlic. Add the chopped vegetables and sauté for 10 minutes. Season with salt, then add the finely chopped thyme, basil and the Espelette pepper. Set aside. In a large pan, heat a little olive oil and lightly toast the coriander seeds. Add the dried lentils and mix until shiny. Add the hot stock and cook for another 15 minutes. Add the vegetables and cook for 3 more minutes before serving.

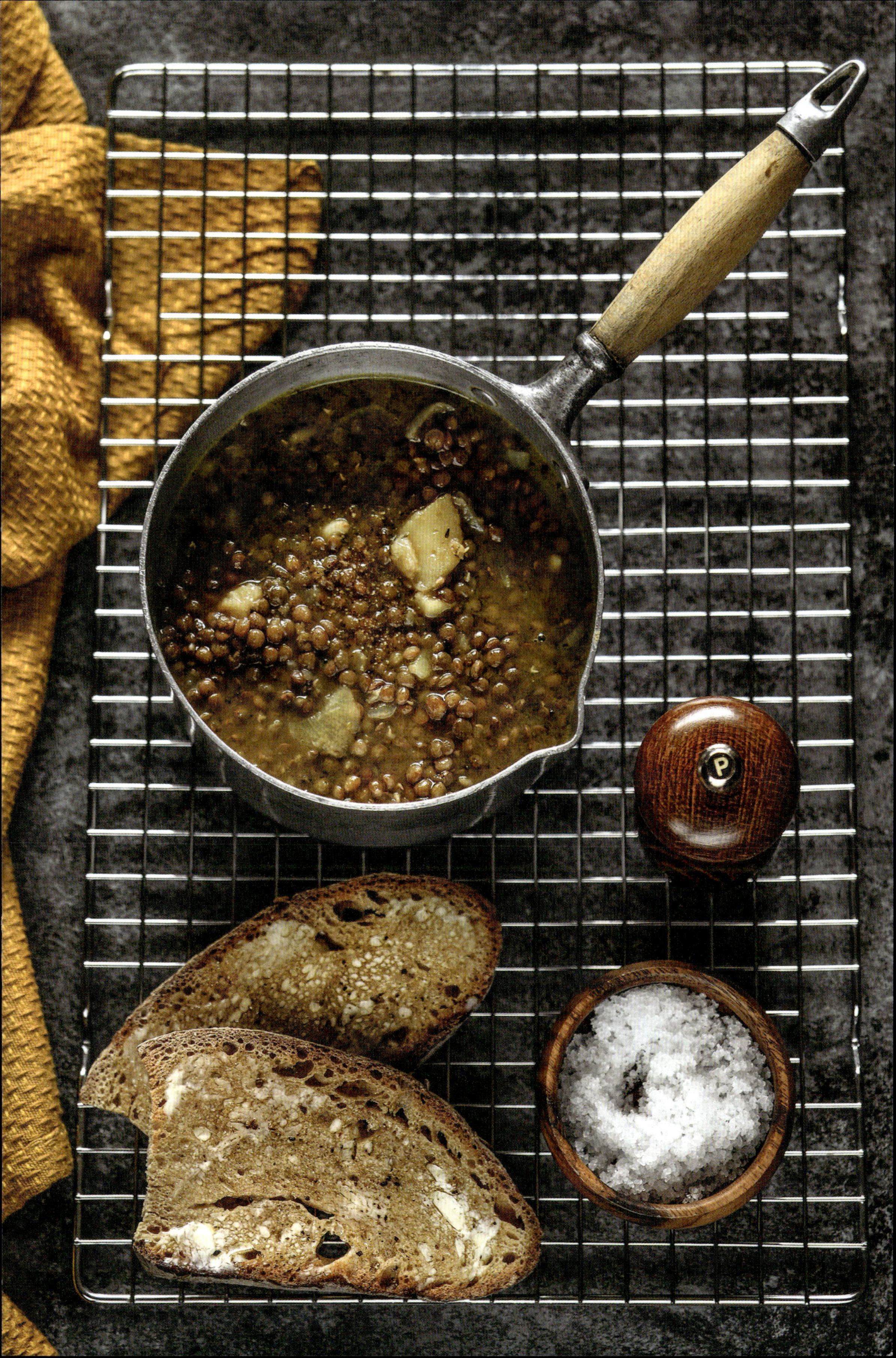

Mayonnaise

Egg-free mayonnaise? Yes it does exist. There is a wide range of ready-made products, plain or flavoured, available. It's a bit like mustard or tomato ketchup, it's something that you should always have in the fridge. Vegan mayonnaise is above all an excellent base to make a variety of gourmet sauces and dressings.

GRAVLAXSAS

- 50 g vegan mayonnaise
- 2 tsp wholegrain mustard
- 1 tsp agave syrup
- ½ tsp ground allspice
- 3 tbsp frozen dill

Mix the mayonnaise with the mustard in a bowl. Thin with agave syrup. Add the allspice and chopped dill. Mix well and transfer to a small jar. Keep in the fridge.

AIOLI

- 50 g vegan mayonnaise
- 2 garlic cloves
- ¼ tsp black pepper
- 2 tsp Dijon mustard
- 2 tbsp olive oil

Mix the mayonnaise with the crushed garlic in a bowl. Add the black pepper and the Dijon mustard. Mix well. Add the olive oil while whisking the sauce with a fork. Transfer to an airtight jar and keep in the fridge.

ANDALUSIAN

- 50 g vegan mayonnaise
- 2 tbsp tomato purée
- 2 tsp jalapeño sauce
- 1 tsp sweet smoked paprika
- 1 tbsp lemon juice

Mix the mayonnaise with the tomato purée and jalapeño sauce in a bowl. Mix the paprika with the lemon juice. Add to the mayonnaise and mix. Transfer to a small jar and keep in the refrigerator.

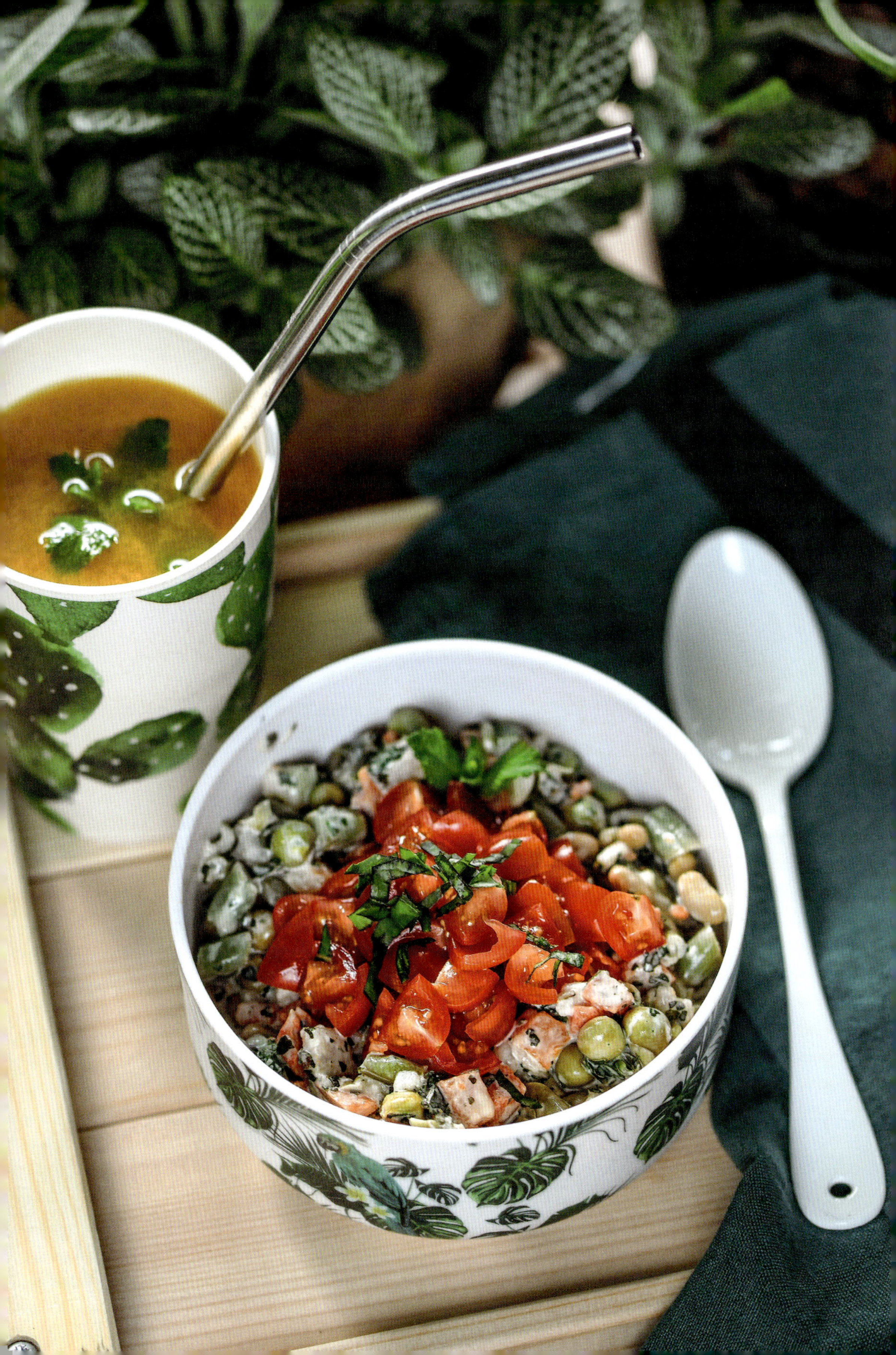

Mayonnaise

SUMMER VEGETABLE SALAD

- 50 g vegan mayonnaise
- 1 tsp apple cider vinegar
- 4 tsp olive oil
- 2 tbsp finely chopped fresh mint
- 2 tbsp finely chopped fresh basil
- 250 g tinned chopped vegetables
- 50 g cherry tomatoes

Mix the mayonnaise with the vinegar and oil in a bowl. Add the finely chopped mint and basil. Drain the vegetables and add to the mayonnaise. Mix and set aside in the fridge for 30 minutes. Finely chop the cherry tomatoes and place on top of the vegetables.

SAUCE GRIBICHE

- 20 g cornichons
- 1 tbsp capers in oil
- 50 g vegan mayonnaise
- 1 tsp Dijon mustard
- 30 g plain tofu
- Fine salt
- 2½ tbsp chopped frozen parsley

Grate the pickles and chop the capers. In a bowl, mix the mayonnaise and mustard with the tofu cut into small pieces. Add the pickles and capers. Season with salt and add the chopped parsley. Mix and transfer to a small jar. Keep in the refrigerator.

TARTARE SAUCE

- 350 g vegan mayonnaise
- 2 tsp Dijon mustard
- 1 tbsp cornichons
- 1 tbsp capers in vinegar
- 1 tbsp chopped frozen shallots
- 3 tbsp chopped frozen parsley
- 4 tbsp chopped frozen chives

Mix the mayonnaise with the Dijon mustard in a bowl. Finely chop the pickles and the capers. Add the mayonnaise along with the shallots, parsley and chives. Mix and transfer to a jar. Store in the refrigerator.

COCKTAIL SAUCE

- 50 g vegan mayonnaise
- 1½ tbsp tomato ketchup
- 1 tsp Cognac
- ¼ tsp Worcestershire sauce
- ¼ tsp Espelette pepper

Mix the mayonnaise with ketchup. Then add the Cognac, Worcestershire sauce and Espelette pepper. Whisk the sauce with a fork, pour into a jar and store in the refrigerator.

BÉARNAISE SAUCE

- 250 g vegan mayonnaise
- 2 tsp apple cider vinegar
- 3 tbsp frozen tarragon
- 2 tbsp chopped frozen shallots
- 1 tbsp white wine
- 1 tbsp olive oil

Mix the mayonnaise with the apple cider vinegar in a bowl. Add the chopped tarragon. Sweat the chopped shallots in a small frying pan. Once they become translucent, deglaze with white wine. Let the liquid evaporate. Add the shallots to the sauce. Pour in the oil while whisking with a fork. Transfer to a small jar and keep in the refrigerator.

HOLLANDAISE SAUCE

- 350 g vegan mayonnaise
- 2 tsp lemon juice
- ¼ tsp turmeric
- ¼ tsp Kala namak (black salt)
- 1 tbsp rapeseed oil

Mix the mayonnaise with the lemon juice, turmeric and Kala namak in a bowl. Loosen with 4 tsp of cold water. Add the rapeseed oil while whisking the sauce with a fork. Transfer to a small jar and keep in the refrigerator.

POTATO SALAD

- 100 g vegan mayonnaise
- 2 tsp apple cider vinegar
- 1½ tbsp chopped frozen parsley
- 500 g pre-cooked potatoes
- Fine salt
- 100 g sweet and sour pickles
- 100 g vegan sausages
- 1 tbsp fried onions
- Black pepper

Mix the mayonnaise with the apple cider vinegar and parsley in a bowl. Set aside.

Cut the potatoes into medium-sized pieces and season with salt to taste. Cut the pickles into thick rounds. Quarter and slice the sausages, then fry them. In a large bowl, mix everything together, add the fried onions and season generously with pepper.

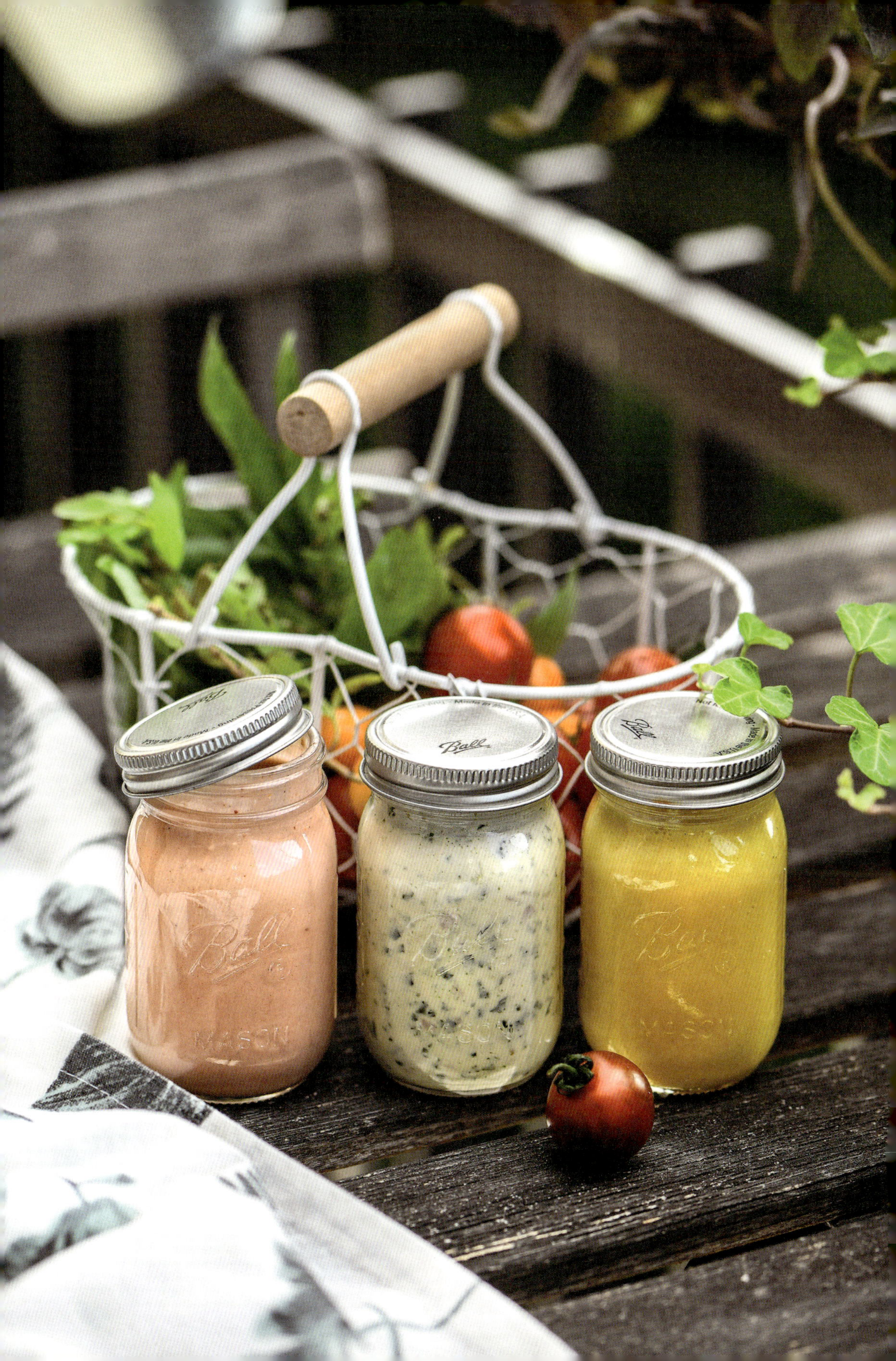
Ball
MASON

Miso

This ingredient is well known thanks to the soup of the same name served in Japanese restaurants. In its original form, it is a fermented paste made from soya, rice or barley, offering very different and interesting possibilities for Western vegan cuisine — as a replacement for meat-based stocks in many recipes, being one of its many uses. With a bit of imagination, it can be used almost anywhere to enhance dishes.

MUSHROOM & HERB SOUP

- 10 button mushrooms
- 1 litre vegetable stock
- 80 g white miso paste
- 2 tbsp wholegrain mustard
- 2½ tbsp fresh tarragon
- 3 tbsp fresh chives

Clean the mushrooms and cut them into 8 pieces. Set aside. Heat the vegetable stock in a pan. When it starts to boil, add the miso paste and mustard. Use a whisk to make sure it dissolves. Add the chopped mushrooms and simmer for 5 minutes before turning off the heat. Finely chop the tarragon and chives, then add to the broth. Serve hot in small bowls.

SALTED PEANUT CUP

- 150 g dark chocolate (60% cocoa solids)
- 90 g peanut butter
- 1 tbsp white miso
- 60 g natural soya/coconut yogurt
- 4 tsp maple syrup
- Peanuts

Melt the chocolate in a bain-marie. Pour a drizzle of chocolate into 4 to 6 cupcake cases (depending on their size) and turn so that the chocolate coats the inside of the case. Put into the freezer for a few minutes to harden. Mix together the peanut butter, miso paste, yogurt and maple syrup in a bowl. Crush several peanuts. When the chocolate is hard, fill with the peanut mixture and add a few pieces of chopped peanuts. Cover with melted chocolate and refrigerate overnight. Remove from the mould and serve.

Miso

RAINBOW SALAD

- 1 tbsp white miso paste
- 1 tbsp tahini
- 2 tsp toasted sesame oil
- 2 tsp mirin
- 2 tsp lemon juice
- 1 tsp maple syrup
- 200 g cucumber
- 150 g yellow pepper
- 12 cherry tomatoes
- 100 g radish
- 50 g baby leaf salad
- 250 g grated carrots
- 60 g blueberries
- Salt
- Pepper
- Toasted almonds
- Fresh coriander

Shake the miso, tahini, sesame oil, mirin, lemon juice and maple syrup together in a jar to make a vinaigrette. Set aside. Cut the cucumber and yellow pepper into small pieces. Halve the cherry tomatoes and slice the radishes.

In a large bowl, arrange the different fruits and vegetables in the colours of the rainbow, and season lightly with salt and pepper. Sprinkle with toasted almonds and coriander. Add the sauce, mix and serve.

BEETROOT RAVIOLI

- 200 g cashew nuts
- 80 g pistachio nuts
- 2 tbsp white miso
- 1 tsp red miso
- 3 tbsp malted yeast
- 5 tsp lemon juice
- 2 tsp Worcestershire sauce
- ½ tsp curry powder
- 1 tbsp olive oil
- ½ tsp garlic powder
- 1 beetroot

Soak the cashews and pistachios in a bowl of hot water for 30 minutes. Rinse and put all the ingredients (except the beetroot) into a food processor with an S blade and add 6 tbsp of cold water. Mix to form a vegan 'cheese' and transfer to a bowl and refrigerate. Use a mandoline to finely slice the beetroot. Place a teaspoon of cheese on each slice and fold over to make a ravioli. Repeat to make several ravioli. Garnish with a dash of olive oil, some fresh herbs and serve with a salad such as a cucumber and mint salad.

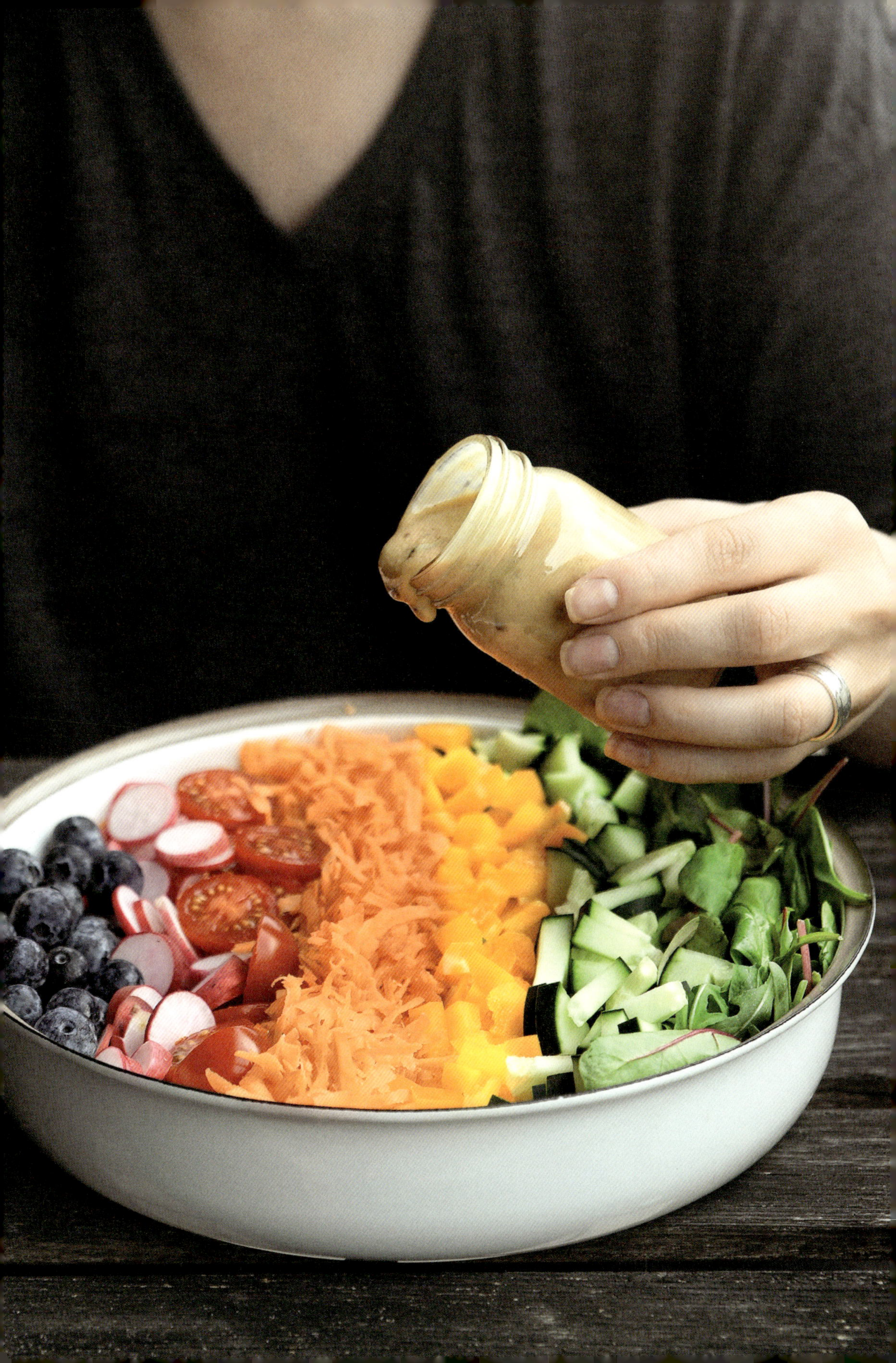

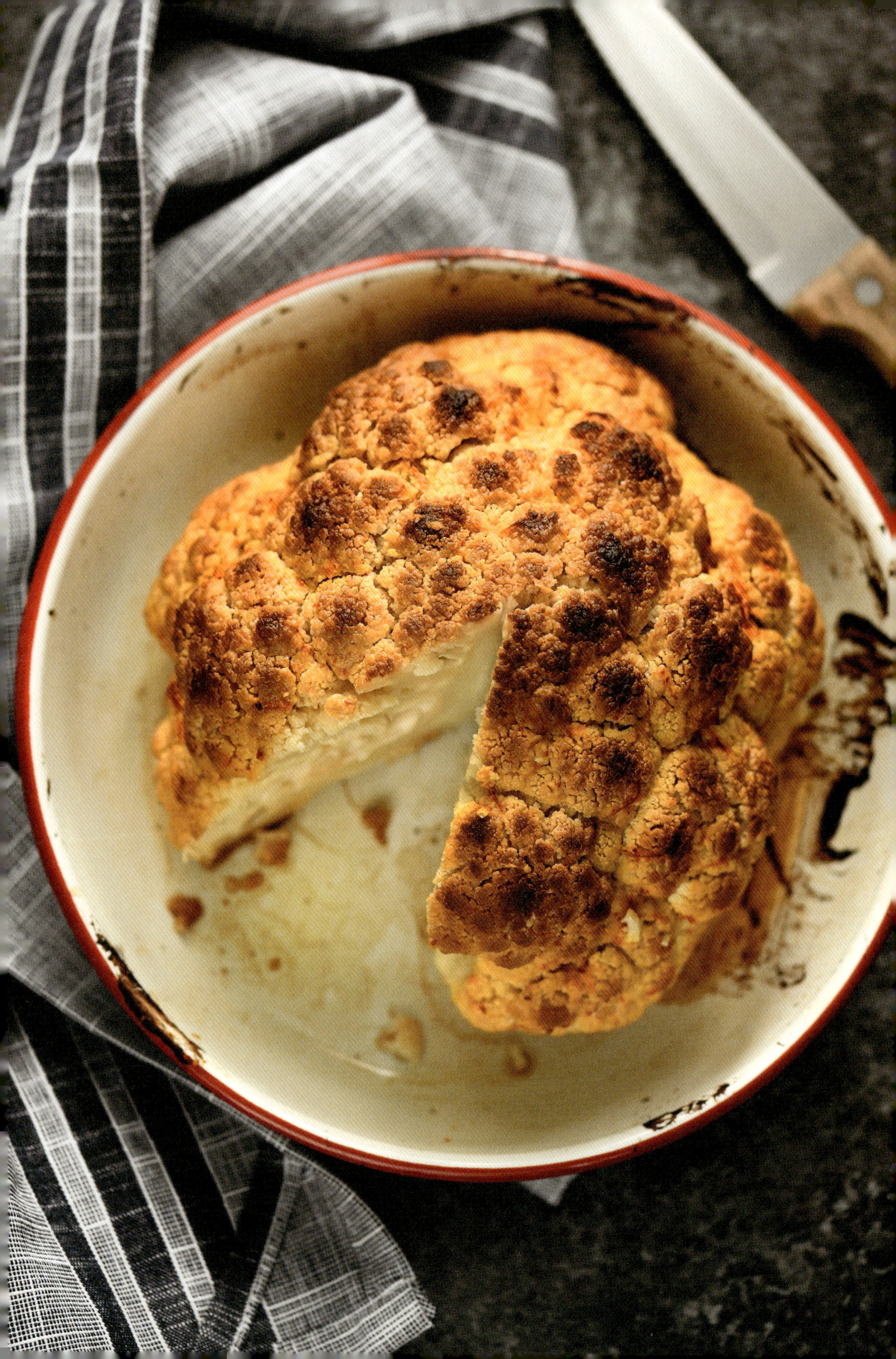

SAFFRON CAULIFLOWER

- Pinch of saffron
- 1.5 kg whole cauliflower
- ¼ tsp Espelette pepper
- ¼ tsp garlic powder
- 1½ tbsp white miso
- 3 tbsp olive oil

Infuse the saffron in 2 tbsp of warm water for 20 minutes. Wash the cauliflower, remove the leaves and the stalk, taking care not to remove too much. Place on a baking tray and preheat the oven to 190°C (gas mark 5). Add the Espelette pepper and garlic powder to the infusion, mix well, then add the miso. Mix well again so that the liquid is smooth. Pour over the whole cauliflower and coat it all over. Put into the oven for 45 minutes. Then add 3 tbsp of olive oil, cover with baking parchment to cook en papillote and continue to bake for another 45 minutes. Serve immediately.

SAUTÉED MUSHROOMS

- 4 tsp vegan margarine • 100 g smoked tofu • 300 g mixed frozen mushrooms • 1 tbsp Cognac • Fine salt • Black pepper • 1 tbsp red miso • 100 ml soya cream • 1½ tbsp chopped fresh parsley

Melt the margarine in a hot frying pan and sauté the tofu cut into pieces. Add the mushrooms and allow to cook for 6 minutes. Deglaze with the Cognac, then season with salt and pepper. Add the miso mixed with the soya cream over a low heat. Stir and scatter with chopped parsley.

MISO-GLAZED AUBERGINES

- 2 large aubergines
- 3 tbsp white miso
- 2 tbsp coconut vinegar
- 1¼ tbsp caster sugar
- 2 tbsp toasted sesame oil
- 1½ tsp toasted sesame seeds
- Fresh coriander

Preheat the oven to 190°C (gas mark 5). Cut the aubergines in half lengthways then make diagonal cuts along the flesh. Place the aubergines on a baking tray. Mix the miso paste with the vinegar, sugar and oil in a bowl. Brush the aubergine halves generously with the marinade so that it goes into the cuts, then add a thick layer of the marinade. Scatter with sesame seeds and bake in the oven for 45-55 minutes. Serve with fresh coriander over the top.

Bread

As an open sandwich, toast or just accompanying a bowl of soup, bread is a staple we all enjoy and can be eaten at every meal no matter where you go in the world. Just because you don't eat butter doesn't mean you have to pass it up! There are so many other ways to top it! It can even be used to cook with.

TOAST WITH MUSHROOMS

- Olive oil
- ¼ tsp black pepper
- ¼ tsp grated nutmeg
- 200 ml natural soya milk
- Salt
- 30 g cornflour
- White wine
- 1 tbsp malted yeast
- 250 g wild or cultivated mushrooms
- 2 tsp chopped frozen garlic
- 1 tbsp chopped frozen shallots
- 4 large slices wholemeal bread

Heat a splash of oil in a frying pan, then sauté the pepper and grated nutmeg for 45 seconds. Add the soya milk, salt to your taste and mix. Mix the cornflour with a little white wine and add to the milk. Mix vigorously on a high heat and allow to thicken. Once it is the desired thickness, add the yeast, mix and set aside. Clean the mushrooms, ensuring that the stems are clean. Sauté the garlic and shallots in a little olive oil, add the mushrooms, salt and mix everything together. Lower the heat to a medium heat. Cook for 5 minutes and deglaze with a splash of white wine. Let the liquid evaporate over a high heat. Toast the bread and add a generous layer of sauce on top. Add a handful of mushrooms on top and serve immediately.

CLUB SANDWICH

- 200 g meatless strips
- 130 ml Worcestershire sauce
- 12 slices sandwich bread
- 60 g vegan mayonnaise
- 60 g piccalilli
- 1 iceberg lettuce
- 8 slices smoked vegan cheese
- 2 tomatoes
- 8 slices vegan ham

Cook the meatless strips in a hot pan without any fat. Deglaze with the Worcestershire sauce and set aside. Toast the bread. Mix the mayonnaise and piccalilli in a bowl (blend the piccalilli if the vegetable pieces are too big). Assembly: spread a layer of mayonnaise on the first slice of bread, add two slices of lettuce, the meatless strips and a slice of smoked cheese. Place a second slice of bread on top, add a layer of mayonnaise, a few tomato slices, two slices of ham and a slice of smoked cheese. Finish with a third slice of bread. Press down, remove the crusts and any filling that sticks out. Cut into four triangles and secure with wooden cocktail sticks. Repeat the process.

Bread

AVOCADO TOAST

- 1 tbsp chopped frozen shallots
- 1 tbsp lemon juice
- 2 ripe avocados
- 1 tbsp olive oil
- 1 tsp jalapeño sauce
- Fine salt
- 4 slices sourdough bread
- ½ tsp Espelette pepper
- Fresh coriander
- Cherry tomatoes

Marinade the shallots in the lemon juice for 10 minutes. Crush the avocados with a fork, then add the olive oil, jalapeño sauce and salt. Add the shallots with the lemon juice and mix well with the avocado. Cut the slices of bread to fit a toaster and toast. Spread a generous layer of crushed avocado on the toasted bread and sprinkle with Espelette pepper. Add a few coriander leaves and the cherry tomatoes cut in half.

GARLIC BREAD

- 1 baguette
- 3 tbsp olive oil
- 2 garlic cloves
- 1 tbsp oregano
- 1 tsp chipotle powder
- Fine salt
- 100 g grated vegan mozzarella

Cut the baguette into roughly 3-cm slices, place on a baking tray and bake in the oven preheated to 180°C (gas mark 4) for 5 minutes. Let it cool. In a bowl, mix together the oil, crushed garlic, oregano, chipotle powder and salt. Brush the mixture onto the slices of bread. Add a small pile of cheese on each piece and put under the grill until the cheese melts.

CHESTNUT FRENCH TOAST

- 20 pieces baguette bread
- 50 g cornflour
- 600 ml vanilla soya milk
- 60 g brown sugar
- 60 g chestnut cream
- 1 tsp cinnamon
- Vegan margarine

Cut the pieces of bread the day before and let them dry out.

In a bowl, dissolve the cornflour in a little soya milk then add the rest of the milk. Add the brown sugar, chestnut cream and cinnamon. Blend with a stick blender to make a smooth mixture. Pour into a large bowl, add the bread and soak it in the mixture. Heat a frying pan with a knob of margarine. Transfer the pieces of bread to the pan and fry over a medium heat for 5 minutes. Turn them so that each side is cooked. The surface of the bread should be golden. Transfer to a plate and sprinkle with brown sugar.

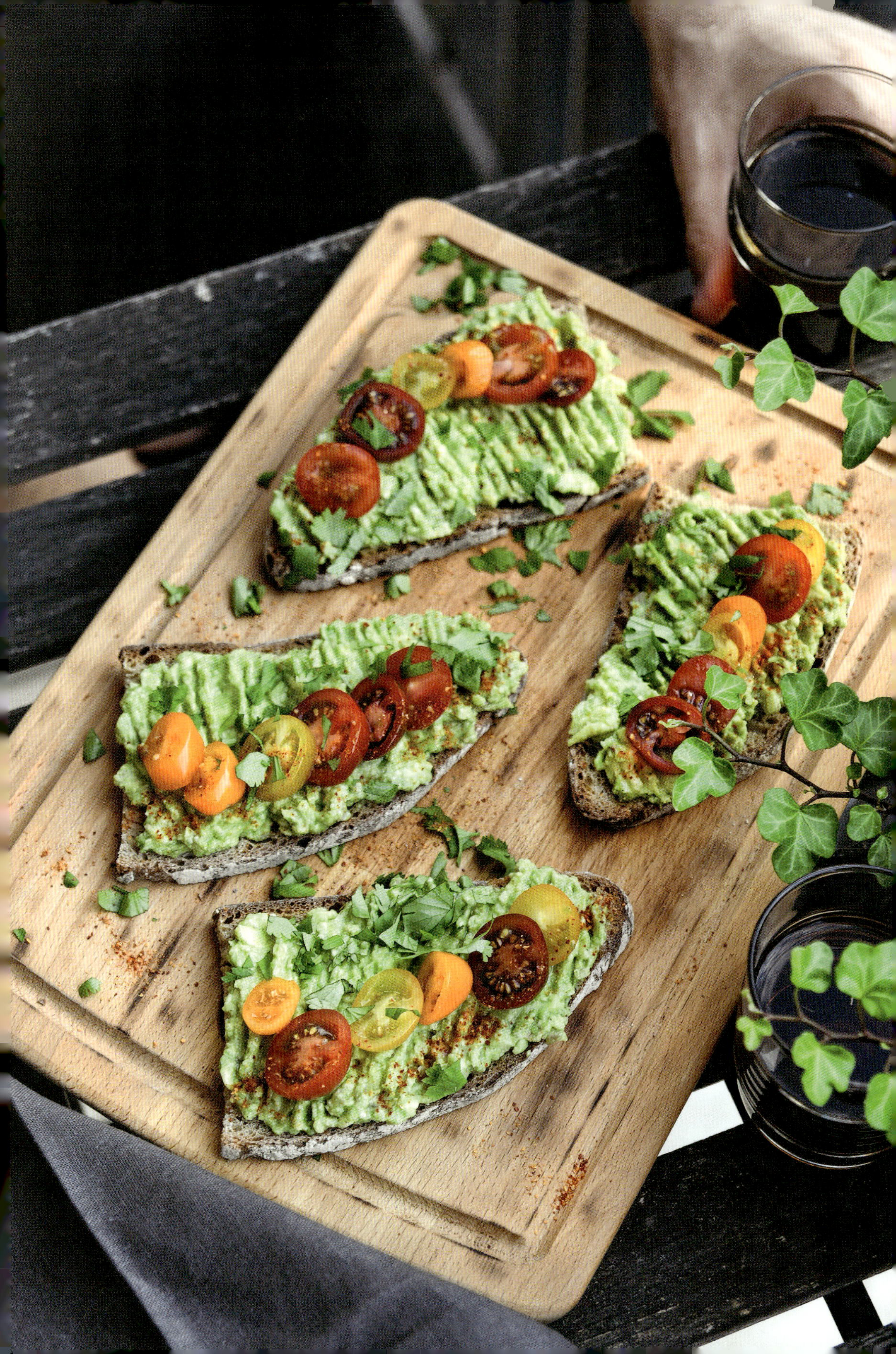

Bread

GAZPACHO

- 400 g tomato passata
- 350 g cucumber
- 2 garlic cloves
- 1 tbsp balsamic vinegar
- ¼ tsp fine salt
- 1¼ tsp Espelette pepper
- 300 g mixed frozen peppers
- Olive oil
- 1 thin baguette

Put the tomato passata and cucumber, cut into small pieces, into a blender. Blend for 30 seconds and add 100 ml of cold water, garlic, vinegar, Espelette pepper and frozen peppers. Blend again for 1 minute. Add 2 tbsp of oil and 50 g of bread. Mix with a spatula and set aside while preparing the croutons. Transfer the rest of the bread, cut into 1-cm slices, to a hot frying pan. Drizzle with 2 tbsp of olive oil and cook over a high heat. Turn the croutons so that they are golden on both sides. Blend the soup one last time for 1 minute and serve with the croutons.

BREAD PUDDING

- 100 g raisins
- 2 tbsp dark rum
- 1 tbsp vanilla extract
- 600 ml vanilla soya milk
- 300 g stale bread
- 70 g caster sugar
- 200 g natural soya yogurt
- 2 tbsp candied lemons
- 2 tbsp candied oranges

Soak the raisins in the rum and vanilla extract. Heat the soya milk in a small pan then pour over the bread already cut into large pieces in a large bowl. Once the bread has absorbed all the milk, crush with a whisk so that it has a porridge-like texture. Add the sugar, yogurt and mix. Add the candied fruits and infused raisins and mix one last time. Grease a 20-cm cake tin, pour in the mixture and bake in the oven for 45 minutes at 180°C (gas mark 4). Check that the pudding is cooked with the tip of a knife. Allow to cool completely before serving. Variation: instead of raisins and candied fruit, add chocolate chips, hazelnuts or other nuts.

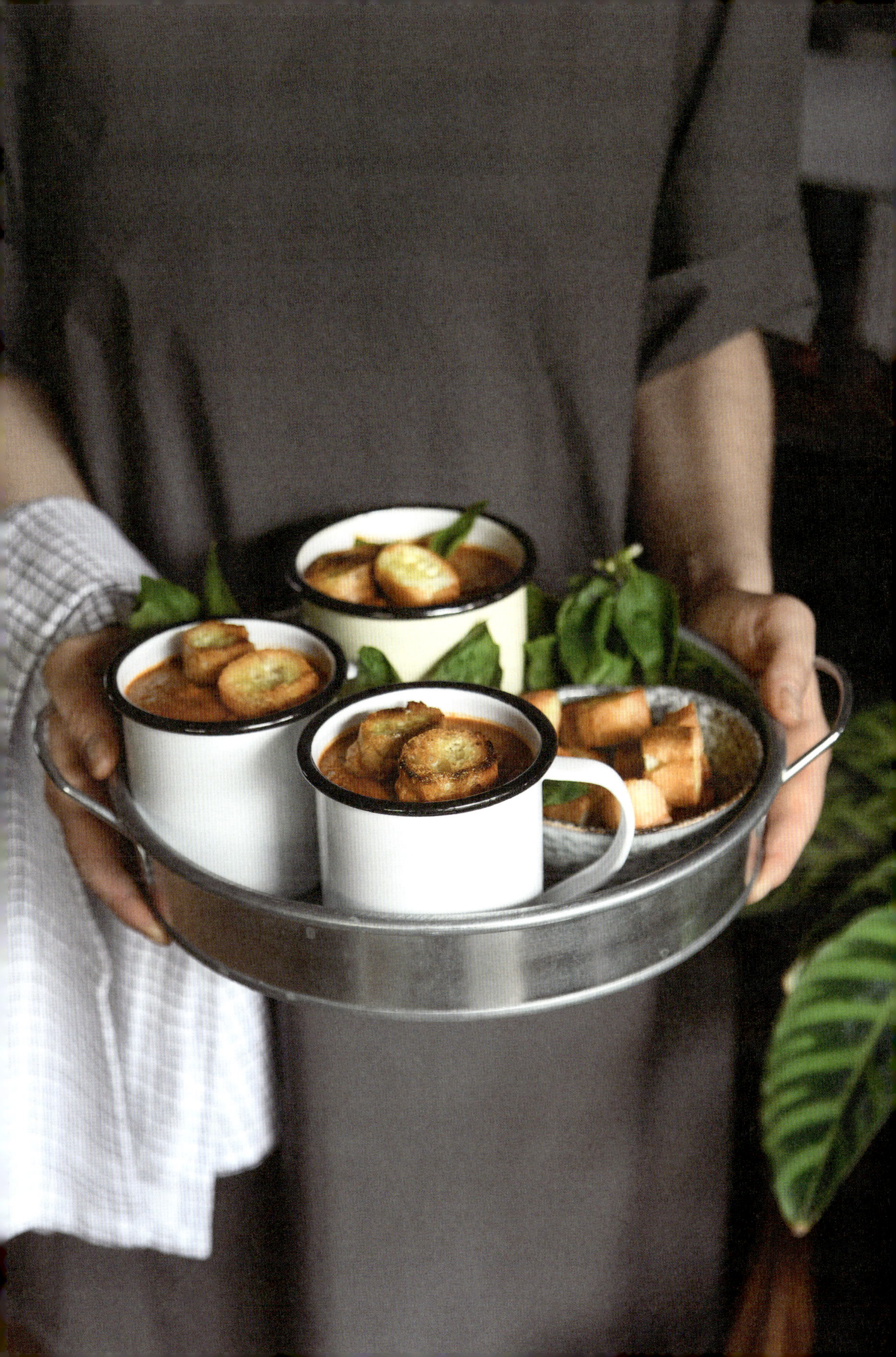

Bread

TOASTIE ROLL UPS

- 8 slices sandwich bread
- Vegan margarine
- Black pepper
- 8 slices vegan cheese
- 4 slices vegan ham

Preheat the oven to 200°C (gas mark 6). Remove the crusts and flatten the bread with a rolling pin. Spread a thin layer of margarine on to each slice, season with pepper, then add a slice of cheese and ½ a slice of ham. Carefully roll the bread and transfer to a baking tray. Brush another layer of margarine on the outside of the roll. Bake in the oven for 10 minutes then finish under the grill for 5 minutes. Trim the rolls with a large knife and serve.

MINI BRUSCHETTA

- 200 g frozen courgettes
- 1 tbsp olive oil
- Generous pinch of fine salt
- 1 tsp oregano
- 1 baguette
- 100 g green pesto
- 100 g grated vegan mozzarella
- Fresh rocket leaves

Sweat the courgette slices in a hot pan. Once thawed, add the oil, salt and oregano. Stir and cook over a high heat for 2 minutes.

Cut the baguette into 10 slices and place on a baking tray. Spread a layer of pesto on the bread. Place the courgette slices on top and cover with mozzarella. Bake under the grill for 6 minutes. Garnish with a few rocket leaves and serve very hot.

BREAD SOUP

- 4 tsp vegan margarine
- 100 g frozen onions
- 200 g stale bread
- 2 cloves
- ¼ tsp grated nutmeg
- 250 ml vegetable stock
- 500 ml natural soya milk
- Black pepper

In a large pan, melt the margarine and sauté the onion for 10 minutes over a low heat. Add the bread broken into pieces. Add the cloves, grated nutmeg and hot vegetable stock. Cook for 5 minutes and pour in the soya milk. Mix well and cook over a low heat for 15 minutes, stirring regularly. Blend the soup with a stick blender. Serve in a soup bowl and season to your taste.

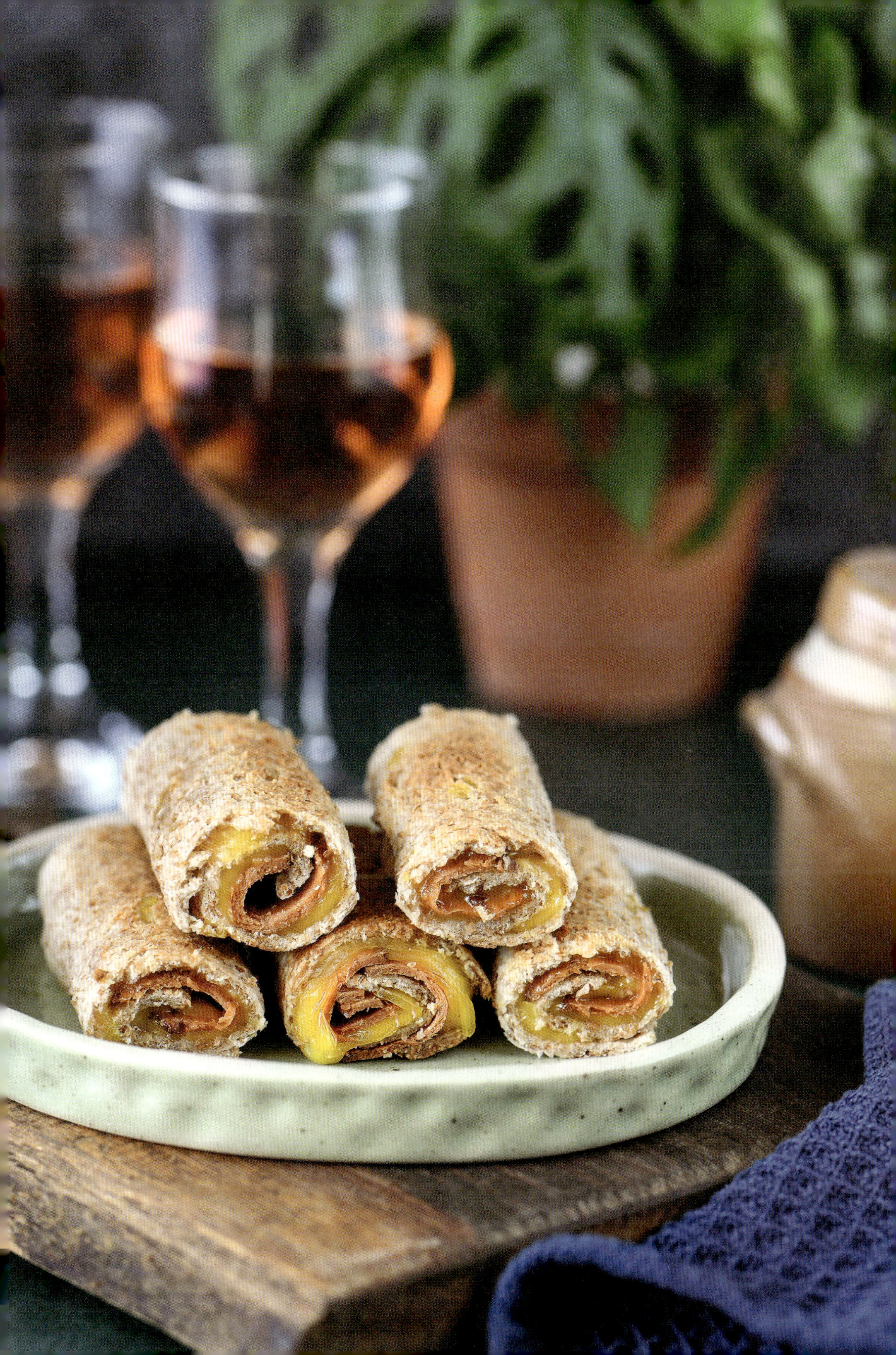

Breaded Treats

Whether shaped like nuggets, bites, batons or escalopes, a crispy breadcrumb coating can add an indulgent touch to any dish that will make your mouth water. It's a classic style of preparation that we are happy to fry quickly in a pan, without needing any more fuss. But we also like to ring the changes in different ways.

CAESAR SALAD

- 1 garlic clove
- 2 slices sandwich bread
- 1 tbsp olive oil
- 300 g mixed leaf salad
- 100 g cherry tomatoes
- 50 g vegan mayonnaise
- ½ lemon
- 2 breaded vegan escalopes
- Vegan parmesan

Cut the garlic clove in half and rub on each side of the bread. Cut the bread into small cubes. In a large frying pan, heat olive oil with the garlic until it starts to brown. Add the bread and mix well. Cook for 5 minutes over a high heat, stirring often. In a salad bowl mix the salad, tomato halves and the croutons. Mix the mayonnaise with the juice of half a lemon and 1 tbsp of cold water in a bowl. Pour into the salad bowl and mix. Fry the breaded escalopes on both sides in a frying pan. Cut into strips and add to the salad. Make parmesan shavings using a vegetable peeler and scatter on top of the salad.

SPINACH ESCALOPES

- 350 g chopped frozen spinach
- 50 g sorrel leaves (optional)
- Fine salt
- Black pepper
- 2 tsp olive oil
- 4 tsp cornflour
- 4 breaded vegan escalopes

In a pan, cook the spinach with the sorrel for 5 minutes over a high heat. Lower the heat, add salt and pepper, then pour in the oil and cornflour dissolved in cold water. Mix well and allow to thicken. Cut the escalopes in half through the middle and fry in a little oil in a frying pan. Place a portion of spinach between the two escalope halves and serve. Serve with a hollandaise sauce (see page 88).

Breaded Treats

VIENNESE BURGER

- 2 tbsp vegan mayonnaise
- 2 tsp creamed horseradish sauce
- 2 tsp lemon juice
- 100 g cooked beetroot
- 60 g pickles
- 2 breaded vegan escalopes
- 2 burger buns
- Green salad
- 4 slices vegan cheese
- 4 slices smoked vegan ham

Mix the mayonnaise with the horseradish and lemon juice in a bowl. Finely slice the beetroot. Finely slice the pickles lengthways. Fry the escalopes in a hot pan with a little oil. Put the buns in the toaster. Assemble as follows: place some salad on the bottom bun, add the escalope on top then 2 slices of cheese and 2 slices of vegan ham. Top with sliced pickles and beetroot. Cover with sauce and close with the top bun.

TOASTED WRAPS

- Oil
- 16 vegan chicken nuggets
- 100 g tomatoes
- 100 g avocado
- 100 g vegan mayonnaise
- 4 tsp za'atar seasoning
- 1 tsp lemon juice
- 4 wheat tortilla wraps
- 8 slices vegan cheese
- Jalapeño sauce

Fry the nuggets in a hot pan with a little oil. Preheat an electric grill or sandwich maker. Slice the tomato and avocado into batons. Mix together the mayonnaise, za'atar and lemon juice in a bowl. On each wrap, place two slices of cheese lengthways, 4 nuggets, 25 g tomato, 25 g avocado (plus jalapeño sauce according to taste). Seal the edges with the mayonnaise sauce. Close the wrap by folding the bottom edge, then folding the right edge and lastly the left edge. Transfer the wraps to the grill and reseal them. Wait 3 minutes until the wraps have grill marks, are sealed and are crispy on the outside.

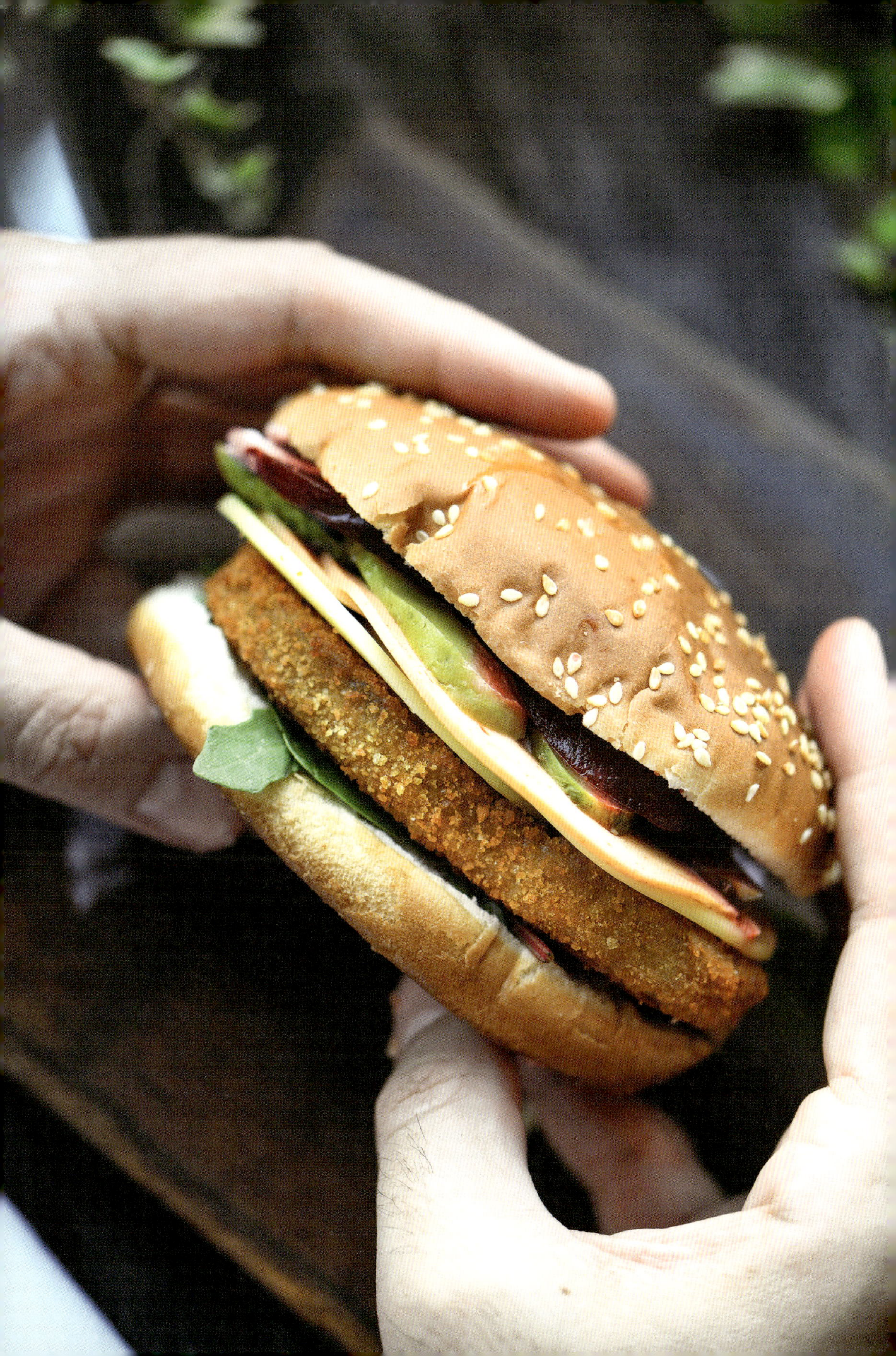

Breaded Treats

BBQ PIZZA

- 250 g frozen chopped tomatoes
- 4 tsp tomato purée
- 100 g frozen mixed peppers
- 100 g frozen red onions
- 100 g frozen diced potatoes
- 8 vegan chicken nuggets
- 1 pizza dough (260 g)
- BBQ sauce
- Fresh basil

In a pan, defrost the tomatoes and add the tomato purée. Mix and set aside. In a small, hot frying pan, sweat the peppers for 5 minutes over a high heat and set aside. In a frying pan, without oil or fat, sauté the onions and diced potatoes for around 5 minutes over a high heat. Set aside. In a frying pan with a little olive oil, brown the nuggets on both sides. Preheat the oven to 200°C (gas mark 6). Unroll the pizza dough on a baking tray lined with baking parchment. Make a rim around the edge of the dough. Spread the tomatoes on the base and evenly distribute the peppers, potatoes, onions and nuggets cut in half. Bake for 40 minutes. 5 minutes before the end, add a thin drizzle of bbq sauce over the pizza. Garnish with a few fresh basil leaves.

TORIKATSU

- 4 breaded vegan escalopes
- 2 tbsp sunflower oil
- 3 tbsp mirin
- 3½ tbsp tomato ketchup
- 2 tbsp Worcestershire sauce
- 1 tsp curry powder
- 1 tbsp tamari

In a hot frying pan, fry the escalopes on both sides in the sunflower oil. Drizzle with 2 tbsp of mirin and leave to evaporate. Mix together the ketchup, Worcestershire sauce, curry, tamari and 1 tbsp of mirin in a bowl. Slice the escalopes into 2-cm strips and cover with sauce. Serve with white rice.

MILANESE

- 60 g capers in oil
- 100 g sun-dried tomatoes in oil
- 150 g cherry tomatoes
- 4 breaded vegan escalopes
- 1 tbsp olive oil
- 4 tbsp lemon juice
- 3 tbsp chopped frozen flat-leaf parsley
- 10 g rocket leaves
- 2 tsp balsamic vinegar

Chop the capers and sun-dried tomatoes, quarter the cherry tomatoes and mix together in a bowl. In a hot frying pan, fry the escalopes on both sides in the olive oil. Drizzle with lemon juice and sprinkle with parsley. Cover the escalopes in the tomato sauce. Distribute the rocket and add a splash of balsamic vinegar.

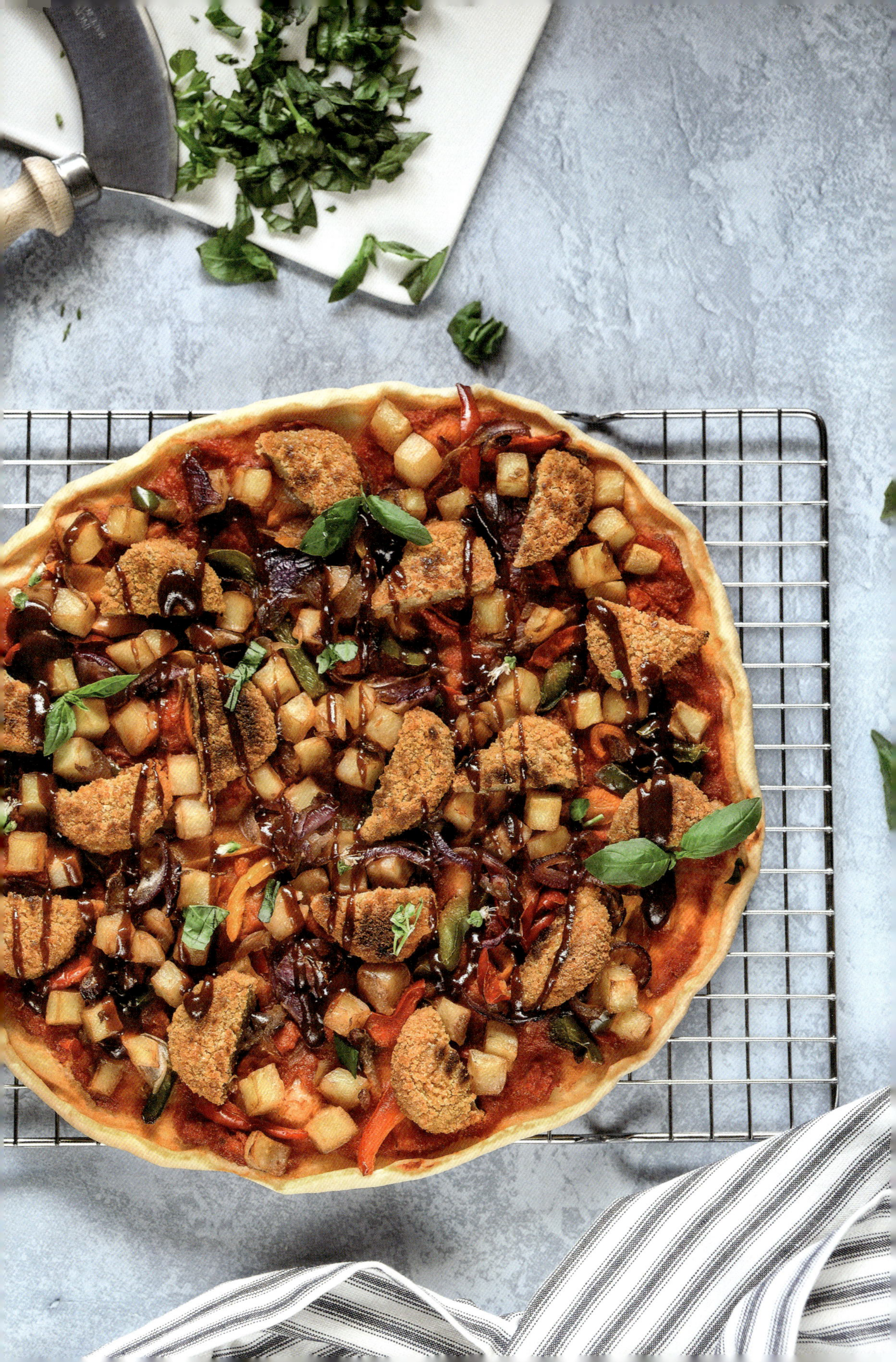

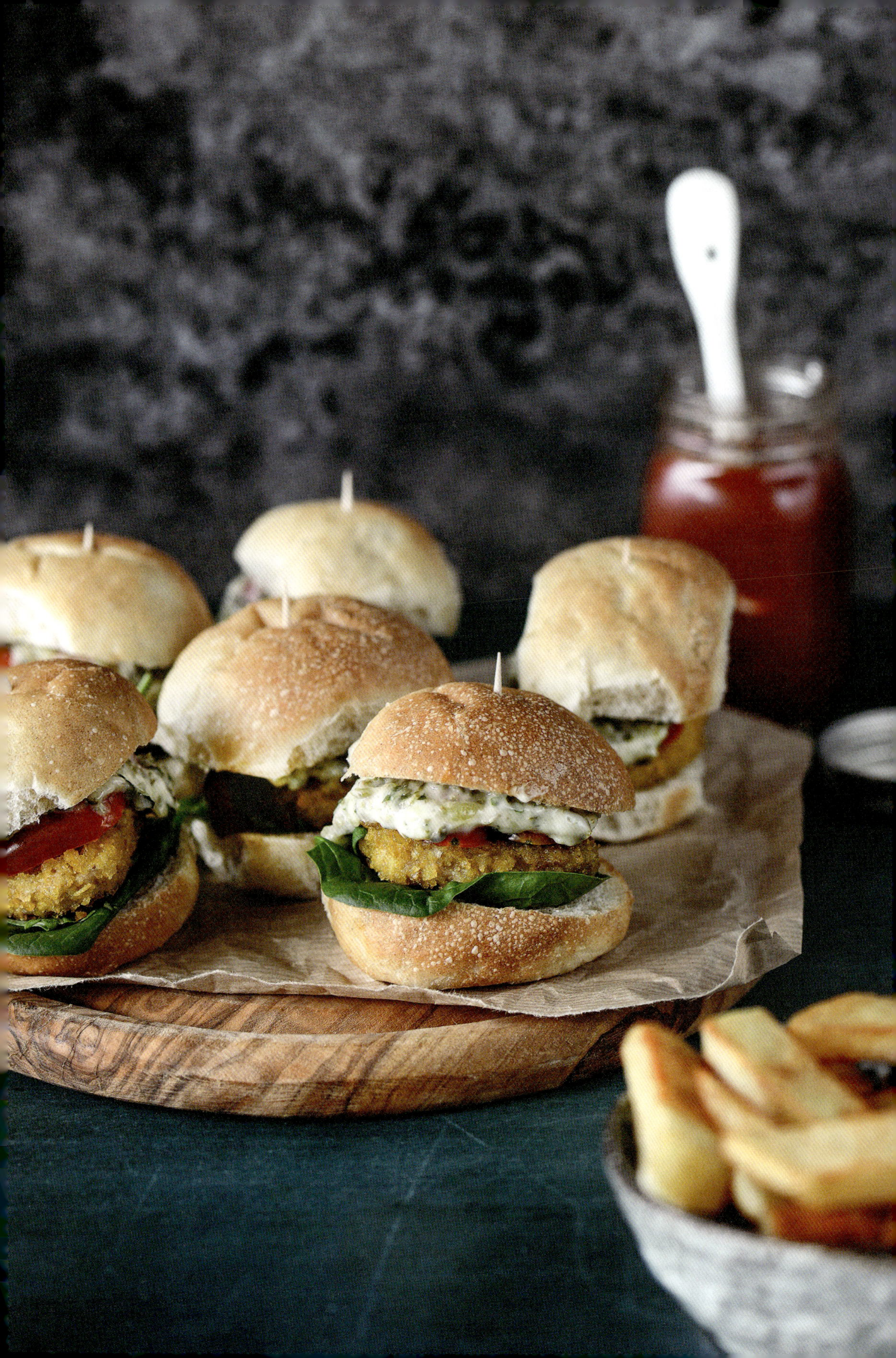

Breaded Treats

MINI BURGERS

- 60 g vegan mayonnaise
- 30 g sweet and sour pickles
- 1 tbsp tarragon
- 2 tbsp capers in vinegar
- 10 cherry tomatoes
- 10 vegan chicken nuggets
- 10 mini burger buns
- Mixed-leaf salad

In a bowl, mix together the mayonnaise with the grated pickles, tarragon and finely chopped capers. Cut the cherry tomatoes in half. Fry the nuggets in a frying pan with oil over a medium heat for 5 minutes until golden. Place the mini burger buns in the oven for 5 minutes at 180°C (gas mark 4), then open in half. Assemble as follows: put a few salad leaves on the bottom bun, place a nugget on top, add two tomato pieces, cover the top bun with a generous layer of mayonnaise sauce, then place on top of the tomatoes. Use a cocktail stick to secure the mini burger.

OCEAN BROCHETTES

- 200 g frozen broccoli
- 200 g frozen cauliflower
- 200 g vegan 'fish' fingers
- 4 tbsp dried nori flakes
- 1½ tbsp frozen tarragon
- 2 tbsp chopped frozen chives
- 100 ml olive oil
- 200 g frozen pearl onions

Bring 2 litres of salted water to the boil in a large pot and add the vegetables. Simmer for about 7 minutes then transfer to a large bowl of ice water. In a hot pan, fry the vegan fish fingers in a little oil then cut into squares. Mix the nori flakes, tarragon, chives and olive oil in a bowl. Place the ingredients on a cocktail stick in the following order: a pearl onion, fish finger square, small piece of broccoli, a fish finger square, a small piece of cauliflower, a fish finger square and then finally another pearl onion. Cover with the infused oil. Place the skewers on a baking tray and bake under the grill for 10 minutes.

RED KEBAB

- 12 vegan nuggets • 2 tsp sweet paprika • 1 tbsp sunflower oil • 3½ tbsp vegan mayonnaise • 1 tbsp sriracha • 100 g cooked beetroot • 200 g fresh tomatoes • 4 pitta breads • 100 g grated red cabbage

Coat the nuggets in paprika and fry in a frying pan with sunflower oil. Mix the mayonnaise with the sriracha in a bowl. Finely slice the beetroot and tomatoes. Put the pitta breads in a toaster. In each pitta, add the beetroot and tomato slices, a bit of red cabbage and three nuggets. Finish with a bit of sriracha mayonnaise.

Pasta

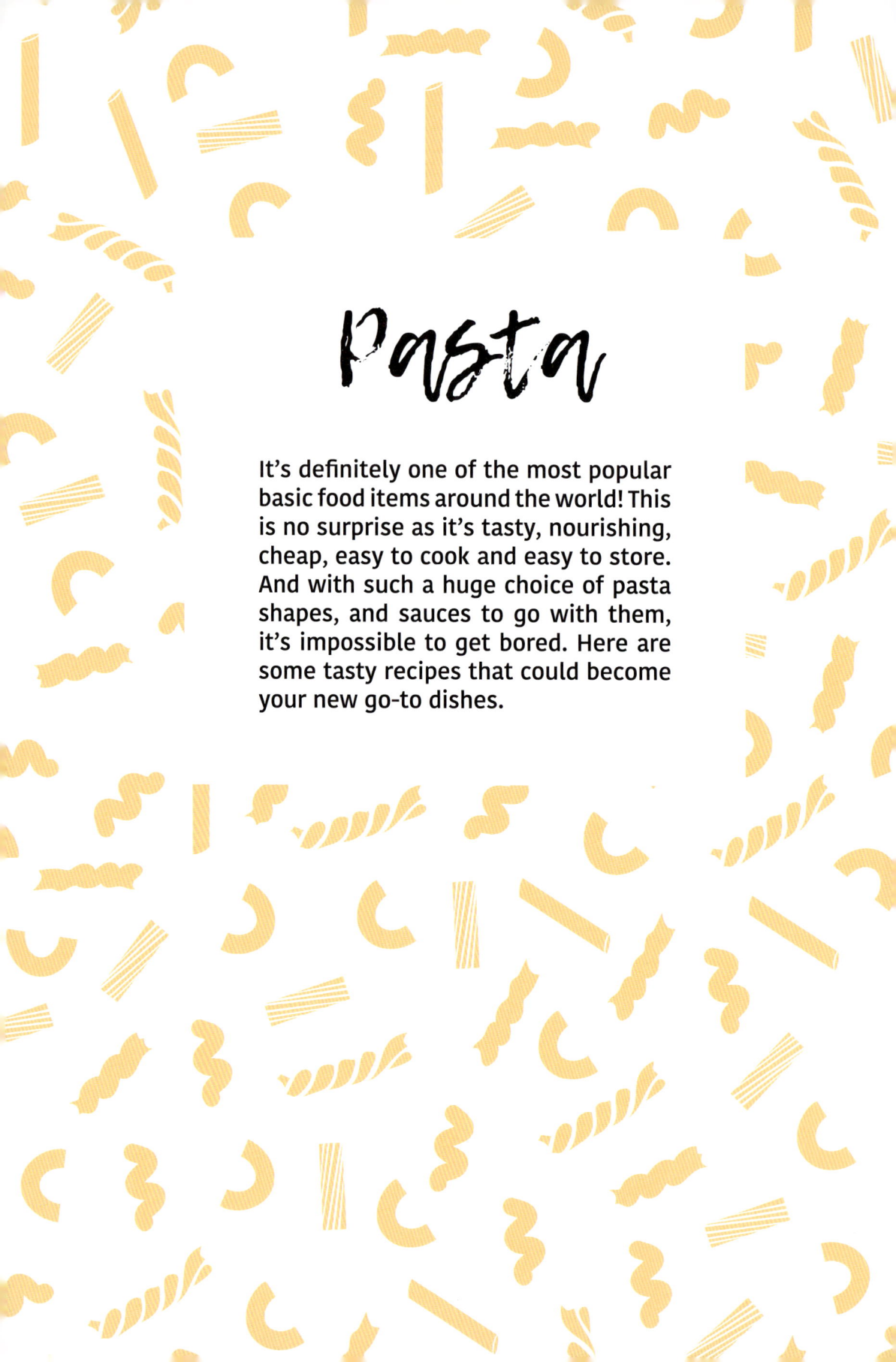

It's definitely one of the most popular basic food items around the world! This is no surprise as it's tasty, nourishing, cheap, easy to cook and easy to store. And with such a huge choice of pasta shapes, and sauces to go with them, it's impossible to get bored. Here are some tasty recipes that could become your new go-to dishes.

PENNE ARRABIATA

- 500 g penne pasta
- 1 tbsp olive oil
- 1 garlic clove
- 400 g tinned chopped tomatoes
- ½ tsp fine salt
- 1¼ tbsp tomato purée
- 2 tsp chilli paste
- 2 tbsp flat-leaf parsley
- Vegan parmesan

In a large pot of salted water, cook the pasta for the time shown on the packet.

In a small pan, heat the olive oil with the chopped garlic for 30 seconds. Add the tomatoes and stir straight away. Add the salt, tomato purée and chilli paste. Stir again and leave to simmer over a low heat. Once the pasta is cooked and drained, add the sauce and serve. Garnish with finely chopped parsley and grated vegan parmesan cheese.

FUSILLI À LA FORESTIÈRE

- 400 g white mushrooms
- 200 g smoked tofu
- 2½ tsp coriander seeds
- 1 clove
- 25 g vegan margarine
- 4 garlic cloves
- Salt
- Pepper
- 1 tbsp white wine
- 200 ml soya cream
- 4 tbsp chopped chives
- ¼ tsp grated nutmeg
- 2 tsp Cognac
- 500 g fusilli pasta

Wash and chop the mushrooms into quarters. Cut the smoked tofu into 1-cm dice. Crush the coriander seeds and clove in a mortar and pestle. Melt the margarine in a hot pan, then add the crushed garlic, coriander and clove. Wait 30 seconds then add the mushrooms and tofu. Stir and sweat the mushrooms over a medium heat for 3 minutes. Season with salt and pepper, then deglaze with white wine. Simmer over a low heat for 2 more minutes and add the soya cream, chopped chives, grated nutmeg and Cognac. Turn off the heat and cover. Bring 3 litres of salted water to the boil in a large pot. Once boiling, add the pasta and stir. Cook the pasta according to the time shown on the packet. Drain the pasta, gently mix with the sauce and mushrooms then serve.

TAGLIATELLE CARBONARA

- 500 g tagliatelle pasta
- 100 g smoked tofu
- 1 tsp olive oil
- 4 tsp soya cream
- ½ tsp turmeric
- 1 tsp Kala namak (black salt)
- 1 tbsp malted yeast
- 1½ tsp cornflour

Cook the pasta for the time shown on the packet in a large pot of salted water. Slice the smoked tofu into small, long pieces, like lardons. Sauté in olive oil for 5 minutes in a hot frying pan. Mix the soya cream, turmeric, salt, malted yeast and cornflour dissolved in 3 tbsp of cold water. Drain the pasta, reserving 3 tbsp of cooking water. Heat the cream in a pan and loosen with a little cooking water to make a thin, creamy sauce. Add the pasta, mix and serve.

FARFALLE WITH BROCCOLI

- 600 g frozen broccoli • 200 g seitan • 50 g shallots • 1 tbsp olive oil • 200 ml soya cream • 2 tbsp wholegrain mustard • 10 g fresh coriander • 500 g farfalle pasta

Bring 3 litres of salted water to the boil. Once boiling, add the broccoli. Blanch for 4 minutes then quickly remove from the pot and transfer to a bowl of cold water. Cut the seitan into small pieces, finely chop the shallots and sauté together in a hot frying pan with olive oil. Cook for 5 minutes. Mix the cream, mustard and chopped coriander. Lower the heat and add the drained broccoli to the seitan. Bring the water to the boil once more and add the pasta. Stir with a spatula, cover and cook for around 12 minutes. Drain the pasta, gently mix with the cream, seitan and broccoli, then serve.

CONCHIGLIE PESTO

- 120 g cashew nuts
- 100 g basil
- 20 g mint
- 400 ml olive oil
- 4 garlic cloves
- 1 tbsp balsamic vinegar
- 40 g sun-dried tomatoes in oil
- 150 g vegan chorizo
- 1 tsp fine salt
- 500 g conchiglie rigate pasta

Soak the cashew nuts in hot water for 20 minutes. Use a stick blender to blend the basil, mint and olive oil until smooth. Add 10 g of cashew nuts at a time and blend well between each addition. Add the crushed garlic and balsamic vinegar, then blend once more. Rehydrate the dried tomatoes for a few minutes in warm water then cut into slices. Cut the vegan chorizo into small pieces. Bring 3 litres of salted water to the boil in a large pot. Add the pasta and stir. Cover and cook over a medium heat for the time shown on the packet. Drain the pasta, mix with the pesto and sprinkle with pieces of tomato and chorizo.

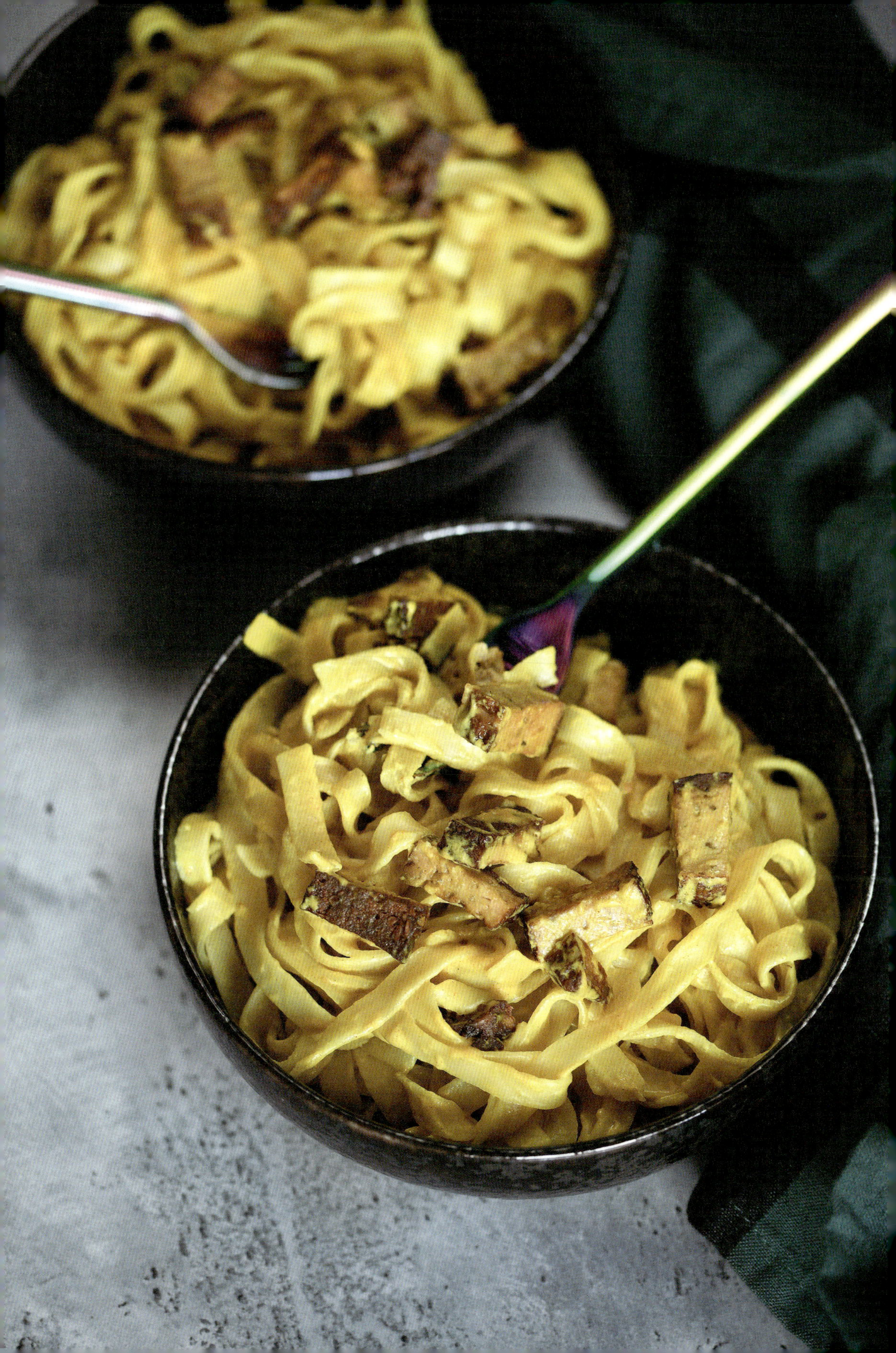

Pasta

INK LINGUINE

- 400 g linguine pasta
- 5 tbsp seaweed flakes
- Salt
- 1½ tsp vegan activated charcoal
- 3 tbsp tomato purée
- 1 tbsp tamari
- 2 garlic cloves
- 1½ tsp cornflour
- 1 tbsp olive oil
- Espelette pepper

Cook the pasta in boiling water according to the instructions on the packet. Rehydrate the seaweed flakes in 3 tbsp lightly salted water. Add the charcoal to a small pan and mix with 1 tbsp of hot water. Add the tomato purée, tamari, crushed garlic and cornflour. Add the seaweed and water to the sauce and mix. Heat over a low heat for 5 minutes while mixing with a whisk. Once the pasta is cooked, add 4 tbsp of cooking water and olive oil to the sauce, then whisk once more. Drain the pasta and gently add to the sauce. Top each dish with a pinch of Espelette pepper.

CONCHIGLIE MELANZANE

- 500 g conchiglie rigate pasta
- 1 large aubergine
- Salt
- Pepper
- 200 g frozen peas
- Olive oil
- 20 sun-dried tomatoes in oil
- Fresh basil
- Espelette pepper

Cook the pasta in boiling water according to the instructions on the packet.

While the pasta is cooking, slice the aubergine, grill each side seasoning with salt and pepper.

Sauté the peas in a frying pan with a little olive oil. Once cooked, add the grilled aubergines. Mix together and add the tomatoes. Turn off the heat and cover. Drain the pasta and mix with the vegetables. Add a drizzle of olive oil and garnish with fresh basil and a pinch of Espelette pepper. Serve.

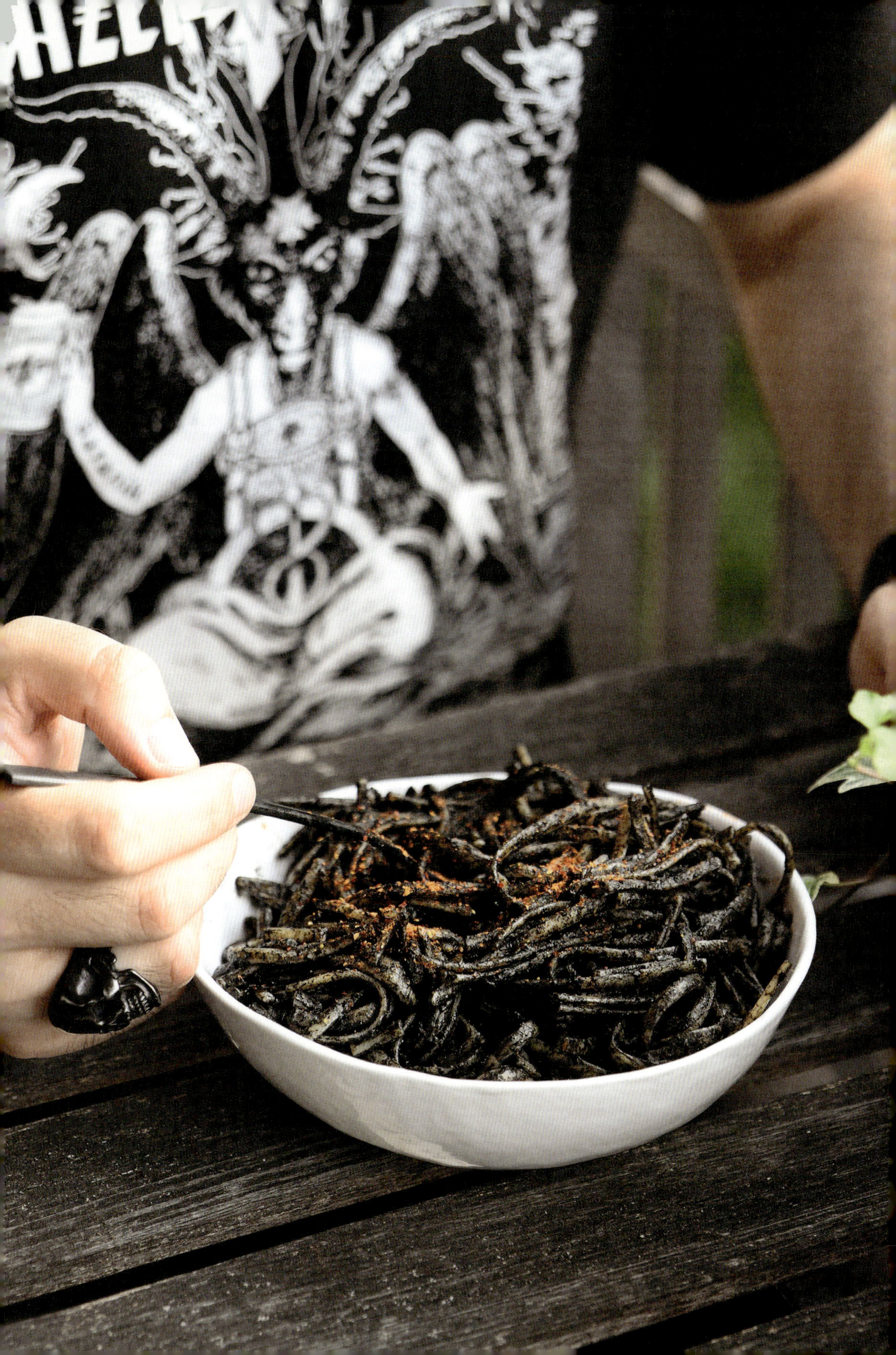

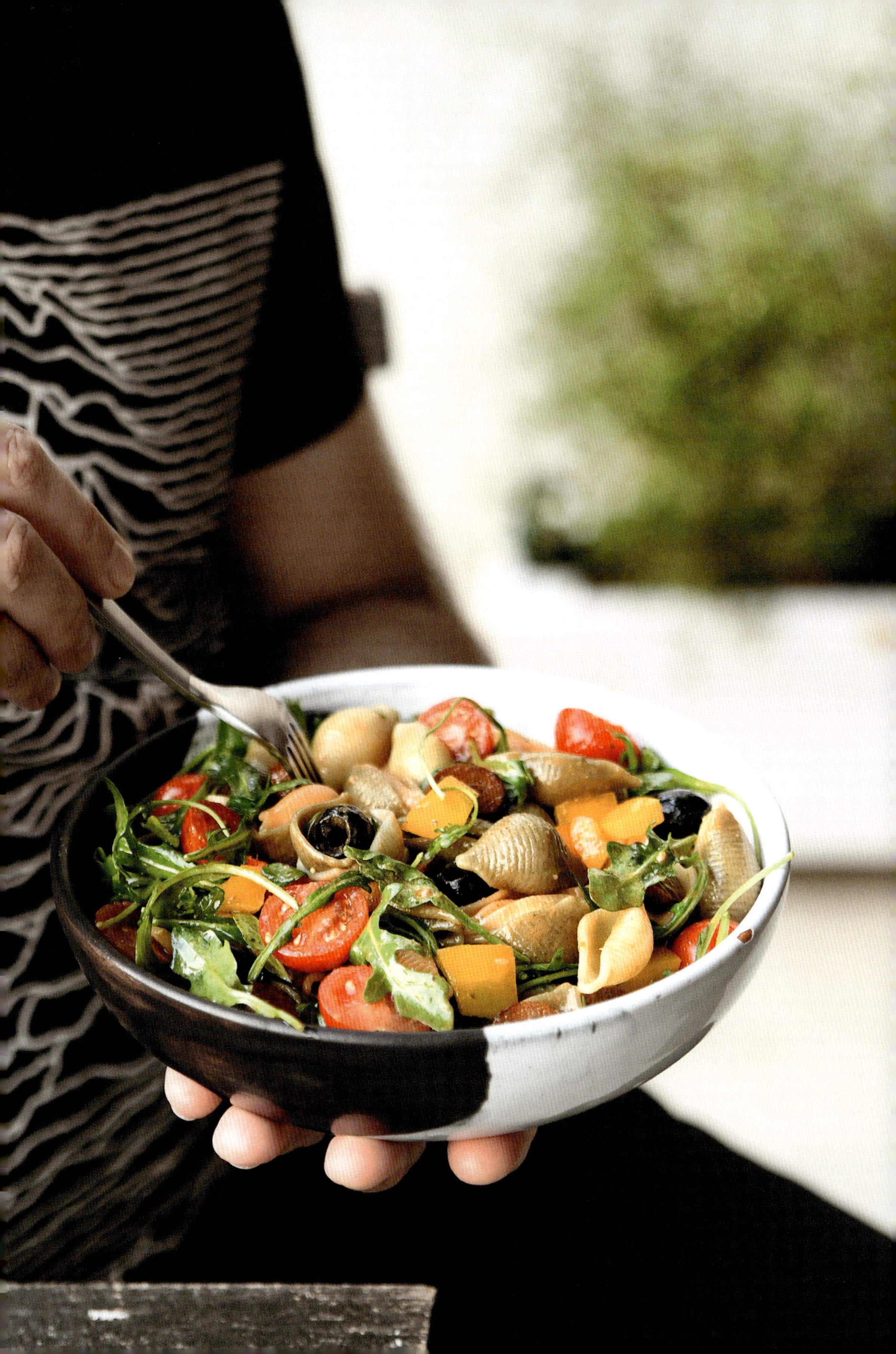

TRICOLOUR SALAD

- 500 g tri-colour pasta • Salt
- 2 tbsp olive oil • 150 g cherry tomatoes • 200 g yellow peppers
- 100 g vegan merguez sausages
- 1 tbsp balsamic vinegar • 1½ tbsp vegan mayonnaise • 4 tsp green pesto • 100 g pitted black olives
- 50 g rocket

Cook the pasta in boiling salted water according to the instructions on the packet. Drain the pasta, lightly coat in oil and leave to cool. Cut the cherry tomatoes in half and slice the peppers. Cut the merguez sausages in 1-cm slices and sauté in a hot pan. Mix the olive oil, vinegar, mayonnaise and pesto in a bowl. Loosen the sauce with 1 tbsp of cold water. Mix all the ingredients together in a salad bowl and serve.

ONE-POT PASTA

- 2 tbsp olive oil
- 100 g frozen sliced onions
- 1 garlic clove
- 150 g frozen peas
- 150 g frozen courgettes
- 150 g frozen green asparagus
- 1 litre soya milk
- 25 g vegetable stock cube
- 15 g frozen chives
- 500 g wholewheat pasta
- Pepper

Heat olive oil in a large pot then add the finely sliced onion and crushed garlic. Mix and cook for 2 minutes before adding peas, courgettes and green asparagus cut into three. Mix and cook for 5 minutes. Add the soya milk, 3 tbsp of water, the stock, chives and the pasta. Mix and cook over a medium/high heat for 15 minutes, checking that the pasta is cooked.

The liquid should have reduced and become thicker. Serve and season with freshly ground pepper.

OVEN-BAKED RAVIOLI

- 2 tbsp olive oil • 2 tbsp dried oregano • Salt • 450 g frozen mixed julienne vegetables • 1 tsp Espelette pepper • 4 tbsp white wine • 200 ml soya cream • 4 tbsp fresh basil
- 100 g grated vegan cheese
- 1 kg vegetable ravioli in tomato sauce

Preheat the oven to 180°C (gas mark 4). Heat the olive oil in a wok and add the oregano, salt and frozen vegetables. Cook for 10 minutes, add the pepper and deglaze with white wine. Reduce for 5 minutes and add the soya cream and chopped basil. Off the heat, add the cheese, then add the ravioli and gently mix together. Transfer to a gratin dish and bake for 15 minutes.

Pastry Dough

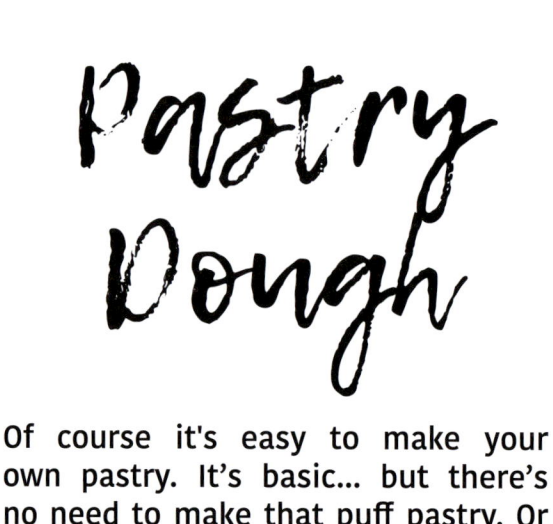

Of course it's easy to make your own pastry. It's basic... but there's no need to make that puff pastry. Or shortcrust pastry. Or a pizza dough. It's quicker to buy pastry that simply needs to be unrolled and baked. It can be bought ready-rolled in circles or rectangles according to your needs! The good news is that it's easy to find different types of pastry without animal products, despite what many people think.

BREAD STICKS

- 4 ready-rolled vegan puff pastry sheets
- 100 g green pesto
- 50 g grated vegan mozzarella
- 30 g vegan margarine
- 100 g tomato salsa
- 50 g grated vegan cheddar cheese

Preheat the oven to 180°C (gas mark 4). Unroll the pastry and cover the surface with a layer of pesto. Cover with grated vegan mozzarella and unroll another pastry on top. Brush with melted margarine. Cut into 3-cm strips and twist. Place on a baking tray. Bake for 20 minutes. Repeat the process using salsa and cheddar cheese instead of pesto and mozzarella.

CHICKPEA PASTIES

- 350 g TVP mince
- 200 ml vegetable stock
- 100 g frozen onions
- 1 tsp chopped frozen garlic
- 1 tbsp rapeseed oil
- 1 tbsp tamari
- 100 g tinned/jarred chickpeas
- 1 tbsp chopped frozen parsley
- 1 rectangular vegan puff pastry sheet

Rehydrate the TVP with the vegetable stock in a large bowl. Drain and squeeze to remove as much liquid as possible. Sauté the onions and garlic with rapeseed oil in a frying pan for 5 minutes. Add the TVP, mix and add the tamari. Use a food processor with an S blade to blend the chickpeas and parsley. Add the contents of the frying pan to the mixture and blend again for a few seconds. Preheat the oven to 180°C (gas mark 4). Unroll the pastry and cut into 16-cm squares. Place the filling on one half of the square, leaving a small border around the edge. Fold over the other half of pastry to make a rectangle. Seal the edges with a fork. Brush the surface with a little tamari. Place on a baking tray and bake in the oven for 30 minutes.

Pastry Dough

VEGETABLE PIE

- 200 g frozen carrots
- 200 g frozen parsnips
- 600 g frozen sweet potatoes
- 2 tbsp olive oil
- 150 g TVP
- 2 tbsp fried onions
- 1 tsp frozen thyme
- ½ tsp salt
- 60 g tomato coulis
- 1 tbsp malted yeast
- 2 ready-rolled vegan shortcrust pastry sheets
- Coconut margarine

Preheat the oven to 180°C (gas mark 4). In a large pot, sweat all the vegetables over a high heat for 10 minutes. Once the sweet potato is soft, add the olive oil and mix well. Add the TVP, fried onions, thyme and season with salt. Mix everything together and leave to stew for 5 minutes. Off the heat, add the tomato coulis and malted yeast. Line a deep pie dish with a sheet of pastry, prick it with a fork and add the filling. Cover with the second pastry sheet and pinch the edges together to make a thick rim around the edge. Remove any excess pastry if it is larger that the pie dish. Brush the top of the pastry with melted margarine. Bake for 45 minutes. Remove from the pie dish, cut into slices and serve.

PIZZA BIANCA

- 200 ml soya cream
- 4 tsp dried rosemary
- Salt
- 50 g frozen grilled aubergine
- 50 g frozen button mushrooms
- 1 pizza dough base
- 100 g grated vegan mozzarella

Mix the thick soya cream, rosemary and salt in a bowl. In a hot pan without oil, defrost the aubergine slices, then the mushrooms. Preheat the oven to 200°C (gas mark 6). Unroll the pizza dough on a baking tray. Spread the cream over the surface leaving a 2-cm border. Distribute the aubergines and mushrooms and scatter vegan cheese on top. Bake for 40 minutes.

EMPANADAS

- 200 g seitan
- 100 g cooked carrots
- 1 tbsp olive oil
- 100 g frozen peas
- 2 tsp frozen thyme
- ¼ tsp fine salt
- 2 tbsp fried onions
- 2 pizza dough bases

Chop the seitan and carrots in a food processor with an S blade. Heat the olive oil in a frying pan and sauté the peas and thyme. Season with salt, add the chopped seitan mixture and fried onions. Preheat the oven to 200°C (gas mark 6). Unroll the dough and cut into 18-cm-diameter circles. Place a small amount of filling on half of each circle Fold the dough over to create a semi-circle. Seal the edges with a fork. Brush the top of the pastry with a little olive oil. Transfer to a baking tray and bake in the oven for 30 to 40 minutes.

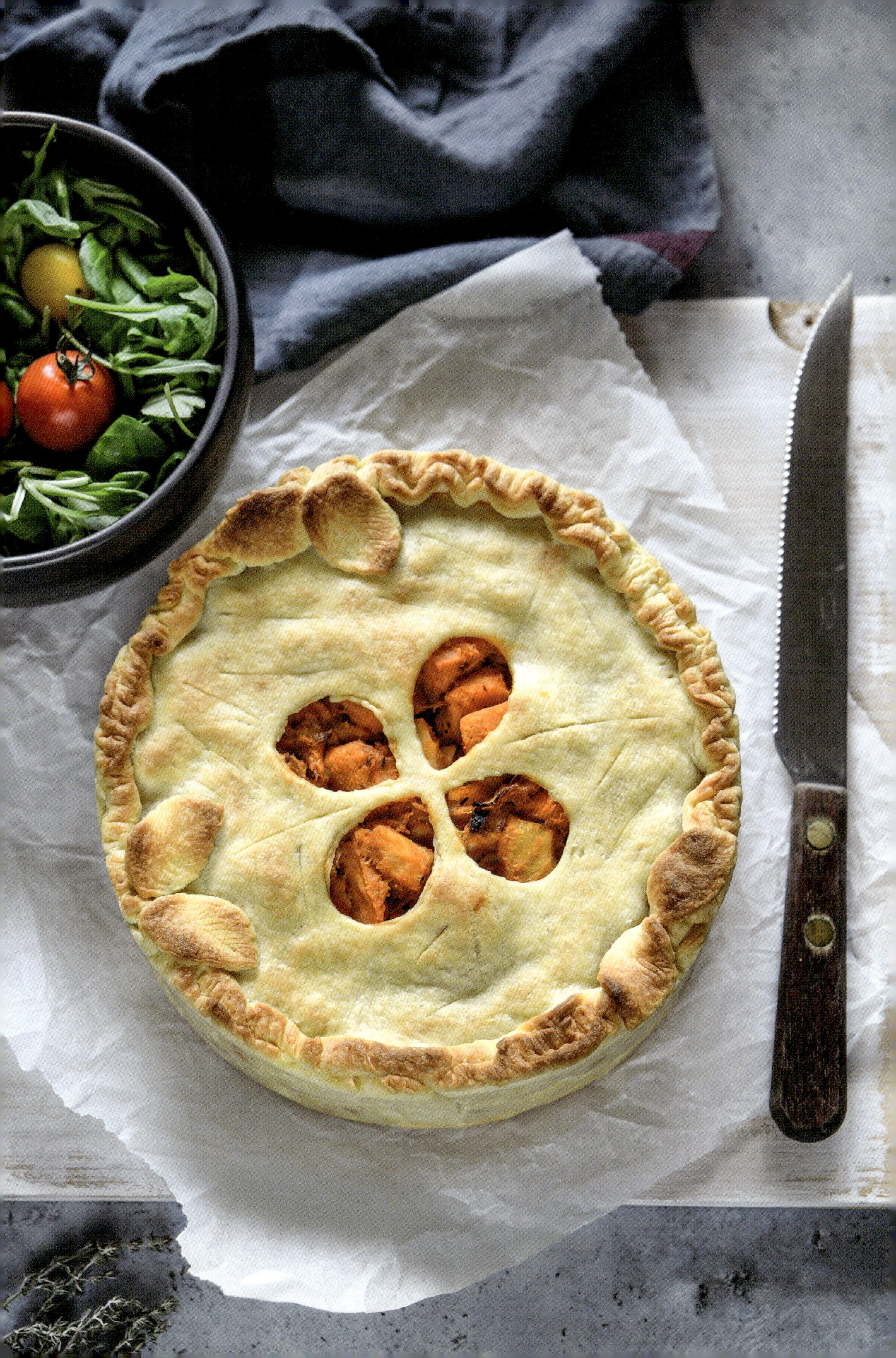

Pastry Dough

APPLE & BLUEBERRY TART

- 3 Gala apples
- 100 g vanilla soya yogurt
- 100 g ground almonds
- 80 g sugar
- 1½ tbsp cornflour
- 100 ml non-dairy milk
- 1 tbsp vanilla extract
- 1 sweet vegan shortcrust pastry sheet (round)
- 100 g blueberries

Preheat the oven to 180°C (gas mark 4). Peel and core the apples. Chop into small pieces and set aside. Pour the yogurt, ground almonds, sugar, cornflour, dairy-free milk and vanilla extract into a large mixing bowl. Whisk well to combine all the ingredients together. Line a 20-cm or 23-cm tart mould with the pastry without removing the baking parchment. Prick the pastry with a fork then add a layer of apples, then add some blueberries and cover with the remaining apples and blueberries. Pour the almond mixture on top, spread it out evenly so that the fruit is completely covered and bake for 45 to 60 minutes depending on the oven. Allow to cool before serving.

FRUIT TART

- 1 sweet vegan shortcrust pastry sheet (round)
- 100 g sugar
- 6 tbsp cornflour
- Ground turmeric
- 500 ml vanilla soya milk
- 50 g vegan margarine
- ½ lemon
- 150 g fresh strawberries
- 150 g fresh raspberries
- Fresh mint

Line a tart tin with the pastry, prick with a fork and bake blind for 25 minutes in an oven preheated to 180°C (gas mark 4). Leave to cool. Put the sugar, cornflour and 5 pinches of turmeric into a bowl. Add the soya milk and mix well. Pour into a pan and continue to stir over a medium heat to make a cream. Turn off the heat, add the margarine, the zest of half a lemon and stir. Pour the cream over the dough. Cover the tart by alternating between strawberries and raspberries. Garnish with a few fresh mint leaves. Leave to cool in the fridge before slicing and serving.

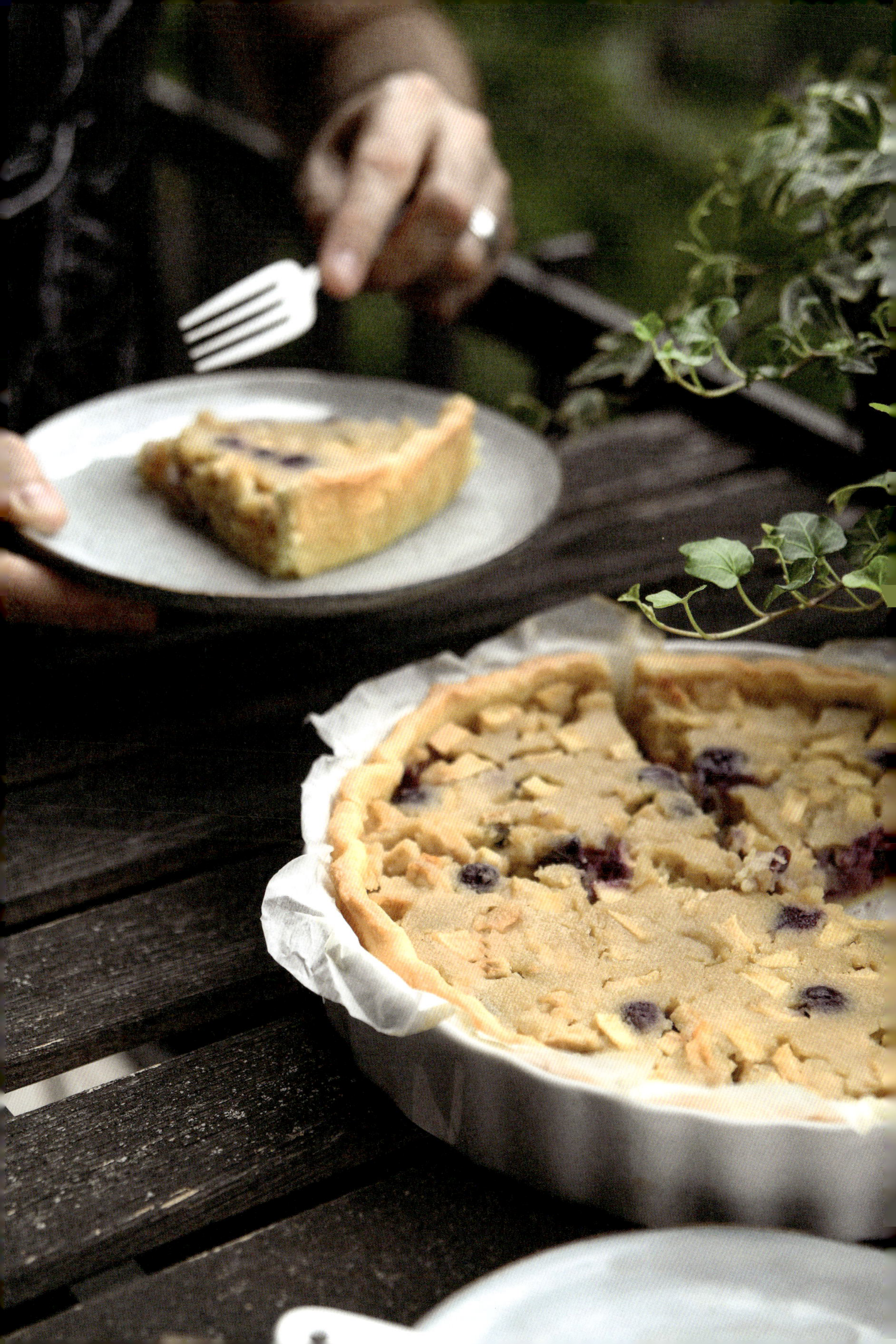

Pastry Dough

QUICK MINI CROISSANTS

- 1 round vegan puff pastry sheet
- Praline paste
- Dark chocolate chips
- 1 tbsp agave syrup
- 2 tsp soya milk

Preheat the oven to 180°C (gas mark 4). Unroll the pastry but don't remove from the baking parchment. Cut into 16 equal triangles. Spread a small amount of praline paste on each wide end and add a few chocolate chips on top. Roll the wide ends towards the tip to make mini croissants. Brush with agave syrup diluted with soya milk and bake for 25 minutes. Allow to cool before serving.

KINGS' & QUEENS' CAKE

- 125 g ground almonds
- 125 g ground toasted hazelnuts
- 100 g caster sugar
- 4 tbsp cornflour
- 90 g vegan margarine
- 50 g dark chocolate chips
- 2 round vegan puff pastry sheets
- 100 g praline paste
- Maple syrup

Mix the ground almonds, hazelnuts and sugar in a large mixing bowl. Dilute the cornflour with a little water, melt the margarine and add to the sugar and nut mixture. Mix, then add the chocolate chips. Unroll the first pastry sheet on a baking tray. Spread the 'frangipane' evenly on top leaving a border around the edge. Add the praline paste on top. Unroll the second pastry sheet on top. Seal the edges. Make a dip in the middle and brush the top with maple syrup. Bake for 45 to 50 minutes in an oven preheated to 180°C (gas mark 4).

THIN BANANA TART

- 200 g apple compote
- 2 tsp vanilla sugar
- 2 tsp Calvados
- 3 large bananas
- 1 round vegan puff pastry sheet
- ½ tsp ground cinnamon

Preheat the oven to 180°C (gas mark 4). Mix the apple compote, vanilla sugar and Calvados in a bowl. Cut the bananas into 5-mm slices. Transfer the pastry to a baking tray, prick with a fork and fold the edge. Spread a thin layer of compote on the pastry base and place the banana slices on top to make a pretty spiral. Dust with cinnamon and bake for 30 minutes.

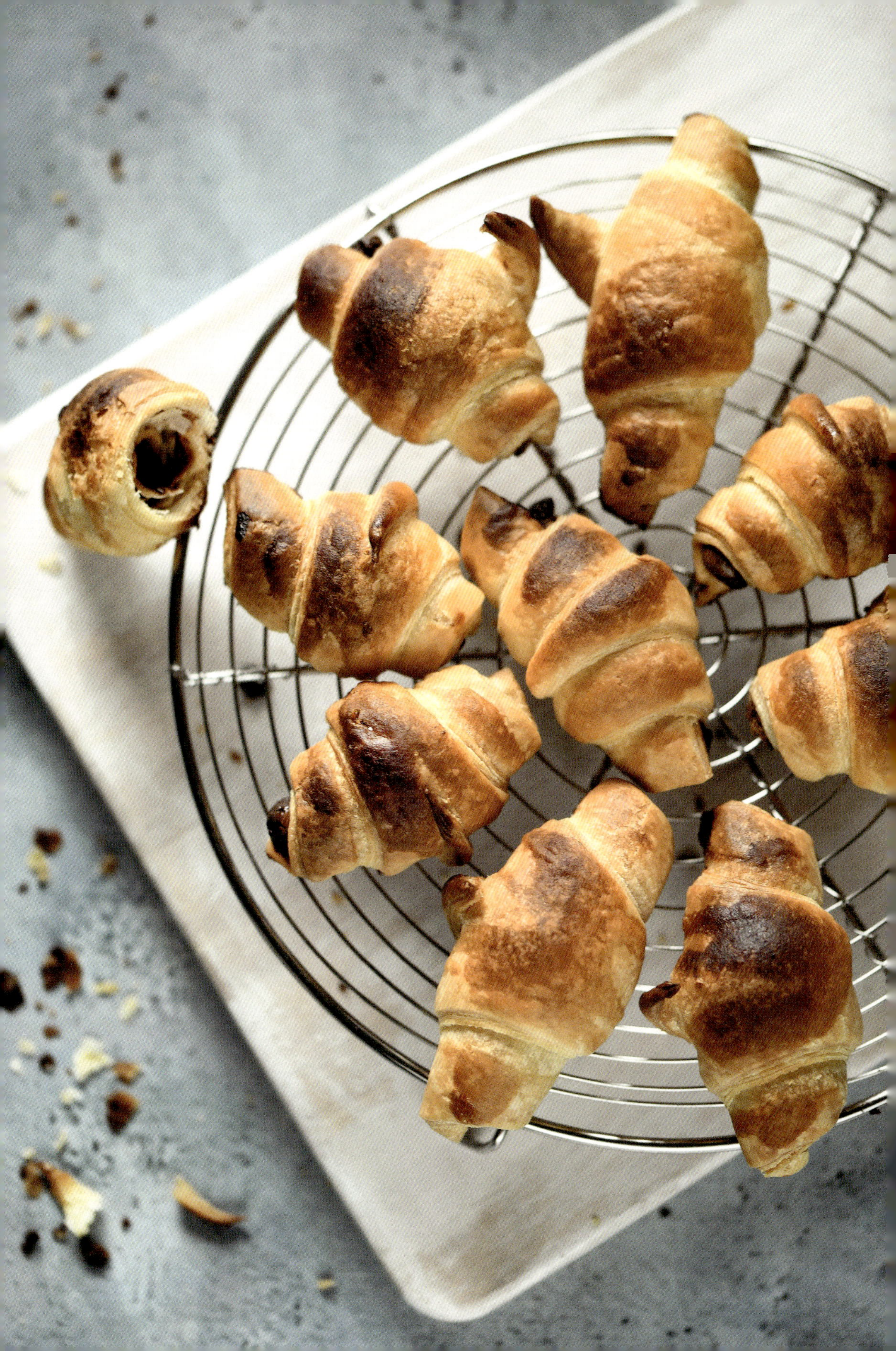

Vegan Pâtés

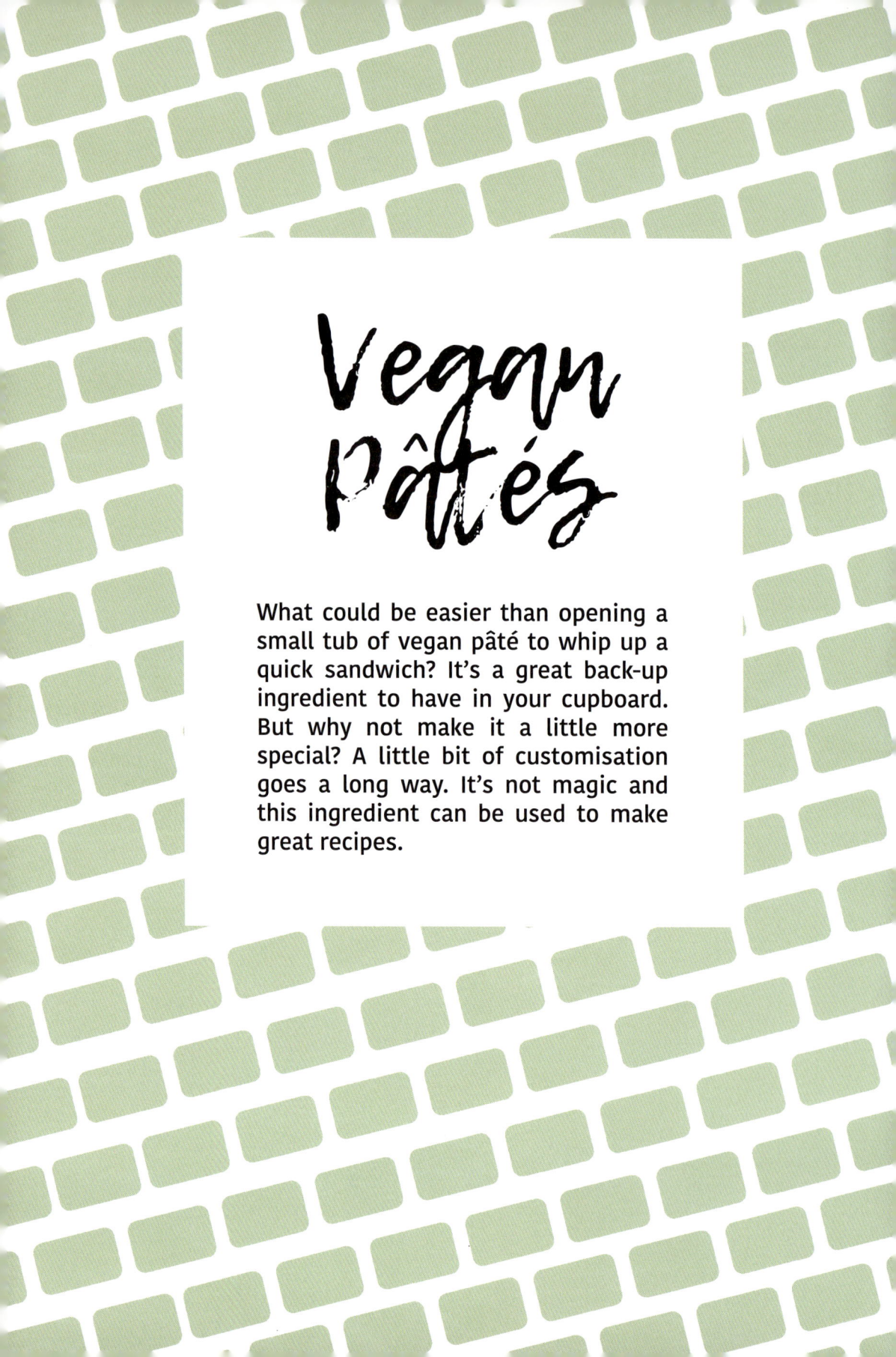

What could be easier than opening a small tub of vegan pâté to whip up a quick sandwich? It's a great back-up ingredient to have in your cupboard. But why not make it a little more special? A little bit of customisation goes a long way. It's not magic and this ingredient can be used to make great recipes.

Vegan Pâtés

RUSTIC SANDWICH

- 50 g frozen red onions
- ½ tsp cumin seeds
- 1½ tsp pink peppercorns
- 125 g vegan paprika pâté
- 1 bunch fresh radishes
- 1 seeded baguette
- 2 tsp vegan margarine
- Lamb's leaf lettuce

Sweat the onions in a hot pan with the cumin seeds and pink peppercorns. Empty the pâté jar into a bowl and add the cooked onions. Mix with a fork. Cut the radishes lengthways. Split the baguette and cut it in half. Make a sandwich by spreading margarine on both halves of the baguette, cover with half the pâté, and add a few lettuce leaves and some radishes. Top with the other half of the baguette.

PUFF PASTRY CANAPÉS

- 125 g vegan green pepper pâté
- 4 tbsp chopped frozen chives
- 1 jar small pickled onions
- 2 rectangular vegan puff pastry sheets
- Olive oil

Empty the pâté into a bowl and add the chopped chives. Mix with a fork. Halve the onions. Preheat the oven to 200°C (gas mark 6). Unroll the pastry and place a level teaspoon of pâté in regular intervals on top. Place half an onion on each spoonful of pâté. Cover with the second pastry sheet and cut into small squares (similar to ravioli) with a pastry crimper. Press gently around the edges to seal the pastries. Place the canapés on a baking tray. Brush the surface of the canapés with a little olive oil. Bake for 20 to 25 minutes.

Vegan Pâtés

POSH SALAD

- 100 g vegan foie gras
- 200 g extra fine frozen green beans
- 2 tbsp olive oil
- 1 tbsp sherry vinegar
- 2 tsp Dijon mustard
- Generous pinch of fine salt
- ¼ tsp black pepper
- 100 g fresh button mushrooms
- 100 g mixed leaf salad

Remove the foie gras from its container and freeze for 15 minutes. Cut the foie gras into large pieces and separate them before putting back in the freezer for 15 minutes. Blanch the green beans in a pot of boiling water for 5 minutes then submerge in cold water. Drain and set aside. Mix the oil, vinegar, mustard, salt and pepper in a bowl. Add 1 tbsp of cold water. Finely slice the mushrooms. Mix the salad leaves, beans, mushrooms and dressing in a salad bowl. Add the foie gras and serve.

SURPRISE MUFFINS

- 120 g plain flour
- 4 tsp cornflour
- 6 tbsp malted yeast
- 3½ tsp dried yeast
- ¼ tsp bicarbonate of soda
- ¼ tsp garlic powder
- ¼ tsp four spice mix
- Freshly ground black pepper
- 120 ml soya milk
- 4 tbsp olive oil
- 25 ml tamari
- 100 g vegan foie gras

Preheat the oven to 180°C (gas mark 4). Mix the dry ingredients together (flour, cornflour, yeast, bicarbonate of soda, garlic, and four spice mix) and season generously with pepper. Set aside. Mix the wet ingredients together (soya milk, olive oil and tamari). Combine the two mixtures and mix vigorously. Pour into six muffin moulds and bake for 25 minutes. Leave to cool. Remove the muffins from the mould and make a hole in the top with a spoon. Fill the inside with foie gras (already mixed with a fork), put in muffin cases, then serve.

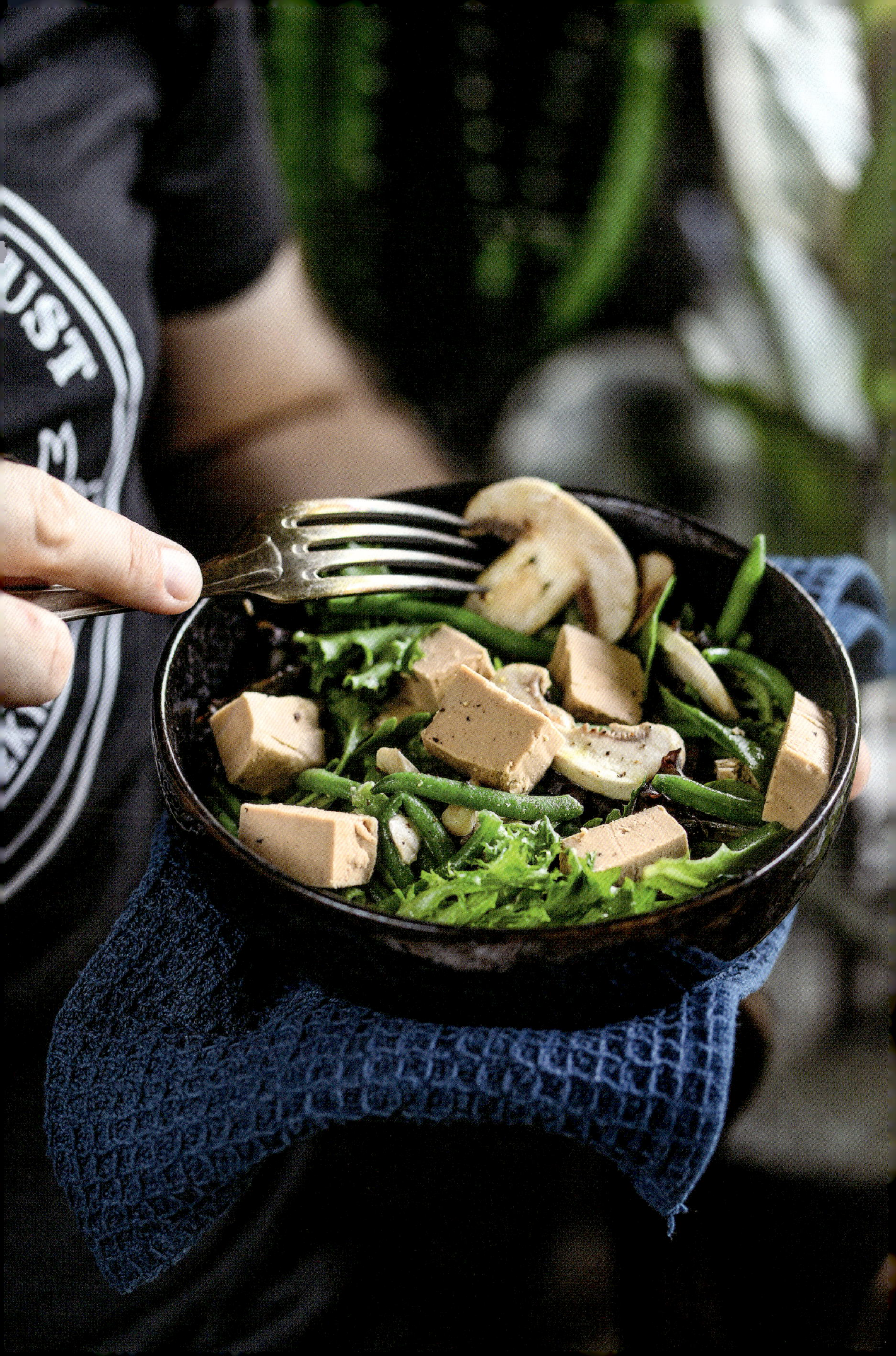

Vegan Pâtés

BLACK FOREST TOAST →

- 100 g firm smoked tofu
- 3½ tbsp vegan mayonnaise
- 1 tbsp creamed horseradish sauce
- 2 tbsp chopped frozen chives
- Grated red cabbage
- 125 g vegan pâté with herbs
- 50 g sweet and sour pickles
- 4 slices whole rye bread

Slice the tofu and brown in a frying pan without oil for 2 minutes. Mix the mayonnaise with the horseradish and chives in a bowl. Tip the grated red cabbage into a large bowl and mix with the mayonnaise. Use a fork to mix the pâté and finely chopped pickles in a bowl. Toast the bread, then spread with pâté, red cabbage and finish with two pieces of tofu.

QUICK & FANCY SAUCE

- 500 ml natural soya milk
- 4 tsp Cognac
- 1 tsp black pepper
- 125 g mushroom pâté
- 4 tsp chopped frozen parsley
- 30 g cornflour
- 30 g vegan margarine

Pour the soya milk, Cognac and black pepper into a stick blender beaker. Add the mushroom pâté cut into small pieces, parsley and cornflour. Blend to a smooth mixture. Pour into a pan and simmer while mixing with a whisk. Once the mixture thickens, turn off the heat and add the margarine. Serve immediately over seitan or simply over pasta.

CREAM OF SHIITAKE MUSHROOM SOUP

- 100 g frozen parsnips
- 2 tsp vegan margarine
- 100 g shiitake mushroom pâté
- 200 ml soya cream
- 300 ml vegetable stock
- ¼ tsp Espelette pepper
- Fresh chervil

Sauté the parsnips with margarine in a frying pan until they start to brown. Mix the pâté with the cooked parsnips and soya cream. Mix the mushroom cream with the hot vegetable stock in a pan. Heat over a low heat for 5 minutes. Serve in small bowls, dust with a little Espelette pepper and add two sprigs of chervil.

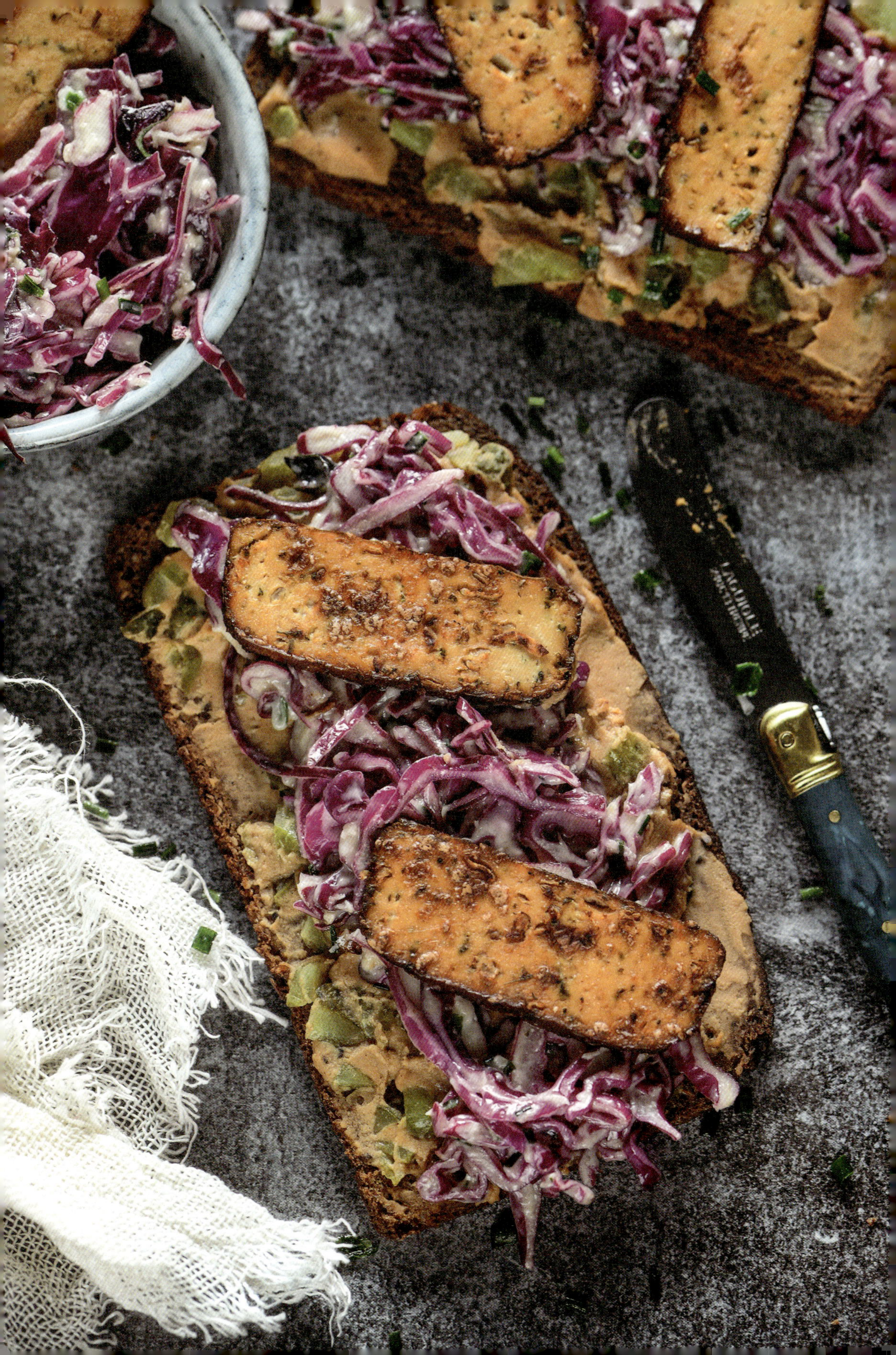

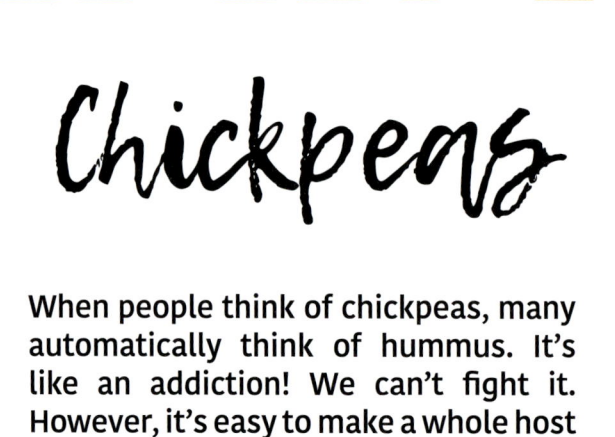

Chickpeas

When people think of chickpeas, many automatically think of hummus. It's like an addiction! We can't fight it. However, it's easy to make a whole host of tasty dishes with chickpeas. Just sit back for a moment, clear your mind and forget about the word hummus... Breathe, open your eyes and let's go. Oops! We're starting with hummus...

RED HUMMUS

- 500 g cooked chickpeas
- 50 g tahini
- 2 garlic cloves
- ½ tsp fine salt
- 2 tsp smoked paprika
- 3 tbsp lemon juice
- 150 g grilled peppers in oil

Pour the drained chickpeas into a food processor with an S blade. Add 3 tbsp of water, tahini and crushed garlic. Blend to make a purée. Add the salt, smoked paprika, lemon juice and grilled peppers. Blend again until smooth.

MOROCCAN HARIRA SOUP

- 1 tbsp olive oil
- 100 g frozen onions
- 50 g celery
- 2 tsp ras-el-hanout
- 100 g 'chicken' meat alternative
- 250 g cooked chickpeas
- 500 ml vegetable stock
- 300 g frozen or tinned chopped tomatoes
- 2 tbsp chopped frozen coriander
- 4 tsp chopped frozen parsley
- 1 tbsp lemon juice

Heat the oil in a large pot with finely chopped onions and celery. Add the ras-el-hanout, meat substitute cut into small pieces and chickpeas. Mix and cook for 5 minutes. Add the vegetable stock and tomatoes. Cover and simmer over a low heat for 20 minutes. At the end, add the coriander, parsley and lemon juice. Serve hot.

Red hummus (page 135)

FALAFEL TERRINE

- 1 tbsp olive oil
- 100 g frozen onions
- 2 tsp chopped frozen garlic
- 1 tbsp coriander seeds
- 1 tbsp cumin seeds
- 500 g cooked chickpeas
- 3 tbsp cornflour
- 2 tsp jalapeño sauce
- 15 g frozen parsley
- 15 g frozen coriander
- ¼ tsp fine salt

Preheat the oven to 180°C (gas mark 4). Heat the olive oil in a pan and sauté the onions and garlic. Add the coriander and cumin seeds ground to a powder. Add the chickpeas and mix. Cook over a medium heat for 5 minutes. Pour everything into a large mixing bowl and crush coarsely with a potato masher. Add the cornflour diluted in a little water, jalapeño sauce, parsley, coriander and salt. Mix well and shape into a dough. Fill a terrine mould and bake in the oven for 40 minutes. Leave to cool completely before serving.

BURRITO

- 250 g cooked chickpeas
- 2 tsp Mexican spice seasoning
- 2½ tbsp tomato passata
- Olive oil
- 100 g pre-cooked rice
- Salt
- Pepper
- 1 avocado
- ½ fresh lemon
- Fresh coriander
- 200 g cherry tomatoes
- 4 wholemeal tortilla wraps
- 50 g rocket leaves
- 80 g vegan cheddar, grated
- Fresh mint

Rinse and drain the chickpeas, then mix with the Mexican seasoning and tomato passata in a large bowl. Heat a splash of olive oil in a wok and sauté the chickpea mixture over a medium heat. Mix well and cook for 5 minutes. Add the rice, season with salt and pepper, mix well and turn off the heat. Set aside. Peel and crush the avocado, add the zest of half a lemon, add salt and pepper and a few chopped coriander leaves. Cut the tomatoes in half. Assembly: soften the tortillas by heating them in a frying pan for several minutes. Cover with a thick layer of crushed avocado, and some rocket, then 2 to 3 tablespoonfuls of the rice/chickpea mixture, a quarter of the vegan cheddar, a few cherry tomato halves and some chopped mint. Close the wrap by folding the ends over the filling then rolling the wrap.

Repeat with the remaining wraps.

Chickpeas

LEBANESE SALAD

- 250 g cooked chickpeas
- 2 tbsp za'atar
- 150 g cherry tomatoes
- 40 g fresh flat-leaf parsley
- 4 tbsp chopped fresh coriander
- 2 tbsp chopped fresh mint
- 2 tbsp olive oil
- 1 tbsp lemon juice
- Generous pinch of fine salt

Drain the chickpeas and mix with the za'atar in a large mixing bowl. Sauté in a frying pan for 3 minutes and leave to cool. Halve the cherry tomatoes. Remove the stalks from the parsley, coriander and mint. Chop the herbs and add to the bowl with the tomatoes and chickpeas. Mix the olive oil, lemon juice and salt in a bowl. Pour the dressing into the bowl and mix everything together. Refrigerate until serving.

SPICED 'STEAKS'

- 50 g cooked beetroot
- 250 g cooked chickpeas
- 4 tsp tomato ketchup
- 2 tsp olive oil
- 2 tsp jalapeño sauce
- ¼ tsp fine salt
- 1 tbsp garam masala
- 1 tbsp malted yeast
- 1 tbsp chopped frozen shallots

Finely grate the beetroot. Crush the chickpeas in a bowl with a potato masher. Add the ketchup, olive oil, jalapeño sauce and mix. Add the salt, garam masala, malted yeast and mix. Finally, add the beetroot and shallots. Mix well one last time and shape into four steaks. Fry in a frying pan with a little oil for 2 to 3 minutes on each side.

SAUTÉED GREENS

- 2 tbsp olive oil
- 2 tsp chopped frozen garlic
- 100 g frozen onions
- 250 g cooked chickpeas
- 100 g frozen courgettes
- 100 g frozen peas
- 100 g frozen fine green beans
- ½ tsp fine salt
- 100 g green pesto
- 3 tbsp white wine

Heat the olive oil in a large frying pan with the garlic and onions. Sauté the chickpeas over a high heat for 3 minutes. Add the courgettes, peas and green beans cut into 3-cm pieces. Mix, season with salt and cook over a medium heat for 15 minutes. Mix the pesto with the white wine and add to the frying pan. Mix and simmer over a low heat for 5 minutes.

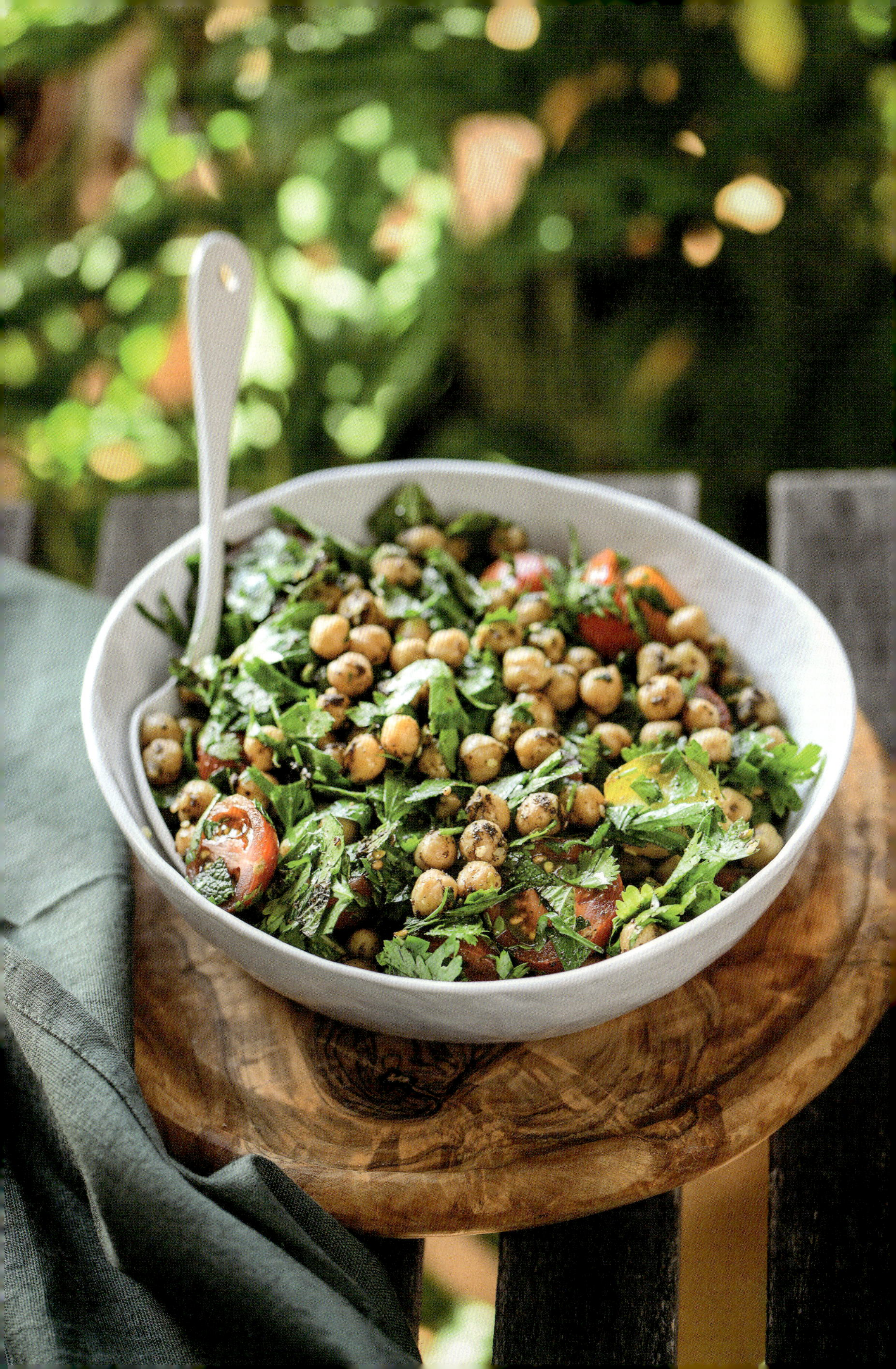

Potatoes

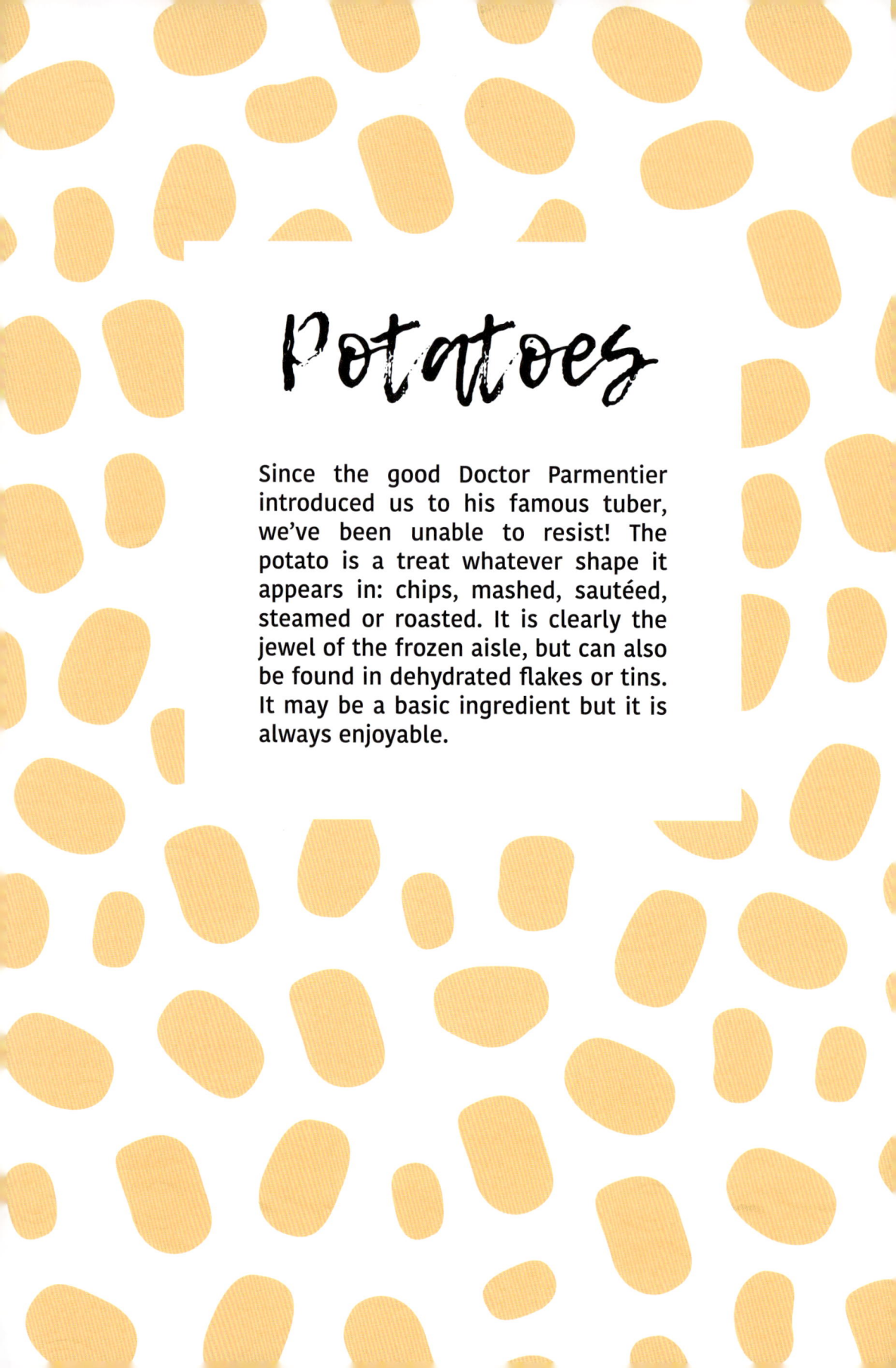

Since the good Doctor Parmentier introduced us to his famous tuber, we've been unable to resist! The potato is a treat whatever shape it appears in: chips, mashed, sautéed, steamed or roasted. It is clearly the jewel of the frozen aisle, but can also be found in dehydrated flakes or tins. It may be a basic ingredient but it is always enjoyable.

SPANISH-STYLE POTATOES

- 2 tbsp olive oil • 100 g frozen onions • 4 tsp chopped frozen garlic
- 2 tsp sweet smoked paprika
- 500 g frozen diced potatoes • ½ tsp fine salt • 2 tbsp fresh coriander

In a large pot, heat the oil and add the onions and garlic. Cook to reduce for 3 minutes. Sprinkle with smoked paprika and mix. Add the diced potatoes and mix again so that they become a red/orange colour. Cook for about 20 minutes over a medium heat and stir regularly. Once cooked, season with salt and add the chopped coriander.

POTATO HOTPOT

- 2 tbsp olive oil
- 500 g cooked sliced potatoes
- 150 g frozen carrots
- 100 g frozen onions
- 100 g frozen peas
- 4 tsp chopped frozen garlic
- ¼ tsp frozen thyme
- ½ tsp sage
- ¼ tsp fine salt
- 2 tsp wholegrain mustard
- 1 tbsp white miso

Heat a large pot with oil and add the sliced potatoes, sliced carrots, onions, peas and crushed garlic. Cook over a high heat for 5 minutes and stir regularly. Add the thyme, sage and salt. Cover and cook over a medium heat for 15 minutes. Mix the mustard and miso with 100 ml of hot water, then add to the pot. Mix and cook over a high heat until the liquid evaporates.

Potatoes

SAUTÉED COUNTRY VEG

- 200 g frozen fine green beans
- 2 tbsp olive oil
- 2 tsp chopped frozen garlic
- 500 cooked whole potatoes
- 100 g smoked tofu
- 1 tbsp chopped frozen shallots
- 1 tbsp fried onions
- 3 tbsp frozen chives
- 2 tbsp chopped frozen parsley
- Fine salt
- Black pepper

Put the green beans in a large bowl of boiling water. Wait for 2 minutes and drain.

Gently squeeze the beans with your hands to extract the maximum amount of water. Heat the oil in a large frying pan with the garlic. Add the potatoes and brown. Once the potatoes are golden, move to the edge of the pan and add diced tofu to the centre. Brown the tofu for 2 minutes and add the shallots. Mix everything together. Add the green beans and fried onions, sprinkle with chives and parsley, then mix. Season with salt and pepper according to taste.

ALOO PIE

- 4 tsp coconut oil
- 1 garlic clove
- 1 small piece fresh ginger
- 500 g frozen diced potatoes
- Salt
- Pepper
- 100 g frozen peas
- 2 tsp sweet curry powder
- 1 tbsp chopped fresh parsley
- 1 tbsp chopped fresh coriander
- 1 pack vegan shortcrust pastry
- 200 g sliced green olives
- 200 ml soya cream
- 2 tsp cornflour
- 2 tbsp malted yeast
- ¼ tsp grated nutmeg

Preheat the oven to 190°C (gas mark 5). Heat the coconut oil in a wok, then lightly brown the crushed garlic and finely chopped ginger. Sauté the potatoes for 15 minutes until well browned. Season with salt and pepper, then add the peas and curry powder and mix. Cover and cook for another 5 minutes. Once cooked, add the chopped parsley and coriander. Unroll the pastry in a deep tart tin 26 cm in diameter without removing the baking parchment. Press into the mould to make a high-sided edge. Prick the dough with a fork. Cover the base with sliced olives and add the potatoes. Mix the soya cream and the cornflour, season with salt and pepper, then add the malted yeast and grated nutmeg. Pour evenly over the potatoes and bake in the oven for 45 minutes.

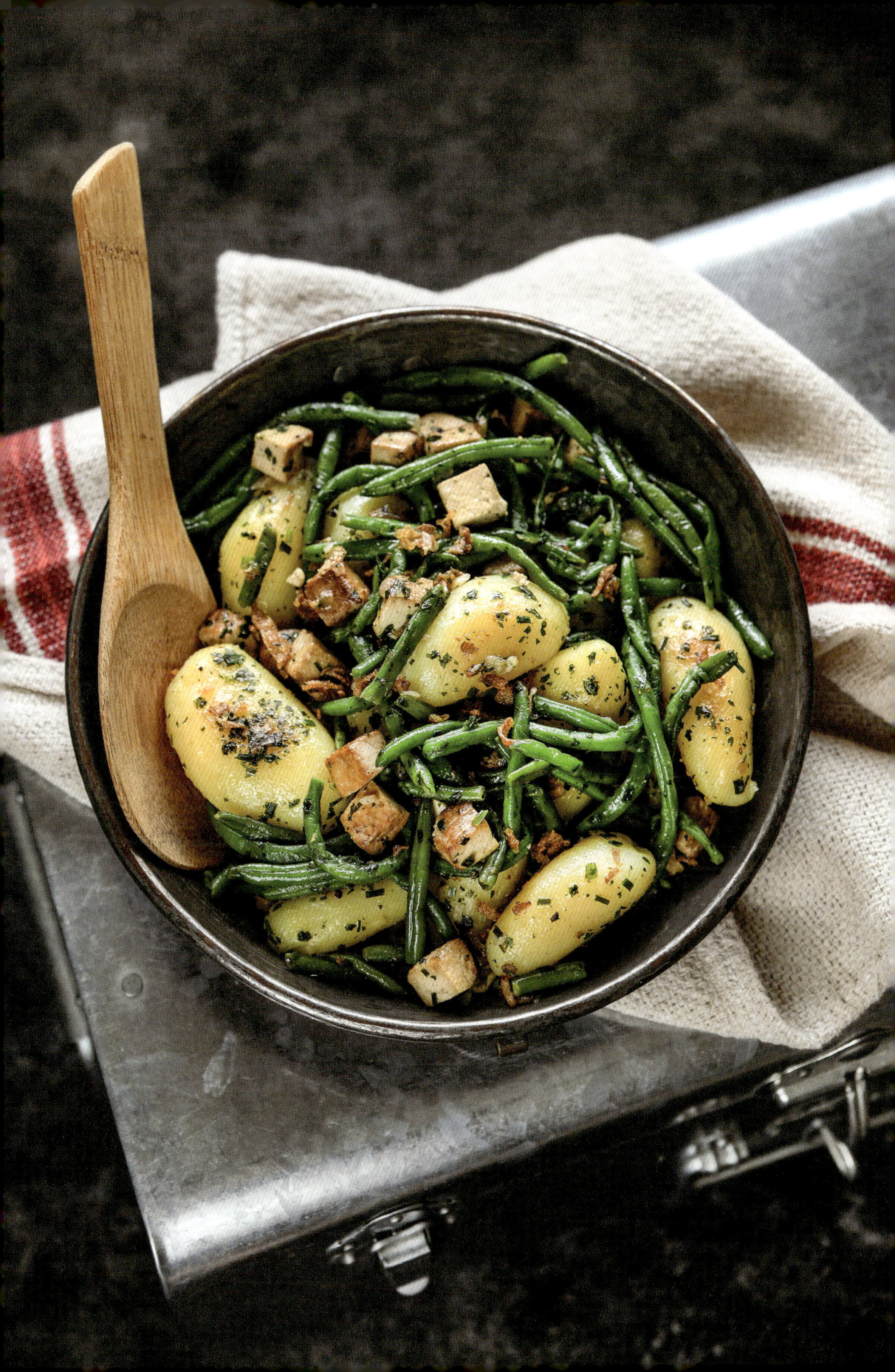

Potatoes

POTATO BURGER

- 150 g frozen onions
- 1 tbsp vegan margarine
- Fine salt
- 2 tbsp fresh coriander
- 8 frozen potato pancakes
- 1 tbsp olive oil
- 150 g fresh tomatoes
- 2 slices vegan cheese
- 1 tbsp vegan mayonnaise

Sweat the onions in a hot pan over a medium heat. Once the onions are soft, add the margarine and salt. When the margarine is melted, add 2 tbsp of cold water and leave to stew. Finish with chopped coriander and set aside. Cook the potato pancakes for 10 minutes in a large frying pan with olive oil. Cut four thick slices from each tomato. Quarter the cheese slices. Assembly: place a little mayonnaise on a pancake, then a slice of tomato, onion compote, two slices of cheese, and place another pancake on top.

POTATO GRATIN

- 500 g frozen potato wedges
- 200 g grated vegan cheese
- 3 tbsp soya cream
- 20 g flat-leaf parsley
- 1 tbsp cornflour

Preheat the oven to 200°C (gas mark 6), cook the wedges for 20 minutes. Mix 100 g of vegan cheese, cream, parsley and cornflour diluted in a little water in a large mixing bowl. Add the wedges to the bowl and mix well to coat the potatoes. Transfer everything to a gratin dish, scatter the rest of the cheese on top and bake for 15 minutes.

POTATO CROQUETTES

- 300 g frozen mashed potato
- 100 g grated vegan cheese
- 15 g frozen chives
- Fine salt
- ½ tsp pepper
- ¼ tsp grated nutmeg
- 100 g wheat flour
- 1 tsp garlic powder
- Breadcrumbs

Defrost the mashed potatoes in a pan. Dry out the potatoes by continuing to cook them a bit longer. Add the cheese, chives, salt, pepper and nutmeg. Mix again and let cool. Shape into twenty 5-cm-diameter balls. In a bowl, mix the flour, garlic powder, salt and 200 ml of cold water. Coat the balls in the batter then roll in the breadcrumbs. Coat in the batter and breadcrumbs once more. Cook in the deep fryer for 3 minutes in oil heated to 180°C.

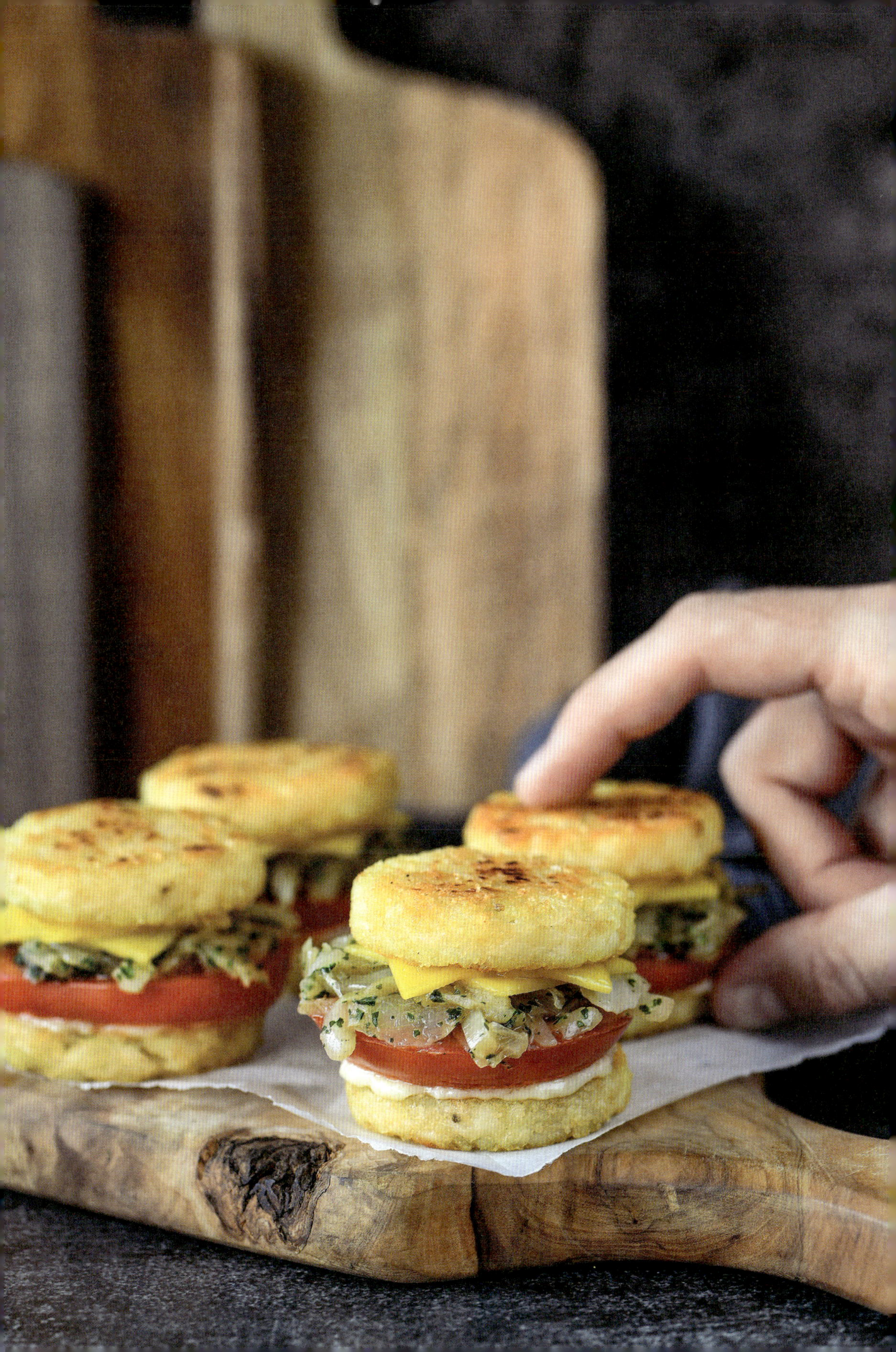

Textured Vegetable Protein

Usually referred to as TVP, and sometimes called textured soy protein (TSP) or soy meat, this is an excellent meat substitute which livens up dishes in so many ways. It is quick to cook, with a protein content comparable to certain meats. So here are some tasty recipes featuring the different forms of TVP.

MARENGO SAUTÉ

- 100 g TVP medallions
- 1 litre vegetable stock
- 2 tbsp olive oil
- 4 tsp chopped frozen garlic
- 1 sprig thyme
- 2 bay leaves
- 200 g frozen spring onions
- 4 tsp wheat flour
- 150 ml white wine
- 50 g chopped tomatoes
- Black pepper
- 200 g frozen button mushrooms
- 150 g frozen chopped tomatoes

In a pan, rehydrate the TVP with the stock over a high heat for 10 minutes.

In a large pot, heat the oil with the garlic, thyme and bay leaves. Add the spring onions and TVP. Sweat for 5 minutes and add the flour. Add the white wine as well as a little TVP broth so that the spring onions and TVP are covered. Add the tomatoes, season with pepper according to taste, and mix. Add the mushrooms and tomatoes. Cover and cook over a medium heat for 20 minutes.

SPAGHETTI BOLOGNESE

- 100 g TVP mince
- 2 tsp sweet paprika
- 4 tsp olive oil
- 300 g frozen red onions
- 2 garlic cloves
- 100 ml red wine
- 800 g peeled tomatoes
- ¾ tsp fine salt
- 2 tbsp balsamic vinegar
- 10 drops jalapeño sauce
- 500 g spaghetti
- 15 g fresh basil

Place the TVP in a bowl and sprinkle with paprika. Cover with salted boiling water and soak for 5 minutes. Drain and squeeze with the back of a spoon to remove the excess liquid. Heat a little oil in a pan and sauté the onions and crushed garlic. Once the onions start to brown, deglaze with wine. Add the tomatoes, salt, balsamic vinegar and jalapeño sauce. Leave to simmer over a low heat for 10 minutes. Add the TVP and mix everything thoroughly. Leave to simmer again over a low heat. Bring 3 litres of salted water to the boil in a large pot. Once boiling, add the spaghetti and stir with a wooden spoon. Cook the spaghetti according to the time shown on the packet. Drain the spaghetti, add a splash of olive oil and serve. Cover with sauce and sprinkle with chopped basil.

Textured Vegetable Protein

FLORENTINE LASAGNE ➡

- 1 kg chopped frozen spinach
- 2 tsp chopped frozen garlic
- 3 tbsp chopped frozen tarragon
- 100 g TVP mince
- 300 ml vegetable stock
- 200 ml soya cream
- 2 tsp Dijon mustard
- 2 tbsp cornflour
- 250 g vegan lasagne sheets
- 100 g grated vegan cheese

In a large pot, defrost the spinach, then add the garlic and tarragon. Mix and cook over a medium heat for 10 minutes. In a large bowl, cover the TVP with vegetable stock. Soak for 5 minutes, then drain.

Mix the soya cream, mustard and cornflour diluted in a little cold water in a bowl, then add to the TVP. Preheat the oven to 180°C (gas mark 4). In a dish the same size as the lasagne sheets, cover the base with a little spinach. Place the lasagne sheets on top, then a layer of spinach and a layer of TVP. Repeat the layers until the top of the dish. Finish with a thin layer of spinach and cover with cheese. Bake for 35 minutes and finish under the grill for 5 minutes.

PUMPKIN PARMENTIER

- 3 large potatoes • 1 medium squash
- Salt • Pepper • 3 tbsp olive oil
- 3 tbsp soya cream • 4 tbsp chopped frozen chives • 600 ml seasoned vegetable stock • 200 g TVP • 1 tsp paprika • ¾ tsp turmeric • 5 tsp ground coriander • 1 large shallot

Peel the potatoes, cut in half, remove the seeds from the squash, chop up the flesh. Steam the potato and squash. Mash with a potato masher. Season with salt, pepper and add the oil, soya cream and chives. Mix well and cover. Heat the vegetable stock and pour over the TVP and spices to rehydrate. Once the stock is absorbed, finely slice the shallot, then add to the TVP and mix. Transfer to a gratin dish, then add an even layer of purée on top. Bake for 30 minutes in an oven preheated to 180°C (gas mark 4). Serve.

OCEAN SANDWICH

- 50 g TVP mince
- 150 ml seasoned vegetable stock
- Pepper • 2 tbsp chopped frozen chives • 2½ tsp seaweed powder
- 120 g vegan mayonnaise

Rehydrate the TVP in the stock. When the stock is absorbed, season with pepper to your taste then add the chives and seaweed. Mix. Finish by adding the mayonnaise and mix again. Chill until using to fill a baguette with sliced tomatoes and salad leaves.

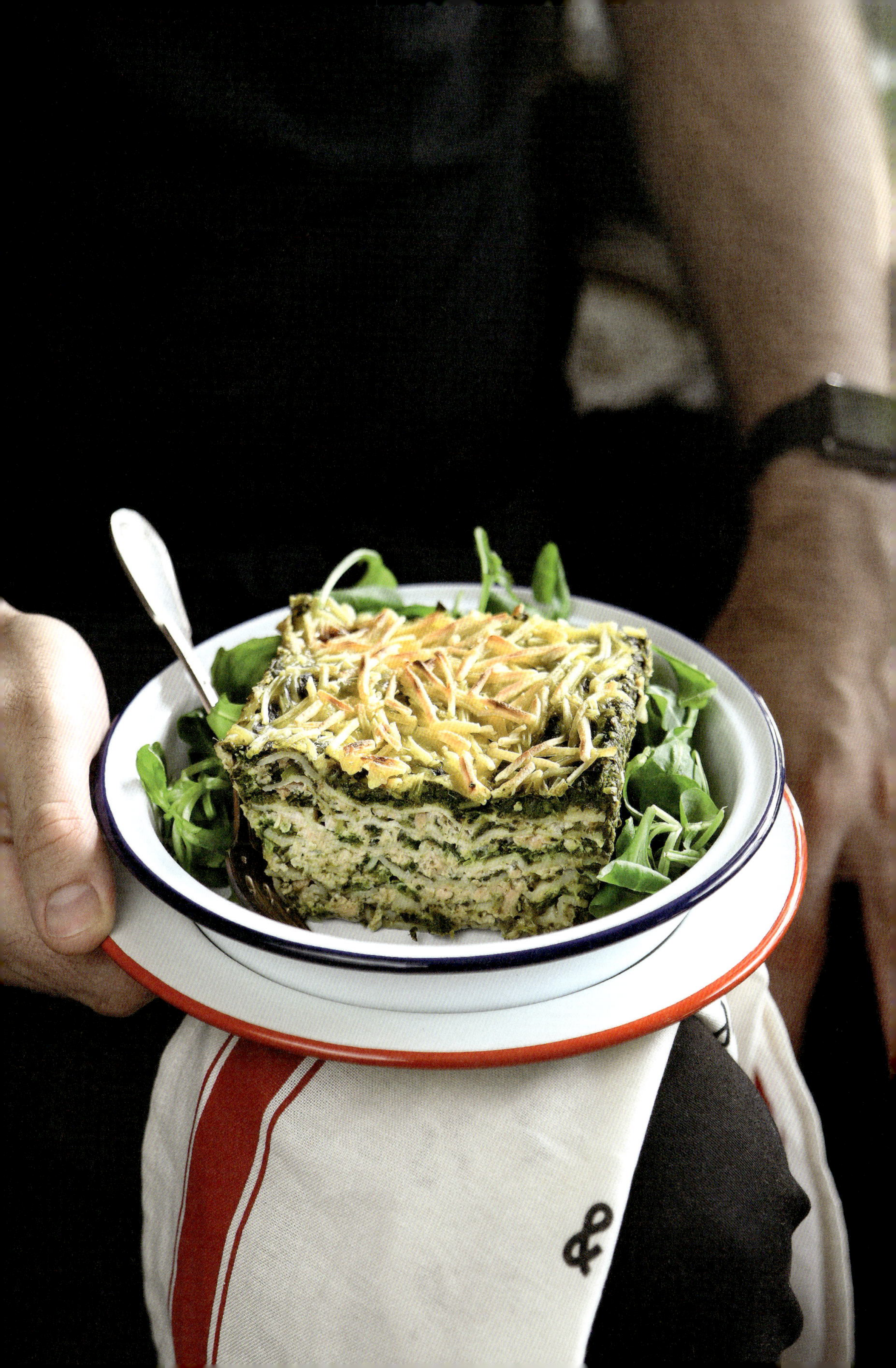

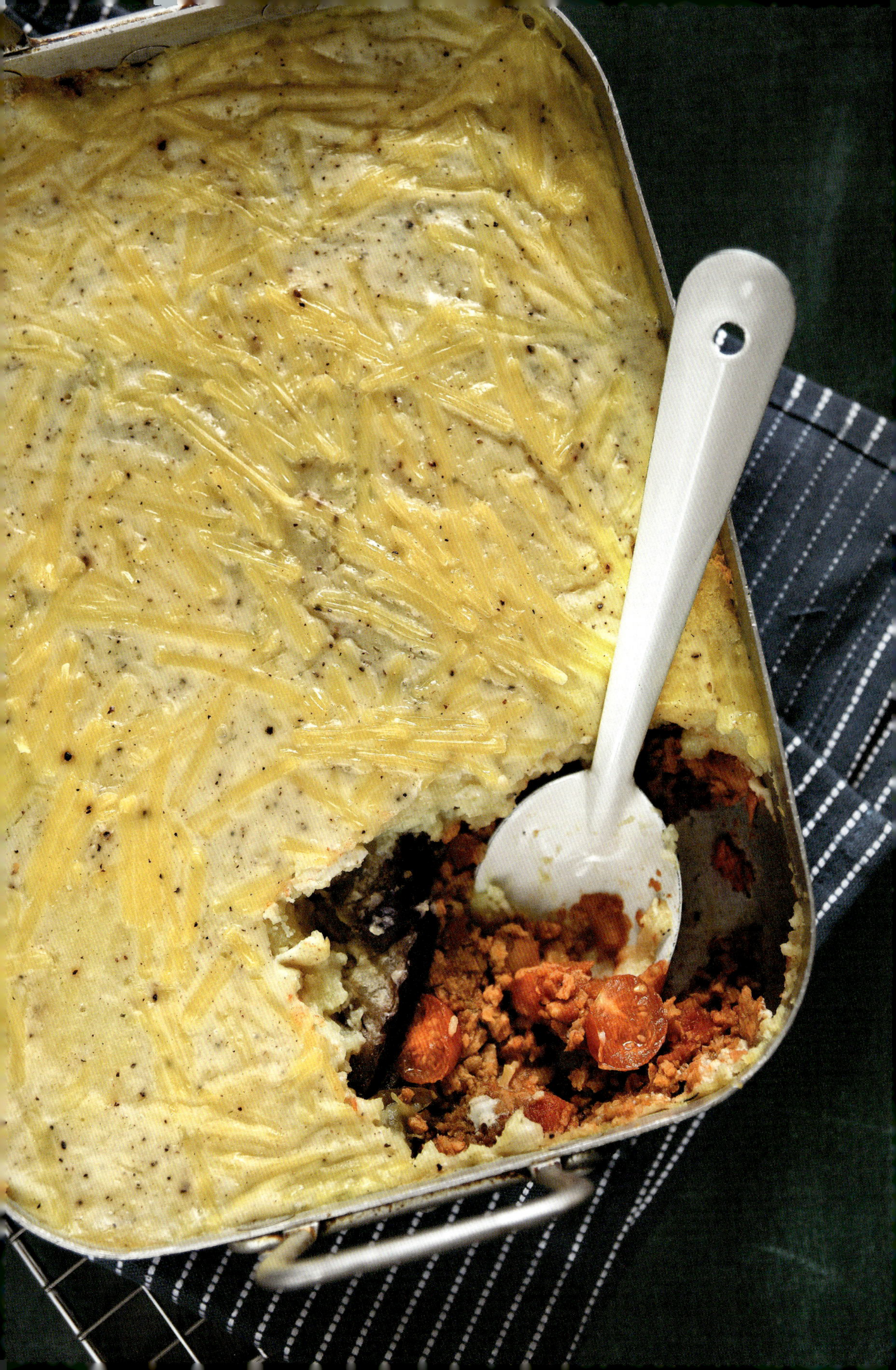

MOUSSAKA

- 550 g tomato passata
- 100 g TVP mince
- 1 tbsp Worcestershire sauce
- Salt
- Pepper
- 20 cherry tomatoes
- 300 g frozen grilled aubergine slices
- 500 g pre-cooked potatoes
- 150 ml soya cream
- 4 tsp vegan margarine
- Frozen thyme
- 4 tsp cornflour
- 50 g grated vegan cheese

Heat the tomato passata in a pan. Add the TVP and Worcestershire sauce, mix well and turn off the heat. Season with salt and pepper if needed. Transfer to an ovenproof dish, halve the tomatoes and place on top of the TVP mixture. Cover with sliced aubergines. Mash the potatoes with 2 tbsp of soya cream, margarine, salt and pepper, then add a few pinches of thyme. Spread evenly over the aubergine. Mix 120 ml of soya cream with cornflour diluted in a little cold water, then season with salt and pepper. Add the grated cheese, mix and pour over the potatoes. Bake in an oven preheated to 180°C (gas mark 4) for 45 minutes.

WARM BROCCOLI SALAD

- 50 g TVP mince
- 500 ml vegetable stock
- Sunflower oil
- Black pepper
- 2 tsp basil-infused olive oil
- 2 tbsp balsamic vinegar
- 2 drops red chilli sauce
- 2 tsp tamari
- 1 kg fresh broccoli

Cook the TVP with 500 ml of vegetable stock in a pan. Reduce over a high heat until the stock is fully absorbed. Dry off the TVP in a hot frying pan with a tablespoon of sunflower oil for 2 minutes. Season with pepper and set aside. Make the sauce by whisking together the basil-infused olive oil, balsamic vinegar, chilli sauce and tamari. Wash the broccoli and cut into florets. Bring 3 litres of salted water to the boil. Submerge the broccoli in the water, cover and cook for 5 minutes. Meanwhile, fill a large bowl with ice cold water. After 5 minutes, drain the broccoli and transfer to the cold water for 1 minute. Drain well. Mix the broccoli, TVP, and the sauce. Serve immediately.

Textured Vegetable Protein

GRILLED TVP WITH SHALLOT SAUCE →

- 200 g TVP (large pieces)
- 500 ml vegetable stock
- 50 g frozen shallots
- 2 tbsp white wine
- 1 tbsp white miso
- 100 ml port
- 4 tsp vegan margarine
- Olive oil
- Oregano
- Black pepper

In a large pot, rehydrate the TVP in the vegetable stock for 15 minutes over a high heat, then strain. Sweat the shallots in a small pan over a medium heat for 3 minutes and deglaze with white wine.

Let the wine evaporate completely. Add the miso, mix and add the port. Reduce over a low heat for 5 minutes. Remove from the heat, add the margarine and set aside. Preheat an electric grill on the highest setting. Brush the TVP pieces with a little olive oil, sprinkle with oregano and black pepper. Grill for 3 minutes and transfer to a plate. Cover with a tablespoonful of sauce and serve.

MODERN BLANQUETTE

- 1 tbsp olive oil • 2 tsp chopped frozen garlic • 1 sprig thyme • 1 bay leaf • 100 g frozen onions • 100 g frozen carrots • 50 g frozen leeks • 100 g frozen button mushrooms • 1 litre vegetable stock • 100 g TVP medallions • 250 ml soya cream • 1 lemon • 2 tsp cornflour • 4 tsp chopped flat-leaf parsley

Heat the oil in a large pot with the garlic, thyme and bay leaf. Add the onions and carrots, mix and cook for 5 minutes. Add the leeks and mushrooms and cook for 5 minutes. Add the hot vegetable stock and TVP. Cover and cook over a high heat for 10 minutes. In a bowl, mix the soya cream, 1 tbsp of lemon juice and cornflour dissolved in a little cold water. Remove the thyme and bay leaf from the pot, add the cream, chopped parsley, zest of half a lemon and mix. Wait for 2 minutes and serve.

CIDER CASSEROLE

- 100 g TVP medallions • 1 litre vegetable stock • 4 tsp vegan margarine • 2 cloves • 2 tsp chopped frozen garlic • 100 g frozen onions • 300 ml dry cider • 250 g cooked potatoes • 4 tsp chopped flat-leaf parsley • 300 g mixed frozen mushrooms

In a pan, rehydrate the TVP with the stock for 15 minutes over a high heat.

Melt the margarine with the cloves and garlic in a large pot. Sauté the onions over a medium heat for 5 minutes. Add the TVP already drained and squeezed. Sauté for 3 minutes, then add the cider. Add the potatoes, parsley and mushrooms. Mix gently, then simmer over a low heat for 15 minutes.

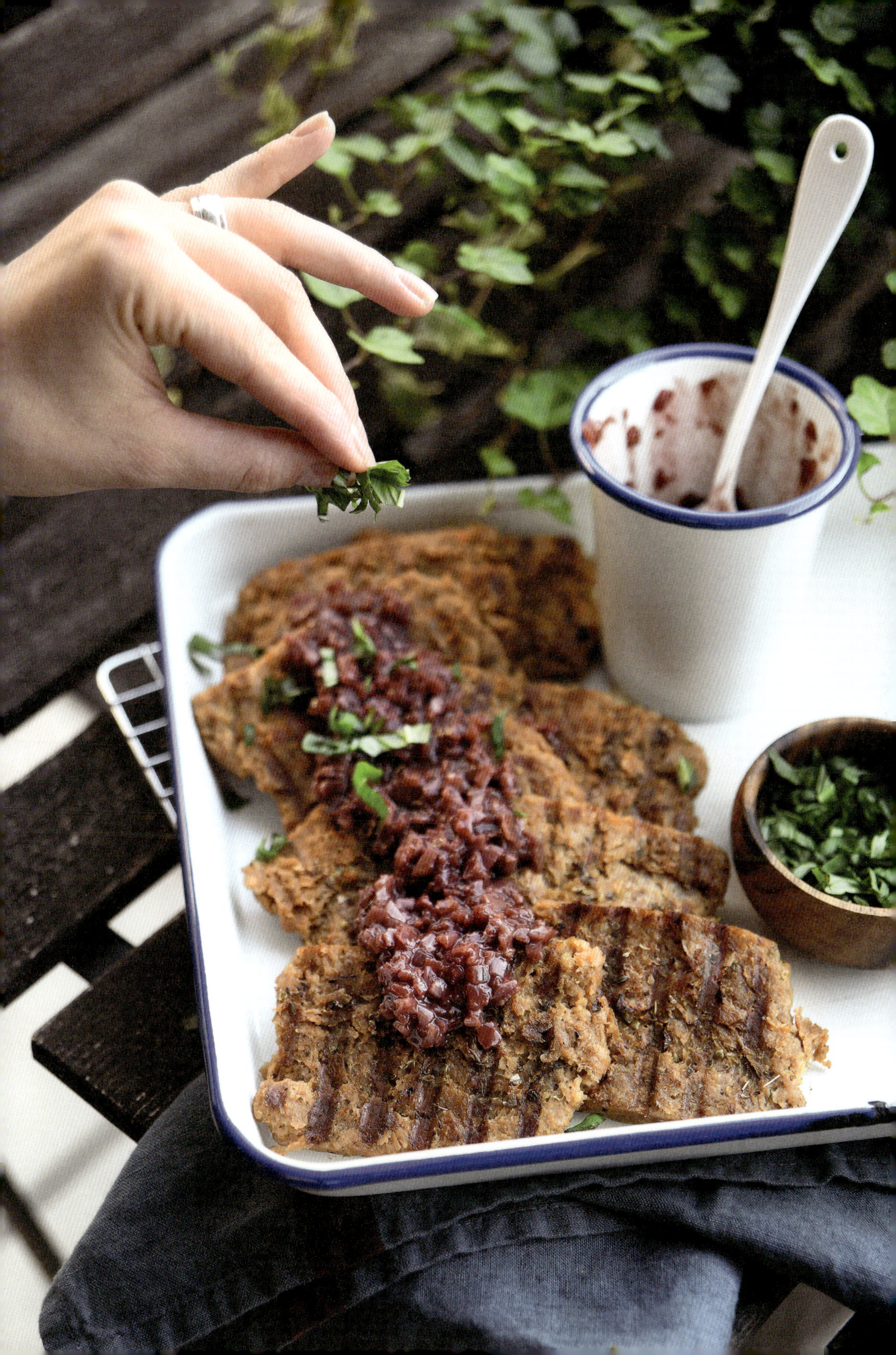

Ratatouille

This famous recipe comes from the south of France. It can be eaten on its own or it can accompany almost everything! But it is also an excellent base for preparing tasty dishes. We prefer it frozen, but it can also be found in tins or jars.

Ratatouille

POLENTA

- 500 g frozen ratatouille
- 100 ml white wine
- 2 tsp olive oil
- 1 pinch Espelette pepper
- Fine salt
- 4 tsp chopped flat-leaf parsley
- 100 g instant polenta

Defrost the ratatouille in a large pot with the lid on over a high heat. Add the white wine, olive oil and Espelette pepper, then mix. Cover and cook over a low heat for 5 minutes. Season according to taste and add the finely chopped parsley. Add the polenta in four batches, mixing well between each addition. Turn off the heat, cover and leave to thicken for 2 minutes. Mix and serve.

RATA-TOAST

- 500 g frozen ratatouille
- 2 tbsp green pesto
- 1 tsp oregano
- 8 slices sandwich bread
- 4 slices vegan cheese
- Olive oil

Defrost the ratatouille in a large pot with the lid on over a high heat. Add the pesto and oregano, mix and cook over a low heat for 5 minutes. Spread an even layer of ratatouille on 4 slices of bread. Cover with a slice of cheese and another slice of bread. Brush an electric sandwich maker or lidded grill with olive oil. Once hot, place the sandwiches on the grill, close the lid and cook at a medium heat for about 4 minutes.

Ratatouille

SAVOURY PORRIDGE →

- 1 kg frozen cooked ratatouille
- 1½ tsp ras-el-hanout
- 200 g vegan 'chicken' nuggets
- Olive oil
- 220 g porridge
- 1.2 litres of soya milk
- 1½ tsp vegetable stock paste
- Rocket leaves
- 12 small tomatoes

Cook the ratatouille over a medium heat in a wok without oil. Once soft, add the ras-el-hanout, mix and set aside. Brown the nuggets on each side in a hot frying pan with a little olive oil and set aside. Cook the porridge over a medium heat in milk with the stock paste and stir regularly. Once the liquid thickens, turn off the heat and divide between four soup bowls. Add the ratatouille, a little sauce, the tomatoes cut in half, rocket leaves and the nuggets. Finish with a drizzle of olive oil and serve.

VEGETABLE LASAGNE

- 1 kg frozen ratatouille
- 1 tbsp olive oil
- 150 ml red wine
- 40 g TVP mince
- 200 ml soya cream
- 50 g basil
- ¼ tsp fine salt
- 180 g vegan lasagne sheets (12 sheets)
- 120 g vegan cheese, grated

Defrost the ratatouille in a large pot with a lid on over a high heat. Add the olive oil and red wine. Mix and leave to simmer for 5 minutes. Add the TVP, cover and leave to soak off the heat. Preheat the oven to 180°C (gas mark 4). Mix the soya cream with the chopped basil and salt in a bowl. Place a first layer of pasta (2 sheets) in a lasagne dish, spread a thin layer of ratatouille on top and cover with pasta. Repeat with the remaining ratatouille and pasta. Pour the basil cream on top and cover with grated cheese. Bake for 30 minutes.

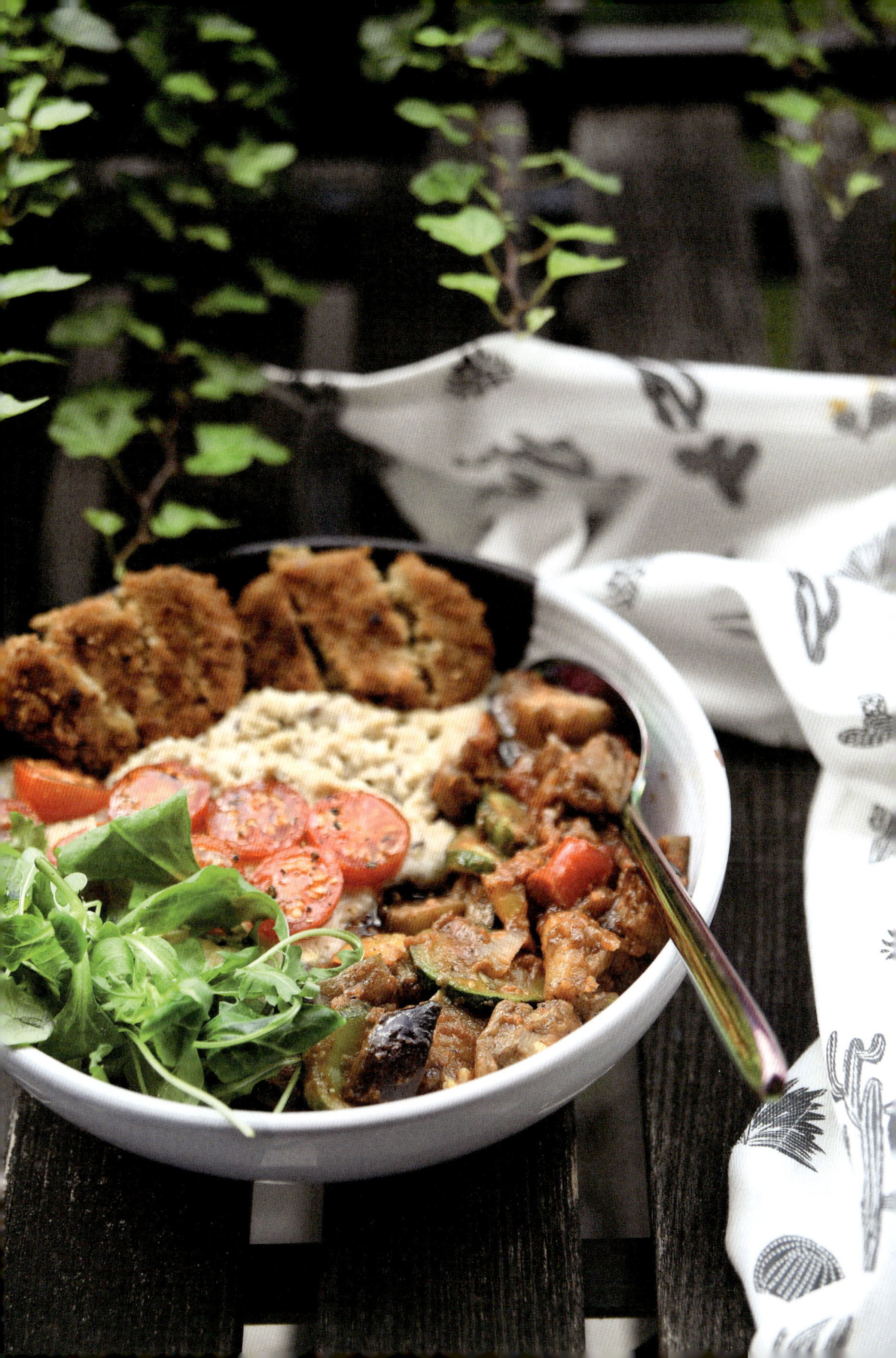

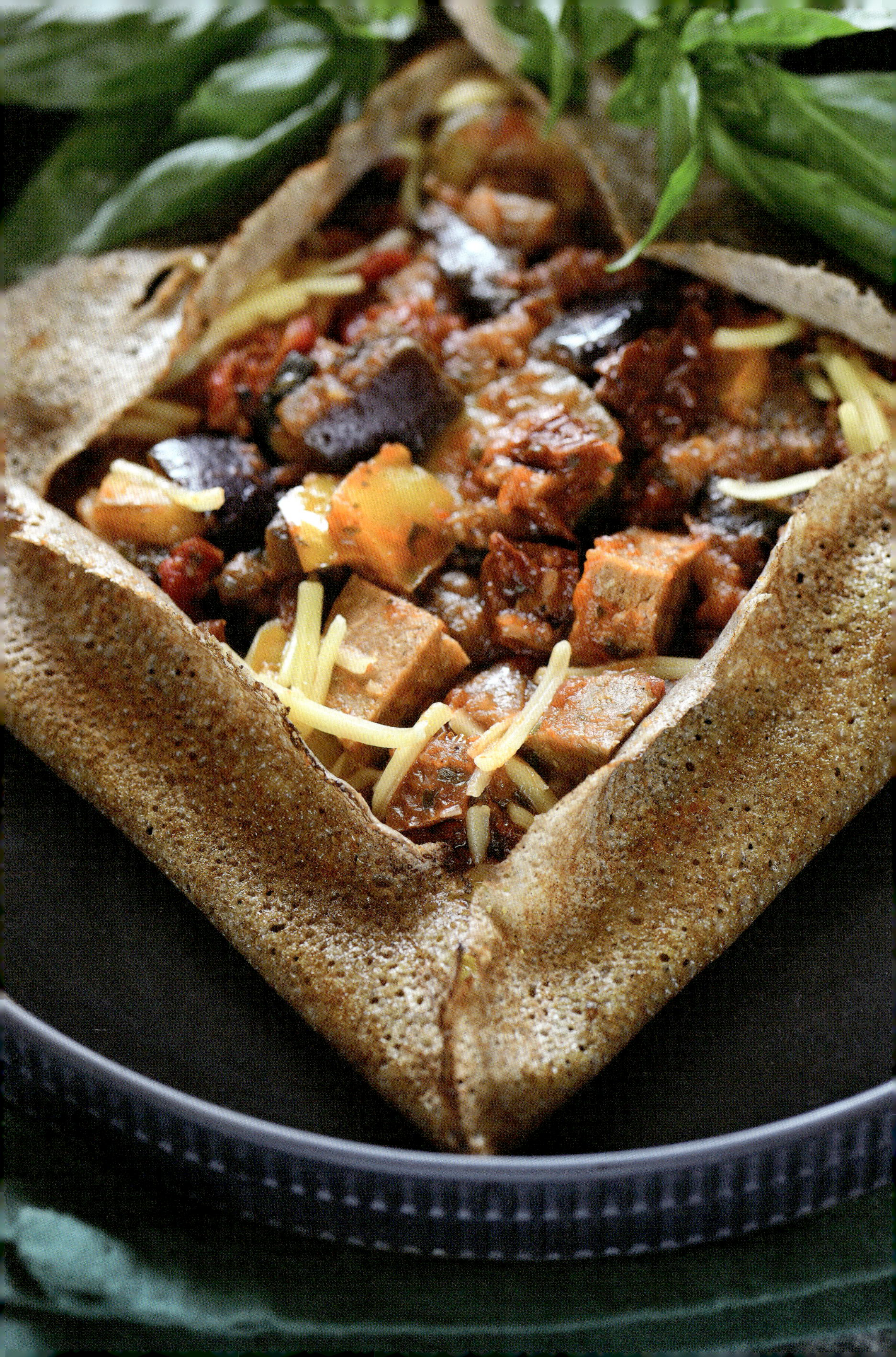

Ratatouille

GALETTES

- 1 kg frozen ratatouille
- 200 g seitan
- 3 tbsp chopped flat-leaf parsley
- 100 g sun-dried tomatoes in oil
- 300 g French buckweat galettes
- 200 g grated vegan cheese

Heat the ratatouille in a pan over a high heat to enable as much liquid to evaporate as possible. Reduce for 10 minutes. Lower the heat and add the seitan cut into small pieces as well as the chopped parsley. Cook for another 5 minutes and add the sun-dried tomatoes. Set aside. Place a galette in a hot frying pan, scatter cheese over the surface and add a serving of ratatouille. Fold over the edges of the galette and serve.

GOURMET SAUCE

- 500 g frozen ratatouille
- ½ tsp frozen thyme
- 2 tbsp olive oil
- 100 ml red wine
- 100 ml tomato passata
- 50 g vegan chorizo
- 50 g smoked tofu
- 1¼ tsp Espelette pepper

Cook the ratatouille in a large pot with the thyme and olive oil. Once soft, add the wine and tomato passata. Cover and leave to simmer over a low heat for 10 minutes. Blend to make a sauce. Cut the chorizo and smoked tofu into small pieces and sauté for several minutes in a frying pan with a little oil. Add to the sauce, along with the Espelette pepper, mix and reheat everything before serving with pasta, for example. If the consistency is too thick, add a little water to loosen the sauce.

MEDITERRANEAN VEGETABLE SOUP

- 1 litre vegetable stock
- 4 tsp chopped frozen garlic
- 2 thyme sprigs
- 2 bay leaves
- 1 kg frozen ratatouille
- 1 tbsp caster sugar
- Black pepper
- Olive oil
- Fresh basil

Heat the vegetable stock in a large pot with the garlic, thyme and bay leaves. Leave to boil for a few minutes and add the ratatouille. Once it starts to boil again, remove the thyme and bay leaves and add the sugar. Cook over a medium heat for 10 minutes then blend with a stick blender. Serve in soup bowls and garnish with pepper, a drizzle of olive oil and a few chopped basil leaves.

Rice

It would be impossible to forget this food that is a staple in the diet of a large part of our planet's population. It's good, nutritious and inexpensive... And the great thing is that it can be used in endless different ways. Whether it's dried, cooked or frozen, no matter the type, rice will always have a place in our cupboards!

VINEYARD RISOTTO

- 350 g frozen red onions
- 200 g tinned or frozen chopped tomatoes
- Olive oil
- 2 tsp frozen thyme
- Pepper
- 200 ml red wine
- 2 tsp chopped frozen garlic
- 3 cloves
- 200 g arborio rice
- 1 litre vegetable stock
- 2 tbsp malted yeast

Sauté 50 g onions with the tomatoes with a little olive oil in a frying pan. Add the thyme, season with pepper and deglaze with 5 tbsp of red wine. Simmer over a low heat for 15 minutes. Bring the stock to the boil in a pan, then lower the heat and leave it to simmer. Heat 1 tbsp of olive oil in a large pot. Sauté 300 g of onions with the garlic and cloves for 5 minutes. Add the rice, stir and add 130 ml of red wine. Stir until the liquid evaporates. Add a ladle of vegetable stock, stir until the liquid is almost fully absorbed then add another ladle of stock. Repeat the process until the rice is cooked. Add the tomatoes, gently mix with the rice, then add the malted yeast and cover for 2 minutes.

VEGETABLE CURRY RICE

- 200 g frozen carrots
- 200 g frozen cauliflower
- 2 tbsp sunflower oil
- 15 cardamom pods
- 1 tbsp cumin seeds
- 2½ tsp coriander seeds
- 1½ tbsp chopped frozen ginger
- 1½ tbsp Madras curry powder
- 100 g frozen onions
- 100 g frozen peas
- 300 g cooked basmati rice
- Fine salt
- 50 g fresh coriander

Blanch the carrots and cauliflower in a pan of salted boiling water for 10 minutes. Drain, then cut the cauliflower florets into small pieces. Set aside. Heat the oil in a large pot. Sauté the cardamom, cumin and coriander seeds for 1 minute, then add the chopped ginger and curry powder. Add the onions and peas. Mix well and cook for 5 minutes. Add the basmati rice, season according to taste, mix again and cook over a low heat for 3 more minutes. Finally, add the carrots and cauliflower, then mix gently and sprinkle with fresh coriander.

Rice

THAI RICE SALAD

- 80 g cashew nuts
- 450 g cooked jasmine rice
- 115 g red peppers
- 90 g grated red cabbage
- 80 g grated carrots
- 25 g spring onion
- 25 g coconut flakes
- 4 tbsp chopped fresh coriander
- 50 g peanut butter
- 1 tbsp agave syrup
- 1 tbsp rice vinegar
- 1 tbsp tamari
- 1 tsp ginger juice
- Pepper
- ½ lime

Toast the cashew nuts for several minutes in a hot frying pan without any oil or fat. Pour the rice, chopped peppers, red cabbage, carrots, cashews, finely chopped spring onion, coconut flakes and chopped coriander into a large mixing bowl and mix. Blend the peanut butter with the agave syrup, rice wine vinegar, tamari, ginger juice, pepper and 3 tbsp of water in a measuring jug. Pour the sauce over the salad, mix well and finish by squeezing the juice of half a lime on top.

TRIO OF MAKI

- 150 g sushi rice
- 4 tsp rice wine vinegar
- 1 tbsp caster sugar
- Generous pinch of salt
- Nori seaweed sheets
- Dijon mustard
- Toasted sesame seeds
- 100 g grated carrots
- 100 g cooked beetroot
- Cornichons in vinegar

Rinse the rice and boil in a large pot with 150 ml water, the rice wine vinegar, sugar and salt for 12 to 15 minutes. The rice should have absorbed almost all the liquid. Leave to cool down. Place a sheet of nori on a chopping board and cover a quarter of the surface with rice. Add a little mustard, toasted sesame seeds and the grated carrot. Roll everything, wetting the end to seal. Repeat the process with the other ingredients, ensuring the cornichons and beetroot are cut lengthways into batons. Serve with a little soy sauce.

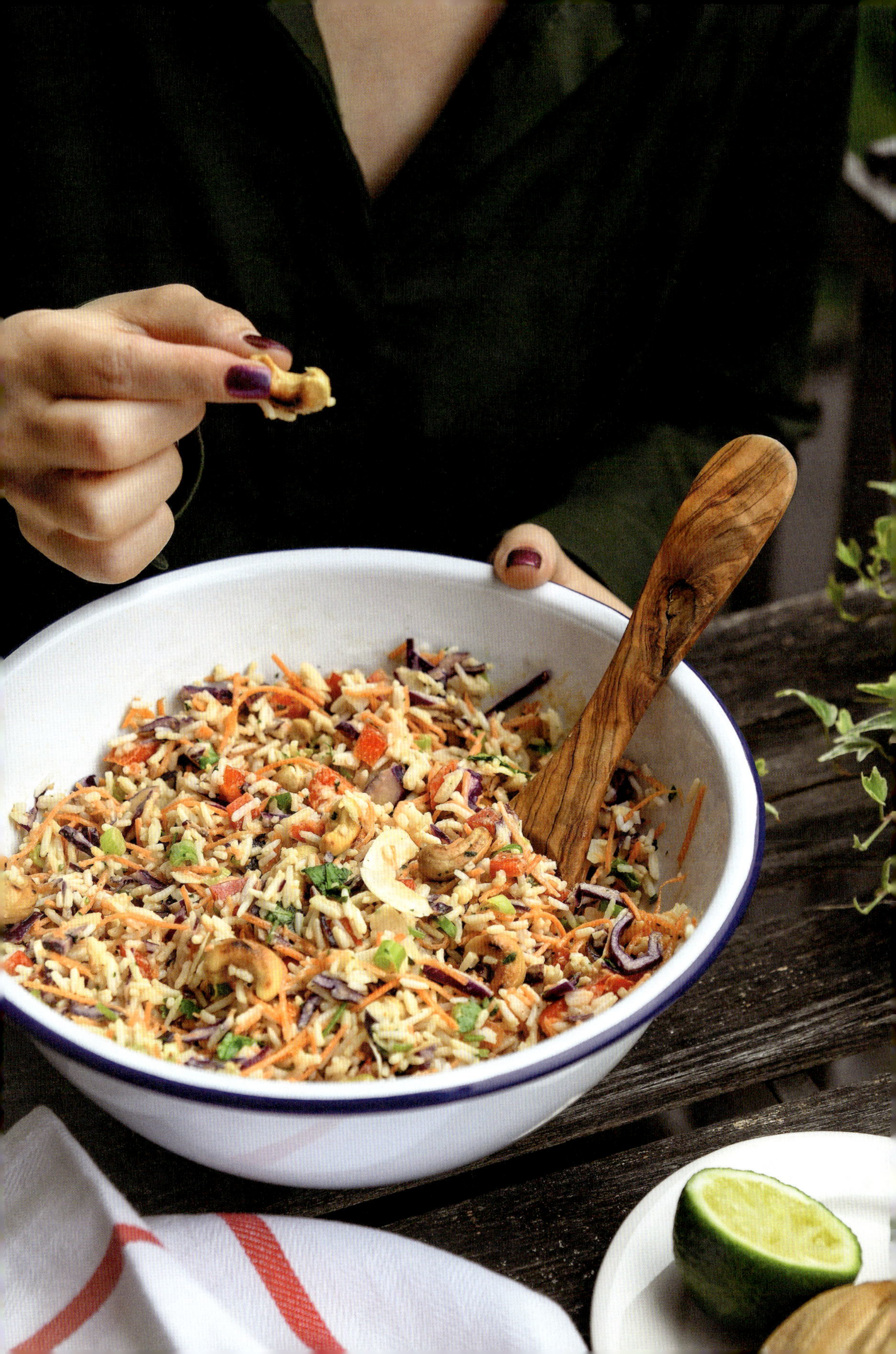

Rice

KIMCHI ONIGIRI →

- 150 g sushi rice • ½ tsp salt • 2 tsp rice vinegar • 1¾ tsp black sesame gomasio
- 80 g kimchi • Toasted sesame oil

Rinse the rice, then boil in a large pot of salted boiling water for 15 minutes. Once the rice is cooked, drain and set aside on a large plate. Add the rice vinegar and gomasio, mix and leave to cool down. Chop up the kimchi and squeeze to remove as much liquid as possible. Use an onigiri mould to shape the onigiri as follows: fill the bottom half of the mould with rice, make a well in the centre, push the rice up the sides of the mould, add a teaspoon of kimchi and cover with rice so that the mould is full. Press firmly with the lid of the mould, then remove from the mould. Leave to rest for 30 minutes. Put a little oil in your hands and coat the onigiri before browning in a hot frying pan with a little sesame oil. Brown for 2 to 3 minutes on both sides, serve immediately.

BROCCOLI & RICE

- 2 tsp chopped frozen garlic
- 100 g frozen onions
- 2 tbsp olive oil
- 600 g frozen broccoli
- 1 litre vegetable stock
- 200 g arborio rice
- 100 ml white wine
- 2 tbsp soya cream
- 3 tbsp malted yeast

Sauté the garlic and onions with olive oil in a large pan. Add the still frozen broccoli and the hot vegetable stock. Bring to the boil and add the rice, mix well. Cook for 15 minutes or until the rice is cooked and add the white wine. Cook for another 3 minutes then add the soya cream and malted yeast. Mix, then cover and leave to rest for 3 minutes off the heat before serving.

PAELLA

- 1 litre vegetable stock
- 20 g mixed dried seaweed
- Pinch of saffron powder
- 50 g frozen red peppers
- 50 g frozen artichoke hearts
- 50 g frozen peas
- 4 tsp chopped frozen garlic
- 2 tbsp olive oil
- 500 ml tomato passata
- 200 g paella rice
- 50 g vegan chorizo, sliced

Heat the vegetable stock in a pan with the seaweed. Simmer for 10 minutes then pass through a sieve to remove the seaweed. Add the saffron and mix. Sauté the peppers, artichokes, peas and garlic in a hot frying pan with oil for 10 minutes. Add the tomato passata, mix and add the rice. Cover with some stock and leave to absorb. Add the sliced chorizo. Cover with more stock and repeat these steps until the rice is fully cooked.

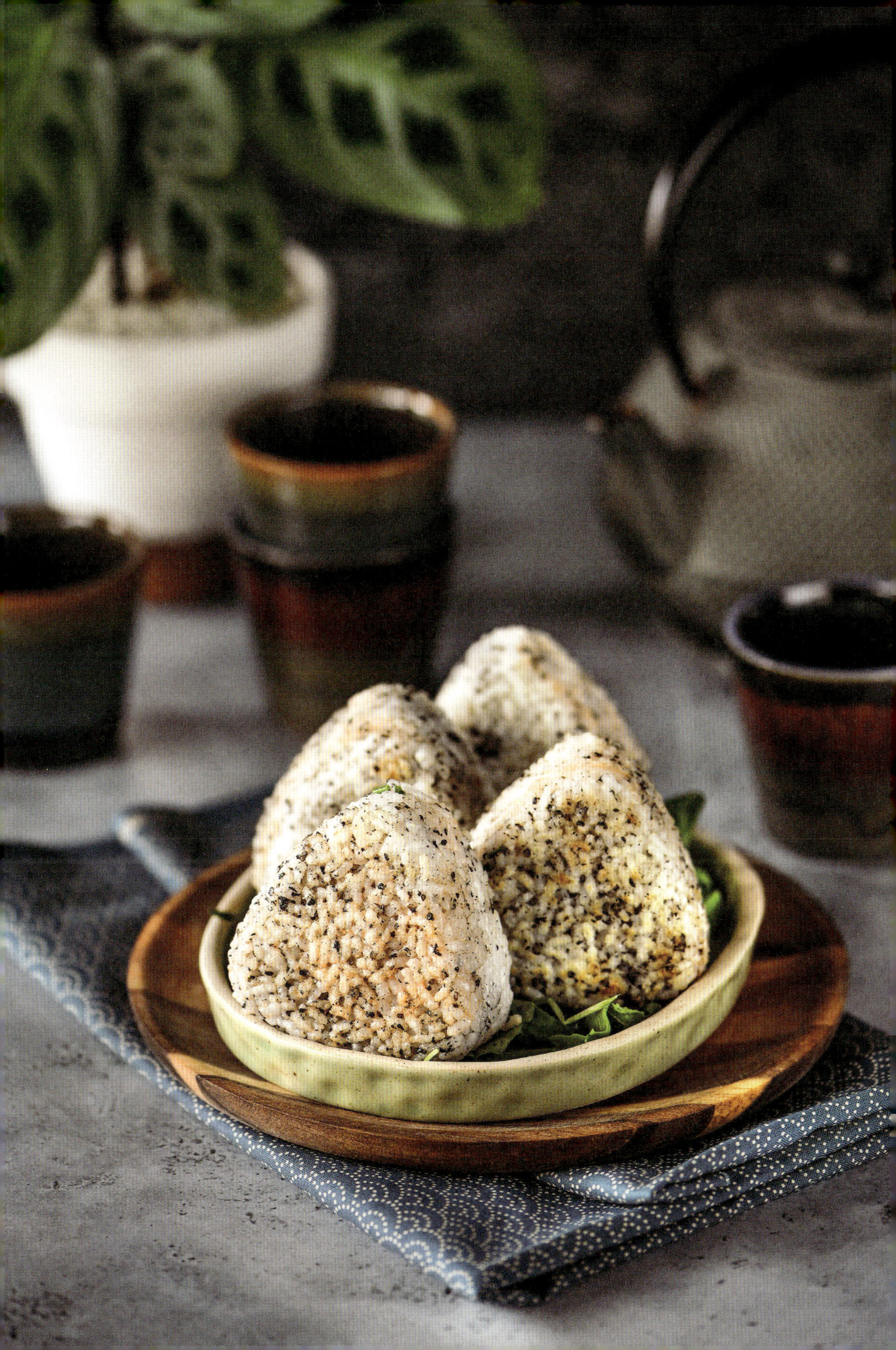

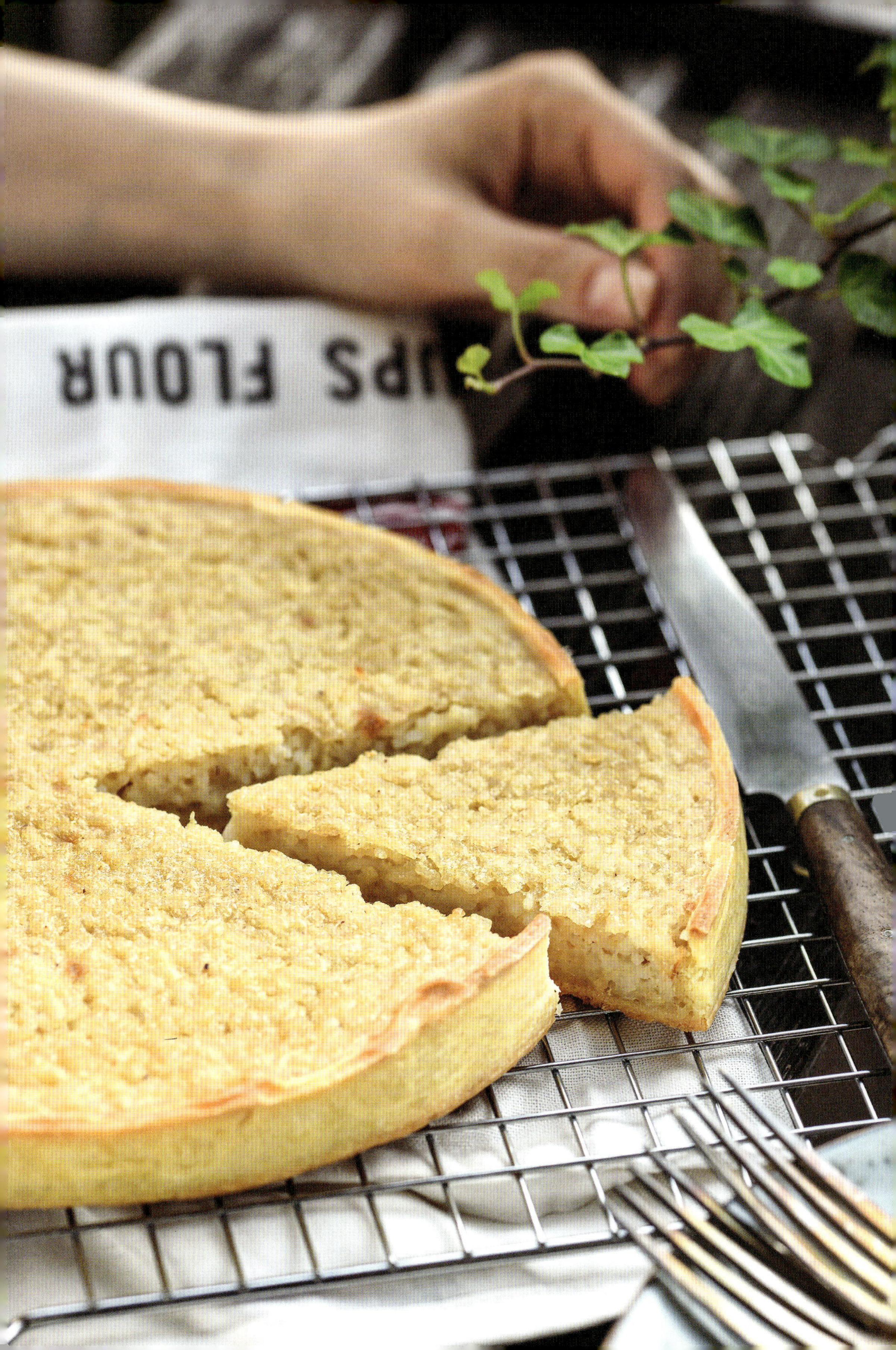
UPS FLOUR

RICE TART

- 250 g cooked jasmine rice
- 500 g vanilla soya custard
- 3 tbsp cornflour
- 2 tbsp non-dairy milk
- 45 g vanilla sugar
- ¼ tonka bean
- 1 cinnamon stick
- 1 ready-rolled sweet vegan shortcrust pastry

Preheat the oven to 180°C (gas mark 4). Mix the rice with the custard and cornflour diluted in dairy-free milk. Add the vanilla sugar, grated tonka bean and a small amount of grated cinnamon then mix again. Line a 20 or 23-cm tart mould with the pastry, prick the base with a fork, add the rice mixture and spread out, sprinkle a little sugar on top and bake for 50 minutes. Allow to cool before removing from the mould and serving.

CHERRY MATCHA RICE PUDDING

- 250 ml vanilla soya milk
- 3 tbsp coconut cream
- 280 g cooked rice
- 60 g caster sugar
- 1 tsp matcha green tea powder
- 100 g Amarena cherries

Bring the soya milk and coconut cream to the boil in a pan. Once boiling, add the cooked rice and sugar. Simmer over a low heat for 5 minutes. Stir regularly.

Once the liquid has thickened and is almost fully absorbed, add the matcha diluted in 2 tbsp of hot water. Mix and cook for a few more minutes. Distribute the cherries between 4 glasses and cover with rice pudding. Chill for several hours.

JAMBALAYA

- 100 g frozen onions
- 4 tbsp chopped frozen garlic
- 100 g mixed frozen peppers
- 3 tbsp olive oil
- 800 g peeled tomatoes
- 50 g celery
- 200 g smoked vegan sausages
- 100 ml vegetable stock
- 200 g cooked long-grain rice
- 1 tbsp jalapeño sauce
- 1½ tsp Cajun spices

Cook the onions, garlic and peppers in a large pot with hot oil for 10 minutes. Add the peeled tomatoes, celery chopped into small pieces and sausages cut into 3-cm slices. Add the stock and let reduce for 5 minutes. Add the rice, jalapeño sauce and Cajun spices. Mix and cook for another 10 minutes over a low heat.

Vegan sausages

Whether made from seitan, TVP or lupin beans, vegan sausages are a must when it comes to meat substitutes. From classic to spiced, smoked or herbed, merguez or bratwurst, the choice is endless!

It would be a shame to simply reheat them so here are some tasty recipes so that you can enjoy them properly.

Vegan Sausages

BASQUAISE

- 4 tsp chopped frozen garlic
- 100 g frozen onions
- 4 tsp olive oil
- 600 g sliced frozen peppers
- Salt
- 100 ml white wine
- 50 g tomato purée
- 1¼ tsp Espelette pepper
- 200 g vegan spicy sausages

Sauté the garlic and onions in a hot frying pan with olive oil. Add the peppers and salt. Reduce for 5 minutes. Add the white wine, tomato purée and Espelette pepper. Mix well, cover and cook for 5 minutes. Cut the sausages in three and add to the pot. Cover and cook over a low heat for 10 minutes. Serve immediately.

BANH MI DOG

- 2½ tbsp vegan mayonnaise
- 1 tbsp rice vinegar
- 1 tsp Worcestershire sauce
- 150 g carrots
- 60 g cucumber
- 4 hotdog buns
- 4 vegan hot dogs (around 200 g)
- 8 sprigs fresh coriander
- Sriracha sauce

Mix the mayonnaise with the rice vinegar and Worcestershire sauce. Grate the carrots and create fine cucumber ribbons using a vegetable peeler. Mix the carrots and sauce together. Heat the hotdog buns in an oven preheated to 180°C (gas mark 4) for 5 minutes. In the meantime, fry the sausages without any fat or oil. Split the hotdog buns lengthways, fill with a few slices of cucumber, then top with grated carrot. Add the sausages to the buns and top with two coriander sprigs and sriracha sauce.

Vegan Sausages

PEA SOUP →

- 2 tsp chopped frozen garlic
- 1 kg frozen peas
- 1 tbsp olive oil
- 1 litre vegetable stock
- 2 cloves
- 1 tsp dried rosemary
- 200 g vegan sausages
- Soya cream
- Black pepper

Sauté the garlic and peas in a large pot with olive oil over a high heat for 5 minutes. Add the hot vegetable stock, cloves and rosemary, then cook for 10 minutes. Transfer the cooked peas and 500 ml of stock to a blender. Blend to make a thick but slightly chunky soup. Cut the sausages into 2-cm slices and sauté in a frying pan. Serve the soup in bowls with a drizzle of soya cream, season generously with pepper and garnish with slices of sausage.

'SAUSAGE' ROLLS

- 200 g vegan puff pastry • 2 tbsp wholegrain mustard • 1 tsp cumin seeds • 3 slices vegan cheese
- 6 vegan sausages (around 200 g)
- Olive oil • 1 tsp sesame seeds
- 1 tsp poppy seeds

Preheat the oven to 180°C (gas mark 4). Unroll the pastry and cut into six rectangles. Brush with mustard and cumin. Place half a cheese slice and one sausage on each rectangle and roll. Transfer to a baking sheet lined with baking parchment, brush lightly with oil and top with sesame and poppy seeds. Cook for 30 minutes.

TOMATO & CHILLI 'SAUSAGES'

- 1 tbsp olive oil • ¾ tsp ground turmeric • 1 tsp cumin seeds • 400 g frozen or tinned chopped tomatoes
- 2 tsp chopped frozen garlic
- 2½ tsp grated frozen ginger
- 100 g frozen onions • 4 tsp red chilli paste • Heaped ¼ tsp fine salt
- 250 g spiced and smoked vegan sausages

Heat the oil with the turmeric and cumin seeds in a wok. Add the tomatoes, garlic, ginger and onion. Cook for 10 minutes and add the red chilli paste and salt. Once simmering, add the sausages cut diagonally into 5-cm slices. Cook for another 10 minutes over a low heat and serve immediately.

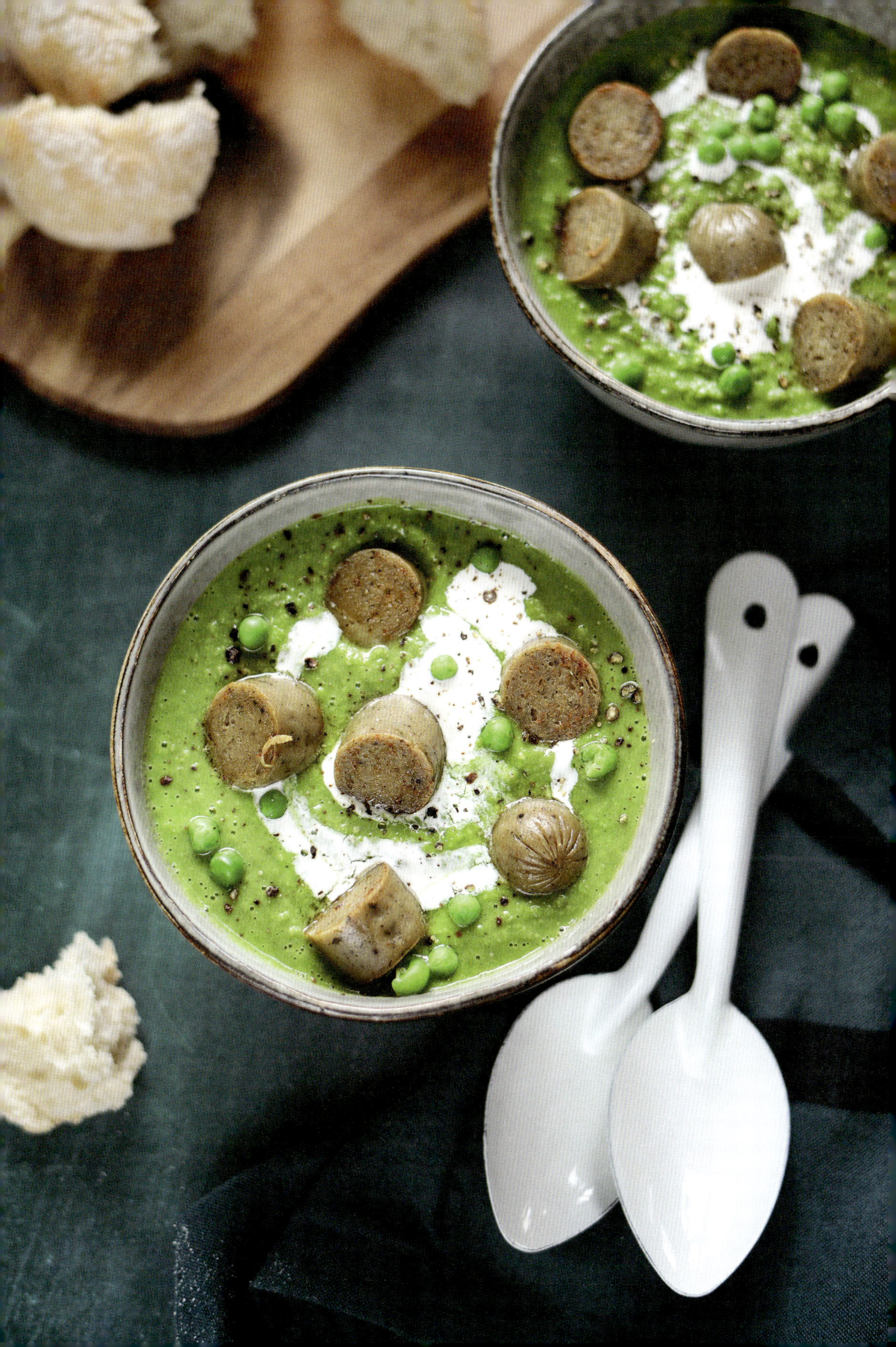

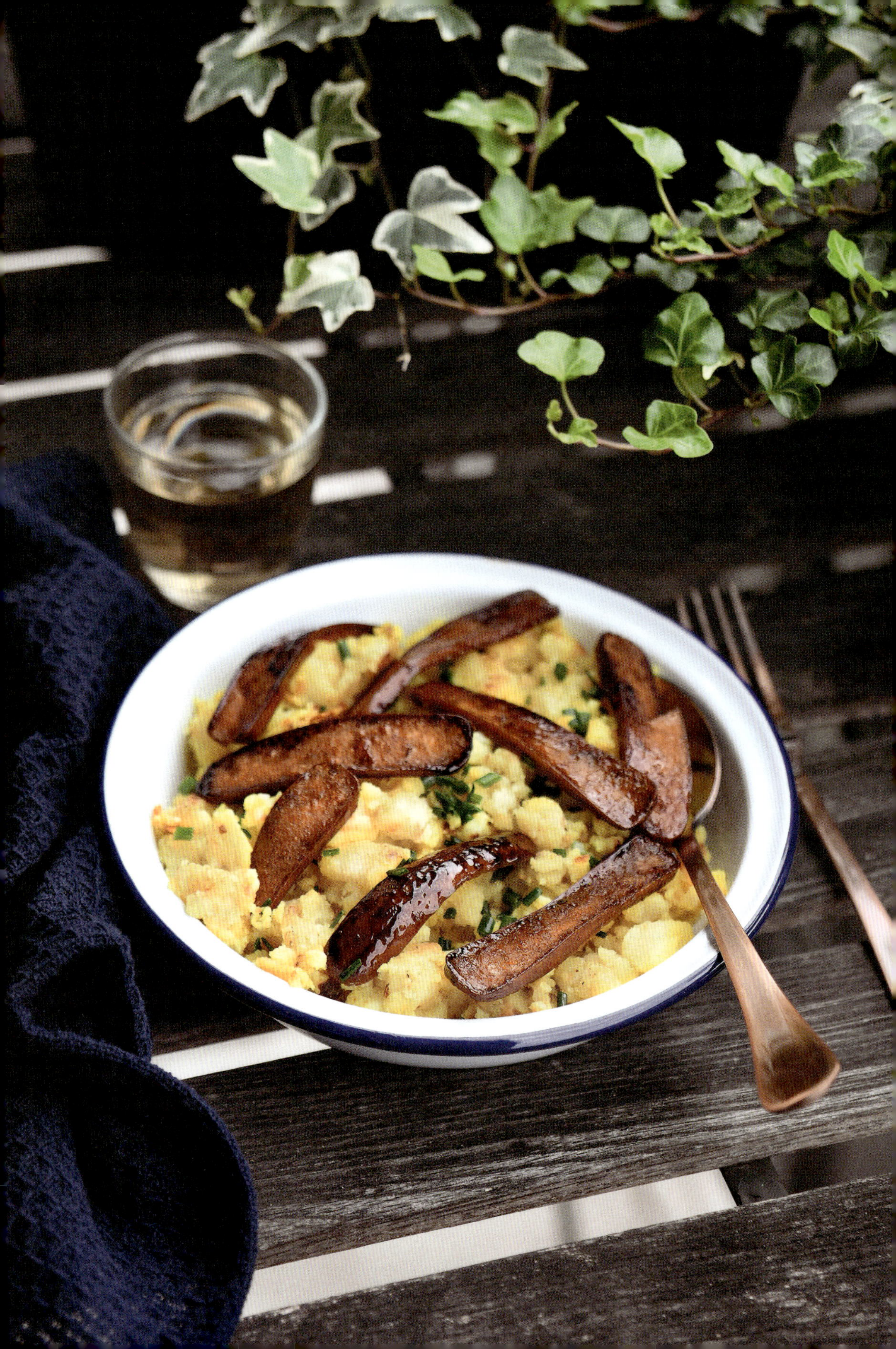

Vegan Sausages

GRILLED 'BACON' & GOLDEN MASH
←

- 1 tbsp vegan margarine
- ½ tsp garlic powder
- ¾ tsp turmeric
- ½ tsp coriander seeds
- 500 g cooked potatoes
- 200 g vegan sausages
- 2 tsp tamari
- 2 tsp maple syrup
- 2 tsp liquid smoke
- Olive oil
- Black pepper
- 4 tbsp chopped frozen chives

Melt the margarine in a hot wok and add the garlic, turmeric and crushed coriander seeds. Add the potatoes and sauté over a medium heat for 10 minutes. Cut the sausages in 1-cm slices lengthways. Mix the tamari, maple syrup and liquid smoke. Sauté the sliced sausages in a frying pan with olive oil. When the sausages start to curl up, deglaze with the sauce and lightly caramelise. Coarsely mash the potatoes, season with pepper and add the chopped chives. Add the sliced sausages on top.

BRUSSELS SPROUTS STEW

- 100 g frozen leeks
- 50 g frozen onions
- 600 g frozen Brussels sprouts
- 4 tsp olive oil
- 500 ml vegetable stock
- 1 sprig thyme
- 2 bay leaves
- 150 g vegan sausages
- Black pepper

In a large pot, sauté the leeks and onions, followed by the frozen Brussels sprouts, with olive oil over a high heat for 5 minutes. Then cover with piping hot vegetable stock. Add the thyme and bay leaves then cover and cook over a medium heat for 10 minutes. Cut the sausages into four pieces and add to the pot. Simmer for 10 minutes over a low heat. Season with plenty of pepper and serve using a skimmer.

Vegan Sausages

CURRYWURST

- 100 g tomato coulis
- 100 g tomato ketchup
- 2 tsp Worcestershire sauce
- 1½ tsp madras curry powder
- 300 g vegan sausages
- Vegetable oil

Mix the tomato coulis with the ketchup, Worcestershire sauce and curry powder in a small pan. Heat over a low heat. In the meantime, sauté the sausages in a frying pan with oil. Cut the sausages into 3-cm-thick slices, transfer to a dish and cover with the sauce. Sprinkle with a little curry powder and a few drops of Worcestershire sauce.

CHOUCROUTE GARNIE

- 100 g frozen onions
- 4 tsp chopped frozen garlic
- 1 tbsp rapeseed oil
- 500 g raw sauerkraut
- 4 juniper berries
- 2 cloves
- 1 bay leaf
- 100 g smoked firm tofu
- 200 g cooked potatoes
- 250 ml white wine
- 150 g vegan sausages

Sauté the onions and garlic in a large pot with rapeseed oil. Once soft, add the sauerkraut (rinsed thoroughly in cold water and drained), juniper berries, cloves and bay leaf. Mix and cook for 5 minutes. Add the diced tofu, potatoes and white wine. Cover and simmer over a low heat for 15 minutes. Add the whole sausages and cook for another 5 minutes. Serve immediately.

'SAUSAGE' SALAD

- 150 g lamb's lettuce
- 200 g tinned green beans
- 150 g fresh cucumber
- 150 g fresh avocado
- 200 g small vegan herb sausages
- 2 tbsp olive oil
- 1 tbsp apple cider vinegar
- 1 tsp lime juice
- 2 tsp Dijon mustard
- Generous pinch of fine salt
- 15 g frozen chives

Add the lamb's lettuce and drained green beans to a salad bowl. Dice the cucumber and avocado, then add to the salad.

Sauté the sausages in a hot frying pan with olive oil, cut them in half, then leave to cool before adding them to the salad. Emulsify 2 tbsp of olive oil with the apple cider vinegar, lime juice, Dijon mustard and salt. Add the chives, mix and pour over the salad. Gently mix everything together and serve.

Seitan

Glorious seitan! Through wheat protein, we are freed from animal flesh without giving up sensory pleasures. It nourishes us and brings us profound satisfaction. It guides our dishes towards the vegetable light, at the dawn of a new culinary day when the dishes will be devoid of suffering. Glorious seitan!

QUICK BOURGUIGNON

- 1 tbsp oil
- 100 g frozen onions
- 200 g frozen carrots
- 2 bay leaves
- 1 sprig thyme
- 300 g seitan
- 4 tsp wheat flour
- 200 ml vegetable stock
- 200 ml red wine
- 4 tsp miso paste

Heat the oil in a large pot. Sauté the onions and carrots with the bay leaves and thyme for 10 minutes. Add the seitan cut into medium-sized pieces. Sprinkle with flour and mix well. Add the vegetable stock and wine. Dissolve the miso in the liquid. Cover and simmer over a low heat for 15 minutes.

'STEAK' TARTARE

- 400 g seitan
- 1 shallot
- 4 cornichons
- 40 capers in oil
- Fresh chervil
- 4 tbsp tomato ketchup
- Worcestershire sauce
- Jalapeño sauce

Chop the seitan in a mini-chopper or coarsely blend. Finely chop the shallot and cornichons, coarsely chop the capers and finely chop the chervil. Put all the chopped ingredients in a bowl and mix together. Season with ketchup, a splash of Worcestershire sauce and a few drops of jalapeño sauce to taste. Shape the mixture into a 'steak haché' or burger with the palm of your hand and serve with fries.

Seitan

BBQ STYLE

- 100 g tomato ketchup
- 2 tbsp peaty whisky
- 2 tbsp liquid smoke
- 2 tbsp maple syrup
- 2 tsp Worcestershire sauce
- 2 tsp jalapeño sauce
- 400 g seitan

Mix the ketchup with the whisky, liquid smoke, maple syrup, Worcestershire sauce and jalapeño sauce in a bowl. Depending on the shape and size of your seitan, it may have to be flattened slightly to make 2-cm thick pieces. Marinate the seitan in the sauce for at least 1 hour. Place the seitan on an electric grill preheated to the highest setting and close the grill. Press firmly to create grill marks on the seitan. Cook for around 5 minutes. Serve the leftover marinade with the seitan as a sauce.

SICHUAN SEITAN SKEWERS

- 4 button mushrooms
- 4 small shallots
- 2 green peppers
- 200 g seitan
- 1 tbsp sunflower oil
- 8 cherry tomatoes
- 2 tsp Sichuan peppercorns
- 1 tbsp rice wine vinegar
- 1 tbsp tamari
- 1¼ tsp Espelette pepper

Clean the mushrooms and remove the stalks. Peel the shallots and remove the ends. Cut the peppers into squares about 4 cm. Chop the seitan into 3-cm cubes. Heat the sunflower oil in a wok and add the vegetables. Sauté until the pepper skins start to brown on the edges. Crush the Sichuan peppercorns and add to the wok. Add the seitan and sauté over a high heat for 5 minutes. Deglaze with the rice wine vinegar and tamari. Add the Espelette pepper. When the liquid has evaporated, turn off the heat and place on skewers in the following order: seitan, cherry tomato, pepper, mushroom, seitan, shallot, pepper, cherry tomato, seitan.

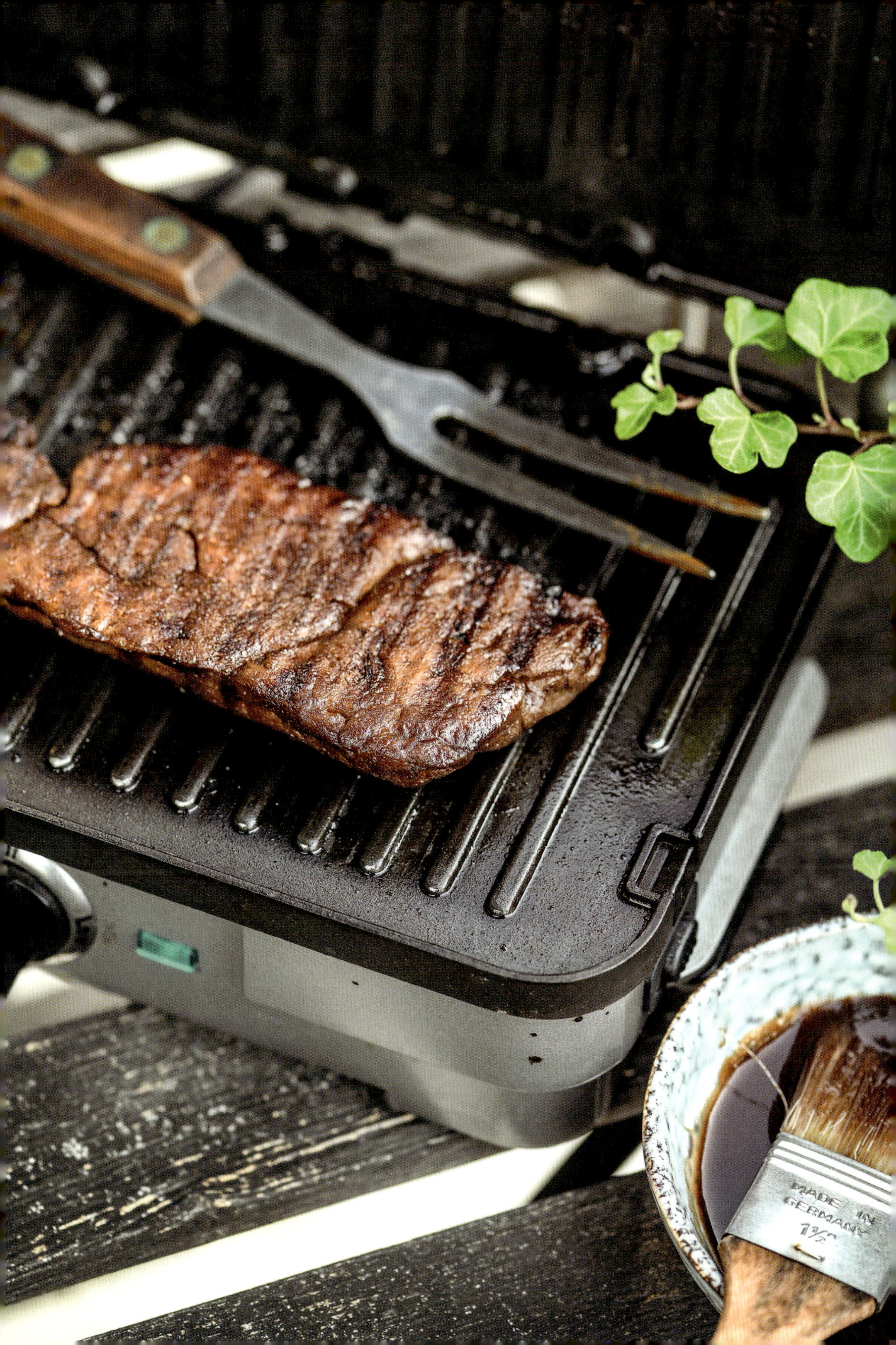
MADE IN
GERMANY
1½

Seitan

PHILLY 'CHEESESTEAK' ⟶

- 500 g seitan • 200 g frozen onions • Rapeseed oil • Fine salt • 200 g frozen button mushrooms • Black pepper • 200 ml Worcestershire sauce • 200 g frozen mixed peppers • 4 tsp tamari • 2 slices vegan cheddar cheese • 2 baguettes

Cut the seitan into 1-cm thick slices. Heat a frying pan over a high heat. Sauté the onions with a little oil until they start to brown. Season with salt and add 2 tsp of water. Once evaporated, set aside. Add the mushrooms to the pan and cook off the water that they release. Once all the water has been released, deglaze with Worcestershire sauce, then set aside. Sauté the sliced peppers in the frying pan until soft. Season with salt and set aside. Pour a splash of oil into the pan and add the seitan. Cook for 1 minute on each side, deglaze with tamari, then cover with cheese. When the cheese is melted, turn off the heat. Slice open a baguette and add a layer of peppers, mushrooms, cheese-topped seitan and finish with onions.

ORANGE SEITAN STRIPS

- 1 pinch of saffron • 250 g seitan • 1 orange • 2 tbsp apple cider vinegar
- 2 tbsp brown cane sugar • 2 shallots • Olive oil • Fine salt • Pepper

Infuse a tablespoon of warm water with the saffron strands. Cut the seitan into strips and set aside. Juice and zest the orange. Bring the vinegar and sugar to the boil in a heavy-based pan. Caramelise and reduce without mixing. Add the orange juice and bring to the boil. Add the saffron strands (without the infusion). Reduce to a thick consistency. Peel and chop the shallots lengthways. Sauté in a hot frying pan with a splash of olive oil. Once browned, deglaze with the saffron infusion. Reduce the liquid until it evaporates. Cook the seitan in a frying pan with a little oil over a medium heat for 5 minutes. Transfer to a plate, add the shallots, cover in sauce, scatter with orange zest and add a twist of salt and pepper.

'STEAK' WITH PEPPERCORN SAUCE

- 250 ml soya cream • 2 tsp crushed black peppercorns • 1½ tsp white miso • 1 tsp tamari • 1 tbsp Cognac • 4 tsp vegan margarine • 400 g seitan

Heat the soya cream in a small pan until simmering and turn off the heat. Add the peppercorns and infuse for 15 minutes. Then add the white miso, tamari and the Cognac. Mix well and reheat over a low heat for 5 minutes. Remove from the heat, add the margarine and mix with a whisk. Slice the seitan into 1-cm thick steak. Sauté the seitan in a hot pan with a little oil. Serve on plates and pour the sauce over the seitan steaks.

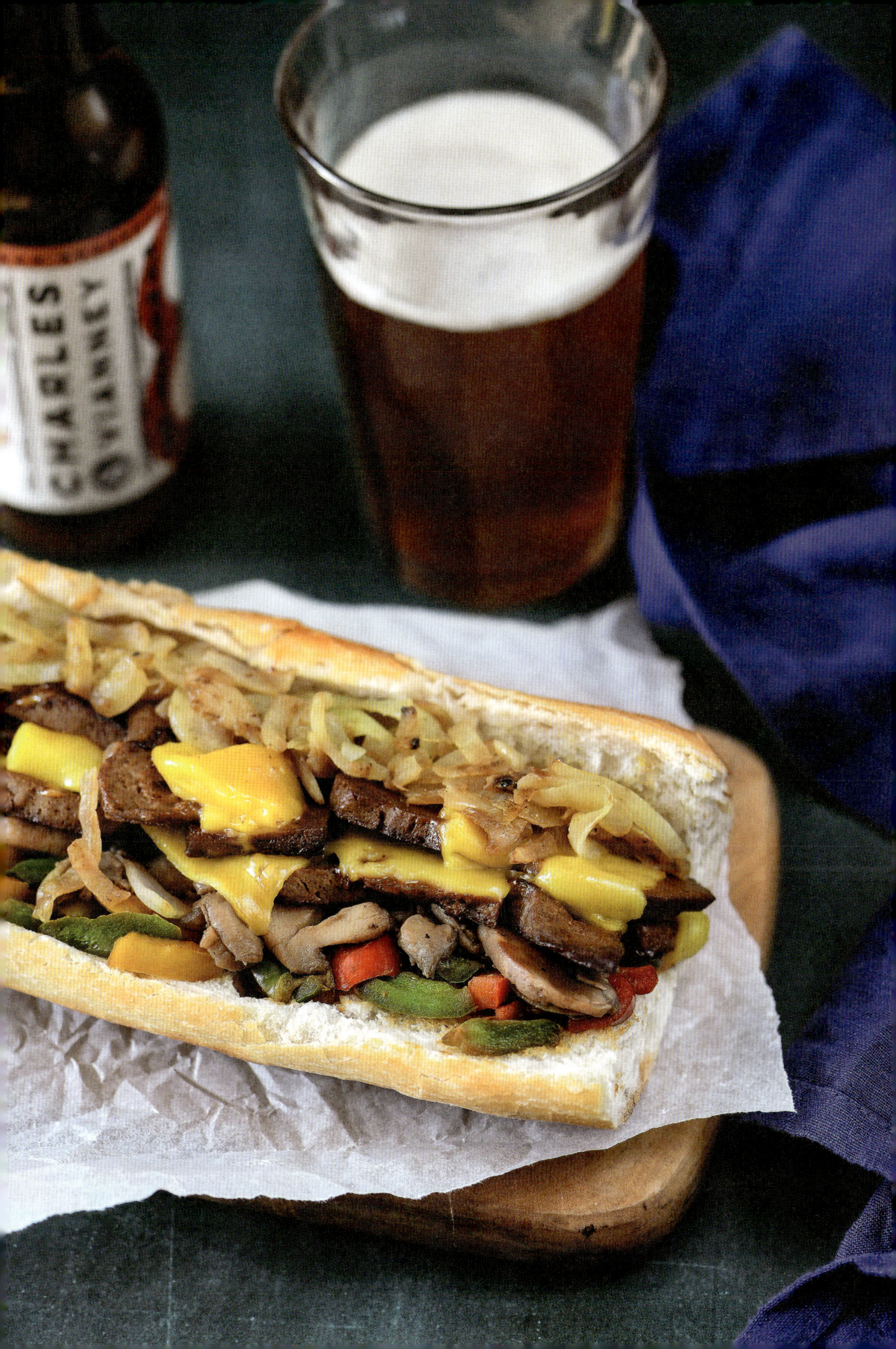
CHARLES

Seitan

ITALIAN STEW

- 100 g frozen carrots
- 100 g frozen onions
- 40 g celery stalk
- 2 tbsp olive oil
- 250 g seitan
- 2 tsp chopped frozen garlic
- 200 ml white wine
- 4 tsp white miso
- 60 g chopped tomatoes
- 2 bay leaves
- 100 g tomatoes in quarters
- Salt • 4 tsp chopped flat-leaf parsley • Black pepper

Chop the carrots, onions and celery into small pieces, set aside. In a large pot, heat the olive oil and sauté the seitan pieces for 3 minutes. Then add the carrots, onions, celery and chopped garlic. Sweat for 5 minutes and deglaze with the white wine. Add the miso, mix and reduce over a high heat for 2 minutes. Lastly add the chopped tomatoes, bay leaves and quartered tomatoes. Gently mix, reduce the heat, cover and simmer for 20 minutes. Adjust the seasoning if necessary. Garnish with parsley and season with pepper.

POT-AU-FEU

- 1.5 litres vegetable stock
- 2 cloves
- 1 sprig thyme
- 1 bay leaf
- 2 tsp chopped frozen garlic
- 200 g frozen leeks
- 200 g frozen turnips
- 200 g frozen carrots
- 100 g frozen onions
- 400 g seitan

Bring the vegetable stock to the boil with the cloves, thyme and bay leaf in a large pot. Add the garlic, leeks and turnips and cook for 5 minutes. Then add the carrots and onions. Cook for 5 more minutes, then add the seitan cut into large pieces.

Cover and cook over a medium heat for 20 minutes. Serve with Dijon mustard.

SAUTÉ PROVENÇAL

- 4 tsp chopped frozen garlic
- 100 g frozen onions • 4 tsp olive oil
- 100 g sliced frozen peppers
- 150 g frozen or tinned chopped tomatoes
- 2 tsp herbes de Provence
- 50 g pitted green olives
- 400 g seitan • 150 ml white wine
- 4 tsp tomato purée

Sauté the garlic and onions in a large pot with olive oil. Add the sliced peppers, tomatoes and herbes de Provence. Cover and cook over a high heat for 5 minutes. Add the olives and seitan cut into large dice. Cook for 5 minutes uncovered and stir regularly. Deglaze with white wine and tomato purée. Cook over a low heat for 5 minutes.

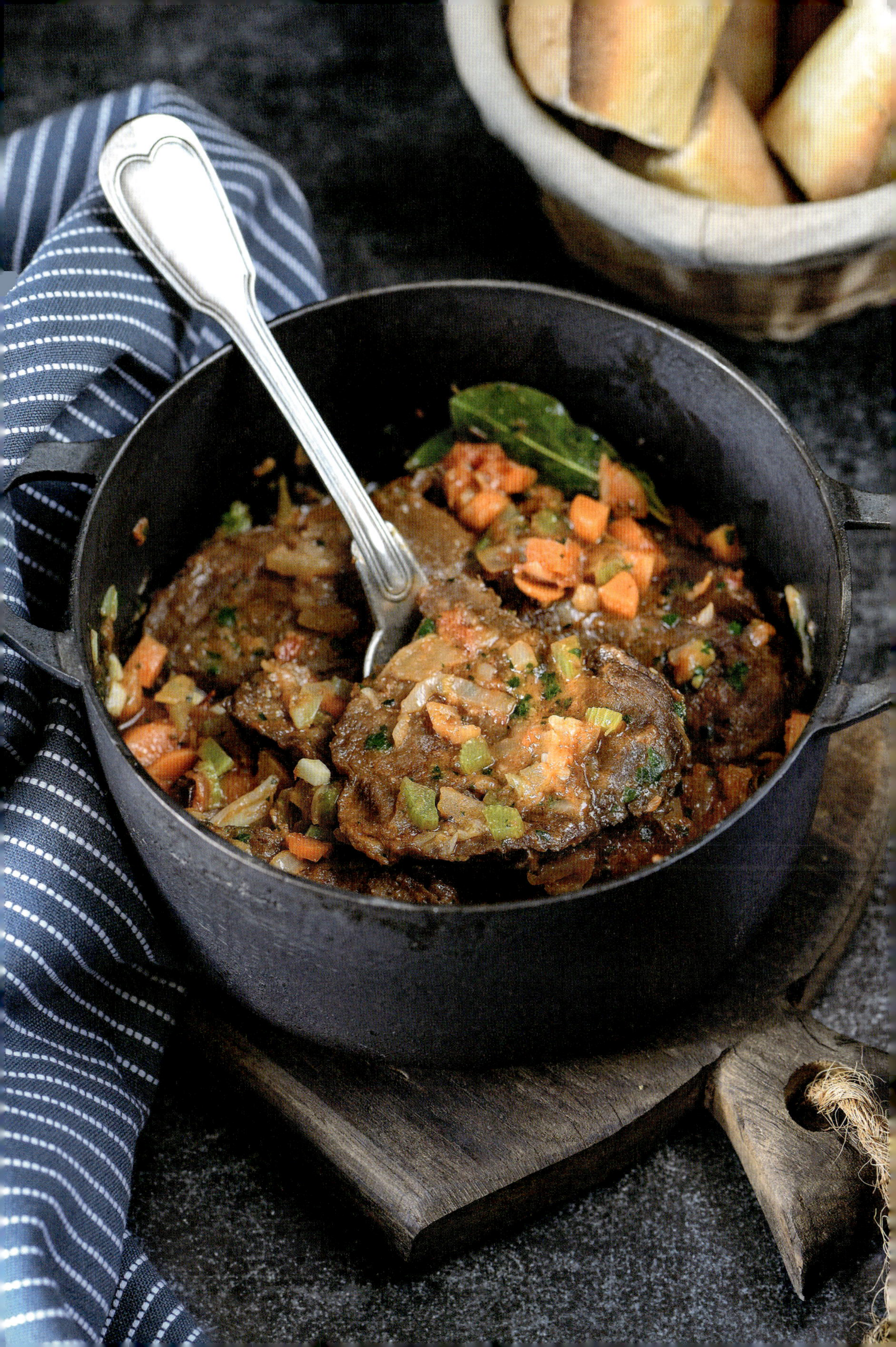

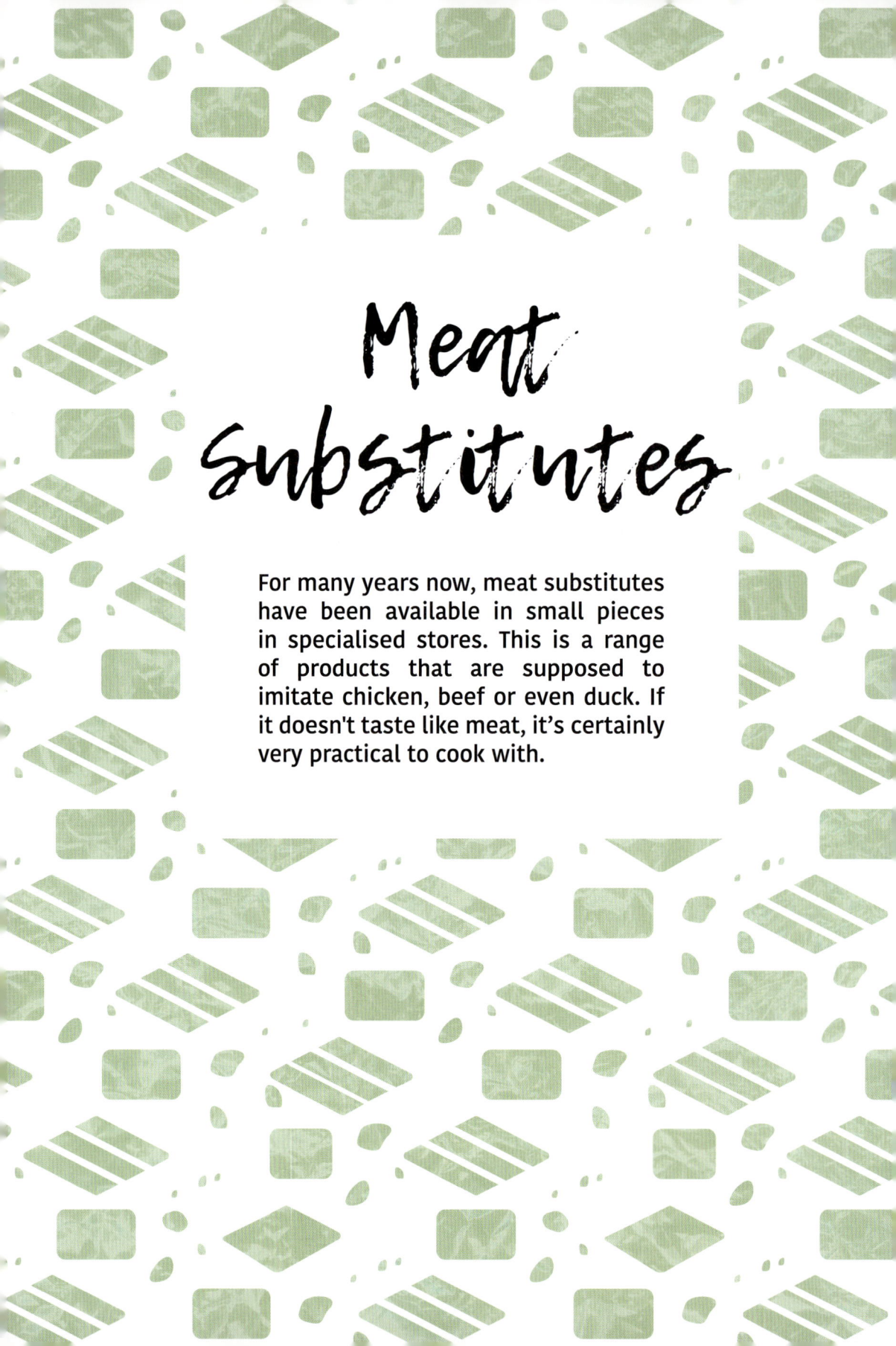

Meat substitutes

For many years now, meat substitutes have been available in small pieces in specialised stores. This is a range of products that are supposed to imitate chicken, beef or even duck. If it doesn't taste like meat, it's certainly very practical to cook with.

Meat substitutes

CHINESE 'CHICKEN'

- 2 tbsp toasted sesame oil
- 250 g 'chicken' meat substitute
- 50 g frozen peas
- 50 g tinned sweetcorn
- 1 tbsp tamari • 300 g cooked rice

Heat the sesame oil over a high heat in a large pot and sauté the meat substitute for 3 minutes. Add the peas and drained sweetcorn. Sauté for 2 minutes and deglaze with tamari. Add the rice and mix. Cook over a low heat until the rice is hot.

TRADITIONAL FRENCH STEW

- 2 tbsp olive oil
- 2 tsp chopped frozen garlic
- 1 bay leaf
- 1 sprig thyme
- 500 g 'beef' meat substitute
- 1½ tsp four spice mix
- 250 g frozen onions
- 250 g frozen button mushrooms
- 200 ml white wine
- 4 tsp white miso
- Fine salt

In a large pot, heat the oil with the garlic, bay leaf and thyme. Sauté the meat substitute for 3 minutes over a high heat with the four spice mix. Add the onions, mushrooms and cook for 5 minutes. Add the wine and white miso. Season with salt to taste and mix well. Simmer over a medium heat for 10 minutes.

Meat substitutes

'CHICKEN' & GINGER

- 2 tbsp tamari • 1 tbsp agave syrup
- 2 tbsp grated frozen ginger
- 1½ tbsp chopped frozen shallot
- 2 tsp chopped frozen garlic
- 250 g 'chicken' meat substitute
- 1 tbsp peanut oil • 2 tsp chilli paste
- 4 tbsp chopped frozen chives

In a mixing bowl, whisk together the tamari and agave syrup. Add the ginger, shallot and garlic. Lastly add the 'chicken' and mix well. Leave to rest for 10 minutes. Heat the peanut oil in a wok and cook the marinated meat substitute for 5 minutes, then add 150 ml of water as well as the chilli paste. Reduce over a low heat. Garnish with chives and serve.

BEAN SATAY

- 100 g frozen green beans
- 1 tbsp rapeseed oil • 3 tbsp satay seasoning mix • 250 g 'beef' meat substitute • 2½ tsp grated frozen ginger • 50 g frozen onions • 1 tbsp tamari • 100 ml coconut milk

Cut the green beans into 3-cm pieces. Heat the oil with the satay seasoning mix in a wok. Add the meat substitute, ginger and onions and sauté over a high heat for 5 minutes. Deglaze with tamari. Add the green beans, mix and add the coconut milk. Simmer for 10 minutes over a low heat.

SAUTÉED 'CHICKEN' WITH OLIVES

- 50 g frozen onions • 1 tsp chopped frozen garlic • 1 tsp fennel seeds
- 1 sprig thyme • 2 tbsp olive oil
- 500 g 'chicken' meat substitute
- 4 tsp tomato purée • 50 g pitted green olives • 50 g pitted black olives • Generous pinch of fine salt
- ½ tsp Espelette pepper

In a large pot, sauté the onions, garlic, fennel seeds and thyme in oil. When the onions turn translucent, add the meat substitute and tomato purée. Cook over a medium heat for 5 minutes before adding the olives. Season with salt and add 100 ml cold water. Cover and simmer over a low heat for 15 minutes. Add the Espelette pepper.

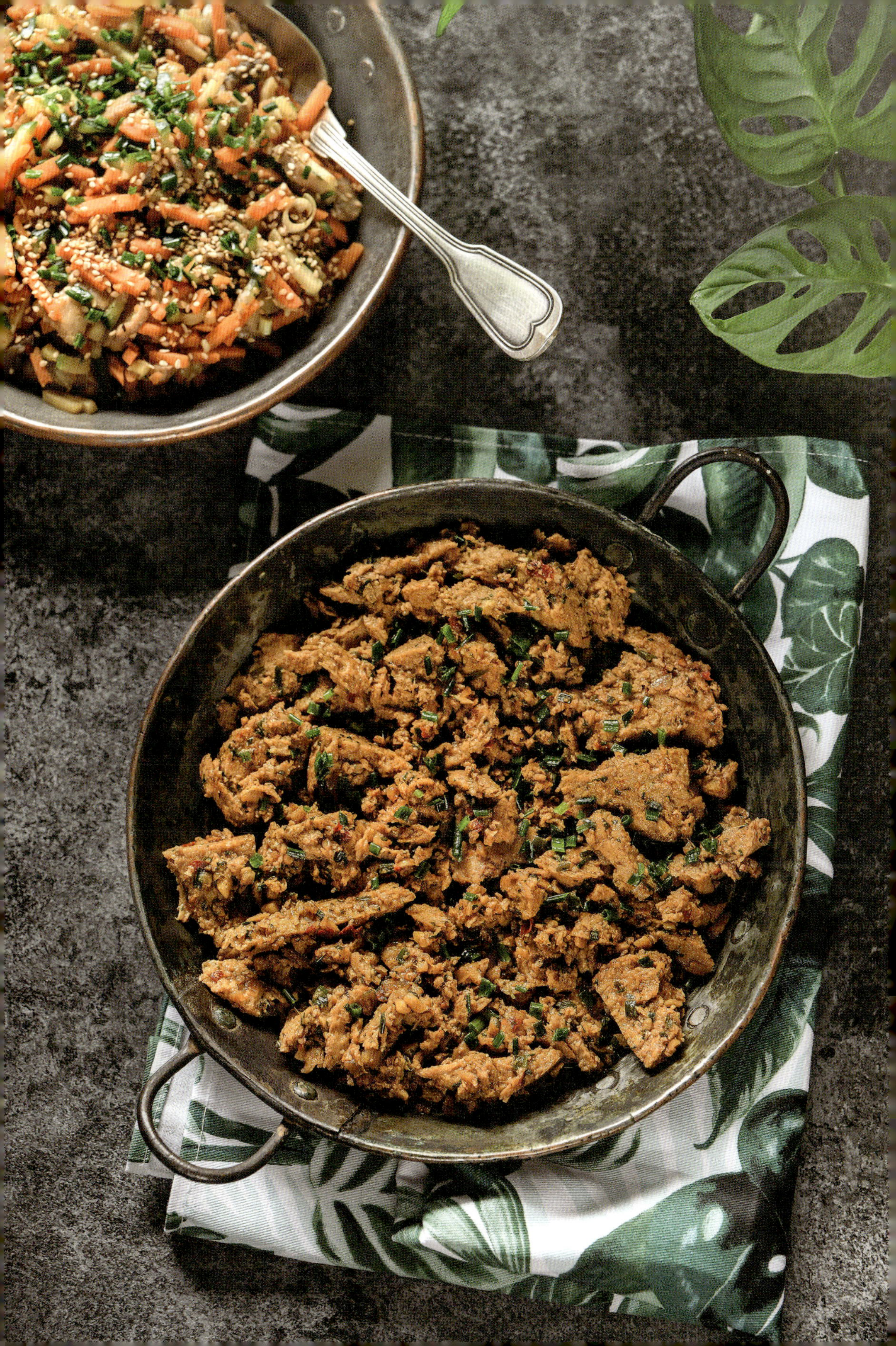

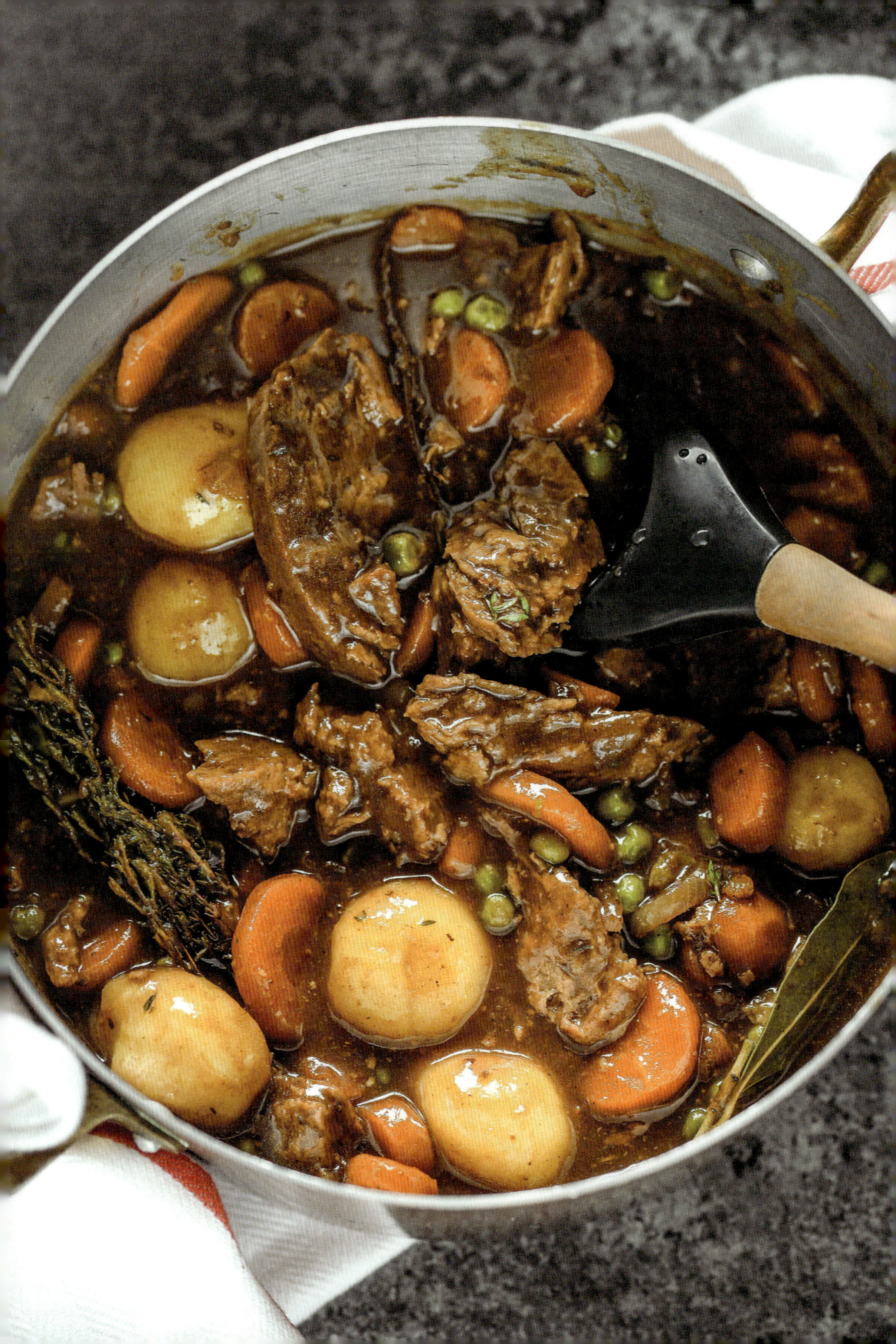

Meat substitutes

BEER STEW

- 2 tbsp oil • 1 sprig thyme
- 2 bay leaves • 300 g 'beef' meat substitute • 100 g frozen onions
- 100 g peas • 2½ tbsp plain flour
- 250 g cooked carrots • 250 g cooked potatoes • 500 ml stout beer
- 1 tsp salt • 2½ tbsp sugar • Pepper
- 4 tsp red miso

In a large pot, heat the oil with the thyme and bay leaves. Sauté the meat substitute over a high heat for 3 minutes. Add the onions and peas. Cook for around 3 minutes. Sprinkle with flour and add the carrots and potatoes straight away. Pour in the beer and lower the heat. Add the salt, sugar, pepper and red miso diluted in 4 tbsp of cold water. Mix, cover and cook for 15 minutes.

AFRICAN PEANUT STEW

- 500 g 'chicken' meat substitute
- 4 tbsp rapeseed oil • 100 g frozen onions • 150 g tomato passata
- 2 tsp chilli paste • 100 g peanut butter • 500 ml vegetable stock
- 300 g frozen sweet potatoes

In a large pot, sauté the meat substitute in hot oil for 3 minutes, then add the onions and cook for another 3 minutes. Add the tomato passata, chilli paste and peanut butter then mix. Cook for another 3 minutes before adding the stock and sweet potatoes. Cover and simmer for 15 minutes over a low heat.

FLAGEOLET BEAN CASSEROLE

- 2 tbsp chopped frozen shallots
- 50 g vegan margarine • 1 sprig thyme • 2 tsp chopped frozen garlic
- 250 g 'beef' meat substitute
- 500 g tinned flageolet beans
- 200 ml soya cream • ½ tsp fine salt
- 1 tsp black pepper

Sauté the shallots in margarine with thyme and garlic in a large pot. Add the meat substitute, mix and cook over a high heat for 3 minutes. Add the beans and 200 ml water. Cover and cook over a low heat for 15 minutes. Add the soya cream, then season with salt and pepper and serve.

Meat substitutes

PAD THAI

- 2 garlic cloves
- 1 tbsp ginger juice
- 2 tbsp kelpamare
- 4 tbsp tamari
- 4 tsp chilli paste
- 250 g 'chicken' meat substitute
- 200 g rice noodles
- 150 g fresh spring onions
- 100 g bean sprouts
- 2 tbsp lime juice
- 40 g peanuts
- 2 tbsp sunflower oil

Mix the crushed garlic, ginger juice, kelpamare, tamari and chilli paste in a large bowl. Add meat substitute and mix. Soak the rice noodles in boiling water for 4 minutes, then drain. Heat the oil in a wok and sauté the finely chopped white part of the spring onions. Then add the meat substitute and cook for 5 minutes. Add the bean sprouts and marinade. Add the noodles to the wok and mix everything together. Sauté over a high heat for 5 minutes. Finish with the lime juice, chopped peanuts and sliced green spring onions.

TARRAGON CASSEROLE

- 2 tbsp rapeseed oil
- 50 g frozen shallots
- 4 tsp chopped garlic
- 250 g 'chicken' meat substitute
- 2½ tbsp plain flour
- 500 ml vegetable stock
- 1½ tbsp frozen tarragon
- 4 tsp Pommery Meaux mustard
- 100 ml soya cream

Heat the oil in a large pot and add the shallots and sliced garlic. When lightly coloured, add the meat substitute. Cook for 3 minutes over a high heat to sauté the meat substitute pieces. Sprinkle with flour and add the hot stock. Mix well and add the tarragon and mustard. Cover and leave to simmer over a low heat for 20 minutes. Add the soya cream, mix and turn off the heat. Serve with rice or potatoes.

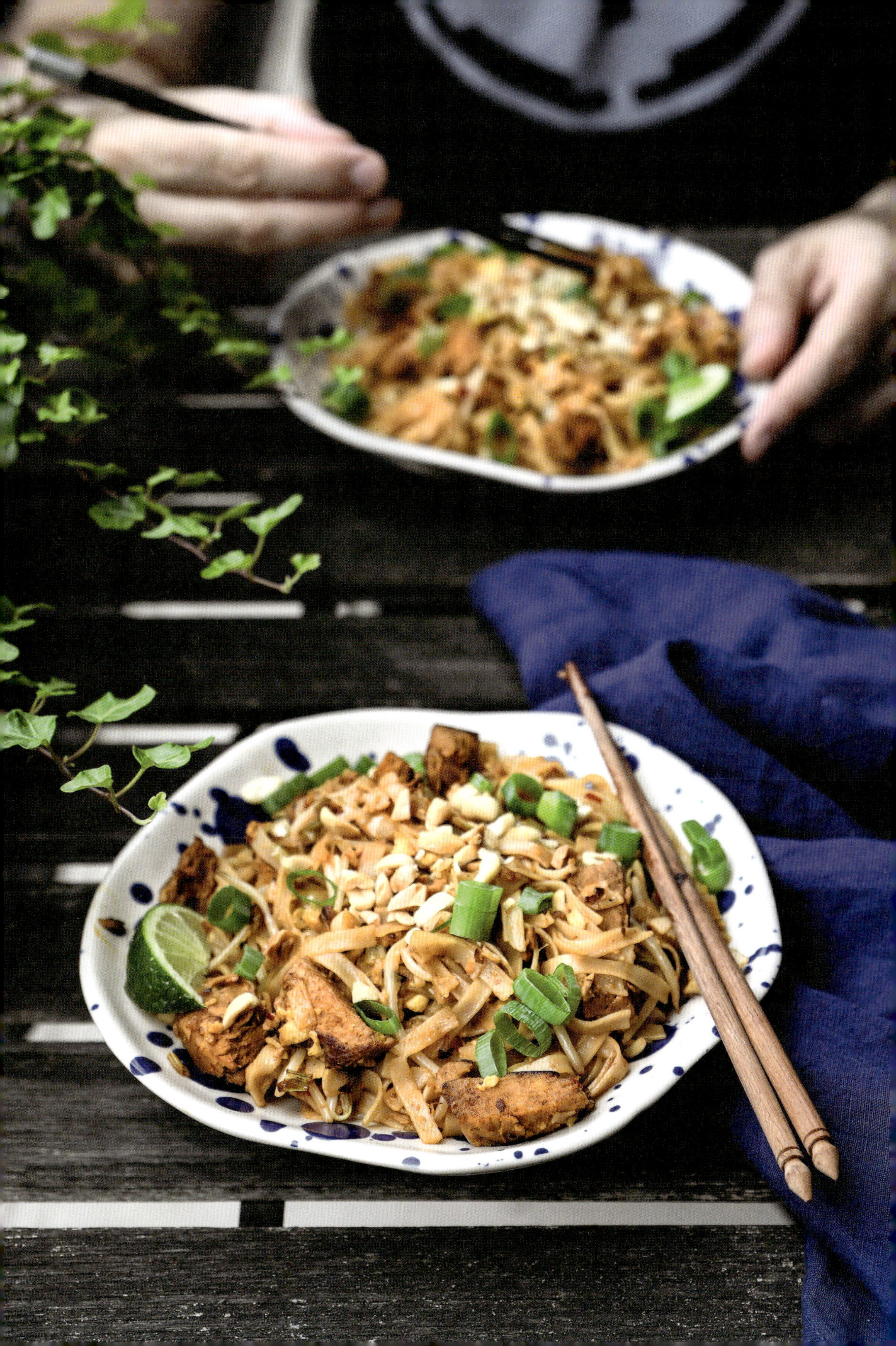

Vegan Steak

Circular in shape, this type of meat substitute is perfect for making burgers! There are classic versions that look like burger patties, but also thicker versions with different spices, herbs and vegetables. Made from seitan or even tofu, vegan steak is a convenient ingredient to cook that allows you to make tasty recipes. See for yourself!

JÄGERBURGER

- 300 g frozen onions
- 2 tbsp oil
- 4 tbsp Jägermeister
- 200 g avocado
- 4 tsp tomato ketchup
- 4 vegan steaks (300 g)
- 4 burger buns
- 20 g rocket leaves
- 8 slices vegan cheddar cheese (80 g)

Sauté the onions in oil in a pan. When they turn translucent, add the Jägermeister and reduce over a low heat for 5 minutes. Mash the avocado and mix with the ketchup. Fry the steaks over a medium heat and toast the burger buns.

Assemble as follows: bottom bun, rocket, steak, slice of cheese (warmed in the frying pan for 5 seconds), onion confit, avocado cream and top bun.

'STEAK' WITH MASH

- 2 tbsp tomato ketchup
- 5 tsp olive oil
- 2 tsp tamari
- 2 tsp Worcestershire sauce
- 400 g frozen mashed potatoes
- 4 tsp wholegrain mustard
- 3 tbsp chopped frozen parsley
- 1 tbsp malted yeast
- ¼ tsp grated nutmeg
- Heaped ¼ tsp fine salt
- ½ tsp black pepper
- 4 vegan steaks (300 g)

Mix the ketchup, 2 tsp of olive oil, tamari, Worcestershire sauce and 1 tbsp of cold water in a bowl, set aside. Defrost the mashed potato in a pan. Once hot, add 3 tsp of olive oil, mustard, parsley, malted yeast, grated nutmeg, salt and pepper. Mix well and divide in four. Cook the steaks for 2 minutes on each side in a frying pan without any oil. Slice the steak into four pieces. Interweave the pieces of one steak with mashed potatoes. Repeat the process with the other steaks and mashed potato. Serve with the sauce.

Vegan Steak

MITRAILETTE SANDWICH →

- 1 kg oven fries
- 300 g onions
- 2 tbsp olive oil
- 4 vegan steaks (300 g)
- 200 g iceberg lettuce
- 2 baguettes
- Andalusian sauce (see page 85)

Cook the fries on a baking tray in an oven at 180°C (gas mark 4) for 25 minutes. Cut the onions into thick slices (1.5 cm) and cook in a frying pan with hot oil for 4 minutes on each side. Fry the steaks for 3 minutes, then cut in two. Chop the lettuce. Cut each baguette in two then slice in half lengthways. Assembly: open the baguette, add some lettuce, onion rings, two steak slices, top with fries and cover in Andalusian sauce.

'STEAK' BAGEL

- 150 g fresh avocados
- 2 tsp lemon juice
- 4 vegan steaks (300 g)
- 4 sesame seed bagels
- 100 g vegan cream cheese
- 100 g baby spinach leaves
- 100 g ploughman's chutney
- 1 tbsp fried onions

Slice the avocado into 0.5-mm slices and cover in lemon juice. Cook the steaks for 2 minutes on each side in a frying pan without any oil. Halve the bagels and toast them. Spread cream cheese on both bagel halves. Assembly: place 25 g baby spinach leaves on the bottom bagel half, then the steak. Add 25 g chutney and avocado slices. Scatter with fried onions and close with the top half of the bagel.

PISTACHIO-CRUSTED 'STEAK'

- 4 vegan steaks (300 g)
- 4 tsp Dijon mustard
- 50 g vegan margarine
- 100 g plain flour
- 100 g pistachio kernels
- Generous pinch of fine salt
- 3 garlic cloves

Preheat the oven to 180°C (gas mark 4). Brush the steaks with mustard and place on a baking tray. Use a fork to mix the cold margarine with the flour in a bowl. Chop the pistachios and add to the bowl. Add the salt, crushed garlic and mix everything together. Spread a layer of mixture on the steaks and bake for 25 minutes.

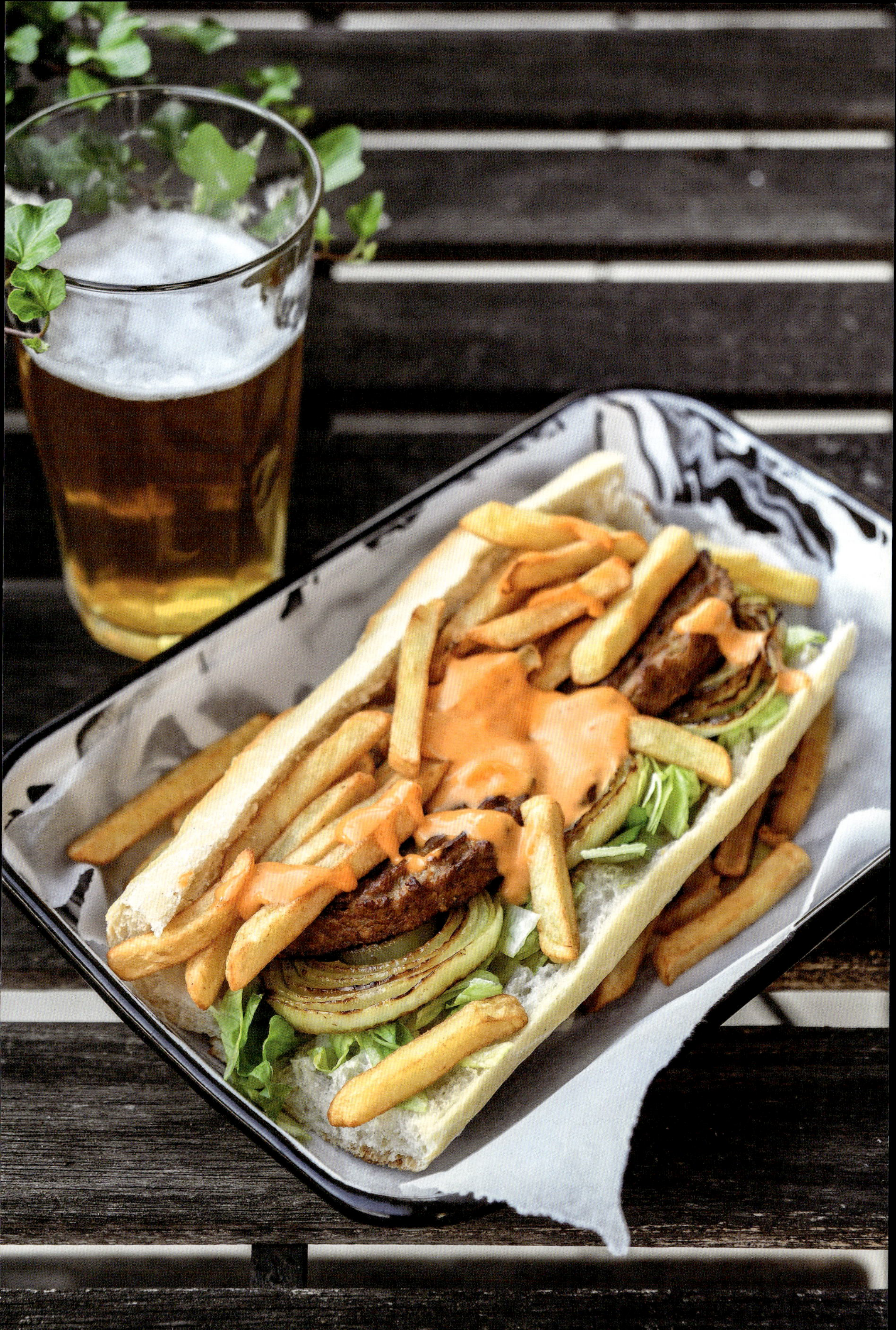

Vegan Steak

ROSSINI →

- 120 ml port • 4 tsp red miso • 1 tbsp cornflour • 2 tbsp vegan margarine
- 4 slices wholemeal bread • 4 vegan steaks (300 g) • 125 g vegan truffle pâté
- Black pepper

Simmer half the port in a small pan with the red miso that has been diluted in 4 tbsp of cold water. When the liquid is hot, add the cornflour diluted in 100 ml cold water. Mix with a whisk and heat until it thickens. Turn off the heat and add the margarine. Whisk, then pass through a conical sieve. Use a biscuit cutter to cut discs out of the bread the same diameter as the steaks. Spread margarine on both sides and toast in a hot frying pan. Set aside on a wire rack. Melt a little margarine in a frying pan and cook the steaks for 1 minute on each side.

Add 2 tbsp of port and let evaporate. Turn the steaks, add another 2 tbsp of port and turn off the heat. Place the steaks on the bread discs.

Use two tablespoons to make 4 dumplings of pâté and place on top of the steaks. Season generously with pepper. Transfer to a plate and add the sauce.

'STEAK' PIE

- 4 vegan steaks (300 g) • 1 tbsp vegan margarine • 250 g button mushrooms
- 2 tbsp tamari • 4 tsp balsamic vinegar • 4 tsp maple syrup • 50 g frozen shallots
- 2 tsp chopped garlic • 1 tbsp olive oil • 1 tbsp white wine • 4 tbsp chopped chives • 2 shortcrust vegan pastry rounds

In a hot frying pan, sauté the steaks in margarine. Brown well on each side then set aside. Slice the mushrooms. Mix together the tamari, vinegar and maple syrup in a bowl. Sauté the shallots and garlic in a hot frying pan with olive oil. Once soft, add the mushrooms and mix. Cook together for 5 minutes then deglaze with the tamari/vinegar/maple syrup. Reduce over a medium heat. Add the white wine and reduce slightly. Add the chives, mix and turn off the heat. Cut out four circles from the pastry. They should be larger than the steaks. Repeat with the rest of the pastry to make 8 circles. Place on a baking tray as follows: a circle of dough, add a bed of mushrooms and place the steak on top. Cover with a circle of dough, seal the edges with a tooth-pick by making small holes and bake in an oven at 180°C (gas mark 4) for 30 to 45 minutes. Serve immediately with, for example, a green salad.

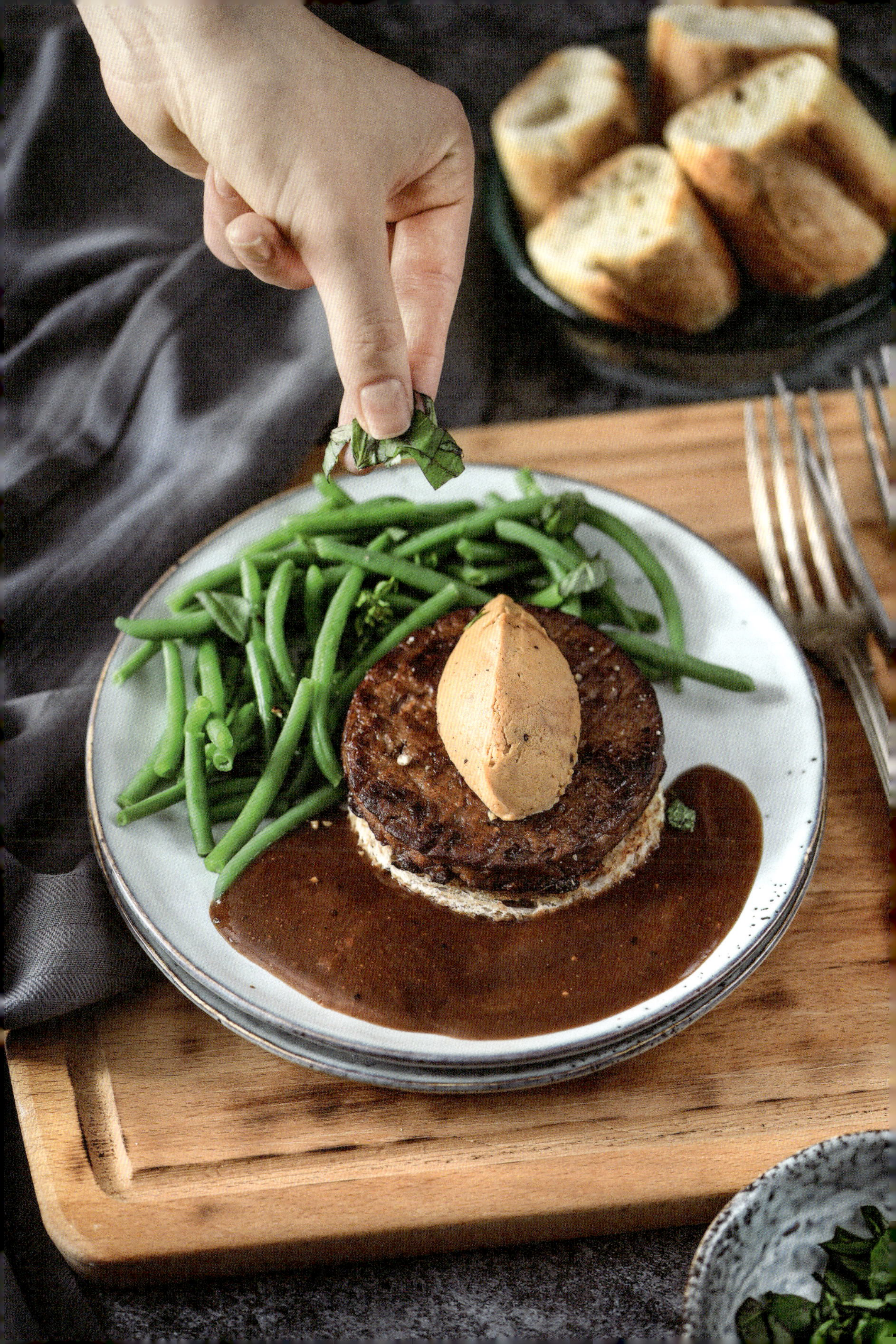

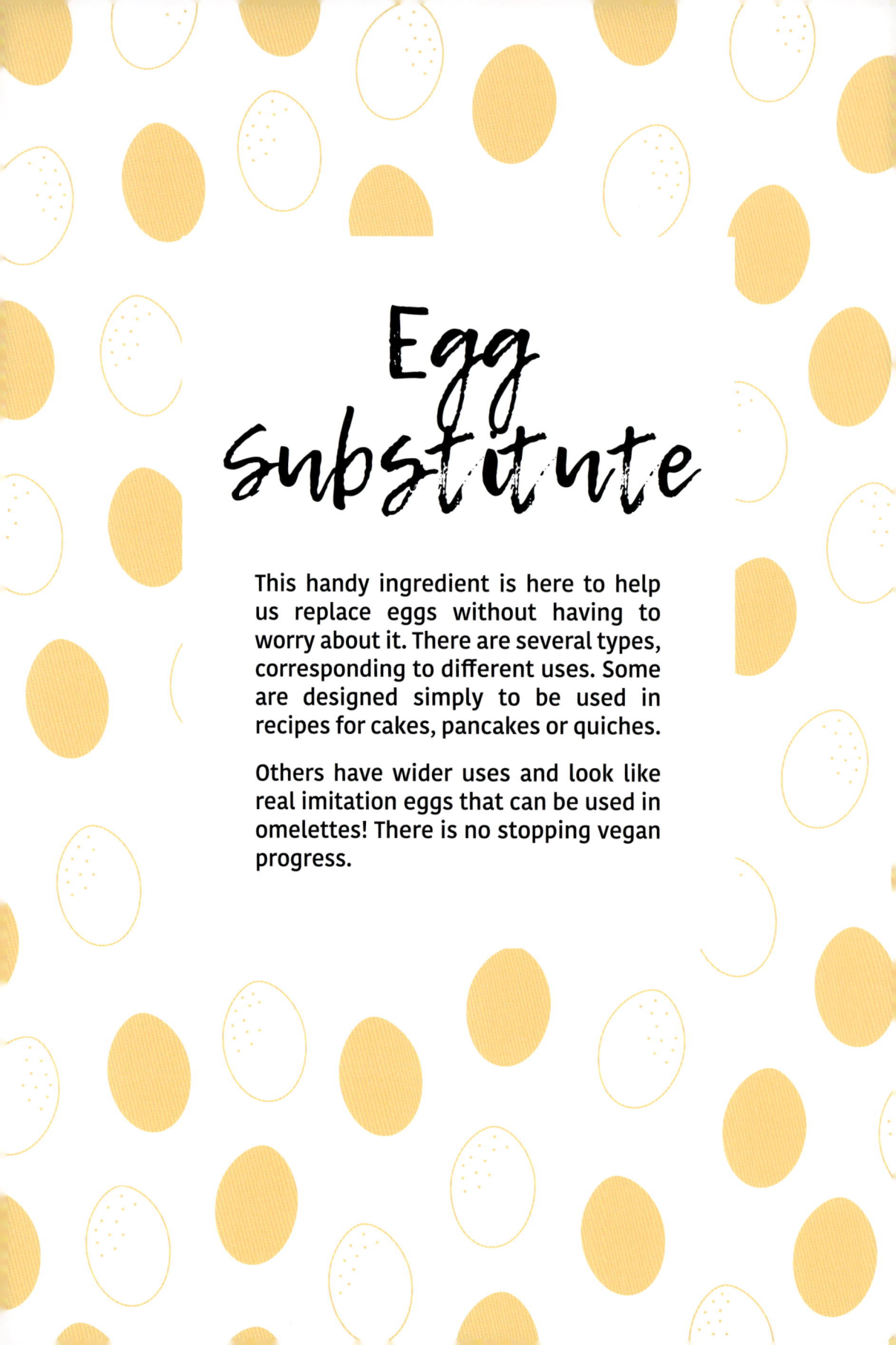

Egg Substitute

This handy ingredient is here to help us replace eggs without having to worry about it. There are several types, corresponding to different uses. Some are designed simply to be used in recipes for cakes, pancakes or quiches.

Others have wider uses and look like real imitation eggs that can be used in omelettes! There is no stopping vegan progress.

Egg substitute

MUSHROOM OMELETTE

- 50 g egg substitute (VeganEgg)
- 550 ml ice water
- Heaped ½ tsp Kala namak (black salt)
- 300 g frozen mixed mushrooms
- 2 tsp vegan margarine
- 2 tbsp chopped chives
- Black pepper

In a bowl, dilute the egg substitute powder with ice water. Add the Kala namak salt and mix well with a whisk. Leave to rest. Sauté the frozen mushrooms in a hot frying pan for 10 minutes and set aside. Melt the margarine in a frying pan and wait until it starts to foam. Pour in the egg mixture and cook over a high heat for 2 minutes. Add the mushrooms and chives, then cover and cook over a medium heat for around 6 minutes. The surface should glossy and slightly creamy. Season with pepper according to taste. Cover and leave to rest for 2 minutes off the heat before serving.

TORTILLA

- 50 g egg substitute (VeganEgg)
- 550 ml ice water
- 1 tsp Kala namak (black salt)
- 4 tbsp olive oil
- 100 g frozen onions
- 500 g pre-cooked sliced potatoes

In a bowl, dilute the egg substitute powder with ice water. Add the Kala namak salt and mix well with a whisk. Leave to rest. Heat oil in a large frying pan and sauté the onions and potatoes for 15 minutes, then add to the bowl with the egg substitute. Mix gently so that the potatoes don't break. Pour everything back into the hot pan and cook for around 7 minutes. Tilt the pan and slide the tortilla onto a large plate. Place the frying pan over the plate, turn quickly and cook the other side for 7 minutes.

Egg Substitute

FRITTATA

- 50 g egg substitute (VeganEgg)
- 550 ml ice water
- Heaped ½ tsp Kala namak (black salt) • 10 g frozen basil
- 100 g frozen courgettes
- 100 g frozen peppers
- 2 tbsp olive oil
- 60 g grated vegan cheese

In a bowl, dilute the egg substitute powder with ice water. Add the Kala namak salt and mix well with a whisk. Add the chopped basil. Leave to rest. Sweat the courgettes and peppers for 5 minutes in a large frying pan. Drizzle with olive oil and mix. Cook for 2 minutes. Pour in the egg mixture and cook over a high heat for 4 minutes. Cover with grated cheese and place the pan under the grill for 5 minutes.

JERUSALEM ARTICHOKE & TRUFFLE OIL CAKE

- 400 g Jerusalem artichokes (peeled)
- 1 shallot
- Olive oil
- Salt
- Pepper
- 1 tbsp balsamic vinegar
- 250 g plain flour
- 40 g maize flour
- 35 g egg substitute (Egg Replacer)
- 1½ tbsp baking powder
- 2 tbsp malted yeast
- 1 tbsp caster sugar
- Fine salt
- Pepper
- 350 ml soya milk
- 1 tbsp tamari
- 4 tsp truffle oil

Peel the Jerusalem artichokes and cut into small pieces. Finely chop the shallot.

Sauté the shallot with 1 tbsp of olive oil in a large pot. Add the diced Jerusalem artichokes, season with salt and pepper, then cover and cook for 10 minutes. Deglaze with balsamic vinegar and cook uncovered for a few minutes. Preheat the oven to 180 °C (gas mark 4).

In a large bowl, mix the dry ingredients together: the flours, egg substitute, baking powder, malted yeast, sugar, salt and pepper.

Mix the liquid ingredients together in another bowl. Combine the two mixtures together to make the cake batter. Add the cooked Jerusalem artichokes and mix once more. Line a 23-cm cake tin. Pour the batter into the tin and bake for 1 hour. After 50 minutes, use a knife to check that it is cooked. Allow to cool before turning out.

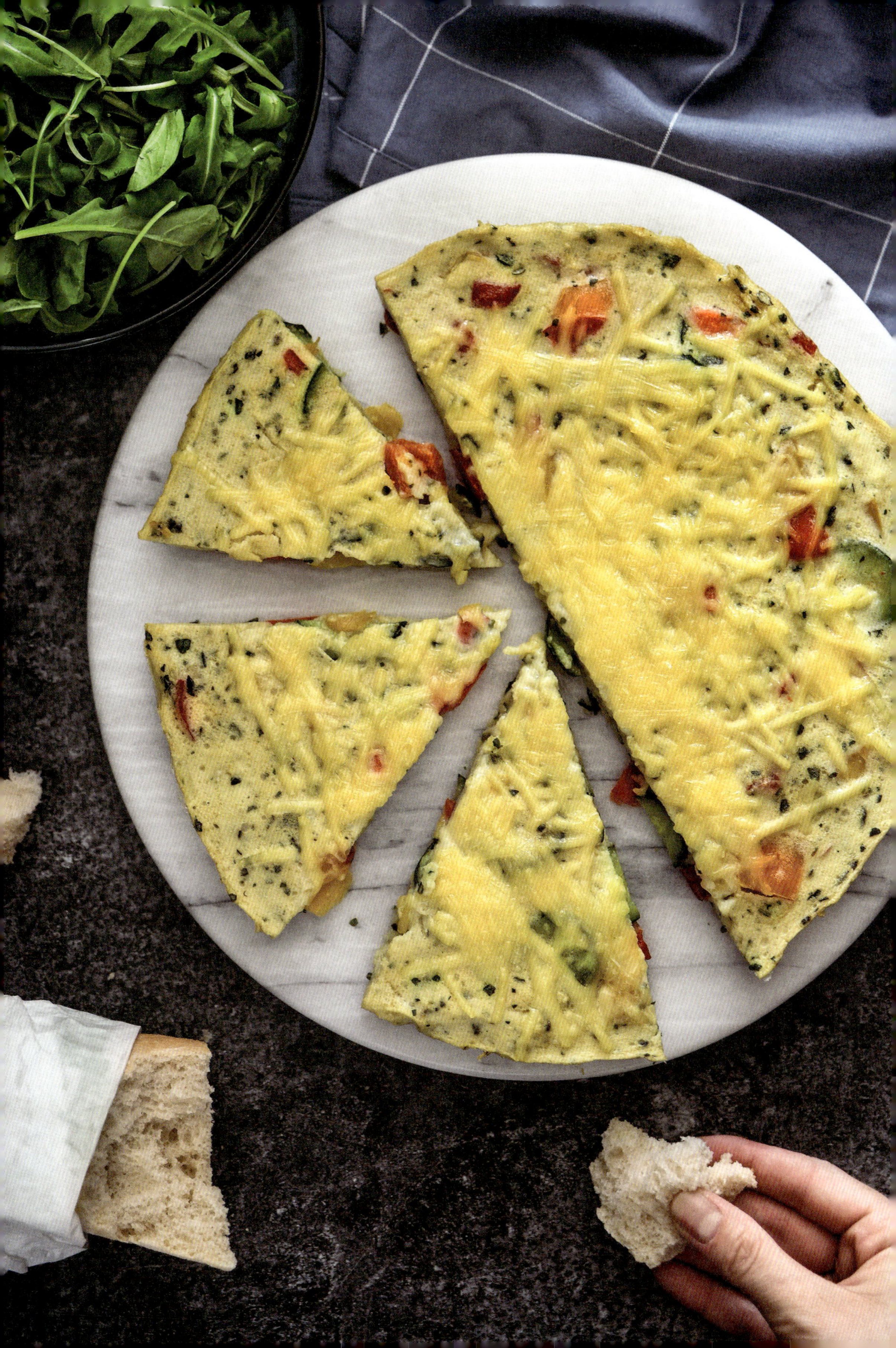

Egg Substitute

COINTREAU FRENCH TOAST

- 2 tbsp egg substitute (VeganEgg)
- 100 ml vanilla soya milk
- 3 tbsp Cointreau
- 1½ tbsp caster sugar
- 1 stale baguette

Dilute the egg substitute in 5 tbsp of cold water, mix well with a whisk then add the milk, Cointreau and sugar and mix again. Slice the bread into 2-cm thick slices and soak in the liquid for several minutes. Cook each side in a hot pan greased with oil. Serve straight away with fresh fruit and agave or maple syrup.

FU-YUNG

- 15 g dried shiitake mushrooms
- 4 tbsp egg substitute (VeganEgg)
- 345 ml ice water
- Heaped ¼ tsp Kala namak (black salt)
- 50 g bean sprouts
- 40 g spring onions
- 1 tbsp toasted sesame oil
- Heaped ¼ tsp fine salt
- 1 tomato, diced

Rehydrate the mushroom in hot water for 30 minutes, then drain. In a bowl, dilute the egg substitute powder with ice water. Add the Kala namak salt and mix well with a whisk. Leave to rest. Sauté the bean sprouts, mushrooms and finely chopped spring onions in a wok with sesame oil. Season with salt and add the diced tomato. Pour in the egg mixture and cook over a high heat for 4 minutes. Serve hot.

MATCHA PANCAKES

- 2 tbsp egg substitute (Egg Replacer)
- 300 ml vanilla soya milk
- 4 tbsp olive oil
- 250 g plain flour
- 50 g caster sugar
- 3½ tsp matcha powder
- 2½ tsp baking powder
- 2 pinches of salt

Mix the egg substitute with 6 tbsp of cold water, then add the milk, oil and mix well. Set aside. Combine the flour, sugar, matcha, baking powder, and salt in a mixing bowl. Combine the two mixtures and mix with a whisk. Pour a ladle of batter into a hot frying pan greased with oil and cook for 2 to 3 minutes on each side. Repeat with the remaining batter and serve with fresh seasonal fruit and maple syrup. You can also add chocolate chips during cooking.

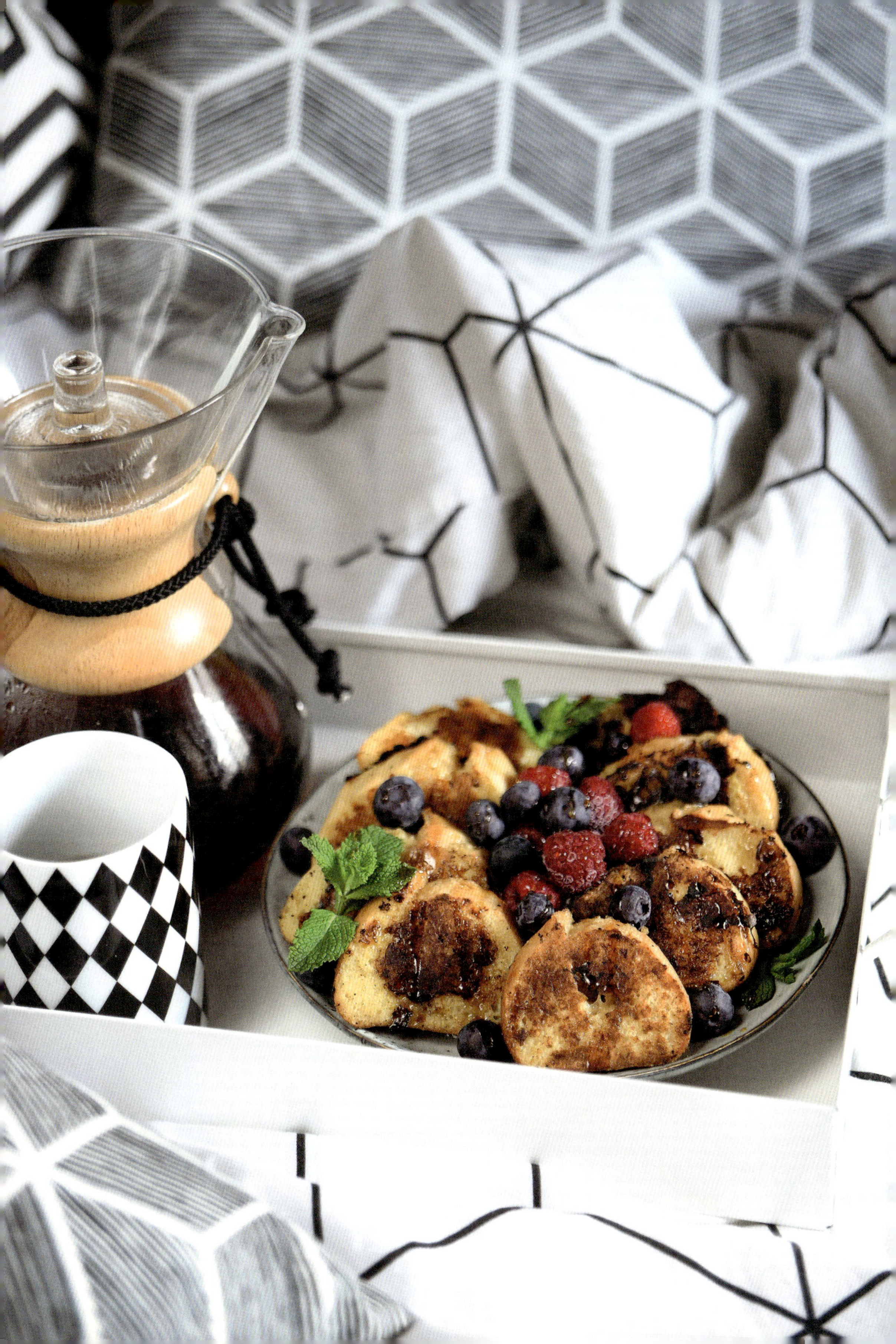

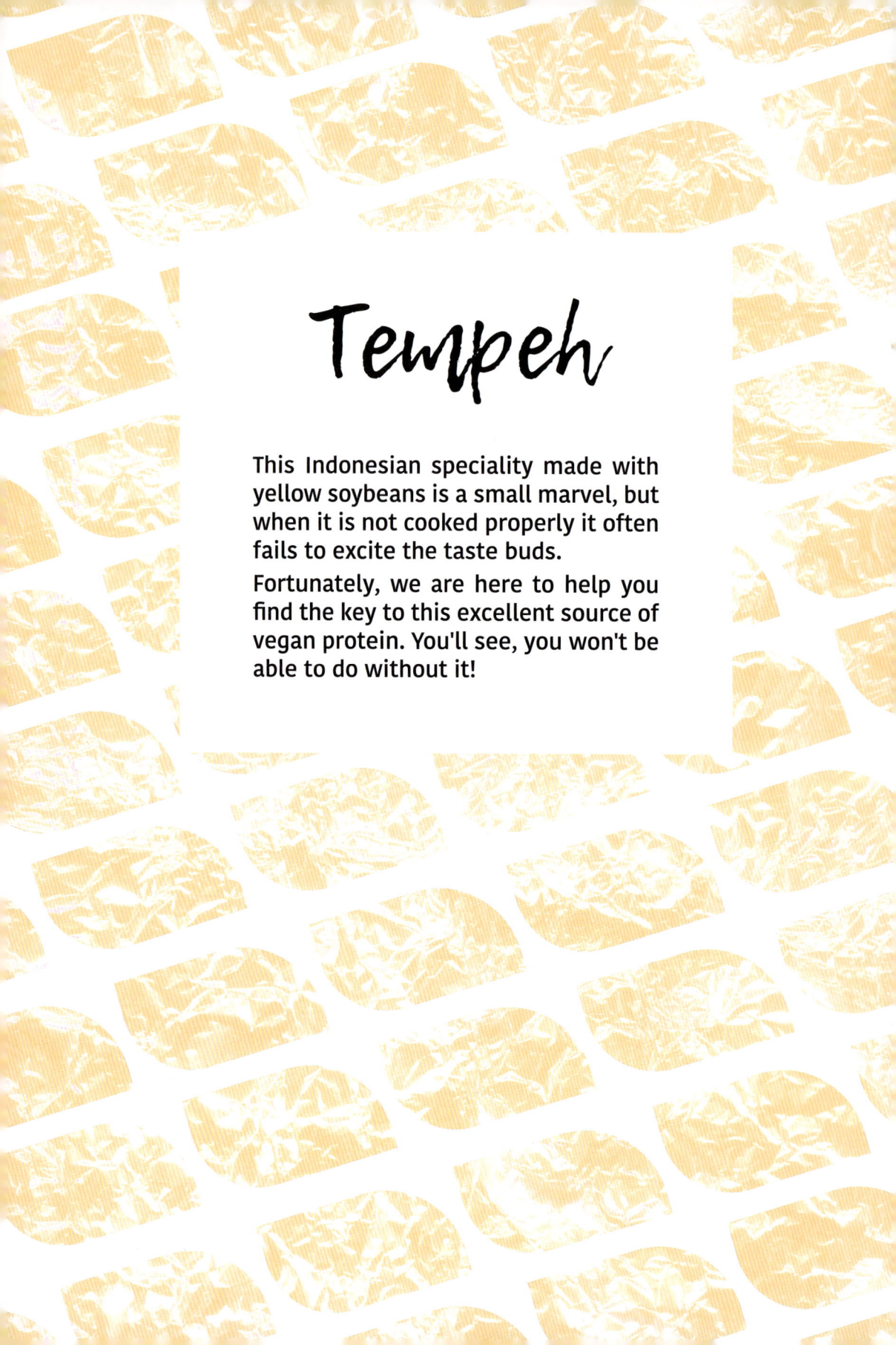

Tempeh

This Indonesian speciality made with yellow soybeans is a small marvel, but when it is not cooked properly it often fails to excite the taste buds.

Fortunately, we are here to help you find the key to this excellent source of vegan protein. You'll see, you won't be able to do without it!

SPRING ROLLS

- 100 g tempeh
- Toasted sesame oil
- Tamari
- 1 medium ripe avocado
- 3 sun-dried tomatoes in oil
- 2 tsp lemon juice
- Salt
- Pepper
- 1 carrot
- 1 small courgette
- ½ apple
- 4 rice paper sheets (28 cm diameter)
- Rocket leaves
- Bean sprouts (of your choice)

Cut the tempeh into batons and sauté in a hot frying pan with toasted sesame oil. Deglaze with a drizzle of tamari. Blend the avocado flesh with the sun-dried tomatoes and lemon juice to make a smooth cream, Season with salt and pepper. Slice the carrot, courgette and half an apple into thin batons. Soak the rice paper in cold water for 30 to 40 seconds. Drain quickly and place on a chopping board. Place a little avocado cream in the centre, some rocket, bean sprouts and 1 to 2 slices of tempeh. Place 3 to 4 carrot, courgette and apple batons on top. Fold over the bottom edge, then the sides and roll tightly. Repeat with the rest of the rice paper sheets. Serve with a dipping sauce made from tamari and wasabi.

TEMPEH TANDOORI

- 250 g smoked tempeh
- 200 g natural soya yogurt
- 1 tbsp tandoori seasoning mix
- 1½ tsp sweet paprika
- Heaped ¼ tsp salt
- 20 g fresh ginger

Preheat the oven to 180ºC (gas mark 4) for 15 minutes. Slice the tempeh lengthways into 6 pieces. Set aside. Mix the soya yogurt, tandoori seasoning, paprika and salt in a bowl. Finely grate the ginger and add the yogurt. Coat the tempeh in the yogurt sauce then place on a baking tray lined with baking parchment. Place on the middle shelf of the oven and bake for 15 minutes.

Tempeh

CAULIFLOWER SOUP →

- 1 kg frozen cauliflower
- 2 tsp chopped frozen garlic
- 1.5 litres vegetable stock
- 2 bay leaves
- 200 g tempeh
- 2 tbsp plain flour
- 1½ tsp madras curry powder
- ½ tsp fine salt
- Black pepper
- Fresh coriander

Cook the cauliflower and garlic in a large pot with the vegetable stock and bay leaves. Bring to the boil and cook for 15 minutes. Cut the tempeh into small pieces. Mix the flour with the curry powder and salt in a large bowl. Add 3 tbsp of cold water. Add the tempeh to the batter and mix. Place on a baking tray and bake in the oven at 180°C (gas mark 4) for 20 minutes. Transfer the cooked cauliflower to a blender, then cover with 1 litre of cooking liquid and blend. Serve the soup in bowls, season with black pepper, chopped coriander and the tempeh pieces.

TEMPEH STEW

- 400 g tempeh
- Olive oil
- 200 g frozen carrots
- 200 g frozen turnips
- 250 g pre-cooked potatoes
- 100 g frozen onions
- Salt
- 250 ml white wine
- 100 g tomato coulis
- Pepper
- ½ tsp thyme
- 2 tsp sweet paprika

Cut the tempeh into six pieces, then set aside. Add a splash of olive oil to a large pot and sauté the carrots and turnip over a high heat for 10 minutes. Add the potatoes, onions and a large pinch of salt. Stir gently. Add the white wine and then add the tomato coulis. Season with pepper, add the thyme and paprika. Cover and simmer over a low heat for 10 minutes. Add the tempeh and cook for 10 minutes. Serve.

SMOKY BURGER PATTY

- 300 g tempeh
- 2 tsp liquid smoke
- 2 tsp oil
- 2 tbsp tomato ketchup
- 1 tsp smoked paprika
- 1 tbsp fresh shallots
- 1 tsp chopped fresh garlic
- 2 tbsp chopped fresh chives

Break up the tempeh in a bowl. Add the liquid smoke, oil and ketchup. Using a fork, mix and crush coarsely. Add the smoked paprika, chopped shallots, crushed garlic and chopped chives. Mix again and compact the mixture with your hands. Divide the mixture into four discs around 1 cm thick. Refrigerate for 20 minutes. Fry in a frying pan with a little oil for 1 minute on each side. Serve in a burger bun.

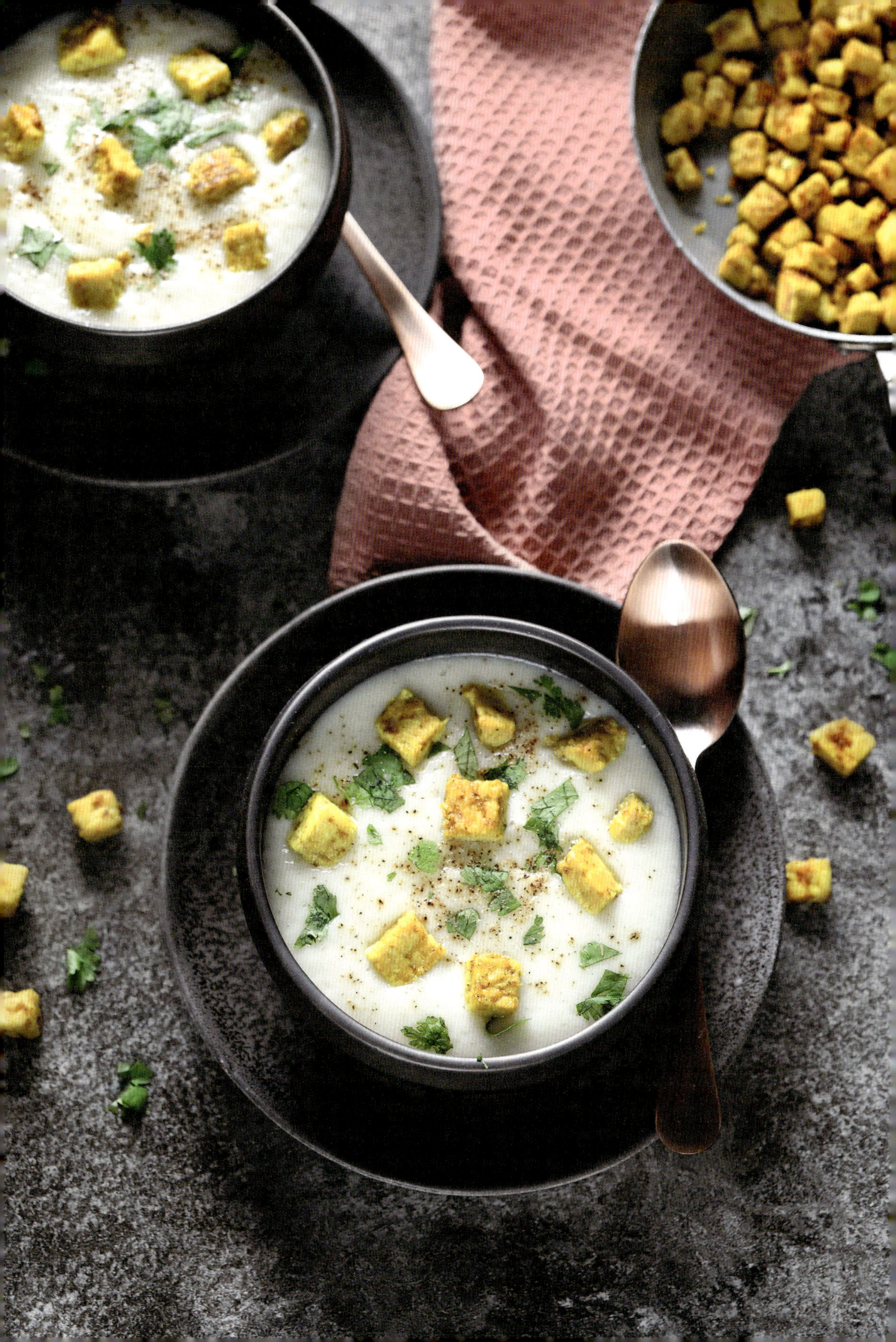

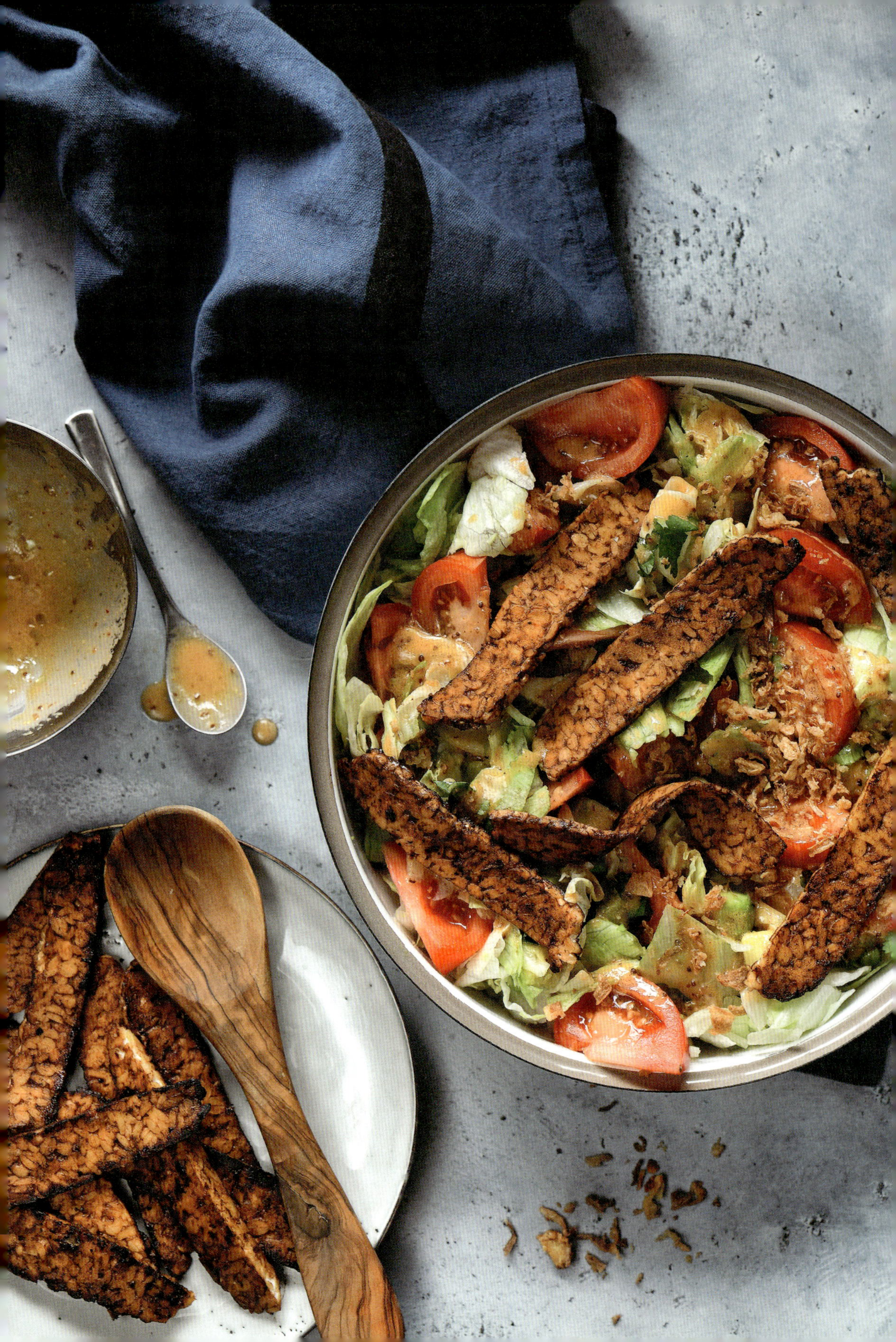

'BACON' SALAD

- 1 tbsp tomato ketchup
- 1 tsp tamari
- 1 tbsp liquid smoke
- ½ tsp garlic powder
- 2 tsp rapeseed oil
- 200 g tempeh
- 1 tbsp apple cider vinegar
- 2 tsp Dijon mustard
- Salt
- ½ tsp Espelette pepper
- 2 tbsp mayonnaise
- 2 tbsp olive oil
- 150 g avocado
- 300 g fresh tomatoes
- 300 g iceberg lettuce
- 1 tbsp fried onions

Mix the ketchup with the tamari, liquid smoke and garlic powder in a large bowl. Add a splash of rapeseed oil and whisk with a fork. Slice the tempeh into 5-mm thick strips and brush marinade on both sides. Leave to rest for 15 minutes. Make the vinaigrette by mixing the apple cider vinegar, mustard, salt, Espelette pepper, mayonnaise and olive oil. Dice the avocados, quarter the tomatoes and separate the lettuce leaves. Mix the vegetables, vinaigrette and fried onions in a large salad bowl. Sauté the marinated tempeh in a hot frying pan without any oil. Place on top of the salad.

ITALIAN-STYLE BURGER

- 200 g frozen onions
- Olive oil
- Salt
- 100 ml white wine
- 4 tbsp chopped frozen basil
- 100 g artichokes in oil
- 100 g sun-dried tomatoes in oil
- 2 tbsp balsamic vinegar
- ¾ tsp Espelette pepper
- 4 tbsp agave syrup
- 2 tbsp tamari
- 2 tbsp rum
- 4 tempeh blocks (400 g)
- 4 burger buns

Brown the onions in a hot frying pan with a drizzle of olive oil. When browned season lightly with salt, deglaze with white wine and add the basil. Drain the artichokes and cut into small pieces, set aside. Blend the sun-dried tomatoes (drain the oil) with the balsamic vinegar, Espelette pepper and 2 tbsp of agave syrup to make a thin paste. Mix the tamari, rum and 2 tbsp of agave syrup in a ramekin. Heat a splash of olive oil in a frying pan and brown the blocks of tempeh on each side. Once cooked, deglaze with tamari mixture. Add gradually so that the tempeh is well coated. Repeat until the liquid fully evaporates. Halve the burger buns and heat in a toaster. For the assembly: on the bottom bun, place a bed of onions with basil, place the tempeh on top and then add the sliced artichoke. Add a layer of sun-dried tomato 'ketchup' on the inside of the top bun. Close the burger and press gently.

TEMPEH SAUTÉED WITH ONIONS

- 1 tbsp olive oil
- 200 g tempeh
- 300 g frozen onions
- 4 tsp sugar
- 2 tbsp tamari
- 4 tbsp white wine
- 2 tbsp chopped fresh chives

In a wok, heat the olive oil and sauté the tempeh cut into large pieces for 5 minutes. Set aside. Add the onions to the wok and cook over a high heat until they caramelise. Add the sugar, tempeh and tamari and mix. Cook for 3 minutes and add the white wine. Mix and reduce until the liquid evaporates. Scatter with chopped chives and serve.

SPICY TEMPEH BALLS

- 200 g tempeh
- 1½ tsp smoked paprika
- 1 tsp dried oregano
- 1 tbsp olive oil
- 2 tsp chopped frozen garlic
- 20 g frozen shallots
- Fine salt
- Black pepper
- 60 g tahini
- 1 tbsp sesame seeds
- 2 tbsp malted yeast

Chop the tempeh in a food processor. Add the smoked paprika, oregano, olive oil, garlic and shallots. Season with salt and pepper. Chop again to make a thick paste. Roll in the palm of your hands to make equal-sized balls. Mix the tahini with 2 tbsp of cold water and a pinch of fine salt in a bowl. In a separate bowl, mix the sesame seeds and malted yeast. Dip the balls in the tahini cream, then in the bowl of sesame seeds to give them an even coating. Cook in a hot frying pan with a splash of olive oil. The balls should be well browned.

TEMPEH CHEESE

- 200 g tempeh
- 40 g white miso
- 1 tbsp apple cider vinegar
- ½ tsp fine salt
- 1 tsp garlic powder
- 6 tbsp malted yeast
- 4 tsp coconut oil

Chop the tempeh in a food processor. Add the white miso, cider vinegar, salt and garlic powder. Blend again to make a smooth paste. Pass the malted yeast through a sieve to obtain a very fine powder. Add the yeast powder to the food processor as well as the coconut oil. Blend again. Shape into the desired form using a mould. Refrigerate for at least 12 hours before turning out.

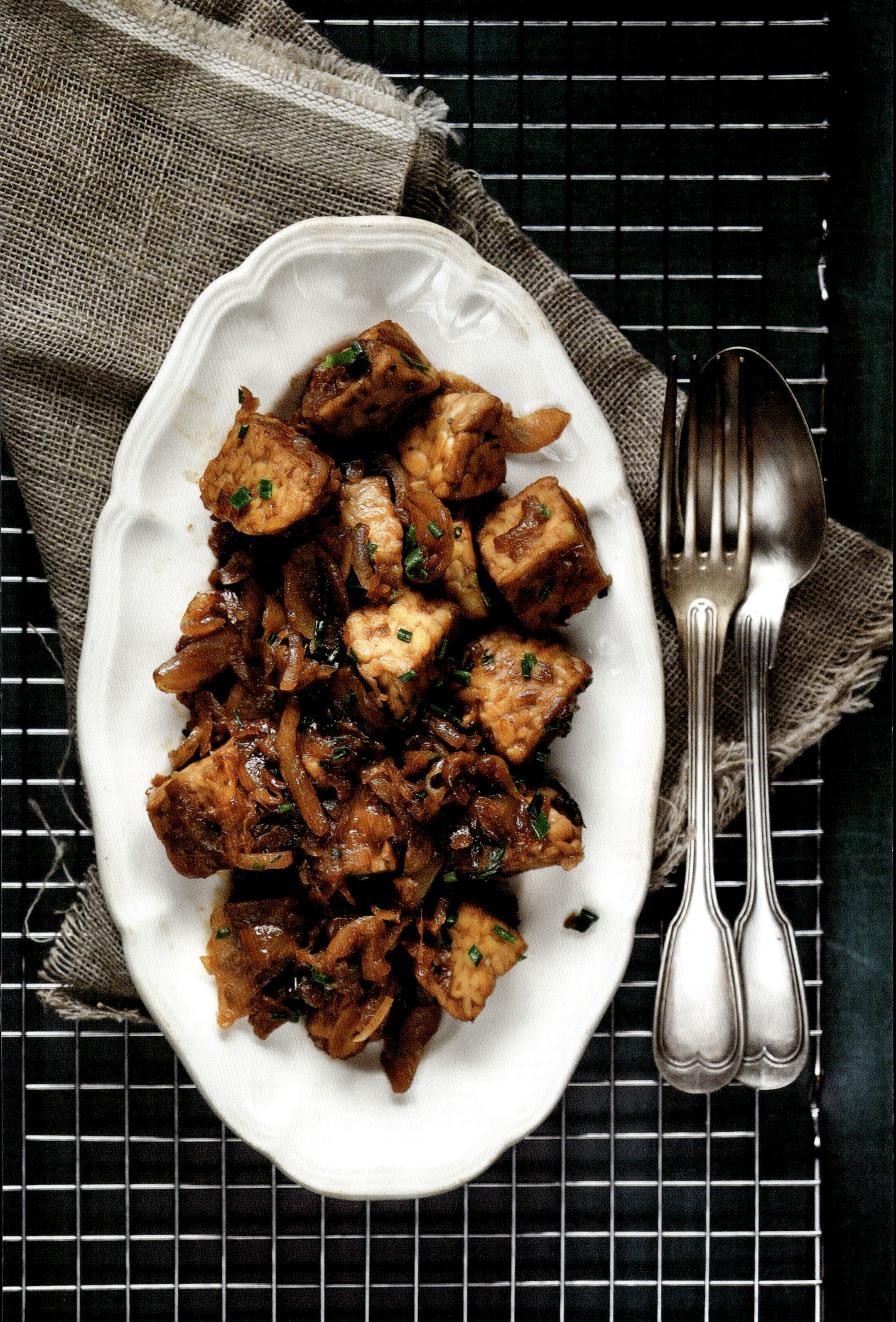

Smoked Tofu

This is certainly the best way to introduce someone to tofu, and even make them appreciate it. Far from the natural blandness of plain tofu, smoked tofu has character! Often smoked with beech wood, this tofu has salty notes and is the perfect replacement for bacon. But not just that...

Smoked Tofu

HAWAIIAN SALAD

- 250 g smoked tofu
- 100 g fresh pineapple
- 6 medium carrots
- Lemon juice
- 4 tbsp soya cream
- 1 tbsp tamari
- 2 tsp chopped fresh coriander
- ½ tsp ground ginger
- 1 tsp curry powder
- Salt
- Black pepper

Dice the smoked tofu and pineapple. Grate the carrots into a salad bowl and add a little lemon juice. Mix everything together. To make the sauce, mix the soya cream with the tamari, coriander, ginger and curry powder in a bowl, season with salt and pepper. Add to the carrots/tofu/pineapple, mix and serve.

CARROT & CUMIN SOUP

- 1 tbsp olive oil
- 1 tsp cumin seeds
- 1 tsp coriander seeds
- 1 kg frozen carrots
- 2 tsp chopped frozen garlic
- 1.5 litres vegetable stock
- 1 tbsp Worcestershire sauce
- 200 g smoked tofu
- 2½ tbsp chervil
- ½ tsp Espelette pepper

In a large pan, heat the oil with the coarsely crushed cumin and coriander seeds. Add the carrots and garlic, sauté for 5 minutes. Add the stock and cook over a medium heat for 15 minutes. Transfer the cooked carrots to a blender, cover with around 1 litre of cooking liquid (including the spices), add the Worcestershire sauce and blend. Cut the smoked tofu into pieces and sauté in a frying pan. Add to the soup and mix. Scatter with chervil leaves and Espelette pepper.

Smoked Tofu

TERRINE

- 200 g smoked tofu
- 1 tbsp malted yeast
- 50 g vegan margarine
- 150 g frozen onions
- ½ tsp fine salt
- ¾ tsp black pepper
- 1 tsp garam masala
- 3 tbsp white wine
- 200 ml vanilla soya milk
- 1 tsp agar-agar powder

Break up the tofu in a stick blender beaker, add the malted yeast and margarine. Sweat the onions in a pan until they are translucent, then add the salt, pepper and garam masala. Deglaze with white wine and leave to reduce for 2 minutes. Add the soya milk and bring to the boil. Add the agar-agar and mix with a whisk for 1 minute without stopping. Pour the hot liquid over the tofu and margarine. Blend until smooth. Pour the mixture into a mould, then leave to cool and refrigerate for 2 hours.

GREEN PEPPERCORN TOFU BURGER

- Sunflower oil
- 200 g frozen red onions
- Fine salt
- 4 tsp Calvados
- 200 g smoked tofu
- 2 tsp tamari
- 1½ tsp green peppercorns
- 4 tbsp malted yeast
- 8 cherry tomatoes
- 4 cornichons
- 4 burger buns
- 4 spinach leaves
- Tomato ketchup

Heat a little oil in a frying pan and sauté the onions. Once the onions start to soften, season with salt and deglaze with Calvados. Let the alcohol evaporate and set aside.

Crush the tofu, add the tamari, green peppercorns and malted yeast. Add half of the cooked onions and knead the mixture together. Shape into burgers that are 8 cm in diameter and 1 cm thick.

Heat 1 tsp of sunflower oil in a frying pan and cook the burgers for 2 minutes on each side over a medium heat. Heat the buns in a griddle pan. Slice the cherry tomatoes and cornichons. Assemble in the following order: bottom bun, ketchup, spinach leaf, cherry tomatoes, tofu burger, onions, cornichons, ketchup, top bun.

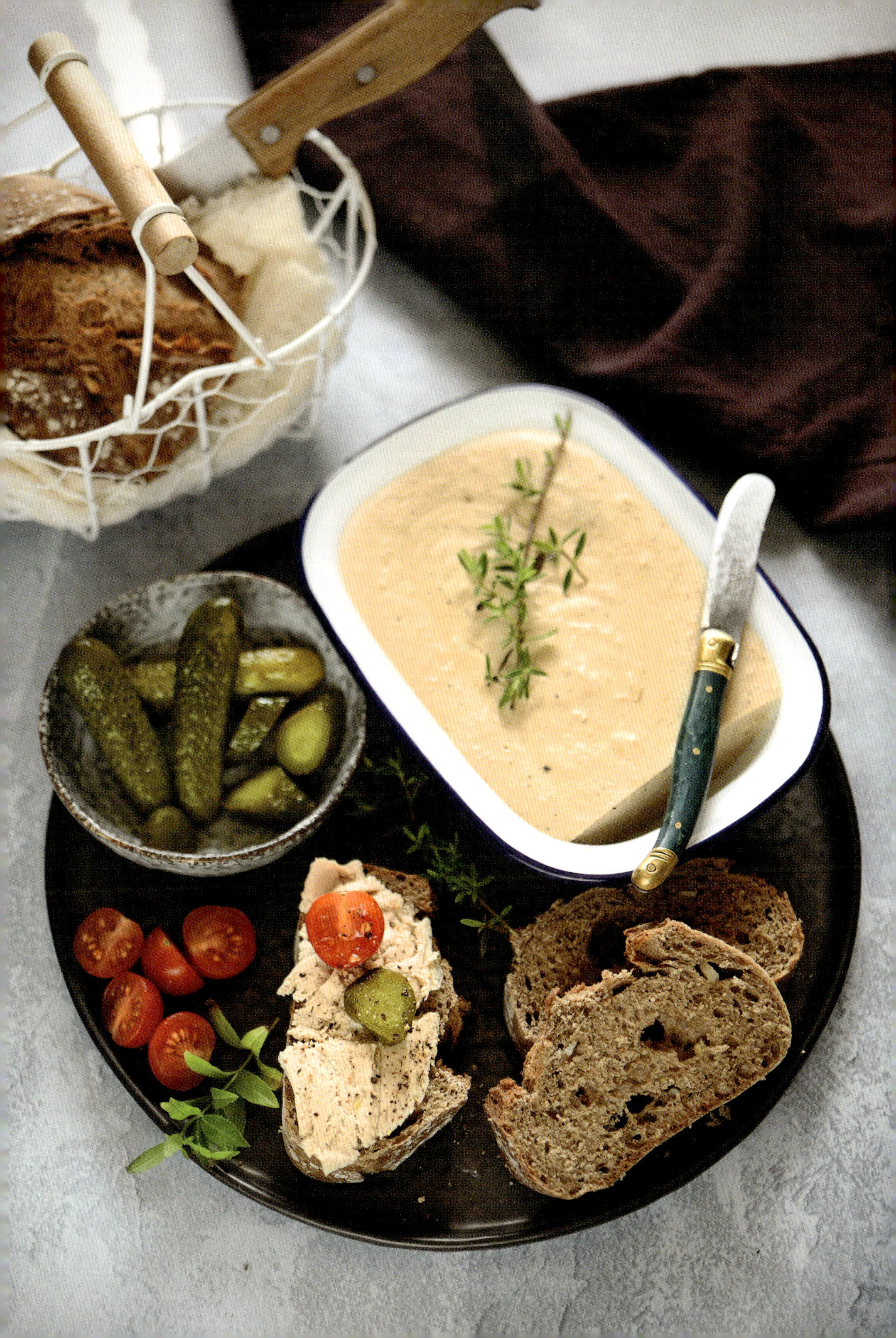

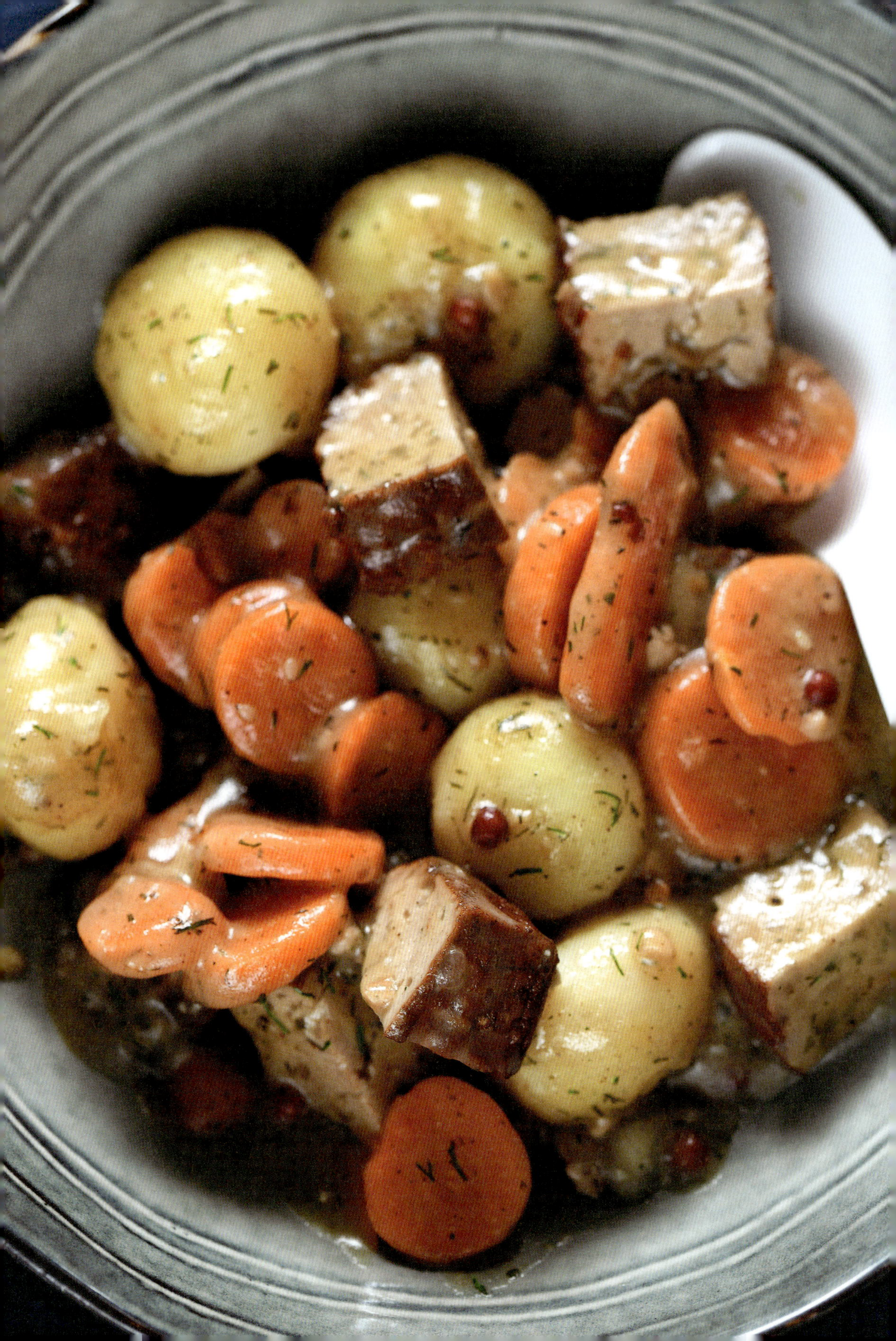

Smoked Tofu

SCANDINAVIAN RAGOUT

- 400 g frozen carrots
- 1 tbsp rapeseed oil
- 400 g smoked tofu
- 500 g cooked potatoes
- 4 tsp pink peppercorns
- 2½ tsp allspice
- 500 ml vegetable stock
- 15 g frozen dill
- 4 tsp soya cream
- 2½ tbsp cornflour

Sauté the carrots in a large pot with rapeseed oil. Cover and cook over a high heat for 5 minutes. Add the tofu cut into large pieces and the potatoes. Add the pink peppercorns and allspice. Add the hot vegetable stock and mix. Cover and simmer over a medium heat for 10 minutes. Add the dill, soya cream and cornflour mixed with a little cold water. Mix and cook for 3 minutes to finish.

TOFU SKEWER

- 400 g smoked tofu
- 1 red pepper
- 100 g pineapple
- 4 tbsp olive oil
- 3 tbsp tamari
- 3 tbsp maple syrup
- 5 tsp sriracha
- 1 garlic clove

Cut the tofu into equal-sized cubes. Wash the pepper, cut in half, remove the seeds and chop into equally sized pieces. Chop the pineapple into triangles. Put all the chopped ingredients in a high-sided bowl. Mix the oil with the tamari, maple syrup, sriracha and crushed garlic in a bowl. Pour over the other ingredients and leave to marinate. Make the skewer alternating the ingredients and bake for 30 minutes at 180°C (gas mark 4) or brown each side in a hot frying pan.

BAKED BAGUETTE

- 200 g frozen onions
- 200 g smoked tofu
- 6 tbsp soya cream
- 2 tsp apple cider vinegar
- 2 tbsp malted yeast
- ¼ tsp grated nutmeg
- Fine salt
- Black pepper
- 1 baguette
- ½ tsp cumin seeds

Cook the onions in a frying pan without any oil for several minutes. Stop when browned. Set aside. Cut the tofu into small rectangles, sear in a hot pan without any fat or oil. Once browned, remove from the heat and set aside. Mix the soya cream with the apple cider vinegar, malted yeast, grated nutmeg, salt and pepper in a bowl. Halve the baguette, split lengthways and spread an even layer of cream on each side. Add the onions, tofu and sprinkle with cumin seeds. Bake for 10 minutes in an oven preheated to 180°C (gas mark 4).

Smoked Tofu

AUTUMN ROLLS

- 500 g cooked potatoes
- 3 tbsp olive oil
- 5 tbsp frozen chives
- 1½ tbsp frozen shallots
- Salt • Pepper
- 200 g smoked tofu with almonds and sesame seeds
- 40 g celery stalk
- 12 rice paper sheets (28 cm diameter)
- Oak leaf lettuce
- 1 tbsp wholegrain mustard
- 1 tbsp water
- 2 tsp peanut butter
- 1 tsp apple cider vinegar
- 1 tsp agave syrup

Crush the potatoes in a large bowl and add the oil, chives and shallots, season with salt and pepper and set aside. Slice the tofu and celery into batons. Soak the rice paper in a bowl of hot water for several seconds to soften, place on a chopping board and fill as follows: 1 to 2 lettuce leaves, 1 tablespoon of crushed potatoes, 1 tofu baton and 2 to 3 celery batons. Roll the front part tightly, fold over the sides and close the roll. Repeat the process to make 12 rolls. In a small ramekin, mix the mustard with the water, peanut butter, vinegar and agave syrup. Serve immediately.

VOL-AU-VENT

- 200 g smoked tofu
- 200 g tinned button mushrooms
- 100 ml soya milk
- 200 ml soya cream
- 2 tbsp cornflour
- ½ tsp black pepper
- Heaped ¼ tsp fine salt
- ¼ tsp grated nutmeg
- 4 frozen round vegan vol-au-vent cases

Cut the tofu into 1-cm pieces and sauté in a hot pan with a little oil. Add the mushrooms and cook over a low heat for 3 minutes. Heat the milk and soya cream with cornflour mixed with a little cold water in a pan. Add the salt, pepper and grated nutmeg. Whisk until the sauce thickens. Add the mushrooms and diced tofu. Fill the vol-au-vent cases and bake in the oven at 180°C (gas mark 4) for 15 minutes and serve.

RED PESTO

- 150 ml olive oil
- 125 g smoked tofu
- 2 tbsp pine nuts
- 50 g sun-dried tomatoes in oil
- 1 tbsp frozen shallots
- 1 tbsp capers in vinegar
- 1 tsp paprika

Put all the ingredients in a blender and blend for 5 minutes to make the pesto. Store in a closed glass jar.

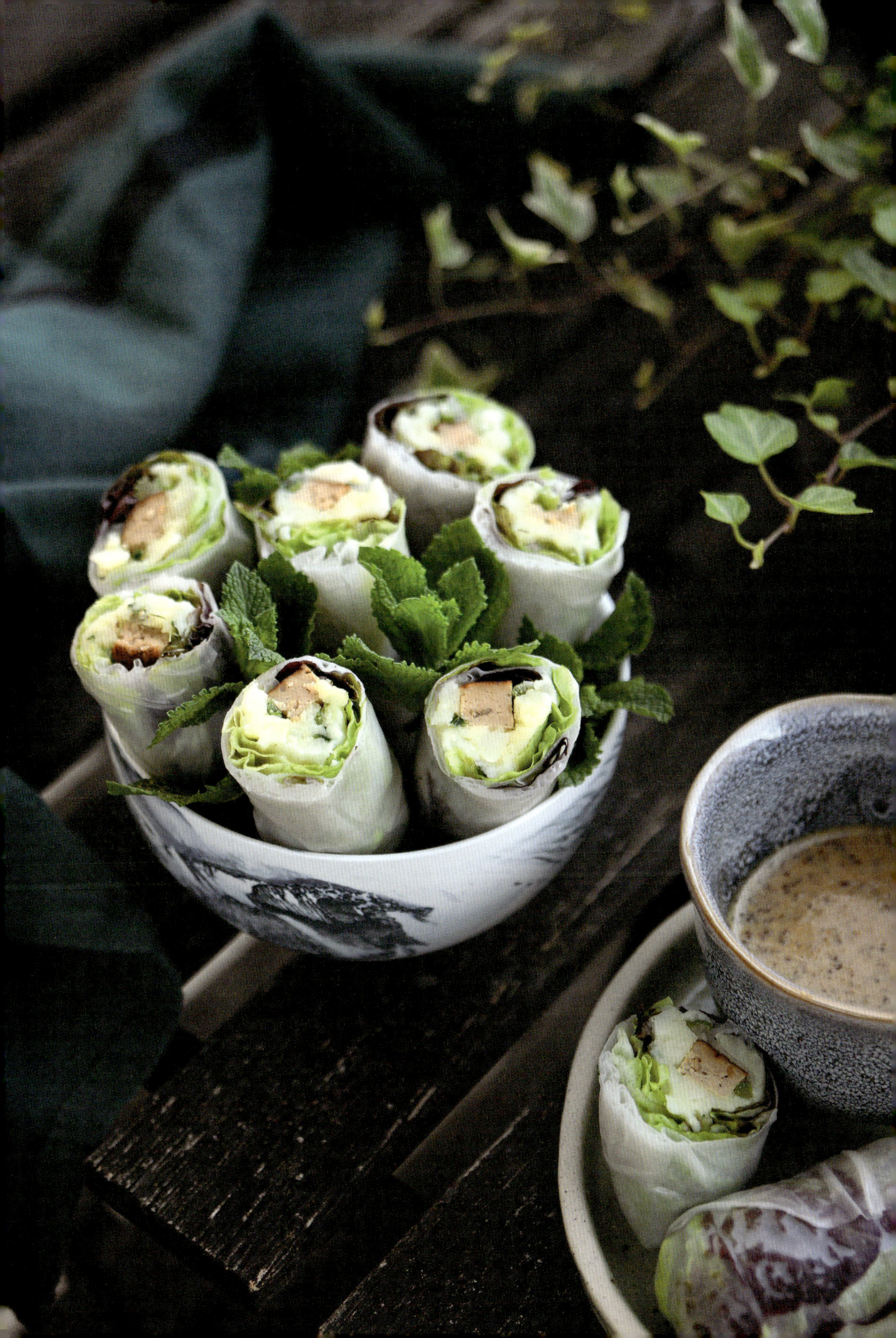

Plain Tofu

This is the most emblematic ingredient in vegan food, the most caricatured. Bland in taste, spongy in texture, our poor tofu has little on its side to excite the taste buds of outsiders. However, it's a great product, as long as you make the effort to cook it well. Give it a chance, you won't be disappointed!

Plain Tofu

SESAME GRILLED TOFU

- 200 g tofu
- 3 tbsp white miso paste
- 3 tbsp tahini
- Sesame seeds
- Olive oil
- 4 tbsp tomato ketchup
- 1 tsp toasted sesame oil
- 1 pinch Espelette pepper
- 3 sprigs of chives

Cut the tofu into equal-sized cubes. Mix the miso, tahini and 3 tbsp of warm water to make a smooth paste. Coat the tofu in the paste and leave to rest for 10 minutes. Pour the sesame seeds onto a plate and coat the tofu in sesame seeds. Cook in a hot frying pan with a splash of olive oil. Brown on each side for a few seconds and set aside. Mix the ketchup, toasted sesame oil, Espelette pepper and chopped chives. Serve the tofu cold with the sauce.

TOFU MARINIÈRE

- 50 g vegan margarine
- 1 bay leaf
- 50 g frozen shallots
- 2 tsp chopped frozen garlic
- 400 g tofu
- 1 tsp fine salt
- 500 ml white wine
- 10 g seaweed flakes
- 3 tbsp chopped frozen flat-leaf parsley
- 1 tsp white miso

Melt the margarine over a medium heat in a large pot and add the bay leaf, shallots and garlic. Cut the tofu into 2-cm pieces and add to the pot with salt. Mix and cook for 5 minutes. Add the white wine, seaweed and chopped parsley. Dissolve the miso in 100 ml water and add to the pot. Cook over a low heat for 10 minutes. Remove the bay leaf and serve with the cooking liquid.

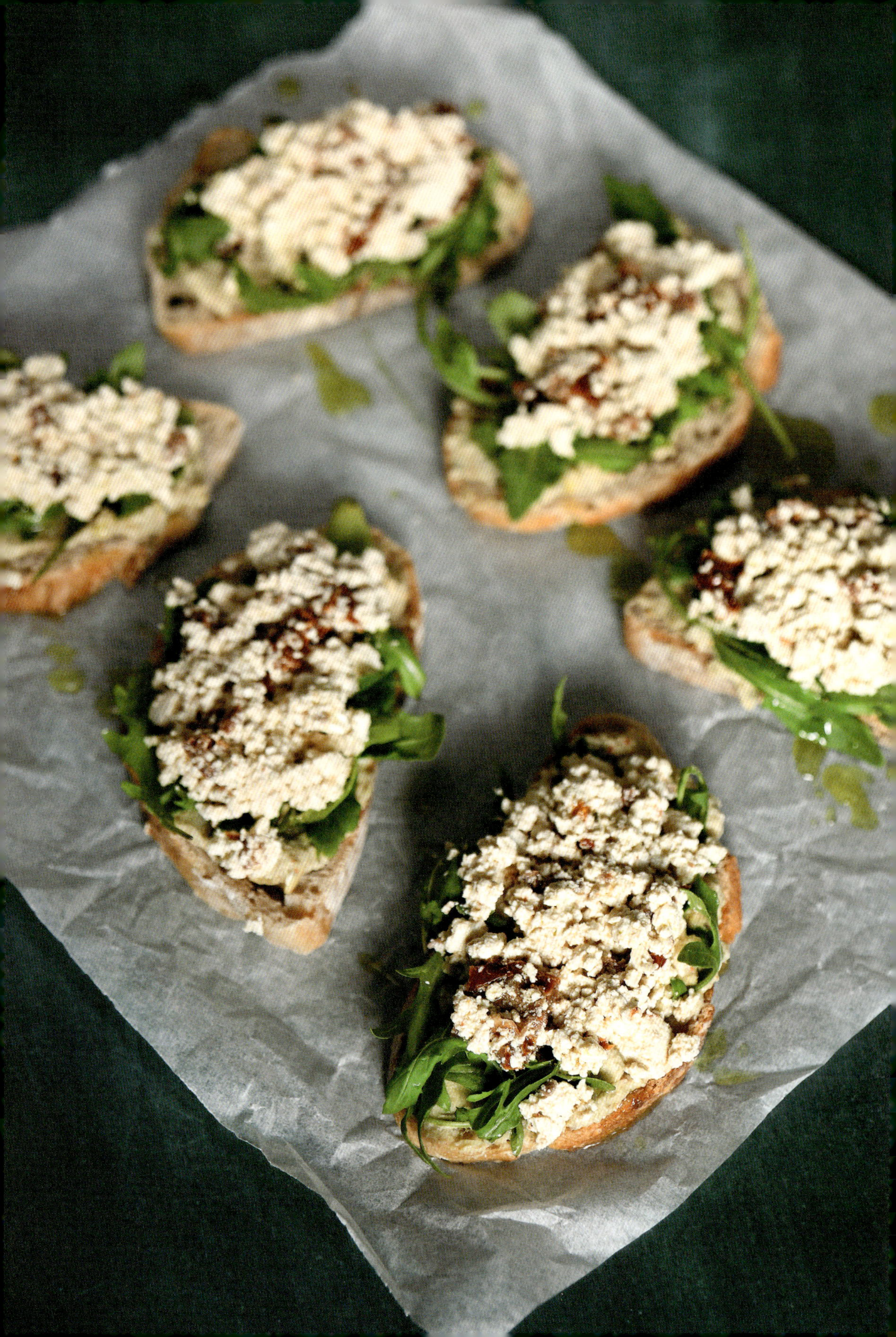

Plain Tofu

SUMMER BRUSCHETTA

- 250 g tofu • Heaped ¼ tsp fine salt
- 4 tsp lemon juice • 2 tsp olive oil
- 50 g sun-dried tomatoes in oil
- 120 g artichokes in oil
- 1 tbsp capers in vinegar
- ¼ tsp Espelette pepper
- 8 slices bread (180 g)
- 30 g rocket leaves

Crumble the tofu in a large bowl, then add the salt, lemon juice and oil. Finely dice the tomatoes. Mix together and refrigerate for 15 minutes. Blend the artichokes with the capers and Espelette pepper to make a cream. Toast the bread and spread with a layer of artichoke cream, then add a layer of rocket and cover with tofu. Finish with a drizzle of olive oil.

BRUSCHETTA

- 200 g tofu
- Heaped ¼ tsp fine salt
- 1 tbsp malted yeast
- 1 tsp balsamic vinegar
- 1 tbsp olive oil
- 100 g fresh button mushrooms
- 1 tbsp oregano
- 400 g bruschetta bread (4 slices)
- 280 g tomato sauce
- 2 tbsp chopped frozen basil
- 1½ tbsp chopped fresh shallots

Preheat the oven to 180°C (gas mark 4). Coarsely crumble the tofu with your fingers. Add the salt, malted yeast, balsamic vinegar and oil then set aside.

Cut the mushrooms into thick slices and cover in oregano. Lightly toast the bread in the oven for 3 minutes. Cover the bread in tomato sauce, basil and finely chopped shallots. Top with the mushrooms and tofu. Bake for 8 minutes.

GOLDEN NUGGETS

- 200 g tofu
- 150 g plain flour
- 30 g cornflour
- 2 tsp fine salt
- 2½ tsp garlic powder
- 2 tsp turmeric
- 2 tsp fennel seeds
- 2 tsp thyme
- 60 g breadcrumbs

Cut the tofu into 12 equal-sized pieces. Drain between two sheets of kitchen paper. Mix the flour, cornflour, salt, garlic, turmeric, fennel seeds and thyme in a bowl. Add 200 ml of cold water and mix well with a whisk until smooth. Add the tofu and leave to rest for 10 minutes. Pour the breadcrumbs into a high-sided bowl. Preheat a deep fryer to 180°C. Coat each tofu piece in breadcrumbs. Quickly dip the tofu in the batter once more before coating in another layer of breadcrumbs. Gently place the breaded tofu in the fryer and deep fry for 3 minutes at 180°C.

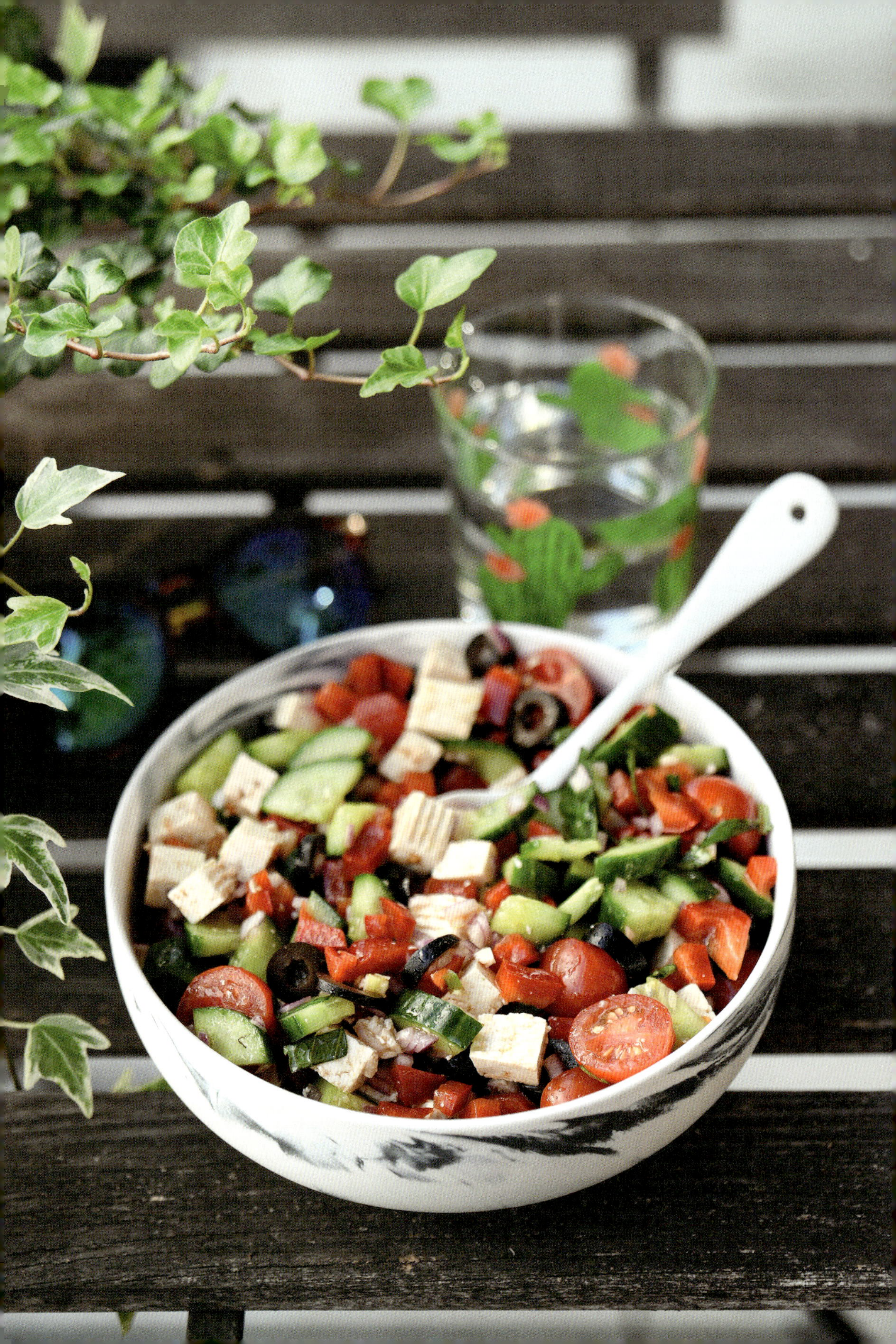

Plain Tofu

CRETAN SALAD

⬅

- 200 g tofu
- 200 g cucumber
- 200 g baby tomatoes
- 200 g peppers
- 100 g black olives
- 90 g red onion
- 2½ tbsp mint leaves
- 4 tbsp olive oil
- 4 tsp lemon juice
- 2 tsp Worcestershire sauce
- 2 tsp agave syrup
- Fine salt

Cut the tofu in cubes, cut the cucumber in four then cut into small pieces, halve the tomatoes, cut the peppers into small pieces, slice the olives and finely chop the red onion. Transfer the chopped ingredients to a salad bowl and mix. Finely chop the mint leaves and mix with the oil, lemon juice, Worcestershire sauce and agave syrup, then season with salt. Pour over the vegetables and tofu. Mix well and serve.

COURGETTE CANNELLONI

- 300 g tofu
- Fine salt
- Black pepper
- 100 ml soya cream
- ¼ tsp grated nutmeg
- 400 g chopped tomatoes
- Olive oil
- 2 tsp balsamic vinegar
- 1 tsp sweet paprika
- 1 tsp thyme
- 4 fresh courgettes
- 60 g fresh shallots
- 1 garlic clove
- 100 ml white wine
- 4 tbsp malted yeast
- 12 cannelloni

Break up the tofu, then season with salt and pepper. Add the soya cream and nutmeg. Mix well and set aside. Simmer the chopped tomatoes with 4 tsp of olive oil, 2 tsp of balsamic vinegar, paprika and thyme in a pan over a low heat and season with salt. Grate the courgettes, chop the shallots and garlic. Cover and cook for 10 minutes in a large pot with olive oil and a pinch of salt. When the courgettes start to reduce, add the white wine and cover until cooked. Add the tofu and malted yeast then mix.

Cook the cannelloni in salted water for about 8 minutes, then gently remove from the water. Fill the cannelloni with the filling. Transfer to plates, cover with tomato sauce and serve.

Plain Tofu

VEGAN EGG MUFFIN →

• 250 g tofu • Heaped ½ tsp Kala namak (black salt) • 1¼ tsp turmeric • 1 tsp apple cider vinegar • 100 g silken tofu • Rapeseed oil • 4 slices smoked vegan ham • 200 g baby spinach leaves • 4 English muffins • Black pepper • 4 tbsp chopped chives • 4 slices vegan cheddar cheese

Break up the tofu with your fingers into a large bowl. Mix the salt, turmeric, vinegar and silken tofu in a bowl. Pour over the broken up tofu and add 1 tsp of rapeseed oil before mixing well. Leave to rest for 5 minutes. Slice the ham into three strips and cook in a frying pan with a little oil. Remove from the pan. Then add the spinach to the frying pan for 1 minute. Halve the muffins and toast them. Heat a frying pan with a little oil and add the tofu. Turn down the heat and cook over a medium heat for 5 minutes while stirring continuously. Season with pepper and add the chopped chives. Assemble as follows: on the bottom muffin, place spinach, followed by the tofu, ham strips, cheddar cheese and close with the top half of the muffin.

PALAK TOFU

• 400 g tofu • 1¼ tsp garam masala • Fine salt • Rapeseed oil • ¾ tsp turmeric • 1 tsp cumin seeds • 1 tsp coriander seeds • 200 g frozen onions • 200 g peeled tomatoes • 200 ml water • 1 kg chopped frozen spinach

Cut the tofu into 2-cm pieces and mix with the garam masala and salt in a bowl. Set aside for 15 minutes. In a large pot, heat 2 tbsp of oil with the turmeric and crushed cumin and coriander seeds. Sauté the onions until translucent. Add the tomatoes and water. Reduce and add the spinach. Stir, add 1 tsp salt, then cook with the lid on for 10 minutes. Brown the tofu in a frying pan on all sides with a little oil. Add the tofu to the spinach and mix.

TOFU & VEGETABLE STEW

• 300 g frozen Brussels sprouts • 200 g fresh button mushrooms • Rapeseed oil • 1 tbsp tamari • 200 g tofu • Salt • Black pepper • 300 g cooked carrots • 100 g frozen onions • 2 tsp thyme • 3 tbsp white wine

Cook the Brussels sprouts in salted boiling water for 6 minutes, then drain. Halve the sprouts and set aside. Clean the mushrooms, quarter them and sauté in a frying pan with oil. Deglaze with tamari, reduce and set aside. Slice the tofu into batons to make around 12 batons. Brown in a pan with a little oil and season with salt and pepper. Sauté the carrots with the onions and thyme in a wok for 5 minutes. Add the tofu, mushrooms, Brussels sprouts and white wine. Sauté over a high heat for 5 minutes. Season with pepper to taste once cooked.

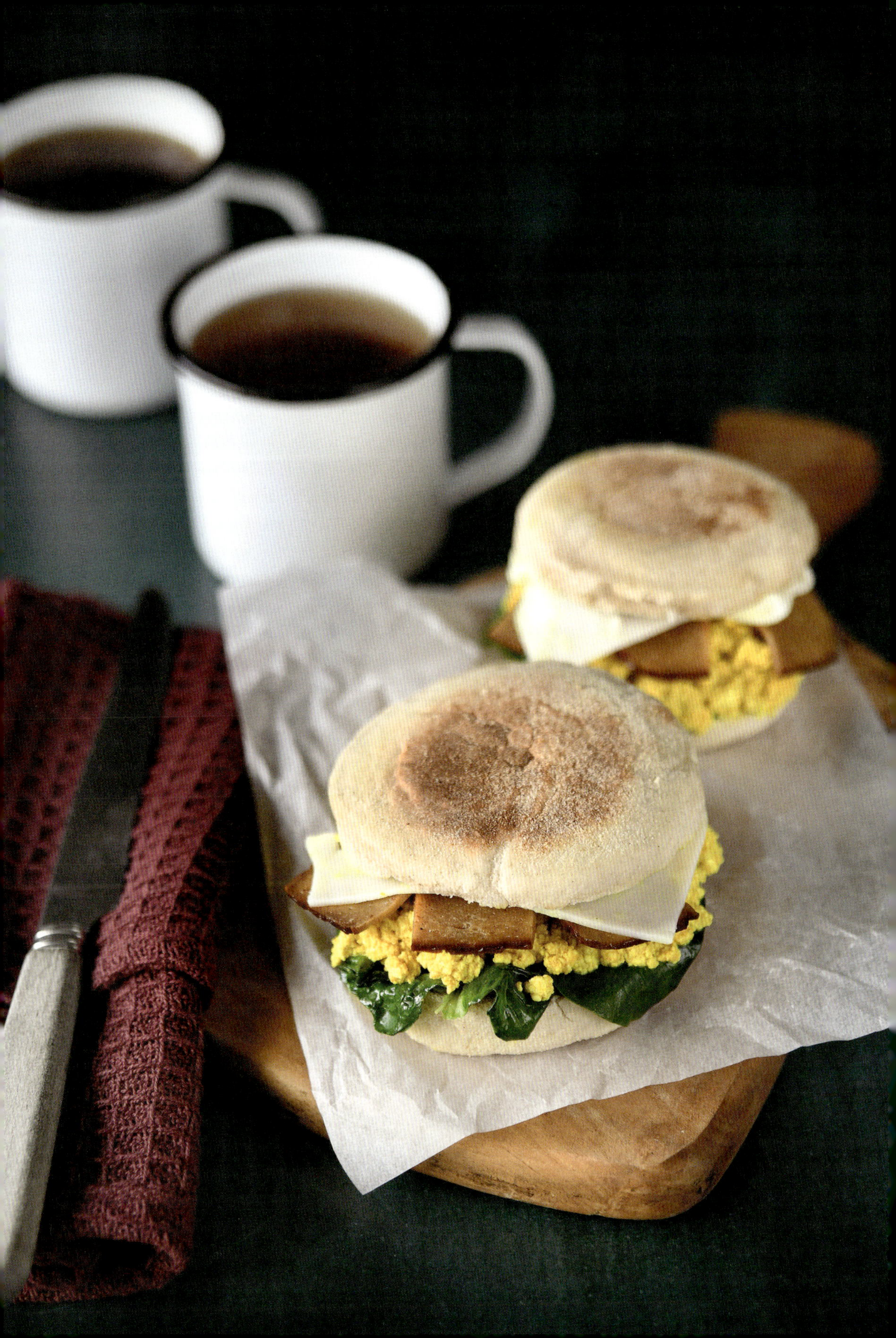

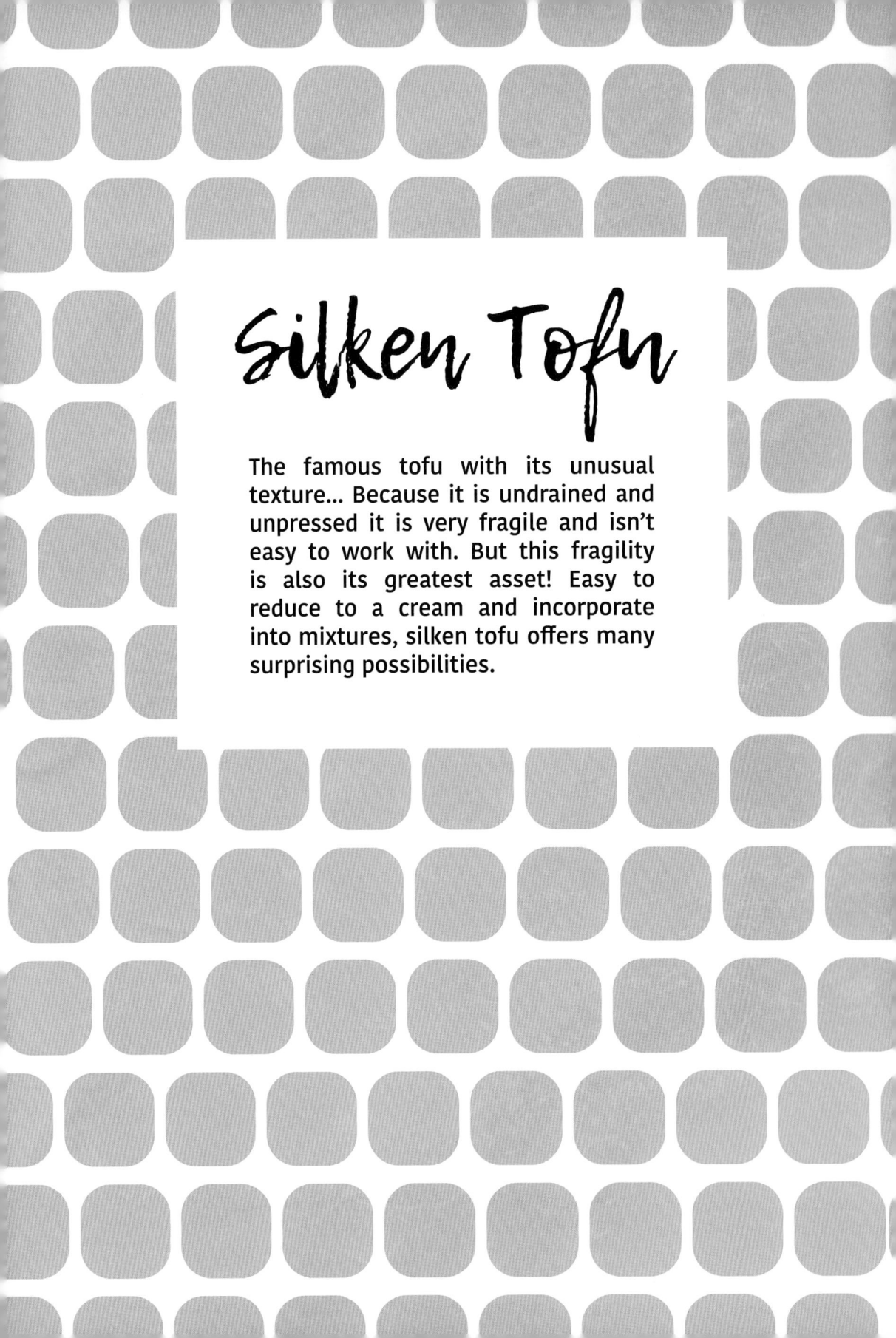

Silken Tofu

The famous tofu with its unusual texture... Because it is undrained and unpressed it is very fragile and isn't easy to work with. But this fragility is also its greatest asset! Easy to reduce to a cream and incorporate into mixtures, silken tofu offers many surprising possibilities.

Silken Tofu

TOFU MAYONNAISE

- 200 g silken tofu
- 2 tsp Dijon mustard
- Heaped ½ tsp Kala namak (black salt)
- 1 tsp apple cider vinegar
- 3 tbsp rapeseed oil

Add the silken tofu, mustard and Kala namak salt to a stick blender beaker. Blend to make a smooth cream, add the vinegar and blend again. Pour in the cold oil while continuing to blend. The mayonnaise can be kept in the fridge for 1 week.

ASPARAGUS TARTLETS

- 12 frozen green asparagus spears
- Olive oil
- Salt
- Pepper
- 1 packet vegan shortcrust pastry
- 150 g silken tofu
- 2 tbsp cornflour
- ¼ tsp grated nutmeg
- 1 lemon

Preheat the oven to 180°C (gas mark 4). Cut the asparagus spears in half and sauté the top half with the tip in a hot pan with a little olive oil, then set aside. Cut the other halves into small lengths and sauté in a hot frying pan with olive oil until soft. Season with salt and pepper. Mash with a fork. Cut the pastry into four pieces the same size as the tartlet moulds and line the moulds. Prick the base of the tartlets and cover with the mashed asparagus. Blend the silken tofu with the cornflour, grated nutmeg and zest of half a lemon, season with salt and pepper and pour over the crushed asparagus. Add three asparagus heads to each tartlet. Cook for 30 minutes. Allow to cool before turning out. Serve.

Silken Tofu

KIMCHI SOUP

- 4 tbsp toasted sesame oil
- 150 g fresh spring onions
- 2 tbsp tamari
- 300 g kimchi
- 60 g white miso
- 1 litre vegetable stock
- 50 g chopped tomatoes
- 300 g silken tofu

In a large pot, heat the sesame oil and sauté the coarsely chopped spring onions. Deglaze with tamari, then add the kimchi and miso. Add the vegetable stock and the tomatoes. Mix and simmer for 5 minutes. Carefully dice the tofu and add to the soup. Cook for another 10 minutes over a medium heat and serve. Take care not to damage the tofu!

LEEK & CORIANDER QUICHE

- 1 kg frozen leeks
- Olive oil
- Fine salt
- 3 tbsp white wine
- 400 g silken tofu
- 4 tbsp soya cream
- 4 tsp cornflour
- ¼ tsp grated nutmeg
- 1 clove
- 4 tbsp fresh coriander
- Black pepper
- 1 packet vegan shortcrust pastry

Cook the leeks in a large pot with a splash of olive oil. Once the leeks start to disintegrate, add salt and white wine, cover and sweat down over a low heat for 10 minutes. Mix the silken tofu with the soya cream and cornflour (mixed with 1 tbsp of cold water). Season with nutmeg, clove and finely chopped coriander. Season with salt and pepper according to taste. Add the leeks and mix. Preheat the oven to 180°C (gas mark 4). Line a 20-cm tart mould with the pastry without removing the baking parchment. Prick the tart base with a fork. Pour the leek/tofu mixture into the mould and spread out evenly. Bake in the oven on the middle shelf for 1 hour.

CHIVE CREAM & CRUDITÉS

- 200 g silken tofu
- 1 tbsp lemon juice
- 1 tsp garlic powder
- 2 tbsp chopped frozen chives
- 2 tbsp frozen mint
- Heaped ¼ tsp fine salt
- ½ tsp black pepper
- 1 tbsp olive oil

Blend the tofu until smooth. Add the lemon juice, garlic powder, herbs, salt and pepper. Blend again for 30 seconds. Add the oil in three batches, a teaspoon at a time blending for 30 seconds between each addition. Pour into a bowl and refrigerate for 20 minutes. Serve with carrot and cucumber batons, radishes and cauliflower florets.

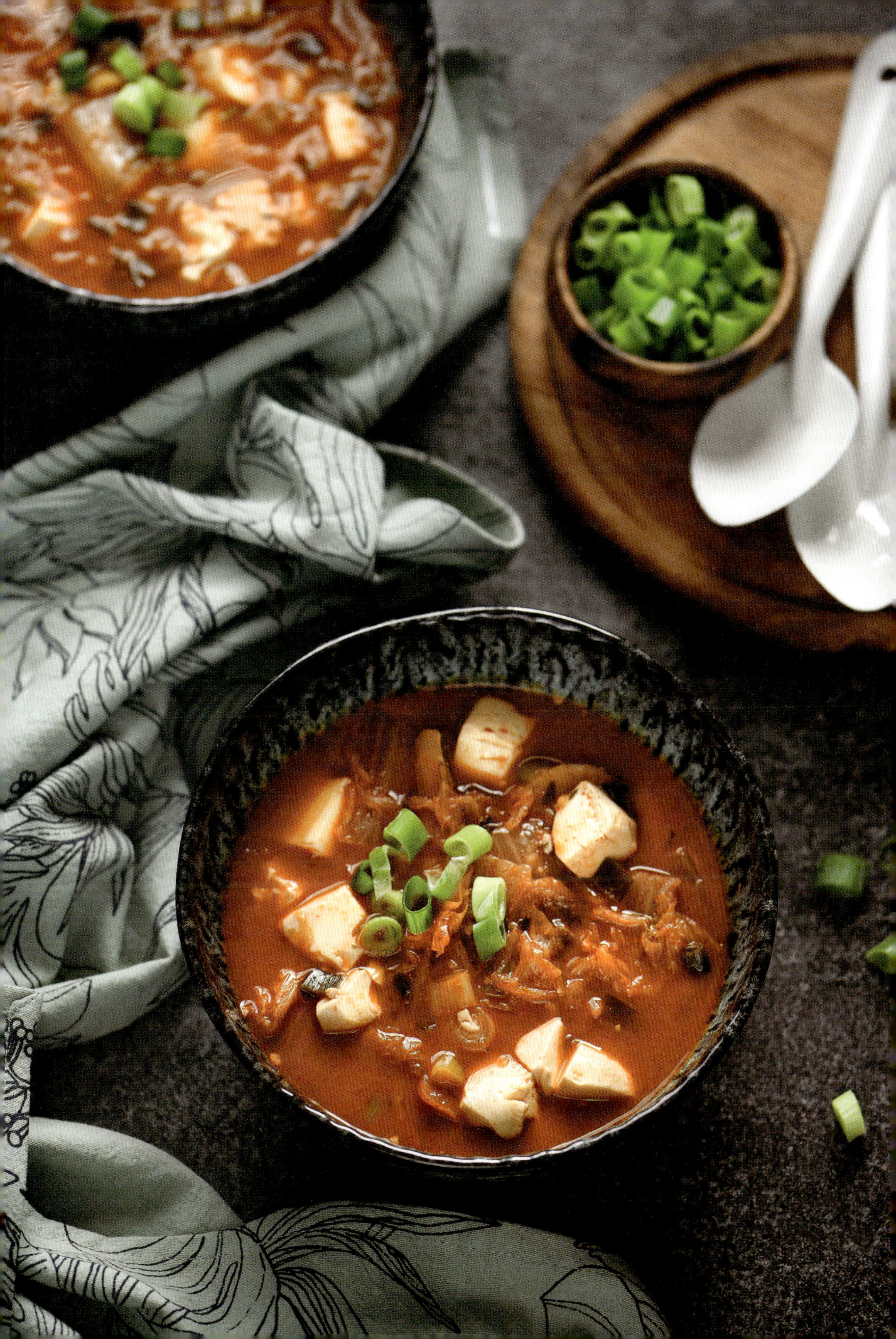

Silken Tofu

BANANA FLAN

- 500 ml vanilla soya milk
- 300 g ripe bananas
- 5 tbsp maple syrup
- 2 tsp agar-agar powder
- 400 g silken tofu
- 1 tsp vanilla extract

Mash the milk with the bananas, maple syrup and agar-agar. Pour into a pan and bring to the boil while stirring continuously. Boil for 2 minutes then add to a blender with the silken tofu and vanilla extract and blend for several minutes. Pour into ramekins and refrigerate for several hours.

IRISH COFFEE CREAM

- 400 g silken tofu
- 4 tbsp espresso
- 2 tbsp maple syrup
- 1 tbsp cocoa powder
- 1 tbsp peaty whisky
- 1 tsp vanilla extract
- 1 can vegan whipped cream

Add 300 g of silken tofu, the espresso, 4 tsp of maple syrup and sieved cocoa powder to a food processor with an S blade. Blend to make a smooth cream. Divide between 4 small ramekins and refrigerate whilst doing the next step. Blend the remaining tofu (100 g) with 2 tsp of maple syrup, whisky and vanilla extract in the food processor to make the cream. Pour over the chocolate cream and refrigerate overnight. Finish with a generous amount of vegan whipped cream.

HIYAYAKKO

- 400 g silken tofu
- 2 tbsp tamari
- 2 tsp yuzu or lime juice
- 2 tsp agave syrup
- Fresh ginger (2 cm)
- 1 spring onion
- 1 fresh shallot
- 1 sheet nori seaweed
- 1½ tsp white sesame seeds

Carefully cut the tofu into four squares and place directly on small plates. Refrigerate. Make the sauce by mixing the tamari, yuzu juice and agave syrup. Finely grate the ginger to make a paste. Finely slice the spring onion and the shallot lengthways. Snip the nori with scissors into small flakes. Remove the plates with the tofu from the fridge. Pour the sauce over the tofu, then scatter with sesame seeds and nori. Add a small spoonful of shallots, another of ginger paste and some spring onion to each plate.

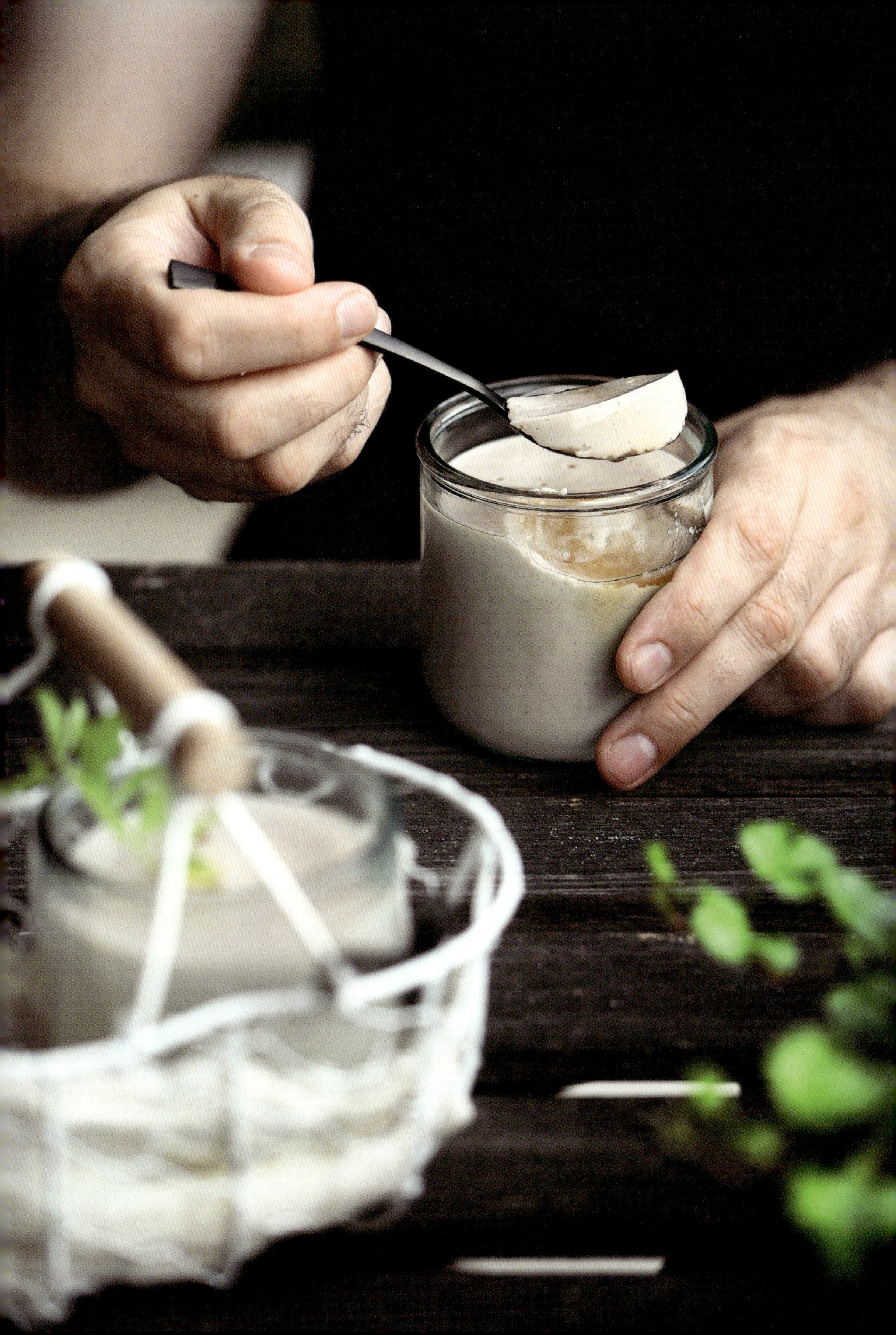

Silken Tofu

CRÈME BRÛLÉE CHARTREUSE

- 250 g vanilla custard dessert
- 200 ml vanilla soya milk
- 60 g caster sugar
- 1 tsp vanilla extract
- 2 tbsp cornflour
- ¾ tsp agar-agar powder
- 3 pinches ground turmeric
- 300 g silken tofu
- 1 tbsp Chartreuse
- Demerara sugar

Add the custard dessert, soya milk, caster sugar, vanilla extract, cornflour diluted in 2 tbsp of water, agar-agar and turmeric to a pan and mix. Heat and boil for several minutes while stirring continuously. Put the silken tofu, Chartreuse and hot mixture into a blender and blend. Pour into six crème brûlée ramekins. Refrigerate for several hours until serving. Cover with a thin layer of demerara sugar and caramelise with a blow torch.

COINTREAU TIRAMISU

- 250 g plain tofu
- 150 g silken tofu
- 130 g caster sugar
- 1 tbsp vanilla extract
- 2 tbsp lemon juice
- 100 ml soya milk
- ¾ tsp agar-agar powder
- 100 ml strong coffee
- 3 tbsp Cointreau
- 200 g plain vegan biscuits
- Cocoa powder

Blend both the tofus, sugar, vanilla extract and lemon juice to make a thick, smooth cream. Boil the soya milk with the agar-agar in a small pan while stirring continuously for 3 minutes. Pour immediately over the cream, mix well and set aside. Pour the strong coffee and Cointreau into a bowl. Dip the biscuits in the liquid one by one and place on the bottom of four verrine glasses. Cover with 2 to 3 tablespoons of cream (1-2-cm thick layer). Repeat the layers. Note: use 4 to 5 biscuits for each glass (depending on the size of the glass). Finish with a creamy layer and dust with cocoa powder. Refrigerate for 2 hours before serving.

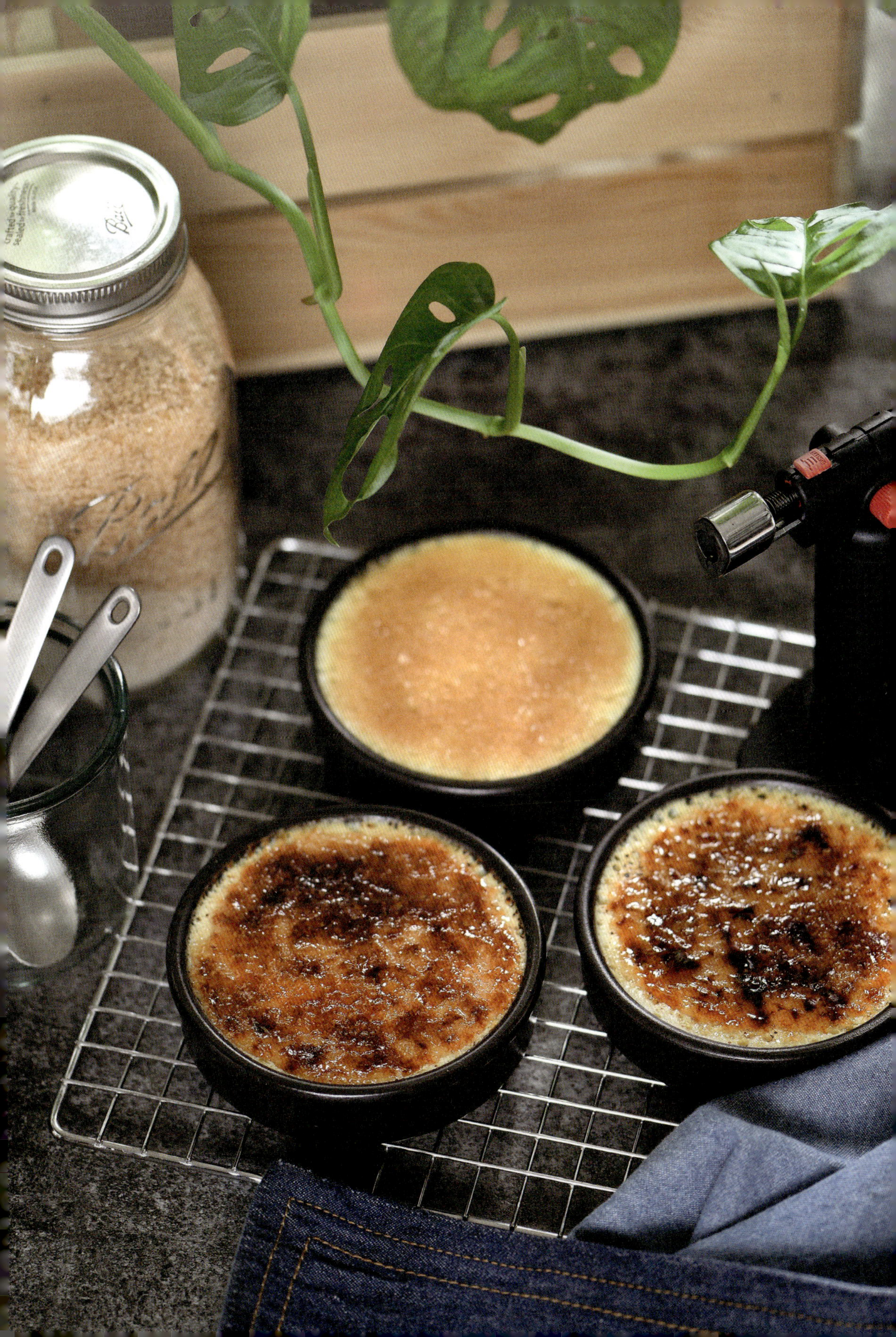

Yogurt

Replacing cow's milk yogurt is child's play thanks to soya!

These days it comes in different styles – natural, sweetened, Greek-style, vanilla flavoured, with fruit, in individual pots and in even one large pot to share. And it's so versatile; in addition to being an easy dessert or to have for breakfast, soya yogurts can also be used in cooking.

Yoghurt

MANGO LASSI

- 150 g frozen mango
- 250 ml rice milk
- 100 g vanilla soya yogurt
- 2 small pinches of ground cardamom

Put the mango, rice milk, yogurt and cardamom into a blender.

Blend for several minutes until creamy and smooth.

Serve in two glasses and enjoy.

MOJITO CURD

- 70 g sugar
- 2 tbsp cornflour
- 2 tbsp rum
- 2 large lemons
- 1½ tbsp vanilla soya yogurt
- 2 tsp vegan margarine
- 4 fresh mint leaves

Put the sugar, cornflour and rum into a small pan. Add the zest of two lemons. Halve the lemons and squeeze to extract around 100 ml of juice and mix everything together. Warm over a medium heat while stirring continuously to make a slightly thick cream. Turn off the heat and add the soya yogurt, margarine and chopped mint leaves then mix everything together. Pour into a glass container and refrigerate for several hours before using. Enjoy on muffins, pancakes or plain biscuits.

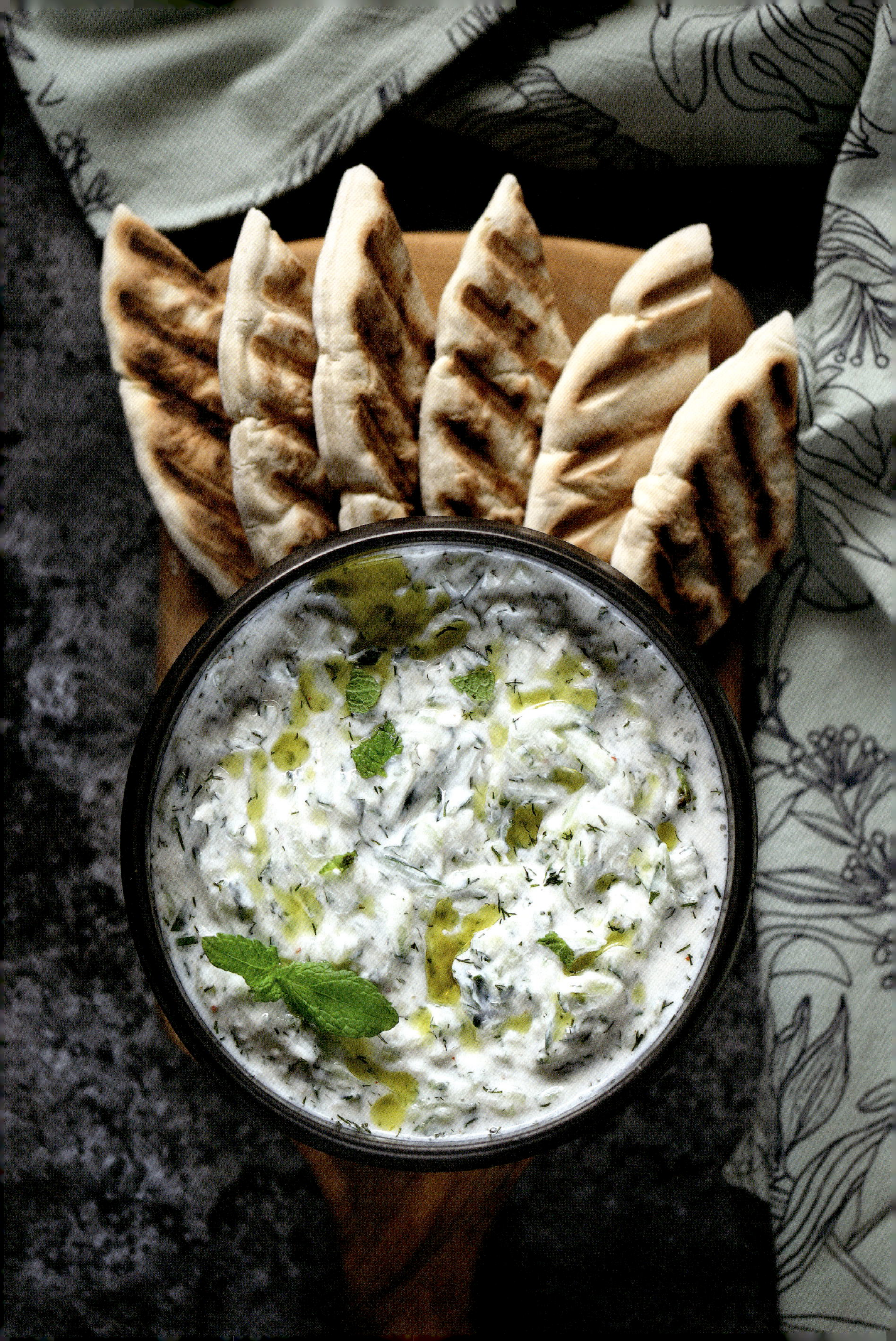

Yoghurt

TZATZIKI

- 500 g cucumber
- 360 g Greek-style soya yogurt
- 2 tsp lemon juice
- 3 garlic cloves
- Heaped ¼ tsp fine salt
- 1½ tbsp fresh dill
- 1 tbsp fresh mint
- Olive oil

Grate the cucumber and leave to stand for 15 minutes. Mix the yogurt, lemon juice and crushed garlic in a bowl. Add the salt, dill and chopped mint. Gently squeeze the cucumber to remove the excess water and add to the bowl. Mix and refrigerate for at least 1 hour. Top with a drizzle of olive oil and serve with grilled pitta breads.

FROMAGE FRAIS

- 400 g natural soya yogurt
- 2 tsp white miso
- 4 tsp plain coconut oil
- ½ tsp fine salt
- 1 tbsp apple cider vinegar
- 1 tsp ground cumin
- 2 tbsp frozen basil
- 2 tbsp chopped frozen chives

Mix the soya yogurt and miso in a bowl, then add the coconut oil, salt and vinegar. When smooth, add the cumin, basil and chives, mix again. Place a muslin cloth in a strainer and place in a large bowl. Pour the mixture into the strainer and drain in the fridge for 24 hours. The whey will be collected in the bowl and the cream will firm up. Store the fromage frais in a glass jar. It can be kept for three days in the fridge.

KTIPITI

- 360 g Greek-style soya yogurt
- ½ tsp fine salt
- 1 tsp sweet paprika
- 1 garlic bulb
- 100 g lacto-fermented tofu
- 150 g grilled peppers marinated in oil

Mix the yogurt with the salt, paprika and crushed garlic in a bowl. Use a food processor with an S blade to blend the lacto-fermented tofu and grilled peppers. Add to the yogurt base. Mix well to make a smooth mixture. Loosen with a little oil from the jar of peppers. Refrigerate for at least 2 hours before serving.

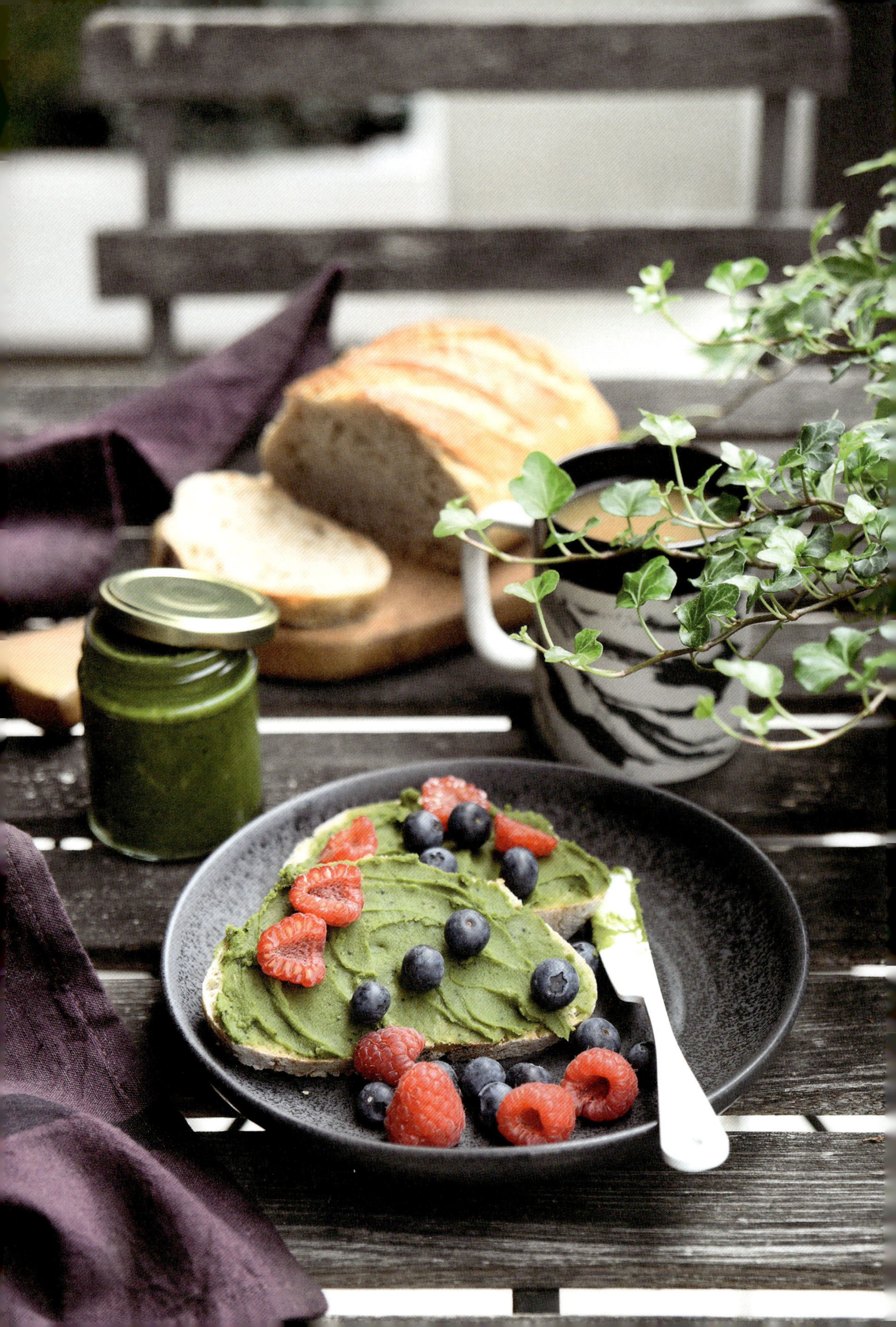

Yoghurt

RAITA

- 100 g fresh carrot
- 150 g cucumber
- 200 g plain soya yogurt
- Generous pinch fine salt
- ½ tsp ground cumin
- 4 tbsp fresh coriander
- 2 tsp mustard seeds

Grate the carrot, chop the cucumber into small dice and mix in a salad bowl. In a bowl, mix the soya yogurt with a pinch of salt, ground cumin, chopped coriander and the mustard seeds ground in a mortar. Pour the seasoned yogurt over the vegetables and mix well. Refrigerate until serving.

'CHICKEN' KORMA

- 200 g soya yogurt
- 1¼ tsp turmeric
- 2 garlic cloves
- 250 g 'chicken' meat substitute
- 1 tbsp coconut oil
- 1 tsp cumin seeds
- 1 tsp garam masala
- 100 g frozen onions
- 2½ tsp grated frozen ginger
- 2½ tbsp cashew nuts
- 1 bunch fresh coriander

Mix the yogurt with the turmeric and crushed garlic in a bowl. Add the meat substitute and leave to stand at least for 15 minutes. In a large pot, heat the coconut oil with the cumin seeds and garam masala. Sauté the onions, ginger and cashew nuts in the oil. Add the meat substitute with all the yogurt sauce and cook over a low heat for 15 minutes. Scatter fresh coriander leaves over as a garnish.

MATCHATELLA

- 200 g vegan white chocolate
- 100 g vanilla soya yogurt
- 4 tsp vegan margarine
- 4 tsp white almond butter
- 1 tbsp matcha powder

Melt the white chocolate with the vanilla yogurt in a bain-marie. Melt over a low heat, stirring from time to time. Turn off the heat when half the chocolate has melted, the rest will melt naturally with the residual heat. Add the margarine and almond butter and mix to combine. Sieve the matcha on top. Mix one last time and refrigerate in a glass jar for several hours to firm up. Enjoy on toast or with pancakes.

Yoghurt

YOGURT LOAF

- 200 g plain flour
- 175 g raw cane sugar
- 1 tbsp baking powder
- 2 tsp vanilla sugar
- 300 g vanilla soya yogurt
- 3 tbsp vegetable oil
- 3 tbsp soya milk

Preheat the oven to 180°C (gas mark 4). Add the dry ingredients to a bowl and mix, then add the wet ingredients and mix to make a smooth batter. Pour into a lined loaf tin or buche mould and bake for 1 hour without opening the oven. Leave to cool completely before slicing. Add some diced apple or chocolate chips, or other ingredients of your choice to personalise the cake. You could also use cinnamon or cocoa, or essential oils such as bergamot, or even diced candied lemon.

AUTUMN CAKE

- 8 dried figs
- 210 g plain flour
- 120 g raw cane sugar
- 40 g cornflour
- 30 g ground almonds
- 1 tbsp baking powder
- 100 g natural soya yogurt
- 200 ml vanilla soya milk
- 100 g almond butter
- 1 tsp caramel flavouring
- 120 g Grenoble walnuts

Preheat the oven to 180°C (gas mark 4), line a cake tin and chop up the figs.

Mix the dry ingredients together in a bowl. Mix the wet ingredients together in another bowl. Combine the two mixtures and add the figs and nuts before mixing again. Pour into the cake tin and bake for 1 hour without opening the oven. Check with the tip of a knife that the cake is cooked. Leave to cool completely before slicing. The cherry on the cake? It will be even better the next day.

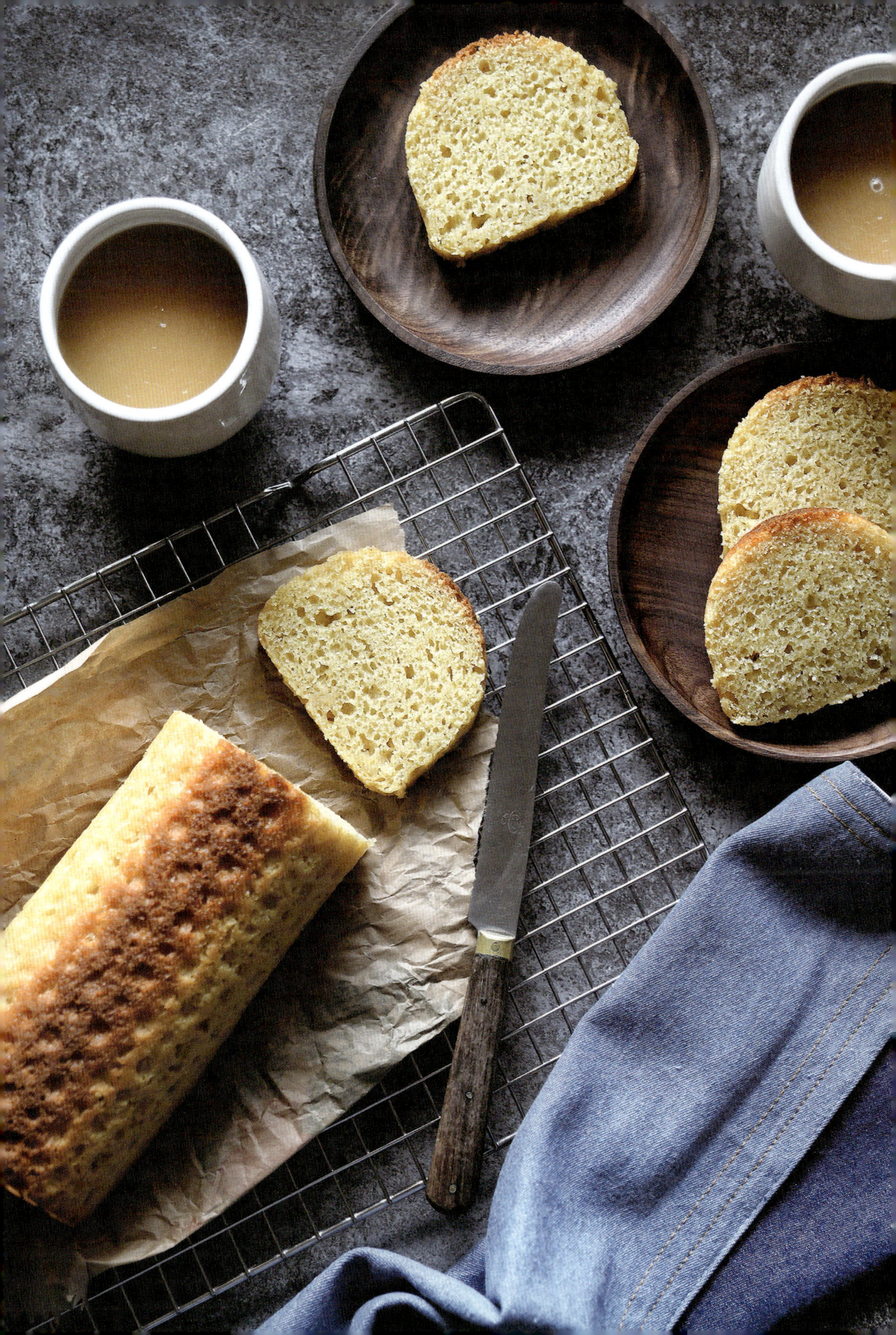

ADDRESS BOOK

As this book reflects our true daily diet, we think it is both logical and practical to share the type of places where we actually shop. Of course, they are all located in Paris, but luckily some brands have locations in other regions or there are local equivalents. And with the internet, we can get rid of geographical barriers!

ORGANIC SHOPS
When it comes to vegan-specific products, organic stores are generally a safe bet, although selection is limited… But it is perfect for things such as tofu, seitan and tempeh. They have a lot of good quality basic ingredients, ingredients in bulk, fresh vegetables, etc.

VEGAN SHOPS
Specifically vegan shops are even better and have the largest offer in terms of meat substitutes, vegan cheeses and other foodstuffs! That's obviously our top choice. No need to read labels three times, it's a safe space.

FROZEN FOOD SUPERMARKETS
Frozen vegetables are the foundation of this book! And we eat them a lot. The same applies to herbs, ice cream, pre-cooked legumes and certain fruits. And there are more and more certified organic products.

SUPERMARKETS
Like most people, we also do our shopping in chain supermarkets. More often than not, that's all there is in the area, but fortunately, supermarkets are offering more and more organic products, certified vegan products, international products, alcohol, basic food items, etc.

SUPERMARKETS & EXOTIC FOOD SHOPS
For us, spice is life! It brings soul to a dish. It would be impossible to live without it! 'Exotic' products can be used to make dishes more authentic, as they are essential to be able to achieve the desired taste. And what's more, they are often available at low prices! Here are some to explore:

• The Spice Shop (https://thespiceshop.co.uk)
• Seasoned Pioneers (https://seasonedpioneers.com)
• Sous Chef (https://www.souschef.co.uk)
• Epices Roellinger (https://www.epices-roellinger.com)
• Kalustyan's (http://kalustyans.com)
• Herbies Spices (https://www.herbies.com.au)

And then there are two essential supply sources in our neighbourhood; the bakery, for all kinds of bread, as well as the greengrocer's where we buy all our fresh fruits and veg, as well as herbs. So we can't give you specific addresses, but don't forget these small businesses have the know-how that you won't find in supermarkets.

INGREDIENTS INDEX

Apple
Apple & blueberry tart 124
Buddha bowl 26
Green salad 37
Spring rolls 205
Thin banana tart 126

Artichoke
Hot & cold salad 17
Italian-style burger 209
Paella 164
Stuffed artichokes 34
Summer bruschetta 223

Aubergine
Conchiglie melanzane 116
Gnocchi alla norma 62
Miso-glazed aubergines 95
Moussaka 151
Pizza bianca 122
Pizza pitta 43

Avocado
Avocado cream 77
Avocado roll 73
Avocado toast 98
'Bacon' salad 209
Buddha bowl 26
Burrito 137
Jägerburger 193
'Sausage' salad 174
Spring rolls 205
'Steak' bagel 194
Toasted wraps 106

Banana
Banana flan 232
Thin banana tart 126

Bean sprouts
Fu-yung 202
Pad thai 190
Spring rolls 205

'Beef' substitute
Bean satay 186
Beer stew 189
Flageolet bean casserole 189
Traditional French stew 185

Beetroot
Beetroot hummus 79
Beetroot ravioli 92
Red kebab 111
Spiced 'steaks' 138
Trio of maki 162
Viennese burger 106

Blueberries
Apple & blueberry tart 124
Rainbow salad 92

Breaded escalopes (substitute)
BBQ pizza 108
Caesar salad 105
Milanese 108
Mini burgers 111
Ocean brochettes 111
Red kebab 111
Spinach escalopes 105
Toasted wraps 106
Torikatsu 108
Viennese burger 106

Broccoli
Broccoli rice 38
Broccoli & rice 164
Buddha bowl 26
Farfalle with broccoli 114
Ocean brochettes 111
Warm broccoli salad 151

Brussels sprouts
Brussels sprouts stew 173
Sauté with brussels sprouts 37
Tofu & vegetable stew 226

Button mushrooms
Bruschetta 223
Fusilli à la forestière 113
Marengo sauté 147
Modern blanquette 152
Mushroom & herb soup 91
Parisian gnocchi 60
Philly 'cheesesteak' 180
Pizza bianca 122
Posh salad 130
Sauté with Brussels sprouts 37
Sichuan seitan skewers 178
'Steak' pie 196

245

Index

Tofu & vegetable stew 226
Traditional French stew 185
Vol-au-vent 218
Wok 71

Cajun spice seasoning
Jambalaya 167
Riboulade 15

Capers
Milanese 108
Mini burgers 111
Red pesto 218
Sauce gribiche 87
'Steak' tartare 177
Summer bruschetta 223
Tartare sauce 87
Vegan meatballs with capers 20

Carrot
Banh mi dog 169
Beer stew 189
Carrot & cumin soup 213
Chilli con corn 80
Empanadas 122
Hawaiian salad 213
Hot & cold salad 17
Italian stew 182
Lentils with smoked tofu 80
Modern blanquette 152
Neo-cassoulet 79
Pot-au-feu 182
Potato hotpot 141
Quick bourguignon 177
Rainbow salad 92
Raita 241
Scandinavian ragout 217
Spring rolls 205
Tempeh stew 206
Thai rice salad 162
Tofu & vegetable stew 226
Trio of maki 162
Vegetable curry rice 161
Wheat biryani 26

Cashew nuts
Beetroot ravioli 92
'Chicken' korma 241
Conchiglie pesto 114
Morning porridge 29

Thai rice salad 162

Cauliflower
Cauliflower soup 206
Ocean brochettes 111
Saffron cauliflower 95
Vegetable curry rice 161
Wheat biryani 26

Celery
Autumn rolls 218
Buddha bowl 26
Italian stew 182
Jambalaya 167
Moroccan harira soup 135

'Chicken' substitute
African peanut stew 189
'Chicken' & ginger 186
'Chicken' korma 241
Chinese 'chicken' 185
Neo-cassoulet 79
Pad thai 190
Sautéed 'chicken' with olives 186
Tarragon casserole 190

Chickpeas
Burrito 137
Chickpea pasties 121
Falafel terrine 137
Lebanese salad 138
Moroccan harira soup 135
Red hummus 135
Sautéed greens 138
Spiced 'steaks' 138

Chicory
Chicory gratin 32

Chilli paste
African peanut stew 189
'Chicken' & ginger 186
Pad thai 190
Penne arrabiata 113
Tomato & chilli 'sausages' 170

Chocolate
Bread pudding 100
Caribbean delight 54
Chocolate granola 29
Cookie sandwich 53

Index

Decadent milkshake 51
Kings' & queens' cake 126
Matcha pancakes 202
Quick mini croissants 126
Salted peanut cup 91

Chorizo (substitute)
'Chorizo' & potato tart 32
'Chorizo' pinwheels 31
Conchiglie pesto 114
Gourmet sauce 159
Paella 164
Quesadillas 46

Coconut
Caribbean delight 54
Chocolate granola 29
Thai rice salad 162

Coconut cream
Cherry matcha rice pudding 167
Thai style 68

Coconut milk
Bean satay 186
Bollywood gnocchi 59
Curry 66
Semolina cake 29
Thai soup 40

Cognac
Cocktail sauce 88
Fusilli à la forestière 113
Quick & fancy sauce 132
Sautéed mushrooms 95
Spicy vegan meatballs 20
'Steak' with peppercorn sauce 180

Courgette
Courgette cannelloni 225
Frittata 200
Gnocchi with pesto 57
Mediterranean dal 82
Mini bruschetta 102
One-pot pasta 119
Oriental vegan meatballs 18
Sautéed greens 138
Spring rolls 205

Cucumber
Banh mi dog 169

Broccoli rice 38
Cretan salad 225
Gazpacho 100
Green salad 37
Rainbow salad 92
Raita 241
'Sausage' salad 174
Tomato salad with lemon sorbet 54
Tzatziki 239

Curry paste
Thai soup 40
Thai style 68

Dill
Gravlaxsas 85
Scandinavian ragout 217
Tzatziki 239

Fennel
Golden nuggets 223
Green salad 37
Parsley butter gnocchi 57
Sautéed 'chicken' with olives 186

Garam Masala
'Chicken' korma 241
Palak tofu 226
Samosas 68
Spiced 'steaks' 138
Sweet potato farmer's pie 38
Terrine 214
Wheat biryani 26

Ginger
Aloo pie 142
Bean satay 186
Broccoli rice 38
'Chicken' & ginger 186
'Chicken' korma 241
Frozen smoothie 53
Hawaiian salad 213
Hiyayakko 232
Pad thai 190
Spicy vegan meatballs 20
Tempeh tandoori 205
Thai rice salad 162
Thai soup 40
Tomato & chilli 'sausages' 170
Vegetable curry rice 161

247

Index

Wok 71

Gnocchi
Bollywood gnocchi 59
Bordelaise Gnocchi 62
Gnocchi alla norma 62
Gnocchi with creamed leeks 59
Gnocchi with peppers 59
Gnocchi with pesto 57
Gnocchi with spinach 60
Parisian gnocchi 60
Parsley butter gnocchi 57
Sea-flavoured gnocchi 62

Green beans
Bean satay 186
Hot & cold salad 17
Posh salad 130
'Sausage' salad 174
Sautéed country veg 142
Sautéed greens 138

Green pesto
Bread sticks 121
Crumble 71
Gnocchi with pesto 57
Minestrone 65
Mini bruschetta 102
Rata-toast 155
Sautéed greens 138
Stuffed tomatoes 24
Tricolour salad 119

Grenoble walnuts
Autumn cake 242
Çiğ köfte 24

Ham (substitute)
'BLT' bagel 31
Chicory gratin 32
Club sandwich 97
Savoury cupcakes 34
Toastie roll ups 102
Vegan egg muffin 226
Viennese burger 106
Welsh rarebit 44

Haricot beans
Avocado cream 77
Beetroot hummus 79

Minestrone 65

Horseradish
Beetroot hummus 79
Black forest toast 132
Sea-flavoured gnocchi 62
Stuffed artichokes 34
Viennese burger 106

Julienne vegetables
Avocado roll 73
Comforting broth 74
Crumble 71
Oven-baked ravioli 119
Puff pastry waffles 73
Stir fry 73
Vegetable pancakes 74
Wok 71

Kala namak salt
Frittata 200
Fu-yung 202
Hollandaise sauce 88
Mushroom omelette 199
Tagliatelle carbonara 114
Tofu mayonnaise 229
Tortilla 199
Vegan egg muffin 226

Kidney beans
Chilli con corn 80
Fajitas 38
Spicy terrine 77

Kimchi
Kimchi onigiri 164
Kimchi soup 230

Leek
Brussels sprouts stew 173
Gnocchi with creamed leeks 59
Leek & coriander quiche 230
Modern blanquette 152
Pot-au-feu 182

Lentils
Lentil cream with truffles 80
Lentil soup 82
Lentils with smoked tofu 80
Mediterranean dal 82

Index

Savoury cupcakes 34

Matcha
Cherry matcha rice pudding 167
Matcha pancakes 202
Matchatella 241

Meatballs (substitute)
Hot & cold salad 17
Moroccan couscous 24
Oriental vegan meatballs 18
Riboulade 15
Spicy vegan meatballs 20
Surprise vegan meatballs 20
Tomato & vegan meatball soup 18
Vegan meatballs with capers 20
Vegan meatballs with mustard 18
Veggie ball gratin 17
Yakitori 15

Meatless strips
Broccoli rice 38
Club sandwich 97
Fajitas 38
Green salad 37
Pitta waffles 40
Sauté with Brussels sprouts 37
Sweet potato farmer's pie 38
Thai soup 40

Mexican spice seasoning
Burrito 137

Miso
Beer stew 189
Beetroot ravioli 92
Bordelaise Gnocchi 62
French onion soup 48
Fromage frais 239
Grilled TVP with shallot sauce 152
Italian stew 182
Kimchi soup 230
Miso-glazed aubergines 95
Mushroom & herb soup 91
Potato hotpot 141
Poutine 46
Rainbow salad 92
Rossini 196
Saffron cauliflower 95
Salted peanut cup 91

Sautéed mushrooms 95
Spicy terrine 77
'Steak' with peppercorn sauce 180
Tempeh cheese 210
Thai soup 40
Tofu marinière 221
Traditional French stew 185

Mixed mushrooms
Cider casserole 152
Mushroom omelette 199
Sautéed mushrooms 95

Mixed vegetables
Creamy vegetables 68
Curry 66
Minestrone 65
Samosas 68
Stuffed peppers 65
Thai style 68
Vegetable tart 66

Mustard
Aioli 85
'Bacon' salad 209
Farfalle with broccoli 114
Florentine lasagne 148
Gravlaxsas 85
Hot & cold salad 17
Mac & cheese 44
Mushroom & herb soup 91
Pistachio-crusted 'steak' 194
Posh salad 130
Sauce gribiche 87
'Sausage' rolls 170
'Sausage' salad 174
'Steak' with mash 193
Tartare sauce 87
Tofu mayonnaise 229
Trio of maki 162
Vegan meatballs with mustard 18
Veggie ball gratin 17
Welsh rarebit 44

Nuggets (substitute)
BBQ pizza 108
Mini burgers 111
Red kebab 111
Savoury porridge 156
Toasted wraps 106

Index

Oats
Chocolate granola 29
Morning porridge 29

Olives
Aloo pie 142
Cretan salad 225
Gnocchi alla norma 62
Sauté Provençal 182
Sautéed chicken with olives 186
Tricolour salad 119

Onion
African peanut stew 189
'Bacon' salad 209
Baked baguette 217
Basquaise 169
Bean satay 186
Beer stew 189
Bread soup 102
Brussels sprouts stew 173
'Chicken' korma 241
Chickpea pasties 121
Chilli con corn 80
Choucroute garnie 174
Cider casserole 152
Comforting broth 74
Fajitas 38
Falafel terrine 137
French onion soup 48
Gnocchi with creamed leeks 59
Gnocchi with peppers 59
Gnocchi with pesto 57
Italian stew 182
Italian-style burger 209
Jägerburger 193
Jambalaya 167
Lentil soup 82
Mediterranean dal 82
Minestrone 65
Mini aperitif brochettes 34
Mitrailette sandwich 194
Modern blanquette 152
Moroccan harira soup 135
Neo-cassoulet 79
Ocean brochettes 111
One-pot pasta 119
Oriental vegan meatballs 18
Palak tofu 226
Parisian gnocchi 60

Philly 'cheesesteak' 180
Pot-au-feu 182
Potato burger 144
Potato hotpot 141
Quick bourguignon 177
Sauté Provençal 182
Sautéed 'chicken' with olives 186
Sautéed greens 138
Spanish-style potatoes 141
Spicy vegan meatballs 20
'Steak' bagel 194
Stuffed peppers 65
Sweet potato farmer's pie 38
Tartiflette 44
Tempeh sautéed with onions 210
Tempeh stew 206
Terrine 214
Tofu & vegetable stew 226
Tomato & chilli 'sausages' 170
Tomato & vegan meatball soup 18
Tortilla 199
Traditional French stew 185
Vegetable curry rice 161
Wheat biryani 26

Parsnip
Cream of shiitake mushroom soup 132
Lentil soup 82
Vegetable pie 122

Pasta
Comforting broth 74
Conchiglie melanzane 116
Conchiglie pesto 114
Courgette cannelloni 225
Farfalle with broccoli 114
Florentine lasagne 148
Fusilli à la forestière 113
Ink linguine 116
Mac & cheese 44
Minestrone 65
One-pot pasta 119
Oven-baked ravioli 119
Pad thai 190
Penne arrabiata 113
Spaghetti bolognese 147
Tagliatelle carbonara 114
Tricolour salad 119
Vegetable lasagne 156

Index

Peas
Aloo pie 142
Beer stew 189
Chinese 'chicken' 185
Conchiglie melanzane 116
Empanadas 122
One-pot pasta 119
Paella 164
Pea soup 170
Pitta waffles 40
Potato hotpot 141
Sautéed greens 138
Stir fry 73
Sweet potato farmer's pie 38
Vegetable curry rice 161
Wheat biryani 26

Peppers
Basquaise 169
BBQ pizza 108
Bollywood gnocchi 59
Broccoli rice 38
Chilli con corn 80
Cretan salad 225
Fajitas 38
Frittata 200
Gazpacho 100
Gnocchi with peppers 59
Jambalaya 167
Ktipiti 239
Mediterranean dal 82
Paella 164
Philly 'cheesesteak' 180
Rainbow salad 92
Red hummus 135
Sauté Provençal 182
Sichuan seitan skewers 178
Stuffed peppers 65
Thai rice salad 162
Tofu skewer 217
Tricolour salad 119

Pineapple
Hawaiian salad 213
Semolina cake 29
Tofu skewer 217

Pistachio
Beetroot ravioli 92
Morning porridge 29

Pistachio-crusted 'steak' 194

Pizza dough
BBQ pizza 108
Empanadas 122
Pizza bianca 122

Plain tofu
Bruschetta 223
Cointreau tiramisu 234
Courgette cannelloni 225
Cretan salad 225
Golden nuggets 223
Palak tofu 226
Sauce gribiche 87
Sesame grilled tofu 221
Stir fry 73
Summer bruschetta 223
Tofu & vegetable stew 226
Tofu marinière 221
Vegan egg muffin 226

Potato
Aligot 48
Aloo pie 142
Autumn rolls 218
BBQ pizza 108
Beer stew 189
'Chorizo' & potato tart 32
Choucroute garnie 174
Cider casserole 152
Grilled 'bacon' & golden mash 173
Hot & cold salad 17
Jacket potatoes 79
Moussaka 151
Potato burger 144
Potato croquettes 144
Potato gratin 144
Potato hotpot 141
Potato salad 88
Sautéed country veg 142
Scandinavian ragout 217
Spanish-style potatoes 141
'Steak' with mash 193
Sweet potato farmer's pie 38
Tartiflette 44
Tempeh stew 206
Tortilla 199
Veggie ball gratin 17

251

Index

Puff pastry
Bread sticks 121
Chickpea pasties 121
'Chorizo' & potato tart 32
'Chorizo' pinwheels 31
Kings' & queens' cake 126
Puff pastry canapés 129
Puff pastry waffles 73
Quick mini croissants 126
'Sausage' rolls 170
Thin banana tart 126
Vol-au-vent 218

Quinoa
Quinoa with black mushrooms 23
Stuffed peppers 65
Stuffed tomatoes 24

Radish
Chive cream & crudités 230
Hot & cold salad 17
Rainbow salad 92
Rustic sandwich 129

Ras-El-Hanout
Oriental vegan meatballs 18
Moroccan couscous 24
Moroccan harira soup 135
Savoury porridge 156

Ratatouille
Galettes 159
Gourmet sauce 159
Mediterranean vegetable soup 159
Polenta 155
Rata-toast 155
Riboulade 15
Savoury porridge 156
Vegetable lasagne 156

Red cabbage
Black forest toast 132
Red kebab 111
Thai rice salad 162

Red onion
BBQ pizza 108
Bordelaise gnocchi 62
Cretan salad 225
Green peppercorn tofu burger 214
Rustic sandwich 129
Spaghetti bolognese 147
Stuffed artichokes 34
Stuffed peppers 65
Vineyard risotto 161

Rice
Broccoli & rice 164
Burrito 137
Cherry matcha rice pudding 167
Chinese 'chicken' 185
Jambalaya 167
Kimchi onigiri 164
Paella 164
Riboulade 15
Rice tart 167
Stir fry 73
Thai rice salad 162
Trio of maki 162
Vegetable curry rice 161
Vineyard risotto 161

Saffron
Orange seitan strips 180
Paella 164
Saffron cauliflower 95

Sausage (substitute)
Banh mi dog 169
Basquaise 169
Brussels sprouts stew 173
Choucroute garnie 174
Currywurst 174
Grilled 'bacon' & golden mash 173
Jambalaya 167
Neo-cassoulet 79
Pea soup 170
Potato salad 88
Tomato & chilli 'sausages' 170
'Sausage' rolls 170
'Sausage' salad 174

Seaweed
Ink linguine 116
Ocean brochettes 111
Ocean sandwich 148
Paella 164
Sea-flavoured gnocchi 62
Tofu marinière 221
Trio of maki 162

Index

Seitan
- BBQ style 178
- Empanadas 122
- Farfalle with broccoli 114
- Galettes 159
- Italian stew 182
- Orange seitan strips 180
- Philly 'cheesesteak' 180
- Pot-au-feu 182
- Quick bourguignon 177
- Sauté Provençal 182
- Sichuan seitan skewers 178
- 'Steak' tartare 177
- 'Steak' with peppercorn sauce 180

Shallots
- Autumn rolls 218
- Avocado toast 98
- Béarnaise sauce 88
- Broccoli rice 38
- Bruschetta 223
- Courgette cannelloni 225
- Farfalle with broccoli 114
- Flageolet bean casserole 189
- Grilled TVP with shallot sauce 152
- Hiyayakko 232
- Orange seitan strips 180
- Poutine 46
- Red pesto 218
- Sauté with Brussels sprouts 37
- Sautéed country veg 142
- Sichuan seitan skewers 178
- Spiced 'steaks' 138
- 'Steak' pie 196
- Tarragon casserole 190
- Tartare sauce 87
- Toast with mushrooms 97
- Tofu marinière 221
- Tomato salad with lemon sorbet 54
- Wheatsotto 23

Shortcrust pastry
- Aloo pie 142
- Asparagus tartlets 229
- Leek & coriander quiche 230
- 'Steak' pie 196
- Vegetable pie 122
- Vegetable tart 66

Silken tofu
- Asparagus tartlets 229
- Banana flan 232
- Chive cream & crudités 230
- 'Chorizo' pinwheels 31
- Cointreau tiramisu 234
- Crème brûlée chartreuse 234
- Hiyayakko 232
- Irish coffee cream 232
- Kimchi soup 230
- Leek & coriander quiche 230
- Tofu mayonnaise 229
- Vegan egg muffin 226

Smoked paprika
- Andalusian 85
- Buddha bowl 26
- Gnocchi with peppers 59
- Red hummus 135
- Smoky burger patty 206
- Spanish-style potatoes 141
- Spicy tempeh balls 210
- Spicy terrine 77
- Surprise vegan meatballs 20
- Vegetable pancakes 74

Smoked tofu
- Autumn rolls 218
- Baked baguette 217
- Black forest toast 132
- Carrot & cumin soup 213
- Choucroute garnie 174
- Fusilli à la forestière 113
- Gourmet sauce 159
- Green peppercorn tofu burger 214
- Hawaiian salad 213
- Lentils with smoked tofu 80
- Neo-cassoulet 79
- Red pesto 218
- Sautéed country veg 142
- Sautéed mushrooms 95
- Scandinavian ragout 217
- Tagliatelle carbonara 114
- Tartiflette 44
- Terrine 214
- Tofu skewer 217
- Vol-au-vent 218

Soya yogurt
- Apple & blueberry tart 124

253

Index

Autumn cake 242
'Chicken' korma 241
Fromage frais 239
Ktipiti 239
Mango lassi 237
Matchatella 241
Mojito curd 237
Raita 241
Tempeh tandoori 205
Tzatziki 239
Wheat biryani 26
Yogurt loaf 242

Spinach
Buddha bowl 26
Curry 66
Florentine lasagne 148
Gnocchi with spinach 60
Hot & cold salad 17
Palak tofu 226
Spinach escalopes 105
'Steak' bagel 194
Vegan egg muffin 226

Spring onion
Fu-yung 202
Hiyayakko 232
Kimchi soup 230
Marengo sauté 147
Pad thai 190
Stir fry 73
Thai rice salad 162
Thai soup 40

Sun-dried tomato
Conchiglie pesto 114
Galettes 159
Italian-style burger 209
Milanese 108
Red pesto 218
Spring rolls 205
Summer bruschetta 223

Sweetcorn
Chilli con corn 80
Chinese 'chicken' 185
Quesadillas 46

Sweet paprika
Çiğ köfte 24

Courgette cannelloni 225
Ktipiti 239
Mediterranean dal 82
Red kebab 111
Spaghetti bolognese 147
Tempeh stew 206
Tempeh tandoori 205
Tomato & vegan meatball soup 18

Sweet potato
African peanut stew 189
Sweet potato farmer's pie 38
Vegetable pie 122

Sweet shortcrust pastry
Apple & blueberry tart 124
Fruit tart 124

Tahini
Lentil cream with truffles 80
Rainbow salad 92
Red hummus 135
Savoury cupcakes 34
Sesame grilled tofu 221
Spicy tempeh balls 210

Tempeh
'Bacon' salad 209
Buddha bowl 26
Cauliflower soup 206
Italian-style burger 209
Smoky burger patty 206
Spicy tempeh balls 210
Spring rolls 205
Tempeh cheese 210
Tempeh sautéed with onions 210
Tempeh stew 206
Tempeh tandoori 205

Textured vegetable protein (TVP)
Chickpea pasties 121
Cider casserole 152
Florentine lasagne 148
Grilled TVP with shallot sauce 152
Marengo sauté 147
Modern blanquette 152
Moussaka 151
Ocean sandwich 148
Pumpkin parmentier 148
Spaghetti bolognese 147

Index

Vegetable pie 122
Warm broccoli salad 151

Tomato
Courgette cannelloni 225
Fajitas 38
Gnocchi alla norma 62
Italian stew 182
Kimchi soup 230
Marengo sauté 147
Oriental vegan meatballs 18
Penne arrabiata 113
Sauté Provençal 182
Tomato & chilli 'sausages' 170

Tortilla
Avocado roll 73
Burrito 137
Fajitas 38
Quesadillas 46
Toasted wraps 106

Turnip
Pot-au-feu 182
Tempeh stew 206

Vegan cheese
Aligot 48
Club sandwich 97
Florentine lasagne 148
French onion soup 48
Frittata 200
Galettes 159
Garlic bread 98
Gnocchi with spinach 60
Grilled cheese 43
Jägerburger 193
Mac & cheese 44
Mini bruschetta 102
Moussaka 151
Oven-baked ravioli 119
Parisian gnocchi 60
Philly 'cheesesteak' 180
Pizza bianca 122
Pizza pitta 43
Potato burger 144
Potato croquettes 144
Potato gratin 144

Poutine 46
Quesadillas 46
Rata-toast 155
Savoury cupcakes 34
'Sausage' rolls 170
'Steak' bagel 194
Surprise vegan meatballs 20
Sweet potato farmer's pie 38
Tartiflette 44
Toasted wraps 106
Toastie roll ups 102
Vegan fondue 48
Vegetable lasagne 156
Vegetable tart 66
Veggie ball gratin 17
Viennese burger 106
Welsh rarebit 44

Vegan mayonnaise
Aioli 85
Andalusian 85
Banh mi dog 169
Béarnaise sauce 88
Black forest toast 132
'BLT' bagel 31
Caesar salad 105
Club sandwich 97
Cocktail sauce 88
Gravlaxsas 85
Hollandaise sauce 88
Mini burgers 111
Ocean sandwich 148
Potato burger 144
Potato salad 88
Red kebab 111
Sauce gribiche 87
Summer vegetable salad 87
Tartare sauce 87
Toasted wraps 106
Viennese burger 106

Vegan merguez sausage
Basquaise 169
Moroccan couscous 24
Tricolour salad 119

Vegan whipped cream
Decadent milkshake 51
Irish coffee cream 232

255

Index

Wheat (grain)
Buddha bowl 26
Wheat biryani 26
Wheatsotto 23

Wine
Basquaise 169
Béarnaise sauce 88
Bordelaise gnocchi 62
Broccoli & rice 164
Choucroute garnie 174
Courgette cannelloni 225
Creamy vegetables 68
French onion soup 48
Fusilli à la forestière 113
Gnocchi with creamed leeks 59
Gnocchi with pesto 57
Gourmet sauce 159
Grilled TVP with shallot sauce 152
Italian stew 182
Italian-style burger 209
Leek & coriander quiche 230
Marengo sauté 147
Oven-baked ravioli 119
Polenta 155
Quick bourguignon 177
Sauté Provençal 182
Sauté with brussels sprouts 37
Sautéed greens 138
Spaghetti bolognese 147
'Steak' pie 196
Stuffed artichokes 34
Sweet potato farmer's pie 38
Tempeh sautéed with onions 210
Tempeh stew 206
Terrine 214
Toast with mushrooms 97
Tofu & vegetable stew 226
Tofu marinière 221
Traditional French stew 185
Vegan fondue 48
Vegetable lasagne 156
Vineyard risotto 161

Worcester sauce
Banh mi dog 169
BBQ style 178
Beetroot ravioli 92
Carrot & cumin soup 213
Club sandwich 97

Cocktail sauce 88
Cretan salad 225
Currywurst 174
Moussaka 151
Philly 'cheesesteak' 180
Poutine 46
Puff pastry waffles 73
Spicy vegan meatballs 20
'Steak' tartare 177
'Steak' with mash 193
Torikatsu 108

Za'atar
Lebanese salad 138
Pizza pitta 43
Toasted wraps 106